P9-DDO-604

THE SOCIAL EVOLUTION OF INTERNATIONAL POLITICS

The Social Evolution of International Politics

SHIPING TANG

JA
76
T345
2013
WEB

OXFORD

UNIVERSITY PRESS

OXFORD
UNIVERSITY PRESS

Great Clarendon Street, Oxford, OX2 6DP,
United Kingdom

Oxford University Press is a department of the University of Oxford.
It furthers the University's objective of excellence in research, scholarship,
and education by publishing worldwide. Oxford is a registered trade mark of
Oxford University Press in the UK and in certain other countries

© Shiping Tang 2013

The moral rights of the author have been asserted

First Edition published in 2013
Impression: 1

All rights reserved. No part of this publication may be reproduced, stored in
a retrieval system, or transmitted, in any form or by any means, without the
prior permission in writing of Oxford University Press, or as expressly permitted
by law, by licence or under terms agreed with the appropriate reprographics
rights organization. Enquiries concerning reproduction outside the scope of the
above should be sent to the Rights Department, Oxford University Press, at the
address above

You must not circulate this work in any other form
and you must impose this same condition on any acquirer

British Library Cataloguing in Publication Data
Data available

ISBN 978-0-19-965833-6

Printed and bound by CPI Group (UK) Ltd, Croydon, CR0 4YY

To Charles Darwin and Jean-Baptiste Lamarck

"One hundred [and fifty] years without Darwinism are enough."
—Hermann. J. Muller, 1959

"Give Darwin his due."
—Philip Kitcher, 2003

Preface

In 1959, the centennial of Darwin's *Origin of Species*, H. J. Muller (Nobel Prize winner in biology and medicine) lamented: "one hundred years without Darwinism are enough". Muller's lamentation rings even more true in social sciences. More than 150 years after *Origin of Species*, most social scientists remain ambivalent, if not hostile, toward applying an evolutionary approach to the understanding of human society. This apologetic mentality for being a social evolutionist, I contend, must be resolutely rejected, if human society is to be adequately understood. Social scientists should unabashedly embrace evolutionary thinking and become social evolutionist, for nothing in human society makes sense unless in the light of social evolution, to paraphrase Dobzhansky (1973).

Elsewhere, I show that when stripped to the bare bone, there are only eleven foundational paradigms in social sciences, and all the major schools or approaches in social sciences have been the product of different combinations of these foundational paradigms (Tang 2011b). I further argue that an evolutionary approach—or more precisely, the social evolution paradigm (hereafter, SEP)—is the most powerful of them all. SEP is the *ultimate* paradigm of social science. And in an accompanying volume, I elaborate what social evolution is as a phenomenon and what social evolution is as a paradigm. That book is designated to help social scientists understand social evolution and deploy SEP in understanding the human society.

In this book, I apply SEP to examine the systemic transformation of international politics from the beginning of human history (c.11,000 BC) to today. Along the way, I also offer an evolutionary (and neat) resolution of the "Great Debates" in IR. By doing so, I seek to showcase the explanatory power of SEP. This book is thus as much a book for IR scholars (and political scientists) as for all social scientists.

Together with other social scientists' work and my other works that deploy SEP (Tang 2008b; 2010a; 2010e; 2011a; Tang and Long 2012), I hope at least some social scientists will be convinced that SEP is a paradigm with great explanatory power, thus ending social sciences' years without social evolutionism after more than 150 years. More than 150 years ought to be more than enough.

This project has taken far longer than I expected. Even with the long hatching time, however, this book would not have been possible without the generous (spiritual and financial) support of several institutions. Let me take this opportunity to express my gratitude to the Institute of Asia-Pacific Studies

(IAPS), Chinese Academy of Social Sciences (CASS), Beijing, and the S. Rajaratnam School of International Studies (RSIS), Nanyang Technological University (NTU), Singapore, with special thanks to Director Prof. Zhang Yunling of IAPS and Dean Ambassador Barry Desker of RSIS. Under their able leadership, these two institutions provided me with a stimulating working environment.

I also thank Prof. Wang Gungwu for hosting me as a visiting fellow at East Asian Institute of National University of Singapore in 2005, so that I could work out some of the details of social evolution and a social evolutionary approach toward international politics and broader human society. More importantly, having the opportunity to learn from a great historian like Prof. Wang who embodies wisdom is something that most students can only dream of, and I have been extremely lucky.

I have benefited greatly from criticism by many individuals. From the broad IR community, they include Amitav Acharya, Barry Buzan, Sen Du, Jeffrey Legro, Bob Jervis, Ned Lebow, Jon Mercer, Xiaoyu Pu, Sow Keat Tow, Alex Wendt, and Li Xue. I also thank Chris Roberts for sharing his unpublished data on ASEAN elite opinion survey.

From anthropology, archaeology, and the broader community on social evolution, Guillermo Algaze, Marion Blute, Geoff Hodgson, and Richard Nelson saved me from some basic mistakes in integrating data and insights from their respective fields into this book.

At Oxford University Press, Dominic Byatt has guided this project with patience, wisdom, and spirited encouragement. By taking on a project that seems to be so out of place with the larger social science literature, Dominic has put his judgment on the line. I can only hope this book vindicates his judgment, at least somewhat.

My gratitude also goes to four special friends: Tao Cui, Hongmei Li, Honglin Li, and Yu Zhang. Their unflinching faith in me has always been an inspiration and an extremely important source of support, encouragement, and understanding. Leslie Fong, Jin Han, Xin Yan—special friends and mentors—taught me things that I could not possibly learn by reading books.

Over the years, I have had the fortune of working with some outstanding research assistants. Yong-peng Fang provided not only excellent research assistance but also useful discussion on the European system. Shan Yang went the extra mile in compiling the bibliography. Beatrice Bieger, Candis Pang, Rongfang Pang, Hon Yang, Yuan Yang, and Lixia Yao have all made my labor less painful. Former and current graduate students of mine, Jiangchun Li, Ruolin Su, Kai Wang, Jingyi Zhang, Min Zhang, and Yiqi Zhou, have also provided some much needed help.

My new colleagues and friends at Fudan Univeristy have made my moving to Fudan a pleasant and productive experience. Yugang Chen, Zhimin Chen, Junzhi He, Zhan Hu, Ruichang Li, Jianjun Liu, Yi Shen, Changhe Su, Chenqiu

Wu, Kaiya Wu, Xinbo Wu, and Qin Zhu have shared coffee, tea, and (unfortunately, sometimes) cigarettes during the numerous but necessary breaks that have made the writing process a bit more lighthearted. Several graduate students have embarrassed their professors ruthlessly, for which I am deeply grateful. I shall name at least Lifeng Xu and Xiyin Zuo.

My deepest gratitude goes to my extended family. My parents not only endowed me with the stamina to tough it out but also tolerated my spending so little time with them over the years. My wife Lin Wang and my parents-in-law have shouldered most of the burden of raising my little boy. And finally, to my son Xiaoyu, who has learned to treasure the very limited play time I can spare for him and taught me to treasure the very limited play time with him.

An earlier version of Chapter 3 was published by the *European Journal of International Relations* (vol. 16, no. 1). I thank Sage publications for permitting me to reuse published material.

Contents

List of Figures   x
List of Tables   xi

Part I Preparing the Ground

Introduction: Why an Evolutionary Approach toward IR?   3
1 From Biological Evolution to Social Evolution   10

Part II The Systemic Transformation of International Politics

2 Paradise Lost and Paradigm Gained: The Making of the Offensive
   Realism World   43
3 From Mearsheimer to Jervis   96
4 A More Rule-based International System Unfolding   110

Part III Implications and Conclusion

5 International Politics as an Evolutionary System   151
Conclusion   179

Appendix I Evidences from Ethnographic Anthropology   187
Appendix II Supplementary Tables for Chapter 2   189
Appendix III The Coming of Warfare to Secondary Systems   197
Endnotes   201
References   237
Subject Index   279

List of Figures

2.1 The Making of the Offensive Realism World 57

4.1 The Institutionalization of (Regional) Peace in a Defensive Realism World 118

5.1 Society as a System 153

List of Tables

1.1   Various Notions of Biological and Social Evolution   14

1.2   Levels of Selection in Biological and Social Evolution   25

2.1   Key Indicators of an Offensive Realism System   63

2.1a The Impact of War upon Societies: Material Manifestations   63

2.1b The Impact of War upon Societies: Ideational Manifestations   63

2.2   Evolution of Man, Human Society, and Warfare, up to 1000 BC   66

3.1   Pattern of State Death in Ancient China, 1045 BC to 1759 AD   100

3.2   Pattern of State Death in post-Roman Europe, 1450–1995 AD   102

4.1   The Institutionalizing of Peace in Three Regions   116

4.2   Debating Institutions in International Politics   125

5.1   Conceptualizations of System (and Structure) Compared   162

S2.1 The Origin and Spread of War in Ancient Mesopotamia and Egypt   189

S2.2 The Origin and Spread of War in Ancient China   191

S2.3 The Origin and Spread of War in North Coastal Peru and Valley
       of Oaxaca   193

S2.4 The Origin and Spread of War in Ancient Anatolia   194

Part I

Preparing the Ground

Introduction: Why an Evolutionary Approach toward IR?

I. THE PUZZLE: "GREAT DEBATES" AND THEIR IRRESOLUTION

In the past century, "great debates" among a few grand theories, offensive realism, defensive realism, and neoliberalism/the English school,[1] have shaped, if not defined, the development of international relations (IR) as a science.[2] After Niebuhr (1932 [1960]) and Carr (1939) (re)ignited the debate between realism and "idealism", Morgenthau (1948) and Wolfers (1962) followed with a more systematic articulation of realism after the Second World War. Next, came Waltz's (1979) neorealism structural revolution, with Keohane and Nye's (1977) neoliberalism joining the foray at about the same time (see also Keohane 1984; 1986). Dissatisfied with both realism's and neoliberalism's lack of attention to the "social", Adler (1991) and Wendt (1992) started the constructivism assault in the early 1990s, while the Copenhagen School (Wæver 1995; Buzan et al. 1998) "securitized" various domains of social life with a constructivism flavor. Along the way, realism decisively split into offensive realism and defensive realism (Jervis 1976; 1978; 1999; Snyder 1991; Glaser 1994–95; Brooks 1997; Taliaferro 2000–1; Mearsheimer 2001; Tang 2008a; 2010a; 2010b).

Although a resolution of these great debates has yet to exist, two important consensuses have emerged from these "great debates". First, excepting a few notable dissenting voices (e.g., Waltz 1979, 66; Mearsheimer 2001, 2), most IR scholars agree that the international system had experienced some kind of fundamental transformation, although they may disagree on the exact timing, extent, degree, and most critically, the causes, of the transformations(s) (e.g., Cox 1981; Ruggie 1983; Schroeder 1994b, xiii; Wendt 1992; 1999; Lebow 2008). Second, some of the fundamental differences that divide the different grand theories are often derived from some hidden assumptions behind the different theories rather than deductive logic (Powell 1994; Taliaferro 2000–1; Tang 2008a).

Yet, an even more fundamental puzzle must be this: how can IR scholars arrive at so vastly different readings into the big picture of international politics, when all along they have been looking at roughly the same human history? This book contends that the key cause behind the irresolution of the "great debates" has been that the transformation power of time has been largely, if not completely, missing in all of the grand theories of international politics. More concretely, because each grand theory explicitly or implicitly claims, or at least, strives, to explain the whole human history, they have essentially assumed that time *cannot* fundamentally transform the nature of the international system and therefore one theory may well fit all. In Robert Cox's Vico-inspired language, all major grand theories of IR have erred in "taking a form of thought from a particular phase of history (and thus from a particular structure of social relations) and assuming it to be universally valid" (Cox 1981, 133).

Putting it differently, by seeking to explain the whole history of international politics with a single grand theory, IR theorists have been implicitly assuming that the fundamental nature of international politics has remained roughly the same, or more precisely, that human society has experienced a single phase of international politics. As such, all major grand IR theories have been non-evolutionary theories.

Waltz provided the clearest statement on this implicit assumption: "*The texture of international politics remains highly constant, patterns recur, and events repeat themselves endlessly.*" Further, Waltz attributed the cause of this "*striking sameness* in the quality of international politics" to "the enduring anarchic character of international politics" (1979, 66; emphasis added). Likewise, Mearsheimer (2001, 2) asserted that "*international politics has always been a ruthless and dangerous business, and it is likely to remain that way*" (emphasis added).

Meanwhile, even theories that admit systemic changes of international politics are inadequate: they do not offer genuinely endogenous explanations of change (e.g., Cox 1981; Ruggie 1983; Wendt 1999; see Chapters 2, 3, and 4 below for details. For a similar take, see Lebow 2008, 96–7). As such, these theories of change are not good theories of changes: good theories of changes must have changes endogenously driven.

The international system, as part of human society, has been an evolutionary system from the very beginning even if some properties of international politics (e.g., anarchy) have persisted even today, contra Waltz (2000, 5).[3] We therefore need a social evolutionary approach toward the history of IR: non-evolutionary theories cannot possibly account for the whole history of international politics. Indeed, as I elaborate in more detail elsewhere, only an evolutionary approach can offer a genuinely endogenous account of changes (Tang 2014–15; see also Chapter 1 below).

This book advances both an account of the transformation of international politics and a macro-sociology of IR theories through the social evolution paradigm (SEP). A social evolutionary approach toward IR not only provides genuinely endogenous explanations for the systemic transformations of international politics but also neatly resolves some of the great debates among IR theories (by advancing a social evolutionary macro-sociology of IR theories): the two tasks are, and can only be, accomplished in one stroke.

II. PLAN OF THE BOOK

This book has three parts in six chapters. Part I, "Preparing the Ground", contains Chapter 1. This part is to lay the foundation for applying SEP to empirical inquiries in the second part. Part II, the empirical part of this book, has three chapters. Armed with SEP, these three chapters examine the systemic transformation of international politics, from c.8000 BC to today, and the future. Consistent with the notion that only genuine evolutionary theorizing can provide a genuinely endogenous explanation for changes, these three chapters provide genuinely endogenous explanations for the transformation of international system through three stages: from a "paradise" to an offensive realism world; from the offensive realism world to a defensive realism world; and from the defensive realism world to a more rule-based world. Part III contains Chapter 5 and the concluding chapter.

Chapter 1, "From Biological Evolution to Social Evolution", summarizes a more detailed discussion on what social evolution is as a phenomenon and as a paradigm (Tang 2014–15). It also provides a brief critique of some of the evolutionary theorizing in IR. This chapter lays the foundation for applying SEP to empirical inquiries in the second part.

Chapter 2, "Paradise Lost and Paradigm Gained: The Making of the Offensive Realism World", examines the process through which major regions on earth were transformed from a paradise-like world in which human groups did not have to fight each other to an offensive realism world in which war became increasingly rampant and brutal, drawing mostly from archaeological (and to a lesser extent, anthropological) evidences. I show that until around 8000–6000 BC, the earth was peaceful because human groups did not have to fight each other, mostly due to abundant supply of readily available food resources and a small population on an open planet. As population increased, readily available food supply depleted, and with finally the coming of settled agriculture, however, human groups had to fight against each other. Gradually, the rule or the logic of offensive realism—that is, "to conquer or be conquered (and there is no middle way)"—originated and then rapidly spread in many subsystems and transformed them into offensive realism worlds.

Chapter 3, "From Mearsheimer to Jervis", examines the transformation of the offensive realism (or Mearsheimer's) world (before 1648 or 1945) to the defensive realism world (or Jervis's) today (post-1945). I present evidences from two regions with clear historical records, ancient China (1046/4 BC to 1759 AD) and post-Holy Roman Empire Europe (1450–1995 AD). I underscore that an offensive realism world is inherently self-destructive. As states pursue conquests and after some (if not many) conquests succeed, two interrelated outcomes become inevitable: (1) the number of states in the system decreased, and (2) the average size of surviving units increased. These two outcomes inevitably make conquest more and more difficult (even though conquests still succeeded from time to time), as measured by the decreasing rate of death within the two systems. The fact that conquest was becoming more and more difficult eventually paved the way for the coming of a defensive realism world, buttressed by three other auxiliary mechanisms, namely selection against offensive realist states and for defensive realist states, negative spreading of ideas that conquest is difficult, and the spread of sovereignty and nationalism.

Chapter 4, "A More Rule-based International System Unfolding", documents the process through which major regions on earth have been institutionalizing peace. I first introduce a general theory of institutional change developed elsewhere (Tang 2011a). Building on this theory of institutional change, I examine three cases of institutionalizing regional peace: the (Old and New) European Union, the Southern Cone, and Southeast Asia. I then draw some implications for studying international institutions (i.e., formal and informal rules) and international order, bringing together insights from the English school, neoliberalism, constructivism, and Foucauldian critical theory.

Building on previous chapters, Chapter 5, "International System as an Evolutionary System", seeks to reinforce the thesis that SEP is a powerful, if not the ultimate, paradigm for social sciences. In light of structuralism's overbearing impact on IR theories (and the broader social sciences), I first single out our past overemphasis on structure as a doomed enterprise that has prevented us from an adequate understanding of the international system. I stress that system, rather than structure, should be our focus: there is no "logic of anarchy" or "logic of structure", there is only *logic of system*. I then explore the five major channels through which a system impacts states' behavior and underscore the implications for theorizing states' behavior of such an understanding. I conclude by underscoring the co-evolution of agent, agents' behavior, and the system as a key for understanding the evolution of social systems.

Finally, in the Conclusion, I summarize the major theses and reiterate that SEP represents a powerful and indispensable paradigm for social sciences. I also draw policy implications for states' seeking security in the present and for the future.

III. KEY DEFINITIONS

No sensible discussion is possible without concepts. Since there has been much disagreement over some of the key concepts below, I shall define them now. For some of the concepts that I have defined in greater detail elsewhere and on which I do not have any second thoughts (Tang 2011a, 3–7), I shall merely restate the definitions without providing detailed rationales.

Society

Statically speaking, society is a system comprising agents or actors (i.e., individuals and collectives of individuals), an institutional system, and the physical environment (with time and space being only part of it).[4] By explicitly including the physical environment as part of our definition of society, our definition makes it abundantly clear that it is profoundly misleading to define society as "stocks of knowledge" or "distribution of knowledge" (e.g., Berger and Luckmann 1966; Barnes 1988; Wendt 1999, 249).

Dynamically, society contains all possible processes within the system (e.g., interactions, units' behaviors, institutionalization, socialization, and internalization). Here, it is important to emphasize three key points regarding processes. First, processes cannot be reduced to properties of units or parts (Archer 1995; Wendt 1999, esp. 147–50). Second, processes within the system are more than interactions among units (including their behaviors) alone: certainly, units' interactions with the physical environment constitute key processes within the system. This is very important because all too often, social scientists merely focus on interactions among units and the interactions between agents and "structure" while completely forgetting interactions between agents and the physical environment (e.g., Archer 1995; Wendt 1999, ch. 4). This easily leads us to the pitfall of ideationalism such as social constructivism. Third, processes (e.g., interactions) produce some "emergent" trends within the system (e.g., industrialization, colonization, decolonization, globalization, global warming, and democratization) and these trends constitute critical properties within the system (see Chapter 5 below for a more detailed discussion). In sum, society as a system exhibits systemic (emergent) properties that cannot be reduced to the sum of the individuals and components within the system (Jervis 1997), but the fact that a society has a system of institutions (i.e., a structure, see below) is one, but not the only, fundamental reason why society cannot be reduced to a sum of individuals (Giddens 1976 [1993], 128; 2006, 106–7).

Institution and Structure

"Institutions are the humanly devised constraints that shape human inter-action" (North 1990, 3). In other words, institutions are social rules, which include both formal rules (e.g., constitutions, laws, and international regimes) and informal rules (e.g., norms, taboos, and conventions). By adopting North's definition, I reject two other definitions of institutions: institutions as behavior or patterned actions or behaviors, institutions as organizations (for a detailed discussion, see Tang 2011a, 3–4).

Human society (or a human system) is underpinned by many rules. Inter-related institutions form a system of institutions, an institutional subsystem (Lin 1989; Lin and Nugent 1995). The whole institutional system of a society or system is the society's "*structure*" or "*social structure*". My definition of structure is thus a narrow "institutional" definition. Again, the fact that a society has a structure is one, but not the only, fundamental reason why society cannot be reduced to a sum of individuals.

Culture

I adopt a purely *ideational* definition of culture, as summarized by Durham (1991, 3–10). For Kroeber and Parsons (1958, 583), culture is the "transmitted and created patterns of value, idea, and other symbolic-meaningful systems as factors in shaping human behavior". For Geertz (1973, 89, 92–4, 144–5), culture is "a historically transmitted pattern of meaning embodied in sym-bols", "an ordered system of meaning and of symbols, in terms of social interaction takes place", or "the fabric of meaning in terms of which human beings interpret their experience and guide their actions". Hence, culture has at least four key properties: it is ideational and symbolic; it is real; it can be socially transmitted, and it has a history. Defined as such, only human beings can have culture (Geertz 1973; Durham 1991, 3–10; Premack and Hauser 2004).

I, however, explicitly reject the notion that culture is necessarily "systemic-ally organized", without denying that some domains of culture may be quite organized (e.g., organized religion, language). The notion that culture is necessarily "systemically organized"—a holistic conceptualization of culture, is a typical functionalism error. Also, cultural artifacts such as monuments are part of our *cultural* heritage, but they are not culture because they have material inputs whereas culture is purely symbolic and ideational although it must have material underpinnings (Tang 2011b).

Culture includes both rule-like components and non-rule-like components (e.g., symbols), and only rule-like components of culture are part of the institutional system (i.e., structure) of a society. Rules within culture have both formal and informal rules, backed or un-backed by sovereign power. Like institutions, culture is not behaviors or patterns of behavior.

Finally, culture makes only part of the ideational part of human society: culture is thus part, but not the whole, of human society. As such, cultural evolution is only part of ideational evolution, and ideational evolution is only part of social evolution. Social evolution subsumes ideational evolution, which in turn subsumes cultural evolution (see Chapter 1 below and the more detailed discussion in Tang 2014–15).

1

From Biological Evolution to Social Evolution

INTRODUCTION

This chapter prepares the ground for the chapters to follow. Essentially, this chapter seeks to equip readers with some basic understanding of biological and social evolution and, most critically, the social evolution paradigm (SEP), by summarizing some of the key points developed in more detail elsewhere (Tang 2014–15). Because the discussion here tends to be brief (and citations have been kept to the minimum), readers who want to gain a more detailed knowledge about the topics discussed here are encouraged to consult the discussion to be advanced in an accompanying volume (Tang 2014–15).

The rest of the chapter unfolds as follows. The first section summarizes some basics about biological evolution. The second section defines what social evolution is as a phenomenon. The third section outlines the core principles of social evolution paradigm (SEP). Based on the discussion in preceding sections, the fourth section makes it clear what does not constitute genuinely evolutionary theorizing. The fifth section presents a brief critical review of some of the existing evolutionary theorizing in IR. A conclusion follows.

Before I proceed further, three caveats are in order. First, I do not deal with mere metaphors that essentially equate evolution with change. For instance, physicists can talk about the evolution of the solar system or the whole universe. Such discussions of evolution of the solar system or the universe are just metaphors because these systems cannot possibly be genuinely evolutionary systems. For any system to be a genuinely evolutionary system, it has to be populated by living creatures (see Section I below), and the solar system is not one such system.

Second, I do not deal with "social evolution" as understood loosely by some evolutionary biologists (e.g., Trivers 1985). These works mostly focus on non-human group species (e.g., ants), and their discussion has little to offer for understanding human society, simply because those organisms do not have minds.

Finally, I do not review statements or applications that claim to be evolutionary but actually have very little to do with a genuine (social) evolutionary approach. Such mishaps have been so rampant that reviewing and critiquing them will be an impossible task. Here, I merely single out two examples.

In the new institutional economics (NIE), Robert Schotter (1981), taking a neoclassical economic approach, nonetheless insists that an evolutionary approach is the way to go for understanding economics and social institutions. Schotter thus implies that a neoclassical economic approach is genuinely evolutionary. As Boland (1979, 988) pointed out, however, the neoclassical economics approach toward institutional change cannot be genuinely evolutionary: it can only be dynamic for one round (reaching equilibrium on the Pareto frontier) and then become static unless some kind of external shock comes along. Changes in NIE thus have to be driven by exogenous events. As such, NIE cannot possibly offer a genuinely evolutionary, which has to be endogenous (and thus adequate), explanation of institutional change (for a more detailed discussion, see Tang 2011a, chs. 1 and 2).

In IR, George Modelski (1978; 1987; 1990; 2005) touted his "long cycles" of power-shift as an evolutionary theory of IR, insisting that international politics is evolutionary because it goes through long cycles of hegemonic rise-and-fall. Yet his whole enterprise is metaphorically evolutionary at best, and pseudo-evolutionary at worst (Falger 2001). Modelski certainly did not grasp the basics of biological or social evolution. Evolution, whether biological or social, does not go through cycles. More critically, the central mechanism of evolution—the mechanism of variation–selection–inheritance—has no role in his whole enterprise. Indeed, even his scheme of "long cycles" is merely an observation with dubious validity.[1]

Neither Modelski's scheme nor Schotter's theory is genuinely evolutionary, and I do not deal with them and their like. Hence, although I deal with some (mis)applications of evolutionary approach to social sciences and IR in some detail in the chapters below, I only deal with those with some genuine evolutionary elements.

I. SOME PRELIMINARIES ABOUT BIOLOGICAL EVOLUTION

To understand social evolution, it is necessary to start with biological evolution, simply because the first coherent and mostly correct theory of evolution came to exist in biological evolution. The modern understanding of biological

evolution, often known as "The Modern Synthesis," is now standard knowledge in any standard biology textbook (e.g., Futuyma 1998). This section
highlights the key aspects of this understanding that are most relevant for
understanding social evolution.

A. Evolution: Essential Conditions

Evolution can only operate with the following three conditions fulfilled.

First, evolution can only operate within a system. A system is a collective of
two or more units that exhibits interconnectedness and emergent properties
(Jervis 1997, 6). Without a system, there will be no diversity among individual
units within the system, no selection pressure (i.e., no environment), and thus
no genuine evolution.[2] Biological evolution operates with an ecosystem (local
and global), which consists of the physical environment and all the organisms
within the system.

Second, evolution can only operate in a system populated by living creatures
or systems developed by living creatures (e.g., human society). In other words,
only systems with living creatures can be genuinely evolutionary.[3] This is so
because a system is evolutionary *only if* its key units (i.e., organisms or
cultural units) change via the mechanism of variation–selection–inheritance,
and units without a biological foundation simply do not do that. Thus, while
one can certainly argue that some non-biological systems (e.g., the solar
system, the cosmos) also "evolve," they evolve only in a metaphorical but
not a substantial sense: To say that these systems evolve is no different from
saying that they change. Genuine evolutionary system not only changes, but
its key units change in a particular way—via the central mechanism of
variation–selection–inheritance.

Third, evolution operates through time and across space (i.e., the ecological
environment in biological evolution and eco-social environment in social
evolution) because changes can only operate through time, and interaction
between units and their environment can only operate in space.[4]

If a system conforms to these three conditions, then it must be an evolutionary system. When this is the case, an evolutionary approach should—and
must—be applied for understanding the system. Indeed, only an evolutionary
approach can provide an adequate understanding of such a system; as Dobzhansky (1973) put it eloquently, "Nothing in biology makes sense except in the
light of evolution."

As far as we can tell, there are only two systems—the biotic system and the
human society (i.e., the social system)—that fulfill the abovementioned three
conditions. In other words, only these two systems are genuinely evolutionary.
Moreover, the human society builds upon the foundation of biotic evolution
on earth (Campbell 1960, 380n2; Bhaskar 1986, 136–43; Hodgson and Knudsen

2010a; 2010b, esp. ch. 1). When this is the case, it is no surprise that the evolutionary approach should and must be applicable to both the biotic system and the human society.

B. Neo-Darwinism on Biological Evolution[5]

a. The Central Mechanism: Variation–Selection–Inheritance

At the micro-level, biological evolution proceeds in three distinctive stages: diversity generation (i.e., variation or mutation of genetic material or genotype), (natural) selection (i.e., eliminating and retaining some phenotypes, and thus some genotypes along with them), and inheritance (i.e., replication, or spreading of the selected genotypes and thus phenotypes).[6] This central mechanism of variation–selection–inheritance was first formulated by Darwin (1959); hence it is often known as "Darwinian".[7]

In natural settings, genetic mutations are generated essentially randomly and there are no artificial forces involved. These different mutations serve as the ultimate basis for the selection process: mutations on genes lead to diversity in phenotypes, and it is these phenotypes that are the direct targets of selection during the phase of selection (Mayr 1997).[8] In other words, selection operates directly on phenotype, but only indirectly on genes. This is so because only phenotype—but not genotype—is visible for selection pressure in the environment. The environment determines whether a particular phenotype is advantageous, disadvantageous, or neutral for an organism's "(inclusive) fitness". *All else being equal,* an organism with an advantageous phenotype is more likely to win the competition versus another organism with a disadvantageous phenotype. By selecting phenotypes, the environment thus also ends up in *indirectly* selecting genetic types: a genotype that underpins an advantageous phenotype will be more likely to survive and spread in a population, while a genotype that underpins a disadvantageous phenotype will be less likely to spread and may eventually disappear completely.

b. The Molecular and Genetic Foundation of Biological Evolution

Gregor Mendel (1822–84) provided us with the first glimpse into the genetic foundation of biological evolution in 1865–6. Unfortunately, his work remained essentially unknown for almost half a century, until it was finally rediscovered in 1900s independently by Hugo De Vries and Carl Correns. In the 1910–20s, Thomas Morgan and his students provided a firmer foundation for Mendel genetics, by locating genes onto chromosomes. In 1937, Thedosius Dobzhansky synthesized evolution biology with genetics into the "Modern Synthesis" or "Neo-Darwinism" as the integrative (or unified) theory of biological evolution.[9]

Inspired by Dobzhansky's book, Ernst Mayr (1942), George Simpson (1944), and G. Ledyard Stebbins (1950), contributed further ideas to and refined the modern synthesis (for a standard introduction to the "Modern Synthesis", see Futuyma 1998, 24–9).[10]

In 1953, Watson and Crick (1953) discovered the key molecular foundation of biological evolution by revealing the famous "double helix" structure of deoxyribonucleic acid (DNA), the most important form of genetic material in the bio-system. Genetic materials are usually in the form of double-strand DNA, but sometimes also in the forms of single-strand or double-strand ribonucleic acid (RNA) in some RNA viruses or retroviruses.[11]

The ultimate basis for the origins of species lies in genetic mutation. Genetic materials, by interacting with the environment through development, give rise to phenotypes. More often than not, there is no simple one-on-one correlation between genes and phenotypes: some phenotypes (e.g., eye color) are controlled by several genes and many genes have multiple copies and can give rise to different phenotypes when combined with other genes.[12]

The establishing that there is a barrier between the nuclei and the cytoplasma of a cell by August Weisman (1834–1914) nullifies the possibility of

Table 1.1. Various Notions of Biological and Social Evolution

Labels\Notions	Organisms desire adaptive variations	Environment induces organisms to have adaptive variations	Direct inheritance of acquired characteristics	Selection: natural or artificial	Evolution as variations toward higher order, progress, and perfection
Lamarckian (e.g., Lamarck)	Ambiguous	Ambiguous	Accept	Ambiguous	Accept
Darwinian (e.g., Darwin)	Reject	Reject	Accept	Natural	Ambivalent
Spencerian (e.g., Spencer)	Accept	Ambivalent	Accept	Ambiguous	Accept
Neo-Darwinian (e.g., Weisman)	Reject	Reject	Reject	Natural	Reject
Neo-Lamarckian (biological evolution)	Reject	Reject	Accept	Natural	Reject
Super-Lamarckian (ideational dimension of social evolution)	Accept	Accept	Accept	Artificial, but with physical constraints	Reject

Note: Ambivalent means that both stands (i.e., accept and reject) can be found in the particular author's elaboration. Ambiguous means that the original author was vague regarding a particular aspect.

direct inheritance of acquired characteristics. The Weisman Barrier dictates that genotypes give rise to phenotypes, but phenotypes cannot directly give rise to genotypes. At the molecular level, the Weisman Barrier means that the information flow in biological evolution is *unidirectional*: from genetic material (DNA or RNA) to protein, but not the other way around. More specifically, genetic information can be translated into proteins, but information stored in protein *cannot* be translated back into genetic information. This uni-directionality of information flow, which precludes the possibility of direct inheritance of acquired characters (i.e., phenotypes) in biological evolution thus ensures only a *Neo-Darwinian* but nullifies a *Darwinian* evolution, and is the "*Central Dogma*" in molecular biology (Crick 1970).[13]

C. The Nature and Power of the Evolutionary Approach

As a body of scientific theory for understanding biological evolution, Neo-Darwinism does not predict the specific outcome or destiny of a particular organism or species, not the least because evolution allows accidents (e.g., the earth being hit by an asteroid and dinosaurs being wiped out).[14] If so, then why has Neo-Darwinism been hailed as one of the two foundational pillars of modern science (the other being Copernican heliocentrism)? To put it differently, where does Neo-Darwinism's power come from? Its power comes from three aspects.

Foremost, Neo-Darwinism is elegant: for explaining the wonders of life (e.g., the great biodiversity, the marvelous adaptation of an organism to its environment, the similarities and differences among organisms of the same species, and the similarities among different but related species) on earth (and other places in the universe), all Neo-Darwinism needs is the single mechanism of variation–selection–inheritance.[15] No other theory or approach (i.e., non-evolutionary and partially evolutionary approaches) comes close.[16] Second, Neo-Darwinism subsumes or unifies all other micro- or meso-level mechanisms in biological evolution. So far, no phenomena in biological evolution have been found to violate the central mechanism of Neo-Darwinism. Neo-Darwinism, as Daniel Dennett (1995, 62) puts it, has proven to be "a universal acid" that dissolves everything. Finally, Neo-Darwinism makes any exogenous (i.e., driven by external factors or force) explanation of life unsatisfactory and, more importantly, unnecessary.[17]

In sum, Neo-Darwinism is elegant, powerful, and endogenous: it triumphs over all other explanations for the wonder of life on (and very likely, beyond) earth.

II. COMMON MISUNDERSTANDINGS ABOUT
BIOLOGICAL EVOLUTION

Though Darwin made his revolutionary theory known to the world over 150 years ago and the advance of genetics and molecular biology in the past half century has established the genetic and molecular foundation of biological evolution beyond any reasonable doubt, misunderstandings about biological evolution and the evolutionary paradigm abound. As Jacques Monod (Nobel Prize winner in biology in 1965) once quipped, "Another curious aspect of the theory of evolution is that everybody thinks that he understands it!" (Quoted in Hodgson 1993, 37.) This section highlights some of the most common misunderstandings about biological evolution, in the hope of eliminating them.

A. "Evolutionary Theory is a Theory, thus Evolution is not a Fact"

A theory—as an ideational construct by scientists—will remain a theory and cannot become a *natural* fact, no matter how established it becomes. Many opponents of evolution, especially creationists in various disguises, have taken this nature of scientific theory as the launch pad not only for their disputing Neo-Darwinism as a theory but also for their rejecting biological evolution as a natural fact. Surely, scientists cannot just show (i.e., run) a historical tape that shows the whole process of evolution from the organic soup to modern human. Worse, even if scientists were to show opponents of evolution such a tape, opponents of evolution can still dismiss the tape as a fake. Is Neo-Darwinism therefore doomed? Not at all![18]

First, the same principles of logical reasoning and demanding for evidences should apply to the theories favored by opponents of Neo-Darwinism (i.e., creationism, "intelligent design"). Can creationism's proponents show us a tape showing the whole process in which God creates everything? Proponents of creationism theory can say: "Yes, we have the *Bible*!" But if they can dismiss the massive evidences that scientists have put together as a fake, we have all the reasons to doubt what the Bible had put together is a fake! After all, scientists have the geological record as a kind of tape carved into rocks (thus it cannot be played back and forth, unfortunately) whereas creationists only have what has been written on paper, and surely things in rocks are more *solid* than things on paper: the former exist independently from humans, and words on paper cannot possibly come before humans. Too often, creationists do not apply the same demanding logic to their own favored "theories".

Second, for a moment, let us assume that neither Neo-Darwinism nor creationism can prove itself by showing a tape; then the battle has to be waged differently: on the ground of scientific logic. Here, the rules of a good scientific theory give an overwhelming advantage to Neo-Darwinism. Neo-Darwinism is logical, parsimonious, and powerful in explaining the wonder of life. Most important of all, Neo-Darwinism is endogenous: it can explain the wonder of life without having to enlist the help of any exogenous force. In contrast, creationism inevitably faces the embarrassing question: where did God (and/or his parents) come from? No amount of infinite regression can let creationism escape from this embarrassing but ultimate question, and creationism has absolutely no answer for it! Ultimately, any theory that relies on general will, natural law, or intelligent design as its final explanation is "mystical and tautological", thus anti-evolutionary (Service 1968, 397). In contrast, Neo-Darwinism eliminates the need of a God or other external forces.

Finally, although Neo-Darwinism will always remain a (very powerful) theory and cannot become a natural fact, *biological evolution is a fact* and scientists have established it beyond any reasonable doubt. I shall mention three sets of evidences here.

First, astronomy, geology, and paleontology have all proven that both the cosmos and life on earth began long before any creationists can imagine. More importantly, life forms in different geological periods have changed greatly, but always with links to life forms that were further back: scientists do have the closest thing to a tape! Second, the living "Tree of Life" shows that different organisms on earth share many similarities, not only in their anatomical structure but also their genetic code.[19] If different life forms had been created separately, they would not share so many similarities, especially at the most fundamental level. Finally, human beings have deployed the principles of genetics in domesticating animals and plants and then cross-breeding them into new species. The principles of genetics, which underpinned Neo-Darwinian evolution, work in these artificial processes. These principles are unlikely to work in artificial settings if they do not have counterparts in the (real) natural environment.

Ultimately, many of those who reject biological evolution as a natural fact and neo-Darwinism as a powerful scientific theory are ideologues, and no amount of logic and scientific evidences can convince them.

B. "Evolution Means 'Survival of the Fittest'"

Perhaps the most prevailing misunderstanding about evolution and evolutionary theory is that biological evolution or Neo-Darwinism dictates "survival of the fittest" because evolution is the "struggle for existence (and/through reproduction)". In truth, as Darwin recognized long ago (1859, 201–2, 472), biological evolution does not dictate survival of the fittest at all: *biological evolution only entails the survival of the fitter among individual organisms within the same species and hence the survival of the fitter species in a specific environment.* As such, *fitness in biological evolution is always relative, never absolute.* In other words, *biological evolution only dictates survival of the fitter, never survival of the fittest.*[20]

Indeed, the notion of a universally fittest phenotype or species violates the fundamental principle of evolution.[21] Even in a specific ecosystem, there is no way to pick the fittest phenotype or species. This is simply because there is usually more than one way to adapt to any given environment: different species adapt to the environment with different tricks that have been selected during the course of evolution.

C. Forms of Bad Adaptationism: Intentional and Induced

An organism's adaptation to its environment is the outcome of evolution. This fact has given rise to two misunderstandings about the causes of adaptation, or two forms of bad adaptationism.

The first form of bad adaptationism holds that adaptation results from organisms' *willful* adapting to their environment (i.e., they intentionally strive to adapt). Unfortunately, this form of adaptationism has no explanation for the origin of organisms' will to adapt in the first place—only a Darwinian adaptationism can do the job (Hodgson 2001, 97–9). As such, after Darwin, this form of willful adaptationism has been firmly rejected. According to (neo-) Darwinism, an organism is "adaptive" because only phenotypes (and genotypes) that are fitter for the environment have been retained, not because an organism consciously develops adaptive phenotypes.

The second form of bad adaptationism holds that organisms adapt because their environment directly or indirectly *induces* adaptive mutations from them. This form of adaptationism proves to be quite attractive even for some of the leading figures in evolutionary theory (e.g., Darwin and Dobzhansky), partially because the molecular foundation of evolution was not well understood back then. With the coming of molecular biology, this second form of bad adaptationism can now be firmly rejected. Environment does not induce adaptive mutations directly or indirectly, even though environment induces mutations not exactly randomly in the most strict sense (i.e., some stretches of DNA are more vulnerable to mutagens than other stretches). Environment induces mutations blindly—in the strictest sense (i.e., the adaptive value of a mutation is not predetermined).

Indeed, taking adaptation as an outcome of willful adaptation on the part of the organism or an outcome induced by the environment is dangerously close to creationism. One can easily contend that God has bestowed all organisms with a will to adapt or commanded the environment to be benevolent to all organisms: God again becomes the ultimate (and benevolent) will or will-giver. Again, any theory that relies on general will, natural law, or intelligent design as its final explanation is fundamentally "mystical and tautological," thus anti-evolutionary (Service 1968, 397). In contrast, Neo-Darwinism eliminates the need of a God or will.

In sum, adaptation in biological evolution is the outcome of natural selection, not the result of willful adaptation on the part of the organism or the environment acting as a purposeful maker of mutation. Adaptation in biological evolution is Darwinian: evolution is a "Blind Watchmaker" (Dawkins 1976), and adaptationist thinking in evolutionary reasoning must be guided by selectionism (Daly and Wilson 1995).

D. Evolution is Complexity or Destiny Unfolding, Progressively

Another prominent misunderstanding about evolution, *which can be understood as a form of bad adaptationism at the level of species or the biotic system*, holds that evolution inevitably leads to greater complexity, more elaborate systemic integration, destiny unfolding, or simply "progress". In short, it holds that evolution is directional toward a higher plateau, if not perfection, thus "progressive". The godfather of all these notions of "evolution as progress" was Herbert Spencer.[22]

Yet, neither a species *as a whole* nor the biotic system can think, thus cannot possibly have a sense of directionality. Without the possibility of conscious adaptation, whether by organisms or the environment, evolution cannot be directional, whether unilinear or multi-linear. Evolution may look directional (in our hindsight), but the seeming "directionality" is merely the unintended consequences of the central mechanism of variation–selection–inheritance. *Biological evolution does not have a sense of direction, at any level.*

Finally, although biological evolution produces adaptations, adaptations cannot be understood as progress in any normative sense. *There is no progress in biological evolution.* The notion of progress in biological evolution essentially reflects our (anthropocentric) concern about our species's position in the tree of life rather than facts of biological evolution (Williams [1966][1996], 35; Levins and Lewontin 1985, 12–29; see also the discussion in Section III below).

E. "Neo-Darwinism Needs Major Corrections" or "There Must Be Some Exceptions"

Perhaps not surprisingly, some of the more "sophisticated" challenges against Neo-Darwinism came from scientists, both natural and social. Some scientists have asserted that Neo-Darwinism needs some major corrections (usually at micro or meso level) to explain some new discoveries. Looking closely, however, these so-called challenges and "corrections" represent minor corrections to Neo-Darwinism at best and rhetorical stunts at worst. Contrary to their bold claims, Neo-Darwinism proves to be readily capable of explaining those phenomena that it supposedly cannot explain, with minor modification at most. In other words, Neo-Darwinism is extremely accommodating thus resilient: it does not need any major corrections.

For instance, Stephen Jay Gould popularized the concept of "punctuated equilibrium" and touted it as an important correction to Darwin's original theory (Eldredge and Gould 1972). Gould charged that Darwinism is strictly gradualism, and yet fossil records have shown that biological evolution has often been a process of general slow changes punctuated by abrupt explosions (i.e., emergence of numerous new species within a "short" geological time frame). Hence, Darwinism needs to be corrected, or at least complemented, by the notion of "punctuated equilibrium". Yet, looking closely, even Darwin's original theory has never been strictly gradualism and has always had "punctuated equilibrium". Darwin just did not use the phraseology: he used the dichotomy of "slow" versus "abrupt" evolution, and "abrupt" evolution is "punctuated equilibrium". Moreover, as Darwin recognized a long time ago, the applicability of these terms critically depends on the time frame with which we look at history. Once we adjust the time frame, punctuated equilibrium disappears (Darwin 1859, esp. 302–29; see also Dennett 1995, 282–312).[23]

III. SOCIAL EVOLUTION AS A PHENOMENON

Both the biotic system and human society fulfill the three essential conditions of evolution. Indeed, human society is an outgrowth of biological evolution: the former is impossible without the latter. As such, both systems are genuinely evolutionary, and both can and should be understood by an evolutionary approach.

At the same time, however, it is also apparent that there is something fundamentally new in social evolution that renders simplistic and mechanistic applications of (Neo-)Darwinism to human society impossible and misleading, if not outright dangerous. A fundamental cause behind the difficulties of directly applying (Neo-)Darwinism to human society is that a fundamentally new force—the ideational force—has come into play in human society and thus in social evolution. *While the coming of this new force itself has been the product of biological evolution, it fundamentally transforms the human system once it is in place.* Of course, the coming of ideational forces does not mean that material forces no longer operate in social evolution. Rather, the two forces interact with each other to drive social evolution, thus making social evolution a phenomenon far more complex than biological evolution. This section only summarizes the points that are most relevant for understanding the evolution of international system, leaving other important aspects of social evolution to a more detailed discussion elsewhere (Tang 2014-15).

A. Genes and Phenotypes in Social Evolution

In biological evolution, there is only one kind of phenotype and gene, the material or biological kind. In social evolution, there are two broad types of phenotype-gene: In addition to the material kind, there is also an ideational kind. Moreover, in the ideational dimension of social evolution, there can be multiple pairs of genes and phenotypes, depending on the level of analysis.

Thus, for understanding technological evolution, Nelson and Winter (1982) take innovation as phenotype, whereas "routine" (i.e., tacit or explicit knowledge for producing things) as gene. For studying the making of habit, Hull (1982, 311) takes idea as gene and habit as phenotype. For understanding institutional change, Veblen (1898) took habit as genes and institutions as phenotype (see also Hodgson 2001, 115, table 6.3; 2006, 13). For understanding the evolution of culture, where one may take meme to be gene (Dawkins 1976; Durham 1991), Hodgson (2001, 109-16) argues that it may be more productive to take habit and idea as genes and cultural traits as phenotypes. For understanding scientific progress, both ideas and theories can be understood as genes (and phenotypes), as the Popperian evolutionary epistemology has long argued (Campbell 1974a; 1974b; see also Hill 1989). For understanding institutional change, Tang (2011a) takes ideas for specific institutional arrangements as genes and institutional arrangements phenotypes. For understanding states' foreign policies, Tang (2008b) and Tang and Long (2012) take ideas for specific policies as genes and policies phenotypes.

Overall, it may be unfeasible, unnecessary, and even undesirable to have a single pair of gene and phenotype in social evolution (for earlier discussions, see Stuart-Fox 1986; Durham 1991, 187-9; Chick 1999). The pragmatic principle should be that as long as an element at a higher level is dependent on the selected expression of an element at a lower level, then the former can be understood as the phenotype and the latter as the gene (for similar views, see Chick 1999; Dopfer 2001, 12-17; Wilkins 2001, 177-9; Hodgson 2002, 269-73; Hodgson and Knudsen 2010b). Indeed, Dawkins's (1976) original definition of "meme" as the unit of cultural inheritance implies multiple pairs of genes and phenotypes in social evolution, because memes can be all sorts of things, from ideas, to words, tunes, and clothing fashions (see also Durham 1991, 176-7; Blackmore 1999, 4-23, 42-6, 59-62).

B. Mutations in Social Evolution: Random and Blind
vs. Non-random and Directed

In biological evolution, mutations are generated *essentially randomly* by three major mechanisms: DNA damages/nucleotide changes, recombination or genetic material exchanges (e.g., chromosome transposition, crossing over of genes), and external invasion (e.g., a virus integrates its genome into its host's genome).[24] More critically, these mutations are also generated *blindly, in the absolute sense*: organisms cannot know whether a mutation is advantageous or not. In the biological dimension of human evolution, these mechanisms and principles still hold.

In the ideational dimension of social evolution, at the most fundamental level, the equivalent of a mutation is simply a new idea (cf. Cavalli-Sforza 1971, 536).[25] In the ideational dimension of social evolution, the equivalent of these three mechanisms also operates. Generation of new ideas corresponds to DNA damages/nucleotide changes; cross-breeding of ideas to genetic material exchange; and importation of foreign ideas (or being imposed by foreign ideas) to external invasion.

Because it is man that invents ideas and the process of inventing ideas involves consciousness, mutations (i.e., new ideas) in the ideational dimension of social evolution are not generated randomly *in the strict sense*. More importantly, individuals quite often generate ideas to solve specific problems and achieve specific goals and they have some expectations about those ideas' potential utilities when being put into practice in the social system (i.e., agents have some expectation of the fitness of their ideas if those ideas are expressed as phenotypes), even though they may not be right all the time. This is especially true when it comes to technical inventions and new institutional designs: agents almost always invent those ideas with goals in mind.

Moreover, existing social structure (i.e., institutions and culture) powerfully shapes what ideas are generated, selected, and inherited (Elias 1939[1994]; Foucault 1980). Hence, many, perhaps even most, mutations in the ideational dimension of social evolution are not generated blindly even *in some broad sense*, although some may be (e.g., through social science research). In other words, *to a very large extent—although not all, ideational mutations in social evolution are nonrandom and directed* (see also Boyd and Richerson 1985, 9–10). As becomes clear below, the fact that ideational mutations in social evolution can be non-random and directed has major implications for the speed of social evolution.

Of course, just because ideas are not generated randomly and blindly does not mean that a phenotype expressed from an idea will always be "fit" in the social system: those ideas (as genes) and phenotypes (e.g., behaviors) will still be subject to selection in the social system. Indeed, equating non-random/

directed mutations with "designed" fitness has been a major source of confusion among many, especially adherents of the Austrian school: implicitly or explicitly, they mistakenly equate *"spontaneous"* with random and blind (e.g., Hakey 1973[1982]).

C. Selection in Social Evolution: A Complex Picture

In biological evolution, there is only one source of selection pressure: the physical environment. In contrast, in social evolution, there are two sources of selection pressure: the physical environment and human beings themselves. These two sources of selection pressure interact with each other to drive social evolution. Furthermore, because of the coming of ideational forces in social evolution, there are also two different types of selection pressure: material and ideational. Coupled with the fact that there can be different pairs of genes and phenotypes in social evolution (see above), selection in social evolution is immensely more complex than that in biological evolution.[26]

a. Natural versus Artificial; Material versus Ideational

Before the coming of humans, the only source of selection pressure in biological evolution was the physical environment. Selection pressure back then was as such exclusively material. Moreover, without human intervention, the physical environment was also entirely natural.

The fact that there are two sources of selection pressure in social evolution adds great complexity to selection in social evolution. To begin with, even the physical environment—which has been increasingly modified by human activities even before the Industrial Revolution—is no longer purely natural. This artificial, although still physical, environment now shapes the biological evolution of human and all other species. The artificial breeding of new species by humans is the most obvious manifestation of humans' impact over the evolution of other species. The coming of global warming represents the most potent manifestation of humans' far-reaching impact over the evolution of other species and humans themselves.

More critically, selection pressure in the ideational dimension of social evolution can be both material and ideational. Material forces still provide the ultimate arbitrator whether an idea improves human welfare or not. At the same time, ideational forces provide the more immediate selection pressure when it comes to picking what ideas are to be put into practice or to be backed. Finally, because ideational forces are ultimately powered by human intelligence, they are purely artificial. As such, *artificial selection rather than natural selection dominates the ideational dimension of social evolution* (Commons 1934, 45, 636, 657–8),[27] although this artificial selection still has to operate within the constraints dictated by the physical environment. In social evolution, artificial selection and natural selection are not incompatible forces as some have insisted (e.g., Hodgson 2002, 266–9; cf. Hodgson and Knudsen 2010b, 50–1). Rather, they work together with each other.

b. Social Power as a Key Selection Force in Social Evolution

From the interaction between material forces and ideational forces, there arises a critical selection force in social evolution: *(social) power.*

As advanced by many, from policy changes (Kingdon 1995; Campbell 2002), to institutional change (Tang 2011a), and to culture (Elias 1939 [1994]; Bourdieu 1980[1990]; Foucault 1976[1990]; 2000; Durham 1991), *power is often one of the key selection forces in social evolution.* Although I cannot elaborate here, suffice to say that without power, it is almost impossible to explain why so many ideational genes and phenotypes (e.g., institutions, cultural traits) have been retained in different human societies despite the fact that these genes and phenotypes fundamentally reduce these societies' welfare (for details, see Tang 2011a). In this sense, any framework on social evolution that does not explicitly admit power as a critical selection force is incomplete (e.g., Boyd and Richerson 1985; Blackmore 1999; Blute 2010; Hodgson and Knudsen 2010b).[28]

Several critical consequences of having social power as a key selection force are obvious. First, selection in the ideational dimension of social evolution, and sometimes in the material (i.e., the genetic) dimension of social evolution is often heavily biased (Durham 1991, 198, 205). Individuals who have more power may determine which idea should spread and which should not. Second, existing ideas, especially those ideas that have been codified, usually backed by power, have a powerful impact on the fitness of (new) ideas and, sometimes genes too (Foucault 1980; North 1990; Tang 2011a).[29] Third, cultural and institutional traits may or may not enhance the inclusive fitness of their hosts.[30]

In sum, whereas there is only material and natural selection in biological evolution, selection in social evolution is both natural and artificial. Human intelligence plays a central role in the ideational dimension of social evolution: it produces not only ideational mutations, but also provides much of the selection pressure. Most importantly, it is due to this artificial selection by human intelligence that *material* progress in social evolution is secured, in the long run (Tang 2011a).

c. Levels of Selection: Gene, Phenotype, Individual, and Group

In biological evolution, selection operates only on the phenotype level, but not on the gene level: only phenotype, but not gene, is "visible" to selection pressure (Mayr 1997). Traditionally, most biologists hold that selection in biological evolution operates almost exclusively on the individual level, but not on the group level (e.g., Williams 1966).[31] After Richard Lewontin's (1970) seminal paper, however, many biologists have also come to admit that there may be multiple levels of selection even in biological evolution (Hull 1980; Brandon 1982; 1998; 1999; Buss 1983; Okasha 2006). The biological evolution of the human species is also governed by multilevel selections.

In contrast, because there are different pairs of genes and phenotypes and different sources and types of selection pressure in the ideational dimension of social evolution, selection in the ideational dimension of social evolution can operate at all four levels: gene, phenotype, individual, group, and many levels within individual and group (for a summary, see Table 1.2).

For example, group selection via war and conquest has been one of the most powerful drivers in social evolution (Darwin 1874, 137–40, Spencer 1873; Campbell 1975; 1976; 1991; Carneiro 1978; Dawson 1999; Diamond 1997; Chaudhry and Garner 2006; Soltis, Boyd, and Richerson 1995; Spencer and Redmond 2001; Nolan and Lenski 2004; for a more detailed discussion, see Chapter 2 below). The central principle might be that groups with more welfare-improving institutions hold more advantage in competitions among groups—especially in organized warfare, all else being equal (Hayek 1967, 67–71; 1973[1982], 44; 1976[1982], 162; 1979[1982], 202).[32] Straightforwardly, better welfare means a larger and better-fed population and thus more technological innovations (Jones 2005), and population size and technological sophistication in turn largely determine groups' war-fighting capabilities (Diamond 1997; for a simulation along this line, see Tang et al., n.d.).

Thus, regarding ideational selection in social evolution, it may be more fruitful to conceive that selection operates on a host of levels that are nested with each other. Selections over phenotypes, both ideational and material, are direct. Meanwhile, whereas selection over biological genes is indirect, selections over ideational genes are mostly direct.

Moreover, within the ideational dimension, different forces of selection may operate at different levels, while at the same time the same force of selection

Table 1.2. Levels of Selection in Biological and Social Evolution

Levels of Selection	Biological Evolution	Social Evolution	
		The Biological Dimension	The Ideational Dimension
Group	?	Yes?	Yes
Individual Organism	Yes	Yes	Yes
Phenotype	Yes	Yes	Yes
Gene	No	No	Yes

may operate differently at different levels. At the individual level, sensation and emotion (e.g., pain and pleasure), instrumental calculation (often in the shadow of social power), habit (socialization and internalization, often backed by power), faith, affection, legality (embedded in existing social structure, often explicitly backed by power), and anti-socialization can all operate as selection forces (Weber 1978, ch. 1). At the collective level (i.e., family, group, corporation, state, and the international system level), selection forces can again range from power (material and ideational combined), to instrumental reason, habit, emotion, and legality. More importantly, the two levels interact with each other: selection forces interact with each other to shape social outcomes at the two levels, outcomes at one level can come back to function as selection forces at the other level (Durham 1991, 204–5). Most prominently, outcomes of selection at higher level impact selection at lower level: ideas are produced under a particular institutional and cultural system (i.e., the social structure), and existing institutions and cultural traits inevitably influence what new ideas are pursued and what new ideas will be retained (Foucault 1972[1977]; 1980; Giddens 1984; Tang 2011a).[33] All these lead to a profoundly complex picture (e.g., Elias 1939[1994]; Bourdieu 1980 [1990]; Foucault 1980; 1976 [1990]; Tang 2011a).

D. Mechanisms of Inheritance in Social Evolution

The two major dimensions of social evolution, the material dimension (which subsumes the biological evolution of human beings) and the ideational dimension, have two fundamentally different mechanisms of inheritance: social evolution has "dual inheritance" (Boyd and Richerson 1985; Durham 1991).

The biological evolution of *Homo sapiens* still obeys the principles of Neo-Darwinism: direct phenotype-to-genotype inheritance remains impossible because the Weisman Barrier remains intact. Even when it comes to the biological evolution of human species, there is a new twist, however. As human activities increasingly reshape our environment, the physical environment as the source of selection pressure for human biological evolution is no longer natural but rather "artificial-natural". In other words, our behaviors also come back to shape our genetic evolution via environment, although this feedback loop from human behavior to human genetic evolution via environment is still poorly understood.

Whereas the Weismann Barrier in the biological dimension of human evolution remains intact, there is no Weismann Barrier in the ideational dimension of social evolution that prevents the flow of information from phenotype to genes. Because human beings have the brain power to absorb and process so much information and they spend a considerable amount of time in nurturing and teaching their progenies, individuals can acquire the product of their ancestors' learning through learning. As such, both ideational genes (e.g., ideas) and phenotypes (e.g., institutions, culture) as acquired characters can now be *directly* transmitted to the next generation. Indeed, institutions (as phenotypes) can be transmitted to the next generation of individuals, almost completely independently from the transmission from one particular individual to his/her progenies: institutions, especially explicitly codified rules, are simply handed down to the next generation, *even if* many individuals refuse to teach their progenies those rules. Inheritance in the ideational dimension of social evolution is thus more than what is captured by the notion of Lamarckian inheritance,[34] and I shall call it *Super-Lamarckian*, in order to differentiate it from the Neo-Lamarckian (or epigenetic) inheritance in biological evolution (see Table 1.1 for details).

Though both ideational genes and phenotypes can be directly inherited, however, inheritance in the ideational dimension of social evolution is *not* purely Super-Lamarckian. Because every generation does some selection over the genes and phenotypes that have been passed to them from the previous generation, the core Darwinian (not Neo-Darwinian) principle of variation-selection-inheritance applies to inheritance in the ideational dimension. As such, the mechanism of inheritance in the ideational dimension of social evolution is *Darwinian nested within Super-Lamarckian*.

A key point must be stressed right away. Exactly because selection in ideational evolution is artificial, this means that not every idea that has been selected for all ideational will improve individuals' or groups' welfare, partly because inheritance of ideas in human society often, if not always, requires the backing of power (for a detailed discussion, see Tang 2011a).

E. Adaptation in the Ideational Dimension of Social Evolution

In both biological evolution and social evolution, a trait is understood to be some kind of adaptation (or fitness), if it can be shown to contribute to an organism's welfare (e.g., survival, reproduction). In biological evolution, organisms cannot attempt to adapt because they lack intelligence. Adaptation in biological evolution is thus produced by the brutal force of natural selection. The same principle still applies to the biological evolution of the human species.

Because we humans do possess intelligence, however, it is only natural that we will consciously strive to adapt to our environment by generating and deploying ideas that improve our welfare, and sometimes we do get things right, although not necessarily immediately. Thus, in the ideational dimension of social evolution, we can indeed have *directed and intended* adaptations. Moreover, some of these adaptations in the ideational dimension can be directly transmitted to the next generation.

Yet, just because we try to adapt consciously does not mean that all of our adaptations are the *immediate* result of our conscious attempts to adapt. Many, if not most, of our adaptations are still the result of a long selection process through trial and error, our conscious attempts to adapt notwithstanding: this process is Darwinian nested within Super-Lamarckian rather than purely Super-Lamarckian. Moreover, just because we try to adapt consciously does not mean that we do not retain ideational impairments: indeed, for a variety of reasons, many of our ideas may actually reduce our welfare (e.g., welfare-decreasing institutions, see Tang 2011a for details).[35] In sum, adaptations in the ideational dimension of social evolution are also produced by a mixture of Darwinian and Lamarckian mechanisms, just like inheritance in the ideational dimension.

F. Stages and Directionality in Social Evolution[36]

A striking observation is that human society has experienced stages. In terms of political organization, human society has experienced band, tribe, chiefdom, and states (Service [1962]1971; for a more differentiated scale, see Johnson and Earle 2000). In terms of the materials and technologies for making tools, human society has experienced at least three stages: stone,[37] bronze, and iron. Similarly, in terms of primary production methods, human society has experienced three key stages: hunting and gathering, (formative and settled) agriculture, and industry.[38] As becomes clear in the chapters below, one can also talk about three or four stages (i.e., phases or eras) in the history of international politics.

What should be emphasized here is that while identifying the various stages of human society is perhaps a useful step for understanding social evolution, merely identifying the stages (or other forms of changes) is not evolutionary theorizing per se: it simply establishes (or captures) the fact of social changes. The hallmark of a genuinely evolutionary theory must explain the shifting from one stage to another with the central mechanism of variation–selection–inheritance (see the chapters below). Many so-called attempts of evolutionary theorizing merely identify the various stages without providing a genuinely evolutionary explanation of the changes.

Once we accept that there are different stages in social evolution and these stages are associated with different levels of social complexities that come sequentially (e.g., from band to tribe to chiefdom to state), it seems inevitable that we must accept that social evolution possesses an apparent "directionality" toward some kind of progress (e.g., Spencer 1857[1891]; White 1949; Huxley 1942, 289; idem., 1956; Sahlins 1960; Carneiro 2003, 169–9, 171–9, 229–39). Such an understanding, however, is incorrect.

Let's recall that the apparent directionality associated with stages is the result brought by the mechanism of variation–selection–inheritance. Most critically, selection, both natural and artificial, still operates in social evolution. *Once we admit this, it is easy to grasp that the seemingly apparent directionality is only apparent because movements in the other direction has been invisible to us (i.e., many social entities have disappeared and left few traces behind), or more likely, we choose to ignore movements in the other direction because we want to believe that evolution must mean movement toward progress.*

Indeed, Carneiro (2003, 165) was only able to claim that evolution has directionality because he explicitly equates evolution with an increase in complexity, but devolution or retrogression with a decrease in complexity. Yet, such a stand of taking only movements to increased complexity as evolution but excluding movements to decreased complexity as part of evolution fundamentally violates the central principle of evolution, biological or social. Because evolution fundamentally depends on selection and selection can only mean some phenotypes, organisms, species, and social entities will be marginalized and eliminated, this movement to decreased complexity is an indispensable part of evolution.[39]

Moreover, once we admit that selection is central to evolution, it becomes apparent that evolution—whether natural or social—does not inevitably lead to greater complexity or moral progress, for three interconnected reasons. First, it does not make sense to argue that all those perished social entities (e.g., tribes and chiefdoms) have been eliminated for the sake of progress by human beings as a whole. Second, the elimination of some social entities certainly does not lead to material progress or moral progress for those who had been eliminated. Finally, can't demise and elimination be understood as directional too?

To reiterate; there is no real directionality in evolution, biological or social. As noted by many (e.g., Williams 1966[1996], 35; Levins and Lewontin 1985; Kaye 1986, 28–33; Fracchia and Lewontin 1999, 60–7), equating biological or social evolution as directional movement toward higher stages and greater complexity essentially reflects our anthropocentric attempt to put our species, "race", and society at the pinnacle of biological and social evolution rather than scientific rigor.

IV. SOCIAL EVOLUTION AS A PARADIGM: CORE PRINCIPLES

Even at the time of publishing the initial exposition of their theory, both Darwin and Alfred Russell Wallace recognized that their theory holds profound implications for understanding human as a species and the human society (Richards 1987, 157–69). Not surprisingly, after their initial discovery, many of their faithful and unfaithful followers had earnestly applied their theory to the understanding of human society (for good historical accounts, see Hodgson 2005; Nelson 2007). Unfortunately, most, if not all, of these earlier (and some later) applications of the evolution paradigm to human society have been misleading, if not outright dangerous (for a more detailed critique, see Tang 2014–15; for earlier critiques, see Campbell 1965[1998]; Hallpike 1986; Kaye 1986; Fracchia and Lewontin 1999). A key cause behind this debacle has been a lack of a systematic statement on what a proper evolutionary approach toward human society should look like, based on a systematic statement on what social evolution is. This section summarizes a more systematic statement on social evolution as a paradigm developed in more detail elsewhere (Tang 2014–15), thus paving the way for applying SEP to examine the evolution of international politics in the chapters follow.

A. Ontological and Epistemological

Ontologically, SEP holds the following core principles. First, human society has always been an evolutionary system. As such, the evolution paradigm expounded by Darwin and his followers can be applied to understand human society. Second, social evolution is fundamentally different from biological evolution. As such, SEP is not, and cannot be a mechanistic transplantation of Darwinian evolution to the human society. Rather, SEP is a fundamentally new paradigm.[40] More concretely, SEP subsumes the social system paradigm (SSP), which organically synthesizes all the nine bedrock paradigms of social sciences and thus provides us with tools for understanding the dynamics within a social system. Ontologically, SEP adds the dimension of time to SSP and gives time the power to transform social systems. As such, SEP organically synthesizes all the other ten foundational paradigms in social sciences, with the core synthesizing principle being the central evolutionary mechanism of variation–selection–inheritance (Tang 2011b; 2014–15).

Epistemologically, SEP holds three principles. First, human society can be productively studied with an evolutionary approach, with its core being the mechanism of *artificial* variation–selection–inheritance. Indeed, SEP holds that the history of human society can only be adequately understood with an evolutionary approach, with SEP as its embodiment. Second, the application of evolutionary thinking to human society must not be metaphorical or purely biological. Third and most importantly, the central explanatory mechanism of social change and stability must be the central mechanism of *artificial* variation–selection–inheritance.

B. SEP's Core Operational Principles toward Systemic Social Change[41]

An evolutionary account of the transformation of a system must have three components: course (history) of evolution, explanation of the transformation with the central mechanisms of variation–selection–retention, and an understanding of the major determinants of evolutionary process (e.g., geography, population, technology, trade, war), without necessarily assigning particular weight to different factors.[42] To achieve such an account, SEP emphasizes the following operational rules.

In principle, SEP can, and should, organically synthesize all the other ten foundational paradigms of social sciences. In practice, however, synthesizing all these paradigms is beyond our capacity. Thus, the first operational principle is that different social scientists looking at different social phenomena will have to combine the foundational paradigms differently but sensibly. In other words, students of human society themselves must decide what paradigms should be deployed for tackling the phenomena they need to tackle, although they must bear all the foundational paradigms in mind. At the same time, however, we must recognize that any framework that ignores those paradigms with ontological priority must necessarily be flawed and cannot possibly be genuinely evolutionary (for details, see Tang 2013). For instance, a purely ideationalism framework (as embodied in social constructivism in IR, e.g., Onuf 1989; Kratochwil 1989; Wendt 1999) cannot be truly evolutionary because it marginalizes, if not totally neglects, material forces.

All in all, as emphasized explicitly earlier and elsewhere (Tang 2011b; 2013), there is no easy guide for which foundational paradigms to deploy: we have to grapple with this challenge for the specific social phenomena we seek to understand, often case by case. Only by doing so can we truly appreciate the potential, but equally if not more important, the limitations of our explanatory framework. Moreover, as we proceed with our research, we may find it necessary to bring more foundational paradigms into our frameworks rather than staying with our preconceived framework stubbornly. Only by doing so can we prevent the search for framework from becoming a hindrance to understanding, as Hirschman (1970) had forewarned us.

Second, SEP insists that changes at one level are fundamentally driven by changes at levels below, although it also admits that changes at a higher level can come back to impact the levels below: changes are thus mostly endogenously driven. Indeed, *only an evolutionary approach can offer genuinely endogenous explanation of change and stability* (Boland 1979, 968; Knudsen 2001, 125).

Third, SEP rejects an adapationism or functionalism approach toward social changes. Just as one cannot conclude that an adaptation is the result of an organism's conscious attempt to adapt in biological evolution, one cannot conclude—as functionalism does—that an "adaptation" in social evolution is the immediate result of an individual or group's conscious attempt to adapt either. Although the possibility that an individual or group's conscious attempt to adapt can succeed is real, it is merely a possibility rather than a predetermined fact. One cannot assume, again as adapationism in biology but especially functionalism in social sciences do, that any phenotype must be an adaptation, if not a perfect adaptation. *Whether a phenotype is an adaptation in social evolution is an empirical question, not a rule.*

Fourth, because social evolution can only operate within a social system, SSP is an integral part of SEP: the latter subsumes the former. As such, SEP accepts all the methodological rules dictated by SSP. In other words, SEP also cautions against simplistic measures for understanding society, such as searching for simple (if not mono-) causal links, linear thinking, assigning weight to particular forces, and adding up effects by individual factors to understand the whole etc. Rather, we should look for interactions, feedbacks, and path dependence, etc. when it comes to social dynamics. When it comes to social outcomes, we should look for indirect/direct, delayed/instant, unintended/intended, and observable (events)/unobservable (non-events) (Jervis 1997).

Finally, in order for a theory to be genuinely evolutionary, it must specify many critical things as noted above, from genes, phenotypes, sources of mutation, sources of selection pressure, and mechanisms through which selection forces select mutations and through which selected phenotypes are inherited. A social evolutionary explanation of a historical outcome must do the same. Most of the earlier applications of evolutionary thinking to social sciences failed because they did not specify these things (e.g., Alchian 1950; Nelson and Winter 1982; Hayek 1967; 1978; 1982; Carneiro 2003; for similar critiques, see Knight 1992, ch. 4; Calvert 1995, 261; Fiani, n.d.).

C. The Power of SEP as a Paradigm

Just as evolutionary theorizing for biological evolution is necessarily *post hoc*, social evolutionary theorizing for social evolution is necessarily *post hoc*. In other words, evolutionary theorizing always theorizes what has already evolved out there. Similarly, just as evolutionary theorizing for biological evolution does not necessarily predict the exact path (e.g., a Spencerian linear progressive process or cycles) and outcome of any particular evolutionary process—whether a species or a fauna—because it allows accidents, social evolutionary theorizing does not necessarily predict the specific path or outcome of any particular evolutionary process in human society because social evolutionary approach too admits accidents. The power of (biological and social) evolutionary theorizing does not lie with its capacity for proving (in the literal sense) the past and predicting the future.

Rather, evolutionary theorizing tries to better non-evolutionary theorizing on four fronts: (1) more effectively and parsimoniously organizing and synthesizing a wider body of evidence than non-evolutionary theorizing; (2) providing a more coherent, integrative, and foundational explanation for a more diverse body of observations than non-evolutionary theorizing; (3) providing more endogenous explanations for social change and stability; and (4) generating predictions about what have been evolved (but yet to be discovered), and these predictions cannot be generated by non-evolutionary theorizing (Dennett 1995; Buss 1995; Caporael and Brewer 1995; Hodgson and Knudsen 2010a; 2010b). More concretely, an evolutionary explanation of social change gains superiority over non-evolutionary explanations by relying on the central mechanism of artificial variation–selection–inheritance.

These properties bestow SEP with great power for understanding human society. Just as Neo-Darwinism claims to be "the universal acid" for understanding biotic evolution, SEP has a legitimate claim to be "the universal acid" for understanding human society across time, space, and level.

V. WHAT IS NOT A SOCIAL EVOLUTIONARY APPROACH?

If there have been numerous areas of confusion about biological evolution even though the theory of biological evolution has been more forcefully established, then it is no surprise that more areas of confusion have bedeviled our understanding of social evolution. After all, social evolution is different from and vastly more complex than biological evolution. Indeed, even some of the biggest names in social sciences one time or another have erred in their understanding of social evolution (e.g., Spencer, Veblen, Marx, Schumpeter, and Hayek). To make SEP a valid paradigm in social sciences, we must rectify these mistakes. This section seeks to state explicitly what does not constitute a genuine social evolutionary approach by applying the criteria outlined in the preceding two sections.

First and foremost, *SEP is not mechanistic application of Neo-Darwinism as the theory of biological evolution to social evolution*, simply because social evolution is fundamentally different from biological evolution. Social evolution is not purely Neo-Darwinian or even largely Darwinian, but really *Darwinian nested within Super-Lamarckian*. Likewise, both genes and phenotypes in the ideational dimension of social evolution are fundamentally different from the two entities in biological evolution. As such, the ideational dimension in social evolution demands a new understanding about gene and phenotype.

Second, *SEP is not biological evolution-determinism or reductionism*,[43] as embodied in (human) sociobiology and Evolutionary Psychology (EP). Both sociobiology and EP insist that natural selection is *the major force*, if not the only force, in shaping human behavior (e.g., Wilson 1978; Alexander 1979; Tooby and Cosmides 1990; 1992; Buss 1995). In contrast, SEP insists that human society has been a product of social evolution, rather than biological evolution alone. In other words, SEP unambiguously rejects the notion that natural selection is *the major force* in shaping human behavior. As such, SEP firmly rejects biological evolution-determinism or reductionism, in any form. Moreover, because social evolution is much more than "not by gene alone" (e.g., Richerson and Boyd 2005) or "co-evolution of gene and culture" (e.g., Boyd and Richerson 1985; Durham 1991; Blute 2006; 2010), merely admitting "not by gene alone" or "co-evolution of gene and culture" is not sufficiently social evolutionary.

Third, *SEP is not Social Darwinism or "Survival of the Fittest"*, as a twisted form of biological evolution determinism. Social Darwinism, which should be more properly labeled Social Spencerism, is based on an erroneous under-standing even at the level of biological evolution. Spencer believed that natural selection leads to "survival of the fittest." Yet, natural selection does not lead to survival of "the fittest", only the "fitter": there is no such thing called "fittest" in biological or social evolution because all adaptations are environment-specific. With "survival of the fittest" refuted, Social Darwinism/Spencerism has no ground to exist.

Fourth, *SEP is not cultural determinism*, either. SEP insists that social evolution is a process driven by both biological evolution and ideational evolution. Because culture is only part of ideational evolution, culture—un-doubtedly a critical force in shaping human society—cannot possibly deter-mine the whole human society. Moreover, contra to Leslie White's notion that culture is self-contained and self-determined (1949, xviii), culture itself is a product of social evolution. Most fundamentally, culture, as mostly an idea-tional existence, must have a material foundation to begin with and operate within the constraints dictated by a material foundation. As such, culture itself cannot possibly be an independent force in shaping human society. When this is the case, there is no ground for "cultural determinism".

Fifth, *SEP is not naive adaptationism or functionalism* (as it is more commonly known in social sciences). Functional explanation is part of any evolutionary approach, but it is not all of it. Most critically, one cannot assume that any phenotype must be an adaptation, if not a perfect adaptation. Whether a phenotype is an adaptation in biological or social evolution is an empirical question, not a preordained rule. In addition, one cannot con-clude—as functionalism does—that an "adaptation" in social evolution is the immediate result of an individual's or group's conscious attempt to adapt either.[44] Adapationism has been firmly rejected even in biological evolution, and functionalism/adapationism is even more untenable in social evolution. Indeed, functionalism is an enemy of evolutionary thinking (Hallpike 1986).

Finally, *SEP is not destiny unfolding/historical inevitability*. One of the most heinous prophecies has been "historical inevitability" or "destiny unfolding" (Berlin 2002). Because Spencer, consistent with his Christian belief, had essentially equated evolution (biological and social) with a higher destiny unfolding, many have continued to believe that social evolution (if not biological evolution) is some kind of "historical inevitability" or "destiny unfolding" (e.g., Sahlins and Service 1960; Carneiro 2003). SEP, just like evolutionary theorizing in biology, admits accidents and contingencies and firmly rejects "historical inevitability" or "destiny unfolding".

VI. EVOLUTIONARY THEORIZING IN IR: A CRITIQUE

There has not been a lack of flirting with evolutionary ideas in international relations (IR), starting with the notorious racist imperialism, Social Darwinism and Geopolitics in the late 19th and early 20th centuries. After explicitly rejecting those devilish doctrines in the second half of the 20th century, IR theorists have gradually brought evolutionary thinking back, so much so that all major schools of IR such as neorealism, neoliberalism, and constructivism all have some evolutionary elements (Kahler 1999; Sterling-Folker 2001; Patrick 2001).[45] Indeed, Kenneth Waltz (1986, 331) famously called for "keep(ing) the notion of 'selection' in a position of central importance [in international politics]" (see also Waltz 1979, 74–7). Similarly, Scott Sagan (1997), when discussing the possibility of combining (neo)realism and (neo)culturalism, singled out selection as a possible link between the two.

In this section, I present a brief critical survey of several important examples and strains of theorizing of international politics with an evolutionary flavor. The key purpose is to highlight that in light of the coherent and systematic statement on SEP advanced above, it is apparent many earlier applications of evolutionary thinking in IR are merely metaphorical, superficial, and pseudo-evolutionary (e.g., Modelski's long cycles). Some are genuinely evolutionary (e.g., Spruyt 1994a; 1994b), but most of them do not measure up to what SEP demands.

Theories of Foreign Policy Change Jeffrey Legro (2005) advanced a theory of foreign policy change that is based on an evolutionary scheme, although he did not use the label. Legro emphasized that states often change their policies when they recognize that their old policies are not working, and during the process of searching for new policies, (old and new) ideas compete for the new policies. A similar scheme is also found in David Welch's book on foreign policy changes, and he actually had a casual reference to evolutionary biology (2005, 16).

The first theory of foreign policy change that is explicitly informed by SEP was developed by Tang (2008a). Surveying China's foreign policy from c.1949 to 2007, Tang argued that a social evolutionary account best explains the slow but profound change from Mao Zedong to Deng Xiaoping. Tang's scheme was further developed and then applied to explain military interventions of the United States after the Second World War (Tang and Long 2012). Here, the authors explicitly synthesize material forces with ideational forces on the one hand and selection and learning on the other hand. More concretely, the authors argued that due to its blessed geographical location and power/technological superiority, the United States has been facing much lower selection pressure than other great powers to behave more moderately. As such, among the major states, the United States has been the more offensive realist state.

Change and Spread of International Institutional and Norms The field that has the most applications of evolutionary elements in IR might have been the studying of the evolution of institutions and norms. Taking institutions and norms as dependent variable rather than independent variable,[46] this literature seeks to explain why and how a particular institution or norm emerges and how it spreads. Because this literature focuses on the ideational dimension of social evolution, works within this literature tend to be more evolutionary: even those that are not explicitly evolutionary depend upon some evolutionary elements to operate their scheme of change.

The first wave of neoliberalism toward institutional change adopts an explicitly functionalism approach (e.g., Keohane and Nye 1977[1989]; Keohane 1984; for a good review, see Sterling-Folker 2000). As such, these theories of institutional change suffer from serious deficiencies that are inherent to a functionalism theory of institutional change (Tang 2011a). More recently, neoliberalists have put more emphasis on power and competition, and their theories now capture more, but still limited, social reality (e.g., Ikenberry 2000; Gruber 2000; for a penetrating critique of the neoliberalism literature on institutions, see Schweller 2001).

Neoliberalism holds that states' preferences over goals are fixed whereas constructivism that both states' and other intra-state agents' identities and goals are subject to change. As a result, constructivism is more evolutionary than neoliberalism (Patrick 2001). Many constructivists have explained the rise and spread of norms (often as part of "collective identities") without labeling their framework evolutionary, but their frameworks are at least somewhat evolutionary (e.g., Wendt 1992; 1999; Checkel 2001; Acharya 2004; Hall 1999; Reus-Smit 1997; 1999; Holsti 2004; Johnston 2008). And several constructivists (e.g., Fiorini 1996; Patrick 2001) have explicitly labeled their approaches as evolutionary.

In light of a general theory of institutional change that is firmly informed by SEP (Tang 2011a), however, these neoliberalism and constructivism theories of institutional change (and diffusion) are only naive or partially evolutionary (see Chapter 4 below for details).

"Cognitive Evolution" Emmanuel Adler's (1991[2005]) "cognitive evolution" paper was an early constructivism statement based explicitly on Popper–Campbell–Toulmin-inspired "evolutionary epistemology" (see also Adler 2005, ch. 1). Adler explicitly deployed the central mechanism of variation–selection–inheritance as the key mechanism for understanding cognitive evolution in international politics. Moreover, he singled out several dichotomous foundational paradigms and (implicitly) argued that we need to synthesize them organically (i.e., "seizing the middle ground"; Adler 1997a). Adler's scheme of cognitive evolution is also a two-level game scheme: states invent new ideas, and some ideas (usually innovative and progressive ones) will be selected and propagated in the international arena. Once these ideas win out in the process of cognitive evolution, they will (gradually but progressively) transform the international subsystem (Adler 1997b). This scheme is a significant (evolutionary) improvement over a purely structural approach toward ideational change in the international system (cf. Wendt 1992; 1999), because only individuals (within states) can invent ideas and the ideas within the international structure itself do not come into existence out of the blue.[47]

Despite its significant evolutionary flavor, however, Adler's scheme is still an incomplete application of SEP. Most importantly, despite his claim that constructivism occupies the middle ground between materialism and ideationalism (Adler 1997a, 336), Adler has little to say about what roles material forces play in his "cognitive evolution". Furthermore, contra his claim that constructivism emphasizes power more than its many utopian predecessors (Adler 1997a, 336; 2005, 14), power and real conflict do not really feature significantly in his discussion. Finally, even if constructivism occupies the middle grounds between those dichotomous paradigms, it does not adequately synthesize those paradigms (cf. Tang and Long 2012). Yet such a synthesis is a must for a genuinely evolutionary approach toward IR and the broader human society.

The Emergence of Nation State In IR, Hendrik Spruyt's explanation for the rise of sovereign territorial state in the European international system between the 14th and 18th centuries comes closest to SEP advocated here (Spruyt 1994a; 1994b). Critically building upon Tilly (1990), Krasner (1984, 1988, 1999), and many others, Spruyt emphasizes variations and selection as two crucial steps for understanding why and how a particular form of state (i.e., the sovereign territorial state) eventually came to dominate the system. Spruyt argues that the sovereign territorial state was more capable of protecting trade and extracting revenue and thus had a long-term advantage in competing against the other two possible forms of governance (i.e., city leagues, city state). Spruyt's overall thesis represents a major step toward a more adequate explanation of the rise of territorial state and sovereignty. Unfortunately, Spruyt mistakenly equates social evolution with mostly institutional evolution, emphasizes periodicalization and pace in evolution, and draws too much inspiration from Fernand Braudel and punctuated equilibrium of Stephen Gould (e.g., Spruyt 1994b, 22–33, 178–9; for critique of Gould, see Dennett 1995). In addition, Spruyt still retains a heavy dose of functionalism that is embedded in "comparative institutional historical analysis (HCIA)", which is in turn informed by neoclassical economics (e.g., North, Williamson; for a detailed critique, see Tang 2011a, ch. 2) Finally, Spruyt does not offer a systematic statement on what constitutes a proper social evolutionary approach toward social changes.

Agent-based Evolutionary Modeling Agent-based modeling (or simulation) is another way of modeling evolutionary change. The widely cited study of Axelrod (1984) was an early influential study. Farkas (1996) provided a simple model of picking policies within a leadership group. More recently, Lars-Erik Cederman and his colleagues have modeled the coming of sovereignty and democratic peace via conquest and regime change as an evolutionary process within the international system (Cederman 1997; 2001a; 2001b; 2002; Cederman and Gleditsch 2004; Cederman and Girardin 2010).[48] Their studies have generated some very interesting findings and shed much new light on the evolution of the international system, and their findings tend to corroborate the thesis developed in this book, although within a shorter time frame (i.e., pre-modern Europe to modern Europe).

Agent-based modeling, however powerful, is only evolutionary in a very limited sense. It generally assigns fixed preferences over goals to agents and allows only preferences over strategies to change during the process. It further assumes the environment to be relatively constant (other than the possible change of preferences over strategies, number of actors in the system). As such, this type of modeling cannot model how agents and the system mutually constitute each other and thus the deeper kind of transformation of the whole system.

Theories of International Systemic Change The system of international politics seems to have experienced profound changes. Hence, an evolutionary approach can be fruitfully applied to it. Nonetheless, none has advanced a truly social evolutionary interpretation regarding the evolution of the international system.

At the system level, some of the most influential voices in IR theory have been anti-evolutionary: both Waltz (1979, 66) and Mearsheimer (2001, 2) have explicitly insisted that the nature of international politics remains the same through time.

Yet, most students of IR have admitted fundamental transformations of the international system. For instance, John Ruggie (1983) noted that the coming of territorial state constituted a systemic transformation. Similarly, John Mueller (1989) noted that states have learned that war does not pay: major wars have become obsolete, even if the nuclear revolution had not occurred (see also Jervis 2002). None of these authors, however, explicitly adopts an evolutionary approach.

Alex Wendt's (1992; 1999) discussion on different anarchies constitutes an interpretation of international politics *at the system level* with a genuine evolutionary flavor. Wendt underscores that anarchy can have different types, thus implying the possibility of systemic transformation (see also Ruggie 1983). Wendt (1999, ch. 7) also singled out several possible forces for driving this transformation, based on a "cultural evolutionary" approach toward identity formation/change and structural change. In addition, Wendt discussed both selection and socialization in cultural evolution. Unfortunately, Wendt (like Adler before him) exclusively depends on ideational factors, although he talks about "rump materialism".[49] Thus, Wendt repeatedly asserts that "the most important structures in which states are embedded are made of ideas, not material forces" (Wendt 1999, 309; for critique of Wendt's ideationalism, see Palan 2000; Copeland 2000b, 191–2). As such, Wendt could not explain how and why those ideas that make different anarchies (i.e., Hobbesian, Lockeian, or Kantian) came to form in the first place and then spread (for more in-depth critique in this context, see Chapters 2 and 5 below).

Jared Diamond's majestic book, *Guns, Germs, and Steel* (1997), is a sweeping macro-history of human society from 11,000 BC to today, thus an account of international system change. His approach is based on a social evolutionary approach, emphasizing both material forces (e.g., geography, population, germs) and ideational forces (ideas embodied in agricultural and industrial revolution). Unfortunately, he did not directly discuss the transformation of international politics, nor did he explicitly spell out his core assumptions and operational principles.

The Origins of War in Human History Based on sociobiology, Thayer (2004) and Gat (2006) advance two similar theories on the origin and the spreading of war in human history. Both correctly point out that much of the IR literature on the origins of war is really about the immediate causes of war (e.g., Blainey 1988; Van Evera 1999; Copeland 2000b), and IR scholars often have a mistaken understanding of the origins of war. Both also correctly emphasize that the origins of war can only be adequately understood from an evolutionary view. Unfortunately, both remain firmly within the sociobiology camp, thus cannot possibly offer an adequate explanation for the origin and the spreading of war in human history (for a more detailed critique, see Chapter 2 below).

Moreover, both fail to state explicitly what social evolution is and what the social evolution paradigm is.

CONCLUDING REMARKS

In this chapter, I have summarized a more coherent and systematic statement on social evolution and SEP advanced elsewhere (Tang 2014–15). SEP synthesizes all the other ten foundational paradigms of social sciences, thus providing us with the necessary power for understanding human history with human society as a product of social evolution. SEP synthesizes and subsumes many micro- and middle-level mechanisms that have been uncovered for understanding human society. SEP is indeed the ultimate paradigm in social sciences.

In the next several chapters, I deploy SEP to understand the evolution of international politics as a system and offer a macro-sociology of major IR schools. I show that SEP offers a genuinely endogenous account for the transformation of the international system across time and space: as noted above, only an evolutionary approach can offer genuinely endogenous explanation of changes (Boland 1979, 968; Knudsen 2001, 125). Moreover, the central mechanisms that drive the systemic transformation of international politics have no viable alternatives.[50] Finally, consistent with its claim to be a "universal acid", the account outlined below, based on SEP, accommodates many less fundamental mechanisms, such as the struggle for survival, rational (strategic) behavior, selection, learning, socialization (through the spreading of ideas), technology, systemic approach, and institutions, as part of our understanding of international politics.[51]

Part II

The Systemic Transformation of International Politics

2

Paradise Lost and Paradigm Gained: The Making of the Offensive Realism World

In this chapter, I advance a social evolutionary account for the making of the offensive realism world (i.e., the Hobbesian or Mearsheimer's world), and by so doing, also a social evolutionary sociology of knowledge of offensive realism as a dominant doctrine of international politics for much of human history. I show that by deploying SEP as specified in the previous chapter, we can solve one of the ultimate puzzles in international politics: How did the offensive realism world that many of us had taken for granted come to exist in the first place?

I argue that the human world before c.8000 BC was mostly a "paradise" in the sense that human groups generally did not (have to) fight each other, most critically because the total population was very small and natural resources (especially food and land) were abundantly and readily available. As population grew and natural resources dwindled, however, *relative population pressure* versus key eco-capacities of the land gradually increased.[1] As a result, human groups eventually had to compete for increasingly scarce sources, and conflicts ensued. When the first group-based violent conflict (i.e., war) broke out within a subsystem of groups, it ignited the process of transforming the (sub)system into an offensive realism world.[2] A key dynamic behind this systemic transformation has been: (1) the spreading and retaining of a real and imagined fear of survival plus (2) making, spreading, and retaining a culture of war among all surviving units within the subsystem. Because the key dynamic behind this transformation is self-reinforcing, the offensive realism world would eventually come to last for about ten millennia and its ideational residues still exert a powerful impact over states' conduct of security-seeking even today.

Several caveats are in order before I proceed.

First, it is essential for us to differentiate war from capital punishment and other forms of violence (i.e., physical aggression), especially intra-group violence (e.g., brawling, capital punishment, dueling, feuding), as emphasized by van der Dennen (1995, 69–94) and Kelly (2000, 1–11). Most critically, whereas violence can be both interpersonal (from the same group or two different groups) and intergroup, war is strictly an intergroup phenomenon. Capital punishment is group-sanctioned execution or violence against an individual or individuals within a group (Kelly 2000, 7–10). Feuding between two individuals (families) within a group or between two individuals (families) from two different groups is not sanctioned by group(s) nor participated in by other group members. Hence, war is group-sanctioned, group-participated, and organized violence between two groups with the aim to do lethal injuries rather than violence in general (Mead [1940]1964; van der Dennen 1995, 92–4; Kelly 2000, 1–11; Otterbein 2004, 9–10). As such, there is no inherent relationship between interpersonal violence and war (Kelly 2000 ch. 1; cf. Fabbro 1978), and it is untenable to extrapolate from interpersonal violence to intergroup war, as many sociobiologists have done (see Section II below). Finally, contra many (e.g., Keegan 1993, 386–7; Dawson 1996a, 13–14), even "primitive" war is not just game or ritual: there is no such thing called "ritual war", although war almost inevitably has a large ritual and religious component (Keeley 1996; Otterbein 1989, 33; 2004, 34–8; see also Appendix I).[3]

Second, the thesis that war did not exist at the beginning of our species and came only later on is not new: it has become an accepted truism among many, if not most, anthropologists and archaeologists, although some hardcore sociobiologists may still disagree. Anthropologists and archaeologists, how-ever, have not been very interested in the role of war in the transformation of international system(s), which is the central question for this chapter. Because I am primarily interested in the transformation of international subsystems, I rely mostly on recent surveys of archeological and, to a lesser extent, anthropological evidences to substantiate my argument without getting into the details.[4] As such, this chapter is not another comparative study of warfare. Readers who are interested in more detailed cross-cultural archeological and anthropological studies of warfare should go to general surveys by M. Ember and C. R. Ember (1994), Reyna and Downs (1994), Keeley (1996), Martin and Frayer (1998), Cioffi-Revilla (2000), Kelly (2000), Bradford (2001), Otterbein (1989; 2004), Ferguson (1998; 2006), Guilaine and Zammit (2005), Arkush and Allen (2006), and Hamblin (2006). Likewise, because I am mostly inter-ested in the first outbreak of organized warfare in a subsystem and its aftermath, I am not too concerned with the different stages of warfare in history, usually classified according to the level of organization, weapon technology, and intensity of warfare.[5] Therefore, this chapter is not a (brief) history of warfare or military technology either. Readers who are interested in history of warfare or military technology should read general surveys by Ferrill (1985), O'Connell (1989), Keegan (1993), and Hamblin (2006).

Third, I take the part of our (human) nature that is determined by biological evolution to be a starting point for any discussion of social facts, including the origins of warfare. This is simply because this part of our human nature underpins our sociability, including warfare. Hence, I reject a "blank slate" notion of human nature (Pinker 2002; Tang 2011b). Because this part of our human nature is universal, however, I do not dwell on it. I merely admit it to be an indispensable component of our theory outlined below, although it alone is insufficient for causing war.

Fourth, I do not deal with every aspect of the extensive effects of war upon the internal developments of political units (e.g., formal institutions, extracting apparatus, and educational apparatus). The impact of war and war-making on the internal evolution of human society has been immense and profound, and anthropologists and sociologists, notwithstanding their many differences, have largely reached a consensus. In Charles Tilly's (1985) aphorism: "War (first) makes states, states make (more) war." (See also Spencer 1873, 194; Ferrill 1985, 34; Carneiro 1970; 1994; Spruyt 1994a; 1994b; Diamond 1997; Johnson and Earle 2000; Spencer 2003; Spencer and Redmond 2001; 2004; Redmond and Spencer 2006; 2012.)[6] Instead, I focus on the spreading of war-making cultures *within* and *across* political units while simply admitting that societies' other internal dimensions have been profoundly shaped by warfare and that they are indispensable for the spreading of war-making cultures. I do underscore that the spreading of war memories and war-making cultures both within and across political units had been the more immediate cause for transforming the Eden-like paradise into an offensive realism world in ancient times. Again, I rely on ancient texts and secondary sources to substantiate my case (e.g., Shang Yang [Lord Shang] c.339 BC; Kautilya c.317–293 BC; Han-Fei-Zi [Han-Fei-Tzu] c.280–233 BC; Kelly 2000; Lebow 2008), without getting into the details.

Fifth, although the general thesis that much of human history had been extremely bloody is indisputable, I am not denying that there might have been some human groups that had been peaceful in historical times. What I do contend is that such groups should be exceptions: peaceful communities in the past should have been mostly eliminated or transformed into warring ones in the course of history. Here, it is also important to note that intra-group peace is not a sign of intergroup peace. Indeed, as Spencer (1873, ch. 8; 1892–3, vol. 1, 118), Sumner (1906[1959]), Simmel (1964), and Coser (1956) had perceptively recognized long ago, intra-group peace may actually be a necessary product of intergroup conflict.

Finally, I use the more rigorous dichotomy of offensive realist state versus defensive realist state to denote the two basic types of states within the international system. I reject other less rigorous and thus misleading dichotomies, such as status-quo state versus revisionist state, power-seeking state versus security-seeking state, satisfied state versus dissatisfied state, that are common in the IR literature (Tang 2010b, ch. 1). Briefly, offensive realist states believe that all states are inherently aggressive and their aggressiveness is only limited by their capabilities. As such, the only viable means toward security is to expand and conquer via preventive war whenever opportunities arise. In contrast, defensive realist states (and other non-offensive realist states) reject the assumption that all states are inherently aggressive. As such, security cooperation is a viable means between two likeminded defensive realist states (Tang 2008a; 2010b, ch. 4).

The rest of the chapter is structured as follows. Section I provides a brief critique of existing explanations for the making of the offensive realism world. Section II advances a social evolutionary account for the transforming of the Eden-like paradise into an offensive realism world. Section III provides general evidences for our new theory. Section IV then presents more detailed evidences for our new theory, highlighting the almost identical path traveled by key ancient international subsystems. Section V underscores key dimensions within the impact of warfare upon the internal development of political units that are crucial for reproducing and retaining offensive realism as a dominant practice and culture and hence, for sustaining the nature of the offensive realism system. Section VI provides evidences for the coming and retaining of offensive realism as a dominant doctrine (or theory) of international politics in different subsystems. A brief conclusion follows.

I. A CRITIQUE OF EXISTING THEORIES
OF THE ORIGINS OF WAR

Our enormous direct and indirect knowledge of warfare, long before the coming of writing, had almost inevitably put war at the heart of social inquiries since ancient times.[7] Yet, because many, if not most, historians, political theorists, and IR theorists have taken the nasty and brutish Hobbesian world to be the natural state of human life (i.e., "state of nature"), they have spilled most ink on the immediate or deep *causes* of specific wars (e.g., Thucydides 1954; Wright [1942]1983; Blainey 1988; Van Evera 1999; Copeland 2000a; Mearsheimer 2001; Lebow 2008; 2010; for reviews, see Levy 1998; Levy and Thompson 2010).[8] Few of them have attempted to understand how the nasty and brutish offensive realism world had come to exist in the first place.

In contrast, although some anthropologists and archaeologists had preferred to treat war as pathologies and thus refused to study war as social facts (see the citations in Carneiro 1994, 3–6; Keeley 1996, 1–3), most anthropologists and archaeologists, especially after the 1970s, have known better: war has been a key driving force of human history and thus has to be studied scientifically. As such, archaeology and anthropology as a whole have explicitly rejected the notion that the "state of nature" is a state of warfare: *war has an origin.* Indeed, *the origin of war* has become an enduring question for archaeology and anthropology, second perhaps only to *the origin of state* (Service 1971; 1975; Wright 1977; 1984; Ember and Ember 1992; Carneiro 1970; 1994; Ferguson 1990; 1994; 1998; 2006; Otterbein 2004; Keeley 1996; Flannery 1999; Flannery and Marcus 2003; Kelly 2000; 2005; Spencer 2003; Spencer and Redmond 2001; 2004; Redmond and Spencer 2006; 2012).[9] Unfortunately, anthropologists and archaeologists have not been too interested in the impact of war upon the international systems. This is a major omission: as becomes clear below, war has been a key driving force behind the transformation of international systems (including the transformation of a paradise-like system into an offensive realism world), and this transformation has been a key driver of human history.

This section provides a brief critique of earlier theories on the origin of war, thus laying part of the foundation for constructing a more adequate theory for the origin and spreading of war and the making of the offensive realism world.[10]

A. Early Speculations: Hobbes versus Rousseau

Among some, a conventional wisdom is that Hobbes formulated the first (proto-)theory on the origin and causes of war in *Leviathan*, thus laying part of the foundation of political realism in IR (e.g., Dawson 1996a, 3–14; Keeley 1996, 5–8; Kelly 2000, 121; Gat 2006, ch. 2). Yet, Hobbes was really talking about conflict *within* a group (or community) rather than war as organized lethal conflict between groups. In addition to Thucydides's "three great things" of human nature,[11] Hobbes singled out anarchy (i.e., without a sovereign) as a key cause of conflict within a community. Hobbes assumed the "state of nature" within a community is a community without a sovereign, and life in "state of nature" would be "solitary, poor, nasty, brutish, and short" because human nature is such and such. Hobbes thus justified the necessity of a Leviathan for peace among individuals within a community.

Understood as such, Hobbes advanced a theory of social order within a community rather than a theory on the origin or even causes of war (Bull 1977, 24–7, 46–51; Beitz 1979, 27–34; Heller 1980; Hanson 1984; Boucher 1990; Williams 1996). Indeed, other than noting that relationships between groups (Kings, Persons of Soveraigne Authority) might have approached the "state of nature" whereas the "state of nature" as anarchy among *individuals* may not have existed at all (ch. 13, 187–8), Hobbes had little to say about the origin and causes of war and the condition for peace among groups.[12] The only place that Hobbes ([1651]1985, ch. 30, 387) might have come close to have something to say about the origin of war has been his hypothesis linking population pressure and conflict within a community: "*when all the world is overcharged with Inhabitants, then the last remedy of all is Warre; which providedth for every man, by Vicotry, or Death"* (emphasis added).

Rousseau ([1762]1993) rejected Hobbes's theory of peace (and order) within a community. For Rousseau, the "state of nature" (i.e., a community without a sovereign) is peaceful because human nature is peaceful (hence, "peaceful savages"). Individuals came to blows against each other only after they were contaminated by evil, and this evil had been the sense of (private) property which necessitates defense and thus conflict (Rousseau 1762[1993], 81, 84). Yet, like Hobbes, Rousseau too said little about the causes, not to mention the origin, of war between communities.

Overall, neither Hobbes nor Rousseau told us much about the origin of war, although Hobbes's thesis had gained more acceptance among social theorists, most likely due to Europeans' ethnocentrism that only Europeans were civilized and progressive (hence peace-loving) whereas all other groups were barbaric (raw) and warlike (e.g., Ferguson 1765[1995], 74–105). Indeed, even on the causes of conflict within a group, Hobbes and Rousseau only managed to get something right (e.g., conflict over material things),[13] but not a whole lot: their theses were mostly just speculations. Genuine scientific theories regarding the origin of war with some kind of empirical support came only after the Second World War.

B. Modern Theories I: From Human Nature to Sociobiology to Evolutionary Psychology

In modern time, Hobbes's notion that war lies within our human nature has been most forcefully taken up by sociobiology, and to a much less extent, by Evolutionary Psychology (EP) as sociobiology's more sophisticated upshot.[14] After Konard Lorenz (1966), several prominent sociobiologists, most notably Edward O. Wilson ([1975]2000) and Richard Alexander (1979), advanced the notion that evolution had made war all but inevitable among human groups: aggression is within our genes (and hence part of our "human nature").[15] Sociologist Van Den Berghe (1974) proposed a sociobiological theory of aggression and projected it into human warfare by emphasizing territoriality and hierarchy as part of human nature and resources competition as the trigger. Van der Dennen (1995) contended that war had its roots in "a facultative male-coalitional reproductive strategy". Wrangham and Petersen (1996) and Wrangham (1999) provided seemingly convincing evidences why war is inevitable: the chimpanzees, as our closest relative, have already developed a sense of territoriality and the will and skills to defend it with collective violence, known as "coalitionary killing". Hence, warfare is "adaptive and rooted in genetic predispositions" (Wrangham 1999, 19; emphasis added). Gat (2000a; 2000b; 2006; 2009), starting with a mixture of sociobiology and EP stand, argued that an "integrated human motivational complex" is all that we need to explain all forms of aggression, including warfare.[16] More recently, Smith (2007), an adherent of EP, made an attempt to connect EP with war (for a critical review, see Ferguson 2008). Among IR theorists, Thayer (2004) advanced a theory on the origins of war and the necessity of offensive realism as states' guiding theory in their pursuit of security, drawing exclusively from sociobiology (see also Shaw and Wong 1987; for critiques, see Kitcher 1985; Goldstein 1987; Bell et al. 2001).

As Ferguson (2010) pointed out, the standard practice of sociobiology-based theories on the origin of war operates like the following. They first provide some evidences on violence (or aggression) from group animals (including our close relatives such as the chimpanzees) and then ask us to believe that human beings are inherently aggressive because we have been biologically programmed to be so. Of course, once we believe that human beings are inherently aggressive because of our biology, explaining war is easy: our inherent aggressiveness inevitably leads to war when competition for resources becomes severe. In other words, human beings fight war because it is within our biology or genes (i.e., "human nature"): different groups of human beings fight with each other because war increases our (inclusive) fitness as individuals and/or groups, most prominently manifested in reproductive success with resources merely serving the purpose of reproduction.

The sociobiological approach toward the origin of war, however, is inherently invalid. Since I offer a more foundational critique of sociobiology and EP elsewhere, I only summarize the most critical part of that critique here. Briefly, theories of the origins of war based on sociobiology and EP suffer from three interrelated fundamental defects. First, they often do not differentiate interpersonal violence (or aggression) within a group (e.g., feuding, even homicide) from war as organized violence between groups (e.g., van den Berghe 1974; Thayer 2004; Gat 2006; Smith 2007).[17] Yet, interpersonal violence is not war. As such, many sociobiological theories on the origin of war are not theories of the origin of war but rather theories of interpersonal violence. Even coalitionary killing among chimpanzees is still not war: at most, coalitionary killing is a group's ambush of an isolated individual from another group (usually a bit far away from its core habitat), but never even comes close to night/dawn raid at the lower end of human ("primitive") warfare.[18] Night/dawn raid invariably deploys a group of warriors to attack another group at the latter's base camp while the whole latter group sleeps and is thus most vulnerable (Gat 1999). Coalitionary killing never approaches this level of daring and sophistication in tactics as raid (Wrangham 1999; Wilson and Wrangham 2003).[19]

Second, all sociobiological theories bank heavily on "inclusive fitness" or some other personal benefits to explain individuals' willingness to fight for groups (hence, war is not just possible but almost inevitable, biologically). Thus, Thayer (2004, ch. 3) repeatedly asserted that we fight wars because war increases our intelligence, prowess (as physical fitness), and inclusive fitness (measured in how many progenies we produce and how many copies of our genes have been inherited within the population). There is only one catch: all those nice increases materialize *only if* you actually survive the combat (and, more often than not, your group wins the war).[20] Yet, war is potentially lethal for its combatants and thus utterly counterproductive to individuals' inclusive fitness even if one's group won the war: being killed in battle eliminated one's chance for more reproduction (Ferguson 2008; Collins 2012).[21] In contrast, intergroup cooperation almost inevitably increases individuals' reproductive success (i.e., fitness) while reducing potential losses (Kelly 2005, 15297). Unsurprisingly, ethnographic and sociological evidences strongly indicate that men do not love war: indeed, they often loathe it (Keeley 1996, 143–7; Collins 2012).

Finally and most fundamentally, sociobiological explanations of the origin of war are all biological or at most, material (i.e., competition for resources), nothing social (and hence, cultural). Indeed, sociobiology is inherently asocial and individualistic in extreme. Hence, Thayer (2004, ch. 5) implies that nationalism, ethnocentrism (which underpins or subsumes group identity), and xenophobia are products of our biological evolution alone (see also Shaw and Wong 1987). Yet, such a stand cannot hold: ever since Sumner ([1906] 1959) and LeVine and Campbell (1972), we have understood that ethnocentrism is a product of social evolution rather than biological evolution alone.[22] Groups need group identity to sustain, and this identity is not a product of biological evolution alone, but a product of social evolution. Certainly, mobilizing an (ethnic) group into warfare takes more than invoking a possible increase of inclusive fitness alone (Darwin 1871[1874], 140; Horowitz 1985; Kelly 2000, 4; cf. Shaw and Wong 1987; Thayer 2004).

Inevitably, sociobiologists take a gigantic leap of faith in projecting what they have learned from other group animals to human by glossing over the vast differences between those animals and human beings and dismissing contradicting evidences. For example, sociobiologists want us to believe that because chimpanzees bend on male domination, we too will: there is no escape from our biological fate (e.g., Wrangham 1999). Yet, whereas male domination is the norm in chimpanzee groups, humans in egalitarian hunting-and-foraging societies actually level against male domination *intentionally and collectively* (Boehm 1999; see also Knauft 1991, 398–402)!

War is not the product of biological evolution alone, but a product of social evolution with biological evolution of the human species being part of it. As such, no amount of (socio)biological research and hence no (socio)biological explanation can be adequate for understanding the unique phenomenon of human warfare, although biological research can shed important (but always limited) light on the origin of human warfare. Our biology has made war possible, not inevitable (UNESCO 1986).

To understand the origin of war, we need a social evolutionary approach rather than a purely biological one. Here, sociobiologists are utterly unhelpful: they either deny a role for social (or cultural, for anthropologists) factors or have no clue for how to synthesize biological factors with social factors (e.g., Wrangham 1999, 23–4).

In ending this subsection, however, I want to emphasize that contra some anthropologists and sociologists, we shall not be afraid of biological foundation per se: some biological foundation is necessary for understanding all social facts, including the origin of war. On this front, sociobiology (or biological approaches in general) does provide us with part of the foundation for understanding the origin of war by highlighting that we the *Homo sapiens sapiens* are capable of war biologically. Because the part of our nature determined by biological evolution holds ontological priority over other parts of our nature (Tang 2011b, 2013),[23] biology is never irrelevant, contra Keeley (1996, 157–9).

C. Modern Theories II: Archaeological Anthropology

It is perhaps no mere coincidence that both Malinowski (1941) and Childe (1941), two foundational figures of modern anthropology and archaeology respectively, had explored the origins of war and its impact. Both concluded that war is a "cultural" (or more accurately, social) rather than a biological phenomenon. Unfortunately, for a period of time before the 1950s, some anthropologists did propagate the myth of "peaceful savages" (e.g., Rousseau).[24] In Keeley's (1996) words, some anthropologists have "pacified" the past (see also Carneiro 1994; Kelly 2000; Ferguson 2006, 470–6). Turney-High ([1949]1971) launched the opening salvo against the myth that primitive people are mostly peaceful. This was followed by several important works along the same line, including Chagnon ([1968]1997), Ross (1985), Otterbein (1989; 2004), Keeley (1996), Ferguson (1998; 2000), and Kelly (2000). Together, these works have firmly established that primitive groups have not been peaceful (for summaries and critiques, see Keeley 1996, 8–24; Kelly 2000; Otterbein 2004, 22–34).

Before I go further, however, a long caveat is in order. Roughly speaking, we can divide anthropology into two sub-fields: physical and cultural. Within some corners in cultural anthropology, a strong dose of cultural relativism (or anti-scientific realism) reigns even today (for complaints, see Keeley 1996, x; Flannery 1999, 4). My discussion below draws little from this branch of anthropology.

Within physical anthropology, we can further differentiate archaeological anthropology from ethnographic anthropology. Although both sub-fields have maintained a keen interest in the origin of war and the state plus a strong flavor of evolutionary theorizing (e.g., Flannery 1999; Kelly 2000; 2005; Carneiro 2003), they are very different. Archaeological anthropology is essentially a branch of archaeology: it is mostly concerned with *the origins of state*, and by necessity, the origin of war, in ancient systems.[25] I shall mostly rely on evidences from this literature below.

Ethnographic anthropology (e.g., Chagnon [1968]1997; Otterbein 1989; Keeley 1996; Kelly 2000; 2005) tends to focus on primitive people today (that is, after the coming of the West to the New World or other subsystems). Although studying whether or not war prevails among primitive groups today sheds important lights on the origins of war and state in ancient systems, it can only produce indirect and equivocal evidences on the origin of war in history. This is so because primitive groups, however isolated, are not equivalent to groups in ancient subsystems. Most importantly, ethnographic surveys of these primitive groups had been usually done *after* their contact with Western colonialists. Worse, even before the coming of Western colonialists, these primitive groups might have come into contact with other external groups that we may or may not know.[26] Yet, contact with external groups inevitably changed the trajectories of indigenous groups and the whole subsystem in which they live, as Ferguson (2006, 476–9) has forcefully noted (see also Ferguson 1994; 1995; 2008; Abler 1991; Knauft 1990a; Rodseth 1991; cf. Chagnon [1968]1997).[27] As such, evidences of warfare from ethnographic surveys of these groups do not constitute firm evidences about the *origins* of war within a system, and I generally do not rely on this literature although I do draw from it occasionally.

I shall, however, forcefully note that the ethnographic anthropology literature has produced abundant evidences that support our theories here (for a brief summary, see Appendix I). First, not all primitive groups are warlike (i.e., war had not been with us all the time): war has an origin. Second, primitive wars can be more brutal and total than modern wars, judged by their high rate of casualty and high percentage of the population mobilized (Keeley 1996, 33–6, 88–94). Third, primitive wars had a similar set of motives as their modern counterparts, namely fear, interest (e.g., land, herds, and other foodstuff), and honor (Keeley 1996, chs. 6 and 7; Kelly 2000, ch. 4). Finally, in the justly famous Seville Statement, anthropologists correctly conclude that "*It is scientifically incorrect* to say that we have inherited a tendency to make war from our animal ancestors . . . The fact that warfare has changed so radically over time indicates that it is a product of culture. Although war is biologically possible, but it is not inevitable . . ." (UNESCO 1986; emphasis in original).

Within archaeological anthropology, the main division has been: do states make war or does war make states, at the very beginning? Those who insist that war had been with us early on implicitly admit that war makes states and only later on states make war (e.g., Keeley 1996; LeBlanc and Register 2003; Guilaine and Zammit 2005). Those who deny that war had not been with us early on are divided into two camps: those who believe that war makes states (e.g., Carneiro 1970; Ferguson 1998) and those who believe that (archaic) states make war (e.g., Otterbein 2004), although they sometimes overlap with each other.[28] Fortunately, a consensus seems to be emerging from archaeological anthropology of war and state, and this consensus is that war did not exist at the beginning: unsegmented groups do not produce organized wars (i.e., two organized *armies* sometimes facing each other on the battlefield, in addition to other tactics such as raid and ambush), but at most raids and ambushes. More organized warfare beyond raid and ambush only began with segmented groups (i.e., chiefdoms) and then produced larger units (e.g., Keeley 1996, ch. 4; Kelly 2000; 2005; Spencer and Redmond 2001; Carneiro 2003). This theory that war first makes states and states make war later on is the theory to be developed below.

Although archaeological anthropology has provided the bulk of the evidences for constructing my theory outlined below, from the point of view of our concern here, the literature suffers from three key defects.

First, because some archaeological anthropologists tend to resist human nature-based explanations of war, they sometimes deny that the origin of war must have some kind of biological foundation (Wrangham 1999, 21). This stand is untenable. Biological factors are indispensable for any theory of the origin of war, just like cultural factors: there would be no culture without the biological foundation of our species (Tang 2011b).

Second, as noted above, some authors almost surely got the causal direction wrong by insisting that it is the forms of political, social, and military organizations that have caused the first war (e.g., Reyna 1994; Otterbein 2004). The causal link must have been the reverse: in the very beginning, warfare drives the evolution of military organizations, and also political and social organizations of human society. Of course, larger and more hierarchical units tend to fight more frequently and effectively. There has been a powerful feedback loop between war-making and state formation (see Section V below), but it is wrongheaded to suggest that it is large units that had caused war in the first place.

Third, archeologists and anthropologists have paid scant attention to the transformation of international systems by warfare. As a result, most of them do not recognize that any regional subsystem would have gained a whole new dynamic after the first outbreak of war within it: the first outbreak of war within a subsystem would have been "a watershed event", "a turning point in human history" (Kelly 2000, 3).

D. Identity All the Way Down: Wendt (1992) and Mercer (1995)

Compared to archeologists and anthropologists, IR scholars' inquiry into the origins of war and the making of the offensive realism world has been utterly lacking. For a long time, many IR theorists have assumed that war had been a constant feature of human society, informed by the IR's formative experiences of the First and Second World Wars. Not surprisingly, most IR theorists (and historians) have focused on the immediate and deep causes of specific wars (e.g., Wright 1942; Blainey 1988; Waltz 1988; Van Evera 1999; Copeland 2000a; Mearsheimer 2001; Lebow 2008; 2010; for reviews, see Levy 1998; Levy and Thompson 2010). Not until Wendt's (1992) path-breaking article did IR theorists begin to pay any attention to the origins of war and the making of the offensive realism world.

Wendt (1992) made a fundamental contribution in recognizing that the anarchy of a "competitive self-help" kind that we have known for most of our recorded history and hence taken for granted is not "a constitutive property of anarchy", but "an institution",[29] or more precisely, a product of social evolution (Wendt 1992, 394–6, 399, 401–3, 407; see also Wendt 1999, ch. 6; Cox 1981; Ruggie 1983; cf. Waltz 1979; Mearsheimer 2001). Because the Hobbesian anarchy is an artifact (created by human beings), it must have been made or constructed by interactive processes within the human society in which anarchy plays only a permissive role (Wendt 1992). As such, the Hobbesian anarchy cannot be taken as an inherent property of anarchy as realists have done: the Hobbesian anarchy is a social outcome to be explained.

Despite recognizing that the Hobbesian anarchy has to be explained, however, Wendt could only offer a loosely crafted and extremely weak explanation, covered by a thin layer of evolutionary cream. More concretely, for Wendt, the random presence of a predator state (as a mutation), or "one bad apple spoils the whole barrel", does the job (Wendt 1992, 407–10; see also Wendt 1999, 313–24).[30] For Wendt, the predator state simply comes out of the blue and transforms a system into an offensive realism world. Yet, the coming of the first predator state too must be endogenously explained. Otherwise, the whole explanation would remain exogenously driven.

A key cause behind Wendt's failure to offer an endogenous explanation for the coming of the first offensive realist state and the making of the offensive realism world is his almost exclusive reliance on ideational forces to explain the transition from one type of anarchy to another. Wendt was adamant on this point: "The most important structures in which states are embedded are made of ideas, not material forces" (1999, 309; see also 41, 157). By doing so, he contradicted his earlier approving citation of Searle that "brutal facts have ontological priority over institutional factors" (Wendt 1999, 110, quoting Searle 1995, 55–6). Because material forces hold ontological priority over ideational forces, Wendt's purely ideational explanation cannot possibly be valid and endogenous (Tang 2011b; 2013).[31] As becomes clear below, material forces such as the scarcity of resources, in addition to our biological nature, are quintessential for the birth of the first offensive realist state and the transformation of the initial paradise-like anarchy into an offensive realism world afterwards, although social identities and constructions too are indispensible.

Mercer (1995), criticizing Wendt, did slightly better. Drawing from social identity theory (SIT), Mercer correctly noted that members of a group inevitably develop in-group bias. When distributing material or symbolical rewards between one's ingroup and an out-group, members of a group inevitably favor their own group: "beating the out-group is more important than sheer profit". (Mercer 1995, 239–40) According to Mercer, this in-group favoritism, which can be understood as a primitive form of ethnocentrism, inevitably leads to a concern for relative gains that has been aptly captured by realism's formulation of cooperation among nations. Hence, "*once we assume that we have two states, we can assume each will compete against each other regardless of the other's behavior. Competition need not to be triggered by economic and security concerns; instead, competition results from categorization, comparison, and a need for positive self-identity*" (ibid. 243–6, quote from 246, emphasis added).[32] Apparently, Mercer's explanation too is a purely psychological and hence ideational explanation, and he implicitly denies any role for material forces in engineering the Hobbesian anarchy.

Yet, as Wendt (1999, 322) rightly pointed out, Mercer confused himself because "in-group identity (cohesion and favoritism) is not the same thing as a tendency toward inter-group aggression" (see also Struch and Schwartz 1989; Brewer 1999). In-group identity thus cannot singe-handedly and automatically lead to intergroup aggression.[33] In fact, in-group identity does not even preclude the possibility of forming a larger collective group identity (Gaertner et al. 1993; 2000).

If in-group bias alone cannot turn interactions among states into a Hobbesian kind (and thus make the Hobbesian anarchy), then other than in-group bias and anarchy, some other factors and mechanisms that had been endogenous to social evolution but were neglected by both Mercer and Wendt must have played a part. Such factors and mechanisms, however, are nowhere to be found in Wendt's or Mercer's explanation.

Recall that all SIT experiments initially had an explicit or implicit distributional dimension in material and symbolic reward: members of a group were asked to distribute points or real money. Without such a distributional dimension, it seems unlikely that intergroup competition will result. Transposed to the real world, it seems likely that another factor, scarcity of resources, has to kick in if competition is to result. When resources are abundant, groups need not compete for resources, and war (conflict) is avoided: there is simply no need. When resources are limited or even scarce, however, war becomes far more likely (Keeley 1996, 138–41). Indeed, groups tend to anticipate scarcity and thus fight more when they experience a natural disaster such as a drought (Ember and Ember 1992).[34]

Comparing to sociobiologists, Wendt and Mercer correctly recognized that war is a group-based and hence a decidedly social phenomenon. As such, biology alone cannot explain the origins of war. Yet, Wendt and Mercer's exclusive identity-based explanations cannot hold either. Both Wendt's and Mercer's explanations are largely, if not purely, ideational or psychological, even though both explicitly acknowledged that "nature trumps over process" (Mercer 1995, 236), or "brutal [material] facts have ontological priority over institutional factors" (Wendt 1999, 110, quoting Searle 1995, 55–6). In their explanations, material forces (including biological forces) have little, if any, weight. Because material forces hold ontological priority over ideational forces (e.g., group identity), however, no purely psychological or ideational explanations of social fact can be valid (Tang 2011b; 2013).

II. EDEN AND ITS UNRAVELING: A NEW THEORY

The debate whether it has been biological human nature, material conditions, or culture that had propelled human groups into war has been mostly unproductive, if not obstructive. An adequate theory of the origin of war has to organically synthesize all these forces, although one must admit that high culture came much later than war in history (indeed, as becomes clear below in section five, war makes high culture). This section outlines our social evolutionary theory on the making of the offensive realism world. Our theory, centering on the origin of war and the transformational impact of war upon systems with many political units, provides a complete and ultimate explanation for not only the origin of war but also the transformation of international systems by the coming of warfare (see Figure 2.1 for an overview).

A. Eden Unmakes Itself, Inevitably: The Central Dynamics

In the early period of human history (up to 10,000–8000 BC), with a small population spreading out over a vast landmass, bands of human beings could not interact with each other regularly (if at all) because of the geographical distances between them. When it is so, there is little interaction, either cooperative or conflictual, between them.[35] Moreover, on a sparsely populated earth with abundant and readily available food resources (primarily in terms of fruits, nuts, games, and wild crops), there was no need for conflict (van der Dennen 1995, 14–15). When confronted by another group, all one group had to do was to move into another piece of virgin land. This was a "paradise" in which "[If] I am driven from one tree, I can go to the next", to paraphrase Rousseau ([1762]1993, 81; for evidences from today's Amazon, see Chagnon

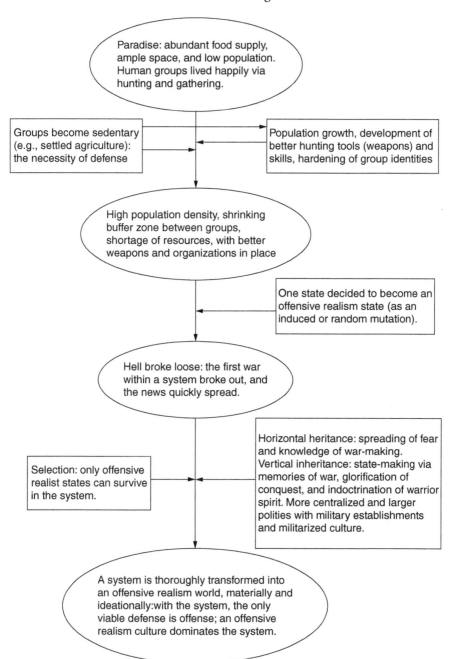

Figure 2.1. The Making of the Offensive Realism World

[1968]1997; Ferguson 1989). These two conditions, a small population and plenty of vast open spaces with abundant food supply, entail a low relative population pressure, which in turn makes the initial stage of human society a happy and peaceful paradise. It was a true Eden-like paradise, even though anarchy reigned and "self-help" was the rule for group survival: the time of plenty (with perhaps the exception of sexual partners) was also a time of happiness.

Unfortunately, all happy things come to an end. Indeed, precisely because it was such a paradise, the paradise would eventually unmake itself, in horrifying fashion.

With abundant supply of food and some skills in obtaining food, the total population of our species slowly but steadily increased. As human beings slowly but steadily increased their population, humans also spread to cover much of the habitable land on earth. Along the way, two fundamental traits that would have decisive influence upon what followed gradually developed (or more precisely, strengthened) within and among human communities. Both traits were conducive to, if not absolutely necessary for, the survival and flourishing of human beings as a species, and thus had been selected for. These two traits are *in-group solidarity and group identity* and *skills (e.g., tactics, hunting as a group) and tools to kill.*[36] Although these two traits did not evolve in order to turn the Eden upside down (they were the unintended consequence of human evolution mostly under the spell of natural selection in this period), they laid the groundwork for the coming of war and the unmaking of Eden.

In-group solidarity and hence group identity, the primitive form of ethnocentrism, are essential to survival because cooperation within one's own band (or tribe) is necessary when facing nature with primitive technologies.[37] Although in-group solidarity does not necessarily (see the discussion on Wendt and Mercer above) entail out-group hostility, the former can be quickly transformed into the latter when situations change (Sumner 1906 [1959]; Levine and Campbell 1972; Brewer 1999).

Meanwhile, better skills and tools to kill large prey also gradually developed by the time of early modern humans (previously known as Cro-Magnons) the latest, so that hunting (and gathering) could support a growing population (Diamond 1997, 38–40; Keegan 1993, 115–26). In the Epipaleolithic (Mesolithic) period and Proto-Neolithic period (c.12,000–8000 BC), five key hunting tools, namely axe, javelin/spear, spear thrower, arrow and bow, and sling, that would later on become standard military weapons, came into existence (Otterbein 2004, 85–90; Hamblin 2006, 19–20), in addition to the already existing club and knife.[38]

Along the way, key hunting tactics such as coordination, concealment/ ambush, encirclement, and tracking that were to become standard military tactics were also invented and perfected (Ferrill 1985, 18–19; Otterbein 2004, ch. 4). Thus, long before the necessity of group conflict came, "the tools of war were ready... With the exception of the sword and body armor, both of which require metal, and the crossbow, all the major implements of personal combat used prior to the invention of firearms were introduced during the hunting-and-gathering stage... Hunting had taught man to kill in groups. It had also nurtured the mechanisms of death" (O'Connell 1989, 26–7). Indeed, initially, all the major weapons and skills for killing fellow humans came directly from tools and skills for hunting beasts, with the mace being the only possible exception (Hamblin 2006, 19–20).

The final blow to the paradise was a combination of three mutually reinforcing factors. The first two factors are population increase and hence depletion of readily available resources (e.g., arable and fertile land, hunting ground, wild fruits, easy prey) within a relatively "circumscribed" area, both naturally and socially (Carneiro 1970; Chagnon [1968]1997, 75; Dickson 1987).[39] The third factor is that more groups become sedentary, often but not always, in the form of settled agriculture (Kelly 2000).[40] Together, these three factors paved the way for the coming of warfare to a subsystem. When all the necessary ingredients were in place, all it needed was a trigger (most likely, an ecological disaster) to unleash the spectre of war.

Population increase within a relatively fixed area leads to depletion of readily available food resources, and in turn increases pressure over fertile (and later on, arable) land. This first leads to migration into virgin (but perhaps less fertile and arable) lands. Migration, however, gradually but inevitably leads to the shrinking of the buffer zone between groups,[41] which in turn increases the chance of contact and thus the possibility of conflict between groups. Moreover, as the whole area becomes largely settled, migration into virgin lands becomes difficult, if not impossible. Yet, steadily increasing population would not let up: it steadily puts more pressure on groups to acquire more arable and fertile land even though the option of spreading or colonizing new territories is no longer easy or viable. When this is the case, some competition for arable and fertile land (and other scarce resources)— now mostly occupied and claimed—becomes necessary for survival and thus inevitable, although perhaps not deadly just yet.

Population increase had also been at least partially responsible for making settled agriculture possible and necessary: agriculture was a major technological leap (i.e., justly known as "the First Economic Revolution"). Increase of population not only demands but also supplies innovation: there is a positive feedback relationship between population increase and technological innovation.[42] Hence, although settled agriculture is actually more laborious than hunting and gathering, settled agriculture eventually increases food production and in turn increases population further.

More critically, the coming of settled agriculture sets several additional positive feedback loops in motion (Ferrill 1985, ch. 1; Otterbein 2004, ch. 5; Guilaine and Zammit 2005, ch. 2).[43] Foremost, circumscribed by natural barriers or human barriers (i.e., other groups), settled agriculture makes fertile and arable land the ultimate scare resource: groups' survival now critically depends on defending (and acquiring, by force if necessary) fertile and arable land (Carneiro 1970; Ferguson 1989, 181). Competition for arable land thus becomes inevitable, and through time, ferocious (Keeley 1996, 106–12; Guilaine and Zammit 2005, ch. 2).[44] Worse, because cultivated land, with its heavy investment in labor and other resources, cannot be easily moved, it becomes a social cage to be defended: "Territory also caged people, because it coincided with substantial labor investment to secure a surplus—*a social cage*" (Mann 1986, 80; italics original).[45]

Moreover, becoming sedentary, especially via settled agriculture, makes defense a necessity: saved foodstuff became a major source of food supply in less productive times of a year (Keeley 1988). Indeed, settled agriculture makes defending what one has cultivated a primary concern for groups because some groups (e.g., some Maori Chiefdoms in New Zealand) may find it always more advantageous to raid other groups' cultivated crops than doing the actual cultivating by themselves (Keegan 1993, 103–6; van der Dennen 1995, 359–62; Miller and Cook 1998, 84). This further compels groups to invent better weapons and tactics for defending via killing other humans. Furthermore, expansion of settled agriculture almost inevitably encroaches upon other groups' hunting and gathering fields, and this encroachment again creates potential sources of conflict (Gullaine and Zammit 2005, ch. 2).

Finally, becoming sedentary (reactivates and) reinforces our sense of territoriality, and a heightened sense of territoriality increases the (real and perceived) necessity of defense, which further moves groups into settled (agriculture) community.[46] Size matters in defense and offense; settled agriculture thus makes larger units desirable. Settled agriculture also makes larger units possible because it not only provides more food output but also facilitates more regular interactions among group members and thus allows a group to gel more cohesively (Knauft 1991, 393–5; see also Knauft 1990b). Being sedentary also stabilizes our reproduction activity and thus leads to further population increase. Sedentary life therefore usually leads to more organized political entities, which in turn increases the available manpower for warfare.

At this stage, the vicious mixture of material forces and ideational forces for transforming Eden into a Hobbesian anarchy is firmly in place. With all these ingredients in place, all that it needed was a trigger, such as a natural disaster that spelled hunger and famine (e.g., drought, flood), the gradual accumulation of ecological pressure by human activities (e.g., forest clearing due to the need for agriculture), or, most likely, a combination of the two. When such a disaster struck, competition for the already scarce resources via organized violence between groups became a necessity, and some groups would inevitably resort to predation (as a form of guided mutation).[47]

B. War as a Self-propellant: Auxiliary Mechanisms

Once the first war broke out between two groups within a region with many groups, it would generate a self-reinforcing dynamic that would eventually transform the system into an offensive realism world: war is self-propelling. In addition to conquest and learning (Otterbein 2004, 177–8), another key mechanism behind this self-reinforcing dynamic is the spreading of a now much heightened fear.

After the first war broke out within a subsystem, news of the conflict will have quickly spread within the system, regardless the actual outcome of the conflict. With the spreading of the news, so does fear, *now significantly heightened*. This spreading of this heightened fear would then quickly transform the paradise-like system into an offensive realism world, although the spreading of actual war might have been gradual (Ferguson 2008, 35).[48]

When two groups in a war have ended with a draw, they may try to regroup and re-engage with each other again. More importantly, other groups in the system would quickly learn that they now need to prepare for war: the region is thus quickly transformed into an offensive realism world (Thayer 2004, 111).

If a conflict ended in a clear victory for one group, its impact might have been more profound. One the one hand, the defeated group would usually have to migrate to another place (if not another region or subsystem) and thus spread the news of the conflict across regions. Moreover, the defeated group most likely would desire revenge. As such, it may well become a predator in another region. This is so because it had learned the lessons from its previous experience: it has to grow stronger, and the easiest, if not the only, way to do so is to conquer others.[49] On the other hand, the victorious group now has to defend what it had gained, not only from possible revenge by its defeated foe but also from aggressions by other groups who would emulate its earlier success. Again, the easiest if not the only way toward such a goal is to further increase its relative power over all other potential foes (i.e., all the groups within the region), and this can only mean more attempts of conquest. Finally, the fact that conquest at the beginning was relatively easy because units were smaller and one mishap (say, overslept guard) could have doomed a group could only magnify the fear, thus turning previous peaceful groups into predators via preventive wars.

Taken together, the very first war would have given birth to the core idea of offensive realism that the only way toward security is to maximize one's relative power over all other groups via conquest: "*the best defense is a good offense*", and it cannot be otherwise (Mearsheimer 2001, 34–6, quote from 36, emphasis added; see also idem, 1994–95, 9–12). Moreover, such an idea, once in place, is hard to dismount: a bad apple can indeed cause the whole barrel to go rotten (Wendt 1992).[50]

Even more profoundly, the impact of the first war within a subsystem does not stop here: *the possibility of war* would fundamentally transform the social fabrics of groups, as sociologists since Herbert Spencer (1873, ch. 8) and Georg Simmel (1964) had recognized (see also Coser 1956; LeVine and Campbell 1972; Collins 2012; for archaeological surveys of this dynamics, see Hamblin 2006 and Sections V and VI below). Simply put, war would come to make states, societies, and thus us, and states, societies, and we would come to make more (and larger) wars. And precisely because war generates such a viciously powerful self-reinforcing dynamic, war tended to engulf a system for a long while once the first war broke out.

Foremost, war gave birth to larger political units, first chiefdoms, and eventually (archaic) state: war makes states, and only later on states came to make (more) war (Spencer 1873, 194; Carneiro 1970; 2000, 12929–12930; Diamond 1997, 291; Keegan 1993, 91).[51] The gradual increase in the size and sophistication of political entities generates two further effects. First, more resources would be devoted to the war machine. Eventually, states came to field a standing army, which requires almost constant grooming, training, and maintaining. States also came to develop specialized professions such as weapon making and strategy crafting (e.g., Sun Tzu), which in turn led to more sophisticated weapons, tactics, organizational innovations. And precisely because war and the war-machine consume an increasing amount of resources, states had to constantly expand to control more resources *and* deny other groups the control of the same resources: again, the best defense is a good offense. Indeed, by the time of chiefdoms and complex chiefdoms, the most important goal of warfare is to expand the political economy by expanding territory and population (Keeley 1996, 106–12; Johnson and Earle 2000, 249). Finally, to maintain the war machine, states would have to install an ever-increasing extraction apparatus.

Second, war can only be fought with supporting ideas: individuals have to be convinced and coerced to fight (Collins 2012). Hence, all states came to install official doctrines, ideologies, cultures and ritual practices for the making of war. At the heart of all these is an indoctrination of subjects with militarism. Doctrine wise, this includes an ideology of offensive realism (as a primitive or crude theory), which insists that conquest and expansion are the only way for survival (Mearsheimer 2001). Culturally, the indoctrination includes glorifying conquest and expansion, severely punishing cowardice on battlefield (usually death), rituals for sending men to the field and honoring the (dead or alive) heroes (often with human sacrifice). The indoctrination further preaches obedience to authority, discipline, immortality and glory via sacrifice for the group. Finally, although primitive religion might have come before war, organized religions had almost inevitably come to support war because religions make individuals more willing to sacrifice for groups in the hope of becoming heroes and legend

Table 2.1. Key Indicators of an Offensive Realism System

Table 2.1a. The Impact of War upon Societies: Material Manifestations

The Impact of War upon Societies: Material Manifestations
Standing army: recruiting, training, and maintaining the army Extraction apparatus: bureaucracies, coercion tools Specialized professions for war-making: weaponry craftsmanship, strategic studies, and spies. More specialized and sophisticated weapons and tactics.

Table 2.1b. The Impact of War upon Societies: Ideational Manifestations

Offensive Realism Doctrine ("Theory")	Offensive Realism Culture ("Practice")
Preaching against defensive realism (as pacifism): it is stupid and immoral because it puts the group in mortal danger (e.g., Shang Yang, Han Fei Tzu, Kautilya, and Machiavelli).	
The Doctrine of Offensive Realism:	1. Glorifying conquest and expansion: the greatest conquerors from our group as saviors of our group. Admiration for heroes and disdain for cowards.
1. In the long run, maximizing relative power over all other units is the only viable way toward security.	
2. Conquest and expansion is the only way for survival. One either expands and conquers or is expended and conquered.	2. Preaching militarism: obedience to authority, discipline, immortality and glory via sacrifice for the group. Severely punishing cowardice on the battlefield (usually by death).
3. The best defense is offense, whenever auspicious situations arise.	
4. The doctrine of preventive war: Preventive wars are necessary and thus just.	3. Warning against pacifism: it corrupts people's soul, weakens our nation, and puts us in danger.
	4. Rigorous military indoctrination and training. Male domination.
	5. Organized rituals (often religious) for honoring heroes and sending men to the battlefield, often with human sacrifice (of captives).
	6. Extreme ethnocentrism (e.g., patriotism, nationalism, racism, xenophobia).
	7. The doctrine of just/holy/sacred war.

and serving God (for a summarization, see Table 2.1). War thus came to penetrate (if not dominate) our individual psychology, group ethos, and the larger social structure (state, religion, education/training, and indoctrination). Literally, war engulfs (almost) everything within a society.

III. MAKING THE OFFENSIVE REALISM WORLD:
GENERAL EVIDENCES

This section provides general evidences for the social evolutionary explanation of the making of the offensive realism world advanced in the last section. I first show that at the beginning, our species had indeed achieved population increase, slowly but steadily. More importantly, during this period of time, war was extremely rare: the Hobbesian world that many took for granted to be "the state of nature" simply did *not* exist. I then show that around 6000–4000 BC, war came to key pristine subsystems and then rapidly became rampant and brutal, often extremely so. Eventually, warfare and ideas of warfare would come to dominate all the major subsystems on earth: all of them were transformed into offensive realism worlds, thoroughly. Finally, I show that conquest had often been successful in the ancient world, connecting with the discussion in the next chapter.

Overall, supporting evidences for our theory came from all major centers of civilization (or subsystems), from Africa, to Asia, Europe, North America, and South America (Cioffi-Revilla 1996; 2000; Carneiro 1994; M. Ember and C. R. Ember 1994; Ember and Ember 1998; Lambert 1998; Maschner 1998; Ferguson 1998; idem, 2006; Smith 1998; Hamblin 2006; Bradford 2001; Otterbein 2004; Raaflaub 2007). These evidences indicate that all major subsystems had gone through roughly the same evolutionary path in different time frames, even though they differed greatly from each other in natural settings.[52]

I present four types of evidences of warfare: (1) *forensic* evidences of organized violence, especially graves with multiple skeletons with fractured bones (cranial and postcranial) inflicted by projectiles, arrows, and sharp blows (usually inflicted by bludgeon/club/mace, machete, and sword), signs of perimortem mutilation (i.e., overkill, mutilated bodies, signs of cannibalism); (2) *weapons and armor*, especially weapons found in burials with a large amount of weapons (merely burials with weapons and tools are less reliable);[53] (3) *structural*: presence of defensive structures such as palisade, walls (especially those with watchtowers, parapets, and ramparts), fortification, trench-embankment features (e.g., moats, baffled gate, guard house), palisaded enclaves, and roof-top habitation (e.g., Catal Huyuk); and (4) *iconographic and epigraphic*: acts and preparations of war depicted in painting (cave, rock, bowl or mural), steles, monuments, bronze, and finally, written texts.[54]

Overall, despite some important exceptions (e.g., "site 117", see below), war rarely existed until the upper Paleolithic age or before 8000 BC (Kelly 2000, 125–33; cf. Keeley 1996, 32, 39; Leblanc 2003, 7–8), although intra-species violence did occur before that (Roper 1975; Ferguson 2006, 470–4). By any measure, widespread and large-scale warfare certainly did not exist back then (Otterbein 2004, 71).[55]

Extensive evidences indicate that the total population of the whole human species was very small before 6000–5000 BC. According to one estimation, the total population hovered around 3–5 million between 250,000 BC and 5000 BC (Kremer 1993, 683). With such a low population and vast empty space, for a very long time after the coming of *Homo erectus* and later *Homo sapiens*, our ancestors were mostly busy in wandering and hunting across the vast empty space further and further away from Africa rather than fighting each other within Africa (Diamond 1997, 37, Fig. 1.1; see also Keegan 1993, 125). Although injuries by projectiles were already present in the Mesolithic age, they were rare (Guilaine and Zammit 2005, 75–7).

Cave/rock paintings from the Upper Paleolithic period to Mesolithic period in Southern Europe (dated to around 35,000–12,000 BC) do show man with weapons (mostly arrow and bow), but the depicted scenes were about hunting, rather than combating (Ferrill 1985, 17–18).[56] Evidences from Mesopotamia during the same period speak of the same lack of warfare (Lamberg-Karolvsky and Sabloff 1995, 49–55; Hamblin 2006, 33–4). Hunting (ritual) also was the predominant scene in wall paintings in Catal Huyuk, dated to around 7000–6500 BC (Guilaine and Zammit 2005, 102). Cave and rock paintings with combat scenes did not clearly emerge until the Neolithic period c.6000–4000 BC; Ferrill 1985, ch. 1; Kelly 2000, 152–156; see also Table 2.2 below and Appendix II).

Indeed, during the Paleolithic age (c.35,000–10,000 BC), other than the famous "site 117" (Jebel Sahaba) in Nubia/Northern Sudan (dated to c.12,000–10,000 BC, Vasilevka in today's Ukraine (dated to c.9000–8000 BC), and a few other sites, there had been few cases with concrete evidences of war (on "site 117" and its implications, see Kelly 2000, 146–61; Guilaine and Zammit 2005, 67–75; on Vasilevka and other sites, see Guilaine and Zammit 2005, 75–81).[57]

During this period of paradise of relative peace, our species had achieved slow but steady increase in its population, starting with a very small population and low (relative) population pressure (Kremer 1993). This steady increase in population eventually culminated in a marked population explosion, often known as the Neolithic demographic transition (Bocquet-Appel and Bar-Yosef 2008).

Evidences from key subsystems unequivocally supported such an interpretation.[58] In ancient Mesopotamia during the Natufian period (13,000 to 11,000 BC), population increased steadily. By 8000 BC, Mesopotamia had been populated by numerous small communities. Between the period of Ubais (5000–4000 BC) and early/middle and late Uruk period (3500–3100 BC), the numbers and the density of settlement within Mesopotamia had increased greatly (Pollock 1999, 56–8, figs. 3.9, after Adams 1981, figs. 9, 12, 13). Population increase in ancient Egypt during roughly the same period too has been well documented (Wenke 2009, 69–71).[59]

Table 2.2. Evolution of Man, Human Society, and Warfare, up to 1000 BC

Archaeological Period (based on technological level)	Approximate date in the Near East and key technological developments	Evidences of warfare
Iron Age	1200 BC on. Iron technologies invented and matured.	Extremely abundant: war became rampant and vicious in most civilizations (e.g., Greece, India, Persia, Rome). War well recorded in written history.
Bronze age: early, middle, late	1600–1200 BC, late 2000–1600 BC, middle 3300–2000 BC, early. Bronze technologies invented and gradually matured. Written language invented and perfected.	Extremely abundant: war became rampant in most ancient civilizations: Egypt, Sumer, Assyria, Babylon, and China. War became well recorded (e.g., Palette of Narmer, monuments, cave paintings, and finally in written history). Fortification became very common.
Chalcolithic (i.e., Copper and Stone Age)	4500–3300 BC. Copper appeared	Abundant: in the later part of this age, war became rampant in Mesopotamia, Egypt, and perhaps China and Spanish Levant. Evidences: burials, weapons, injuries by weapons, executions, stone carving, and rock painting (e.g., Levante Spain and Southern France). Some fortifications were built
Neolithic, pottery (PN, A and B)	6000–4500 BC. Pottery invented. Settled agriculture became common.	Some: war might have appeared in some regions with larger populations (Mesopotamia and Egypt) in the late stage. Evidences: weapons, injuries by weapons, executions.
Neolithic, pre-pottery (PPN, A and B)	8500–6000 BC. Fully settled agriculture villages appeared, irrigation developed later on. More group became sedentary.	Very few. New weapons (e.g., bows and arrows) and military tactics were invented. Some burials with signs of violent deaths.
Mesolithic age or Epipaleolithic (late old stone) age	10,000 BC (or 12,000 BP) to 8500–6000 BC. Domestication of plants and animals began. Some half-settled villages appeared.	Very few (e.g., Vasilevka, Ukraine, 9000–8000 BC; "Site 117," Sudan, 12,000–10,000 BC). Better hunting weapons invented, tactics developed, group identity solidified.
Upper Paleolithic (old stone age): only *Homo sapiens sapiens* survived.	24,000–12,000 BP	None.
		None.[60]

Lower Paleolithic (old stone age): the age of modern human: *Homo sapiens sapiens* & *Homo neanderthalensis*	70,000–24,000 BP. New hunting tools?	
Pre-Homo sapiens: *Homo erectus* (e.g., Java Man and Peking Man)	450,000–70,000 BP. Fire was invented. Club, knife, spear invented.[61]	None.
Pre-Homo sapiens (*Homo habilis*)	2,500,000 to 450,000 BP. Very primitive tools?	None.
Pre-Homo sapiens *Australopithjicus africanus*	5,000,000 to 2,500,000 BP. Very primitive tools?	None.

Notes: Dating archaeological evidences has always been a daunting business, and different authors and sources had different dates. Indeed, even different authors studying the same civilization or subsystems used different periodizations. As such, the exact length and timing of various periods vary from location to location, and the exact dates of various periods do not exactly connect with each other. However, the general trajectory has been consistent and clear. This table draws from van Otterbein 2004, chs. 3 and 4; Hamblin 2006, 4–5; De Mieroop 2007, 10–16; Wenke 2009, 24, 153–66; Trigger 2003. For exact date of post-Mesolithic periods, I use the earliest date known to date from the ancient Near East (Hamblin 2006, 5). BP: before present.

The ancient Chinese system followed a similar trajectory. From the early Neolithic phase to the late Neolithic phase, population within the system steadily increased. Before 7000 BC, only about ten archaeological sites had been discovered (Zhu 2010, 99). By 7000 BC (early Neolithic phase), although human groups had only reached the stage of significant villages in a few regions, the number of sites discovered so far has exceeded one thousand. By 5000 BC (middle Neolithic phase), human settlements had spread to more places, although the distances between many of them were still wide (partly because the size of territory covered by each group was small). By 3000 BC (late Neolithic phase), human groups had occupied far more places, indicated by the more numerous archaeological sites discovered for this period and the increased size of the territory occupied by each group. As a consequence, the average distance between different human groups had been greatly reduced (Chang 1986, 234–42, esp. fig. 197, on p. 235; for more detailed evidence, see Liu 2004, 24–8; Zheng 2005; Zhu 2010). As a result, interaction between human groups inevitably became denser, and eventually more competitive and deadly.

Although population increase within a circumscribed region inevitably reduces readily available sources of food, direct archaeological evidences on this front are hard to come by. We do, however, have extensive evidences indicating that the arrival and subsequent spreading of human population had coincided with rapid and mass extermination of large game animals (especially the easy-to-kill kind) in Polynesia islands, Madagascar, and North/South America within a relatively short period of time (Diamond 1997, 42–7; Otterbein 2004, 12–13, 66–8).

Increase in population within a circumscribed region should also lead to increase in both absolute population density and relative population pressure, and in turn, the chance of contact and the chance and necessity of conflict. Again, direct archaeological evidences on this linkage are hard to come by. Fortunately, the linkage between relative population pressure and war is well substantiated by several in-depth ethnographic surveys of primitive groups. When relative population pressure stays low, war stays rare even though occasional violent competition for resources in the form of murdering and raiding does occur (Chagnon [1968]1997; Keeley 1988; Knauft 1991; see also Kelly 2000, 135–47, ch. 3).[62]

Archaeological evidences that can pinpoint natural disasters as the direct or indirect triggers of war are even hard to come by. So the evidences on this front are more speculative. Recent evidences indicate that a severe drought around 8,200 BC in southern Turkey might have propelled the Pasidia region of southern Turkey into a state of warfare later on: indeed, all four key early sites of warfare, Hacilar, Kurucay Huyuk, Huyucek Huyuk, and Bademagaca Huyuk, are located within this region (Clare et al. 2008). Likewise, violent competition in the heartland of ancient China might have been triggered by a series of climate changes for the worse: between 9000 BC and 3000 BC: East Asian monsoons (from the South China Sea) had steadily weakened and retreated to the south that much of the fertile lands in northwestern China became desiccated by 4000 BC, forcing people to migrate to the more fertile Yellow River valley and the Yantze River valley in the south (Liu 2004, ch. 2).[63]

Although it is impossible to theoretically argue against the notion that group identity *beyond nuclear or even extended family* is necessary for warfare, we again have to rely on indirect evidences on this front. Rock paintings in Spanish Levante depicted that different groups of warriors had different styles, behaviors, and dress. This strongly indicates that group identities—both materially and ideationally—had developed very early on among human groups (Guilaine and Zammit 2005, 103–19), and these identities had played an indispensable role in the making of warfare. On another front, Kelly (2000, ch. 2) assembled impressive anthropological evidences suggesting that groups without group identity beyond nuclear and even extended family do not fight war despite frequent interpersonal violence within these groups.

Eventually, by 6000–4000 BC (the later Neolithic Age) at latest, warfare originated in many major subsystems and came to dominate these systems around 3000–2000 BC. After that, war had remained almost constant in these systems and had maintained an uptrend for at least the next three to four millenniums (for general surveys, see Ferrill 1985, ch. 1; Cioffi-Revilla 1996; 2000; Guilaine and Zammit 2005; Hamblin 2006; see Section IV below for details).[64] Not surprisingly, states also came to exist within all these subsystems, *(long) after* the coming of warfare (for evidences, see Cioffi-Revilla 2000,

71, 85–8; Flannery and Marcus 2003; Spencer 2003; Spencer and Redmond 2001; 2004; Redmond and Spencer 2006; 2012).

Extensive evidences indicate that warfare in the ancient world had been even more total than Clausewitz's time. Killing of captives (often with mutilation), whether military or civilian, had been regular (Otterbein 2000; 2004, 195–8). In ancient Egypt, heads or hands of war prisoners were cut off and bodies mutilated and paraded on chariots, and the "luckier" ones were able to work as slaves and thus lived for another day (Hershey 1911, 905–7). The same barbarianism applied in both republic and imperial Rome: the Romans had regularly killed prisoners, raped women, and plundered treasures (Roth 2009). During the second Punic war, Rome totally dissipated Carthage in 146 BC. Even the more "civilized" ancient Greeks were no different: During the Peloponnesian War (431–404 BC), Athens massacred all the males of the rebellion Mytilene (420 BC) and all the males of the neutral Melos (416 BC) whereas Spartan sacked Corcya in 416 BC (Thucydides 1954). Finally, in ancient China, the kingdom of Qin massacred 240,000 of Kingdom Han's and Wei's troops in one famous battle in 293 BC and then buried 400,000 of surrendered troops of Kingdom Zhao (Yang 2003, 444, 129; see also Hui 2005, 62–3, 86–7).

More importantly, conquests were often successful in these systems, as indicated by the drastic decrease in the numbers of independent political entities through history (Carneiro 1978; see also Chapter 3 below). In ancient Mesopotamia, in the period of late Uruk, Jemdet Nasr, and early dynastic periods, small communities came to be abandoned and larger settlements in the form of walled cities began to dominate (Pollock 1999, 67–77). At least part of this development could only be explained by successful conquests and coerced submissions.

Things were similar in other subsystems. Within ancient Anatolia, the age of the Hittite Empire witnessed a series of successful conquests. From 1402 to 221 BC, the number of independent units within the ancient Chinese system decreased from 1000 to 1. Between 500 BC and 100 BC, Monte Alban conquered the whole Oaxaca valley and then expanded outside the valley after 100 BC. In northeast coast of Peru, Chavin conquered surrounding areas by 200 BC, and eventually came to blow with another emerging state (i.e., Moche). Within the pre-modern European system, from 1450 to 1648, in a span of 199 years, more than 321 states were eliminated, and the average number of states eliminated in a century is 161 (see Chapter 3 below). Finally, in the Indian subsystem, the number of states had dwindled to 15 by 500 BC.

This age of relatively easy conquest would last until 1648 or even 1945 (see Chapter 3 below). This fact and hence the idea that conquest had often been successful had been a crucial factor in sustaining the offensive realism system after the initial transformation of the peaceful paradise into an offensive realism system.[65]

The dynamics underscored above point to a simple outcome: war should have been frequent and rampant for much of our history. Within the ancient Chinese system, according to one count, *Zuo Zhuan* lists some 540 interstate wars and more than 130 major civil wars in a span of only 259 years (Lewis 1990, 36). During the Warring period (which followed the Spring and Autumn period), Hui (2005) counted that from 656 BC to 221 BC (435 years), there were 256 great power wars (i.e., there was at least one great power involved). Things were equally gruesome elsewhere. Within ancient Greece and Rome, war was almost constant (see Appendix II). Within the pre-modern European system, there were 89 great power wars from 1495–1815 alone, or one great power war per 3.65 years (Levy 1983, 88–91).

IV. MAKING THE OFFENSIVE REALISM WORLD: EVIDENCES FROM SUBSYSTEMS

This section presents evidences from six pristine subsystems, namely ancient Mesopotamia, ancient Egypt, ancient China, northeast coastal Peru, the Valley of Oaxaca of Mexico, and Anatolia.[66] All six systems were *circumscribed systems*, and war had most likely originated in these systems endogenously.[67] I also provide a brief survey of four other secondary systems (i.e., war came to these systems via diffusions from other pristine systems) to further buttress our theory (Appendix III).

Overall, although inevitably there are holes in constructing the precise history of these systems,[68] existing evidences overwhelmingly point to a general conclusion: All the systems had undergone from a state without warfare into a state with rampant and brutal warfare, although the scale of conflict in the Valley of Oaxaca and northeast coastal Peru had never reached the scale in the other four subsystems, mostly because these two subsystems never had a very large population.[69]

A. Ancient Mesopotamia (Appendix II, Table S2.1)

Mesopotamia, the area that lies between the two great rivers (i.e., Tigris and Euphrates), is a region within the greater Near East.[70] It is confined by the Zagros Mountains in the east, the Syrian Desert in the northwest, the great Arabia desert in the west, Taurus Mountains in the north, and the Persian Gulf in the south.[71] This region produced some of the most famous imperial civilizations: Sumer, Akkad, Assyria, Babylonia, Elam (Susiana), Hittites, and Mitanni (Hurrians), all came to their age via conquest and expansion.[72]

Before 3500 BC, there were few evidences of warfare. By 3500 BC (the late Uruk period), if not slightly earlier, evidences of warfare became undeniable (Hamblin 2006, ch. 2; McIntosh 2005, 185). By the time of early dynastic period (c.2900–2300 BC), war became endemic (Hamblin 2006, 44). During the age of great powers within the greater Near East between 1600/1500 BC and 1200–1050 BC, several great powers (i.e., Babylon, Assyria, Elam, Hittite, Mitanni, and Egypt) were almost constantly at war (Kuhrt 1995, vol. 1, part 2; McIntosh 2005, ch. 4; Hamblin 2006; van de Mieroop 2007, ch. 7).

Weapons and Forensic Evidences

The earliest copper spearhead discovered in ancient Mesopotamia dated back to early fourth millennium BC. A painting on a bowl dated to roughly the same period showed perhaps the first warrior: he had a bow in one hand and mace in the other (Hamblin 2006, 34). After that, the ancient Mesopotamia developed some of the most important weapons in pre-gun powder age, including war-carts (c.2550 BC), the composite bow (between late third millennium and early second millennium; see Hamblin 2006, 89–95; McIntosh 2005, 188)[73], the sickle-sword after 2,000 BC (Hamblin 2006, 66–71; esp. chs. 5 and 6), and chariots around 1500 BC (Hamblin 2006, ch. 5; van de Mieroop 2007, 122–5). The ancient Mesopotamia also invented some of the earliest battle formations: phalanx appeared in Mesopotamia around 2550 BC the latest (see the "Stele of the Vultures" below).

Traditionally, archaeologists have mostly focused on southern Mesopotamia. More recent discoveries of mass graves in northern Mesopotamia, Tell Brak in today's northeast Syria, however, had pushed back the outbreak of war in ancient Mesopotamia to the early fourth millennium (c.3800–3600 BC). This discovery also raises the possibility that northern Mesopotamia might have experienced brutal and total warfare before southern Mesopotamia (McMahon et al. 2008).[74] Evidences from later periods also indicated that war in the ancient Mesopotamia had often been brutal and total. Both Akkadians and Assyrians were known for their brutality in warfare, and when the Babylonians and the Medes defeated Assyria in 612 BC, they repaid Assyrians with equal brutality. In a well within the Assyrian Review Palace at Kalhu, 180 bodies of manacled Assyrian solders were found. The Babylonians and the Medes also thoroughly sacked the city of Nineveh of Assyria, long a symbol of Assyrian glory and power (McIntosh 2005, 195).

Structural

In the late Ubaid period (c.5000–4000 BC), even the largest city, Eridu, was perhaps not fortified (Hamblin 2006, 34). By the late Uruk period (or pre-dynastic period, c.3500–3100 BC), all major cities within Mesopotamia were fortified with huge mud-brick walls, including walls with ramparts. Walls were initially build with stamped earth, and then both sun-dried and baked bricks (Hamblin 2006, 37–9). By the second millennium BC, integrated defenses with moat, wall, and towers became common and more imposing (McIntosh 2005, 188–9). Major cities, especially capitals, were really huge fortresses with extremely costly and elaborate fortification, as showcased by the city of Babylon (as the capital of Babylonia) and Niveveh (an Assyria fortress) (McIntosh 2005, 191–2). Perhaps fittingly, many of these fortresses and citadels were "named after the dynasty or [its] founder, e.g., 'Dur-Rimush' = 'Fortress of Rimush', 'Dur-Akkade' = 'Stronghold of Agade'" (Kuhrt 1995, vol. 1, 54).

Iconographic and Epigraphic

Numerous documented evidences indicated that war in the cradle of civilization were extremely brutal, if not total. Most prominently, from the Uruk period, the image of priest-king came to dominate martial art: most images of the king showcased his military prowess and success by smiting prisoners (Hamblin 2006, 37–9). Following the appearance of fortification around 3000 BC, siege scenes soon appeared in sculptures and cylinder seals (Hamblin 2006, 37–9, esp. ch. 8). Execution of prisoners also began to appear in late Uruk art (Matthews 2003, 108–26; Hamblin 2006, 34–44; McMahon et al. 2008).

This should not have been a surprise. Within the Sumerian system between 2550 and 2250 BC, four powerful city states (or kingdoms), Kish, Lagash, Umma, and Ur were almost constantly at war with each other. So much so that the Sumerian King-list explicitly stated that "the mechanism by which kingship [of the Sumerian system] is transferred is warfare". (Hamblin 2006, 42) Intra-system warfare had only been punctuated by unifications of southern Mesopotamia by Akkad under Sargon and Naram-Sin (Hamblin 2006, chs. 2 and 3; van de Mieroop 2007, chs. 3 and 4).

Hence, by 2500 BC or so, all kinds of artistic paintings began to depict soldiers, army, and battle scenes from Sumerian and Assyrian periods (Hamblin 2006, chs. 2 and 3), Among these iconographic evidences, the "Standard of Ur," the "Stele of the Vultures," and the "victory stele of Naram-Sin" have been the three most famous.

The "Standard of Ur" (c.2550 BC) depicted not a real battle, but a victorious war by the King of Ur. Within it, axes, clubs, javelins, knives, spears and war-carts all appeared, and Ur's soldiers were depicted to round up prisoners and collect booties while brandishing weapons (Hamblin 2006, 49–50).

The "Stele of the Vultures" (c.2425 BC), justifiably the most famous iconographic evidences of warfare in Mesopotamia, depicted the epic war between king Enantum of Lagash and Enakale of Umma in which the former prevailed (Hamblin 2006, 55–9). The war between Lagash and Umma was perhaps the first war for territory ever recorded, and the rivalry between the two kingdoms might have stretched for 150 years (2500–2350 BC, see van de Mieroop 2007, 48–9).

The "Stele of Naram-Sin" depicted a victorious Naram-Sin, the fourth ruler of the Akkadian empire (reign c.2254–2218 BC) as the unifier of southern Mesopotamia. The stele shows the king and his troops crushing Lullubu highlanders in the Zagros Mountains, with the inscriptions reads in part "Naram-Sin defeated them and heaped up a burial mound over them . . . and dedicated [the stele] to the god [who granted victory]" (Hamblin 2006, 86–7; van de Mieroop 2007, 64–73).[75]

By the late third millennium, warfare became extensively documented, although with exaggeration sometimes. The second ruler of the Akkadian empire, Rimush (reign 2278–2270 BC), claimed to have killed or displaced tends of thousand of men from southern cities (Hamblin 2006, 78–80; van de Mieroop 2007, 69). The fourth ruler of the Akkadian empire, Naram-Sin (reign 2254–2218 BC), boasted to have killed or capture 137,400 in total when trying to suppress a series of rebellions (McIntosh 2005, 78; Hamblin 2006, 81–4).

In the second millennium BC, the greater Mesopotamian system was dotted by several major states and many smaller states. These states (especially major ones) were in a life-and-death struggle with each other. They were engaged in shifting alliances and conspiracies, and their constant and brutal warfare often led to sacking of each other's capitals (e.g., the sacking Babylon in 1595 BC by Hittite King Mursili; van de Mieroop 2007, chs. 5–10). The Amarna Letters among rulers in the 14th century BC in ancient Near East suggest unambiguously that international politics of the Near East then was extremely competitive (Cohen and Westbrook 2002).

In the first millennium BC, the same pattern persisted in the ancient Near East. In 701 BC, Assyria's army under Sennacherib (reign c.704–681 BC) sacked the royal city of Lachish in the Kingdom of Judah: its people were savagely punished as slaves, and the sacking was complete and thorough (Liverani 2005, 143–8; McIntosh 2005, 180). And when the Assyrian empire fell in 612 BC, its enemies sacked the city of Nineveh, massacring many captured Assyrian soldiers (McIntosh 2005, 195).[76]

B. Ancient Egypt (Appendix II, Table S2.1)

Ancient Egypt was separated from Levant/Canaan and Mesopotamia by the Sinai desert and the Red Sea. Although the scenes from Egypt have been less horrifying due to a relative lack of forensic evidences of warfare, we have reason to believe that this was due to the fact that many of these evidences have remained buried (and to some extent, extremely difficult, if not impossible, to be excavated) rather than that life in the ancient Egyptian system was more peaceful. Certainly, the unification of Upper Egypt (Valley/South) and Lower Egypt (Delta/North) achieved under the first dynasty King Narmer (c.3100–3000BC) would have been impossible without war and conquest (Kemp 1989, ch. 1; Kuhrt 1995, 125–34; Wilkinson 1999, ch. 2).

Weapons and Forensic Evidences

Mace, a specialized weapon, first appeared in the Naqada I period (known as the pre-dynastic period, c.4000–3500 BC). By the Naqada II period (c.3500–3150 BC),[77] "maces had become the pre-eminent symbol of kingship and military power", and the smiting of enemies had emerged and stayed as the "norm in Egyptian royal martial iconography for the next three thousand years". In addition to maces, other weapons such as flint knives, flint projective points, and copper harpoons have been uncovered, often in burials (Hamblin 2006, esp. 313–15) During the Naqada II period, artistic depiction of other weapons in the "Painted Tomb" included spear, axe, double-headed axe, bow, and throwing stick, in addition to mace (Wilkinson 1999, 31–4; Hamblin 2006, 315).

Defensive Structures

By the Naqada II period (c.3500–3150 BC), the city of Hierakonpolis was protected by a massive wall made from mud bricks (Hamblin 2006, 312–13; Wenke 2009, 216–25), so did the city of Nagada as the capital of the Nagada kingdom (Kemp 1989, 35–46). This should not be a surprise, for by the time of Nadada II–III period (c.3500–3000 BC), three major kingdoms, Hierakonpolis, Nagada, and This, in the upper Egypt region were already engaged in fierce competition (Kemp 1989, ch. 1; Wilkinson 1999, ch. 2; Hamblin 2006, 317–19; Wenke 2009, 202–29).

The competition between Hierakonpolis, Nagada, and This eventually led to the unification of Upper Egypt by King Narmer around 3050–3000BC, which marked the beginning of the early dynastic I period (c.3000–2686 BC). Narmer built Memphis as the new capital of a unified Egypt, and Memphis literally meant "White Fortress" (Hamblin 2006, 319). During the early dynastic period, the Egyptians constructed a massive fortress in Elephantine along the Nubian border: it had "large, thick mud brick walls with semi-circular projecting bastions, square towers on the corners and a fortified gate". (ibid. 325; Wilkinson 1999, 175–82) By the time of the Old Kingdom period (c.2687–2181 BC), if not before, many towns became protected by a thick brick wall (Kemp 1989, 138–41). Finally, after the re-conquest of Nubia during the Middle Kingdom period (c.2061–1786 BC), the Egyptians built a series of fortresses in order to permanently control the conquered region of lower

Nubia.[78] Among them, the Egyptian fortress at Buhen, built during the reign of Senwosret I (c.1971–1928 BC) stood as an utterly imposing structure (Kemp 1989, 166–78; Hamblin 2006, 443–5).

Iconographic and Epigraphic

Ancient Egypt had also produced some of the most famous iconographic evidences of warfare and conquest. The "Painted Tomb" in Hierakonopolis from the Naqada II period (dated to around 3400–3300 BC), the earliest iconographic evidences of warfare from ancient Egypt, depicts a royal figure standing in a boat with a mace, in addition to several combat scenes (Kemp 1989, 40; Wilkinson 1999, 31–4). From the Naqada II or late pre-dynastic period (c.3500–3150 BC), we have two additional famous artistic representations of warfare, the Gebal-el-Araq knife handle and the "Battlefield Palette" (also known as the "Vultures Palette"). The former showed not only combat scenes between two groups of warriors but also the first evidence of naval warfare. The "Battlefield Palette" depicted not only naked and bound captives "being marched off the battlefield ... by victorious clans" but also naked enemy corpses "being eaten by vultures and a lion" (Hamblin 2006, 314–15; see also Shaw 2000, 316). Obviously, by the pre-Dynastic period, (ritual) sacrifices of prisoners were already present, if not regularly (Wilkinson 1999, 265–7; Wenke 2009, 249–51).

The Narmer Palette (dated to c.3040 BC), justly the most famous palette, perhaps commemorated the unification of Egypt under Narmer around 3010–3050 BC. The palette depicted similar scenes as "Stele of the Vultures" from the Mesopotamia, although the war-god in Egypt was the falcon Horus. On one side of the palette, the Egyptian King is smiting a rival king. On the other side of the palette, the King is inspecting "two rows of bound and decapitated prisoners" (Kemp 1989, 42; Hamblin 2006, 318–20; Wenke 181–8). In addition, the Tjehenu Palette, also known as the "Cities Palette" or "the Libyan Palette" (dated to c.3100 BC), depicted conquests of cities by animals symbolizing Egyptian military gods (lion, scorpion, and falcon), possibly under Narmer (Kemp 1989, 50; Shaw 2000, 4; Hamblin 2006, 319).[79]

An ivory plaque, dated to around 2950 BC, is simply titled "the first occasion of the smiting of the east" by King Den, one of the successors of Narmer (Kemp 1989, 42; Wenke 2009, 243–4; Hamblin 2006, 320–1). During the old kingdom period (c.2687–2171 BC), Egypt's wars with tribes/chiefdoms in southern Palestine and northern Nubia began to feature prominently in Egyptian martial art (Wilkinson 1999, 151–82; Hamblin 2006, chs. 13 and 14). Starting the new kingdom period (c.1539–1075 BC), wars by Egypt had been well recorded (Spalinger 2005; Liverani 2005, 10–17, 101–3; Hamblin 2006, chs. 16 and 17).

C. Ancient China (Appendix II, Table S2.2)

Ancient China, centered within the Yellow River valley, was also a circum-scribed system. It was enclosed by the Tibetan Plateau and the Himalayas in the West, the Yellow Sea in the East, the steppe and Gobi desert in the North, and the Yangtze River in the South. Numerous archeological discoveries have provided irrefutable evidence that war was already rampant within the ancient Chinese system by 3000–2700 BC the latest (for a summary, see Table S2.2; for a comprehensive survey, see Sawyer 2011).

Forensic Evidences and Weapons

Evidences of warfare became irrefutable in the late Long-shan (Lung-shan) phase (c.3000–2200 BC) in the Yellow River valley. In Chien-kon, several abandoned wells were mass graves, with signs of skull scalping, beheaded bodies, victims being buried alive (Chang 1986, 270–1; see also Chang 2005; Zheng 2005). Similar evidences came from the Liang-zhu Culture (c.3000 BC) in the Yangtze Delta (Zhou and Wu 2004, 112–19).

The coming and spreading of warfare gave birth to new and more special-ized and lethal weapons in the ancient Chinese system. Around 3000 BC, a key weapon for close combat made from stone, *yue*, appeared and became stand-ard burial for males in the Liang-zhu culture (Zhou and Wu 2004, 112–19).[80] Late on, more dedicated weapons were invented, and they include fire-arrows, short-knives, and spears (Yates 1999, 9–10). By the late Xia period (c.2200–1700 BC), with the coming of bronze technology and chariot, light bronze weaponries and chariots appeared (Yang 1991; Lin 1990). The dagger-axe (*ge*/戈), a unique bronze weapon and the primary long-handled weapon in ancient Chinese warfare, appeared and became widely adopted around 2000 BC (Shi and Tao 2003; Zheng 2005, 426–7).

Burials with weapons, starting from rare and few in numbers and types, became frequent and many in numbers and types, as cultures moved from later *Long-shan* culture, to *Xin-zai* culture, and to early *Er-li-tou* culture of the late Xia or early Shang dynasty (Shi and Tao 2003; Du 2007, 18–19; J-G Tang 2010, 246–61). Sacrifices were widely practiced from the late Long-shan period, all the way to the Zhou dynasty (Liu 2004, 44–6, 55–7, 105; J-G Tang 2010, 244).

Fortification

During the Pei-li-gang phase (c.7000–5000 BC), villages had yet to be protected by visible walls. By 4000 BC, the later Yan-shao phase or early Long-shan phase, villages were already protected by deep ditches and some towns were protected by walls made from stamped earth. By the late Long-shan phase (the pre-three Dynasties period) and early Xia period (c.3000–2200 BC), many towns were protected by walls made from stamped earth and deep ditches (Chang 1986, 248; Liu 2004, ch. 4; Shao 2005; Zheng 2005, 198–209, 295–305; Zhang 2008). After 2200 BC, almost all major cities and towns were protected by walls with moats and ever more sophisticated fortification (Yang 2003; Liu 2004; Zhang 2008).[81]

Iconographic and Epigraphic

Written language was invented within the ancient Chinese system around 2000 BC. From then, wars were first recorded in inscriptions on oracles and bronze: Indeed, many inscriptions on oracles from the Shang dynasty (c.1700–1046 BC) were about whether it was auspicious to launch a war and many inscriptions on bronze from the Shang and Western Zhou period were to commemorate kings' victories in major wars. After bamboo slips ("竹简/Zhu Jian") came into use after 300BC or so, wars became even more extensively recorded in historical chronicles. Extensive evidences of warfare in the ancient Chinese system had been provided by several classic texts: *Zuo Zhuan* [左传/ Chronicles of Zuo], *Lu Shi Chun Qiu* [鲁氏春秋/Chronicles of Lu, compiled by Confucius], *Zhan Guo Ce* [战国策/Compiles of the Warring Period], *Shi Ji* [史记/Historical Record]. These texts have been extensively reviewed and compiled by Cioffi-Revilla and Lai (1995) and Hui (2005).

Briefly, according to one count, *Zuo Zhuan* recorded 483 wars from the Spring and Autumn time (cited in Yates 1999, 19). According to another, *Zuo Zhuan* lists some 540 interstate wars and more than 130 major civil wars in a span of only 259 years (Lewis 1990, 36). During the Warring period (which followed the Spring and Autumn period), Hui (2005) counted that from 656 to 221 BC (435 years), there were 256 great power wars (i.e., wars in which at least one great power was involved). Overall, there was a marked increase in the frequency of warfare from the age of Legendary Kings to Xia, Shang, Western Zhou, and Eastern Zhou (Cioffi-Revilla and Lai 1995, 480–6, esp. table 2), so much so that by 576 BC, even a minor lord, Kang of Liu, already knew that "The great affairs of the state are sacrifice and warfare" (*Zuo Zhuan*, Duke Cheng year 13).

The prevalence of war can be understood from another angle: the number of states (polities) eliminated through time. My own calculation, which calculated the number of state eliminated and the rate of state death revealed that from 1045–221 BC, more than 800 states were eliminated, and the average number of states eliminated in a century is 97 (see Chapter 3 below). A much earlier estimation revealed an even more drastic decline of the number of states within the Chinese system. Around 1600 AD, Ku Tsu-yu noted that the number of states went from 10,000 at the time of Yu of Xia dynasty, then to

3000 at the time of Cheng Tang of the Shang Dynasty, and then to around 1800 at the time of Wu Wang of the Zhou Dynasty (quoted in Chang 1986, 307; see also Cioffi-Revilla and Lai 1995, 472–3). By any measure, war in the ancient Chinese system was indeed rampant, brutal, and total.

D. North Coast of Peru (Appendix II, Table S2.3)

Until the early Precermamic period (4500–3000 BC), war did not exist in north coast of Peru. War appeared within the system during the late Preceramic Period (the Cotton Preceramic period, 3000/2500–2000/1800 BC). By the Initial Period (2100/1800–900 BC), war had become rampant and brutal. Abundant evidences of warfare from the Initial Period on include weapons (wooden club embedded with shark's teeth, pointed spears and woven slings), headless skeletons, isolated heads, skull scalping, and possible trophy heads (e.g., modified skulls) (Pozorski 1987, 27–8; Burger 1995, 36–7; Stanish 2001, 57–8). During the Early Horizon (c.900–200 BC), there was at least one clear-cut case of conquest within the Casma Valley (Pozorski 1987, 27–8).

Fortifications first appeared in a single site, Salinas de Santa, dated to c.3000 BC, (before the Cotton Preceramic period). By the Early Horizon, fortification had become very common (Pozorski 1987, 27–8; Daggett 1987, esp. 77–8) and stayed so in the Early Intermediate Period (c.200 BC 600 AD, see Topic and Topic 1987, 50; Wilson 1987, 66–8).

Iconographic evidences of warfare first appeared in the Initial Period. In Cerro Sechin (dated to c.1519 BC, within the Initial Period), numerous sculptures depict "a procession of victorious warriors and their mutilated victims", "a victim writhing in agony while his intestines spill from his body", "a successful warrior adorned with severed heads, a large pile of decapitated heads, and the bleeding head of a defeated solider" (Burger 1995, 77–9).[82]

Together, these evidences strongly indicate that rampant and brutal warfare had come to north coast Peru by the Initial Period and the Early Horizon the latest.

E. Valley of Oaxaca, Mexico (Appendix II, Table S2.3)

The Oaxaca Valley of central Mexico had followed the same pattern as other pristine systems, going from a system without war to a system with rampant and brutal war. In 8050–2050 BC (10,000–4000 BP, the Archaic period), the Oaxaca region was a warless world (Flannery and Marcus 2003, 11801).[83] Defensive palisade appeared around 1310–1210 BC (3260–3160 BP, the Tierras Largas phase), shortly after settled agriculture villages appeared around 1650 BC (3600 BP). Inter-village raiding appeared around 1150–850

BC (3100–2800 BP, the San Jose phase) and became intensive around 850–500 BC (2800–2450 BP, Guadalupe phase and Rosario phase). By 500–300 BC (Monte Albán Ia phase, 2450–2250 BP), warfare had become rampant and brutal within the system (Flannery and Marcus 2003, 11801–3).[84]

By 850–500 BC, defensive walls had appeared within the Oaxaca Valley (Marcus and Flannery 1996, 124). The San Jose Mogote village, the largest settlement from the Tierras Largas phase to the Rosario phase, would eventually conquer and expand to form the Zapotec state (Spencer and Redmond 2003). But before that, the San Jose Mogote village had to move to a more defensible site and form a new city, Monte Albán (the first city in Mesoamerica). This strategic relocation, or *Synoikism* as called in ancient Greek city state system, was undoubtedly a defensive reaction against pressing threats from other political units (Marcus and Flannery 1996, ch. 11; Spencer and Redmond 2001). By the end of Monte Albán I [phase, 500–150/100 BC], "more than a third of the valley's population [had come to live] in such sites [i.e., defensible hilltop locations]" (Marcus and Flannery 1996, 150–4, quote from 151; see also Flannery and Marcus 2003, 11804). Eventually, when facing serious threats from other powerful states, around AD 500, 64 per cent of the 115,000 Zapotec individuals had to live in 38 defensible sites (Marcus and Flannery 1996, 228, 243–4).

During the Rosario phase, the first iconographic evidence of warfare appeared: a monument (known as Monument 3) within the village San Jose Mogote, dated to 630–560 BC (2580–2510 BP), depicts the corpse of a captive with his heart removed (Marcus and Flannery 1996, 128–30; Flannery and Marcus 2003, 11802–3). Most gruesomely, in the Monte Albán Ia phase (c.500–300 BC), "more than 300 of the earliest monuments at Monte Alban depict slain or sacrificed enemies like the one we saw earlier at San Jose Mongote" (Marcus and Flannery 1996, 150–54). Evidences of sacrifice were also present (ibid. 183–4).

While consolidating its grip on the heartland of Oaxaca valley, Monte Albán also begun to expand by conquest and colonialization, first within and then outside the valley (Spencer and Redmond 2001). During the Monte Albán II phase (c.150/100 BC to 200 AD), the Zapotec state would erect "Conquest slabs" in the main plaza of Monte Albán to commemorate its numerous conquests and colonies within the valley (Marcus and Flannery 1996, 195–9). "At one village, La Coyotera, the conquerors [i.e., the Zapotecs] erected a feature the Zapotec called *yagabetoo*, a wooden rack displaying the skulls of 61 of the vanquished [dated to 10 BC]" (Flannery and Marcus 2003, 11805; see also Marcus and Flannery 1996, 203–6). The Zapotec state also built a strategic fortress at nearby Cuicatlán Cañada to defend the northern gateway of the valley.[85] From 200 to 500 AD (Monte Albán phases IIIa and IIIb) and on, the Zapotec state began to encounter other similarly powerful and expansionist states (i.e., Mixtecs, Teotihuacan), and these rivals borrowed strategies and tactics from each other in order to compete against each other, through both warfare and diplomacy (Marcus and Flannery 1996, 229–35; Joyce 2010, 173–7).

F. Anatolia as a Possible Pristine System?
(Appendix II, Table S2.4)

In archaeological terms, Anatolia covers much of modern Turkey. Looking from the perspective of state-making, Anatolia traditionally had not been recognized as one of the pristine systems (e.g., Cioffi-Revilla 2000; Otterbein 2004).[86] But from the point view of the origins of war, Anatolia might have been the first system that had decisively crossed the military threshold by 5000 BC, if not earlier (Ferguson 2006, 483; Hamblin 2006, 24–7), although more evidences are needed.

In Pottery Neolithic Anatolia (c.7000/6500–6000/5500 BC), the village of Catal Huyuk (or Hoyuk) was already well fortified: Catal Huyuk was perhaps the world's first fortified village. Yet, wall painting at this time was mostly about hunting and gaming (Guilaine and Zammit 2005, 102; Sagona and Zimansky 2009, 88–99). Later on, however, wall painting began to depict humans being decapitated, vultures hovering above headless bodies, and possibly men carrying a human head. Later on, weapons such as stone daggers, spearheads, arrowheads, maces, and slings appeared (Mellaart 1967, 68–9; 207–9; Ferrill 1985, 24–5). Although these evidences were by no means conclusive, they strongly indicate that war was already present in ancient Anatolia by then (Ferguson 2006, 483; Hamblin 2006, 24–6).

In Hacilar, a site not too far away from Catal Hoyuk and dated to a slightly later time (c.5700–4800 BC), wall painting clearly showed that by then, Anatolia had experienced warfare. "The originally unwalled village was destroyed around 5500 BC, and rebuilt with a wall 1.5–3 meters thick. It was destroyed again in 5250 and rebuilt with stronger 'fortresslike characteristics'. It was destroyed again and abandoned in 4800" (Hamblin 2006, 26). And there had been other similar sites. One site (Kurucay Hoyuk, dated 6000–5500 BC) had "a fortified stone wall with projecting semi-circular towers" (Hamblin 2006, 25; see also Ferguson 2006, 483–4).

By the Chaclolithic age (c.5500–3000 BC) at latest, Anatolia had been firmly transformed into an offensive realism world, perhaps with some input from external forces (i.e., Mesopotamia and Egypt, via Canaan and Levant). By 4500–4300 BC, fortifications had become very sophisticated, and copper spears and daggers had appeared. By 3500–3000 BC, warrior burial had also appeared (Hamblin 2006, 285–6). Mass graves with evidences of massacre dated to the early Bronze Age (3000–2700 BC) at Titrish Huyuk in southeast Turkey indicated that by then war had already ravaged some parts of Anatolia

(Erdal 2012). By the second millennium, Anatolia had produced kingdoms and empires that were constantly at war with other powerful states within the ancient Mesopotamia: many Assyrian texts referred to wars between Assyria and the Anatolian Hittite kingdom known as Urartu (Kuhrt 1995, 547–61; Macqueen 1995; Zimansky 1995; Sagona and Zimansky 2009, ch. 9; Hamblin 2006; van de Mieroop 2007). By this time around, therefore, Anatolia had firmly submerged into the greater Near East international system (Macqueen 1995, 1087).

V. WAR MAKES STATES/SOCIETIES/US AND STATES/ SOCIETIES/WE MAKE WAR

When war has been so rampant and often brutal, it should not be a surprise that societies and civilizations that lie far apart in time and space have been moulded by war into extremely similar entities: almost all of them have become entities of war, literally.[87] To paraphrase Carneiro's (2000, 12929) words on Sparta, virtually every aspect of a society's life becomes subordinated to war. This process of "war making states/societies/us" has mostly proceeded along two key dimensions: molding the state/society into a great war-machine; inoculating among the subjects (i.e., all of us) a culture of war for supporting the great war-machine, generation after generation.

A. The State/Society as a War Machine

The foremost manifestation of war making states/societies is that states/societies had become thoroughly organized for war: fundamentally, all of them they had become war machines. This should not come as a surprise: states/societies could have only survived by doing so. The selection pressure within an offensive realism system had been powerful, if not suffocating.

The backbone of a state as the war machine is a standing army. Indeed, ever since the coming of archaic states, a standing army has always been the true backbone of a state.

At the very beginning of human history, there was of course no standing army. Indeed, even after war had become fairly frequent, standing army might have not become very common: in most societies, all able males were full-time peasants (or hunter-gatherers) and only part-time warriors (i.e., in time of conflict). This is so because a standing army requires a sufficiently large population: the minimum requirement may be a simple chiefdom with a population of about 2000–2500 individuals, if not more (Carneiro 1987, 124;

Earle 1987, 288; Kosse 1990, 295).[88] Indeed, even today, village-level tribes (usually with fewer than 200 individuals) in Amazon have no standing army: all able males are part-time warriors and full-time hunter-gatherers and they drill for conflict only sporadically (Chagnon 1968[1997]). Their small population and economy simply cannot support a standing army.

The first standing army most likely consists only of elite warriors with royal officers. This was the likely case with the Zapotec archaic state and the Moche archaic state (Hassig 1992; Marcus and Flannery 1996; Otterbein 2004, 128, 139–41, 179–182). The next stage is a mixture of elite warriors mixed with conscripts: elite warriors served as commanders whereas conscripts as foot soldiers. This seems to be the case for both ancient Egypt under the Middle Kingdom (Hamblin 2006, 418–22) and ancient China during the Xia period (Yang 1991). During the Xia period, all major chiefdoms/states had fielded a standing army, organized into units of different size, although the size of the army remaining limited. By the Western Zhou period (c.1046–771 BC), armies in the ancient Chinese system were clearly divided into two types of units/ soldiers: elite units made from elite warriors ("huben"/虎贲) and regular units ("jiashi"/甲士) (Si-ma, vol. 1, "Book of Zhou," 822).

Within those larger international systems such as Mesopotamia, Egypt, China, and Europe, the competition among states had been so fierce that even standing armies with elite warriors plus conscripts were not enough: eventually, standing armies with mostly conscripts emerged, although still mostly with elite commanders (Certainly, the size of the population within these systems made a standing army made of mostly conscripts possible.) Most importantly, with these larger systems, the standing army might have quickly moved from armies of conscripts without open social mobility to armies of conscripts with open social mobility, to a various degree: Military prowess and valour can now allow a foot soldier to obtain things that he would not normally be able to obtain.

Indeed, extensive evidences indicated that armies of conscripts with open social mobility had been developed since ancient times. The first such army was perhaps installed in the Akkadian empire under Sargon (Kuhrt 1995, 55; Hamblin 2006, 95–9). Later on, such armies had been in place in Egypt under the New Kingdom the latest (c.1552/1550–1069 BC, Kuhrt 1995, 217–19), the Qin Kingdom after the reform by Lord Shang Yang (Yates 1999, 26–7; Hui 2005, 80–4), Spartan/Macedonia (Carneiro 2000), Persia, and Imperial Rome (and to a lesser extent, in republican Rome, see Roth 2009, ch. 4).

Indeed, in his thoroughgoing reform of the Qin Kingdom, Lord Shang Yang made military prowess and valor the only channel for upward social mobility: "What I mean by the unifying of rewards is that profits and emoluments, office and rank, should be determined *exclusively* by military merit, and nothing else" (Lord Shang c.339 BC, book 17, translation modified from Duyvendak's translation; emphasis added). Similar laws were installed under republican and imperial Rome, especially under Augustus (Rosenstein 1999; Campbell 1999; Eckstein 2007; Roth 2009, ch. 4). Although these two great empires were continents apart, both made military prowess a key, if not the only, channel of social mobility within their societies.

A final note regarding the standing army is that the size of the standing army had steadily increased along the increase of warfare. In ancient Mesopotamia, King Sargon of Akkad (c.2350 BC) had a standing army of 5400 (Kuhrt 1995, 53–5; McIntosh 2005, 188). In the first millennium in ancient Mesopotamia, forces under Shalameser III (9th century BC) reached around 44,000; 73,000 under Tiglath-Pileser III (8th century BC), and 208,000 under Sennacherib 40 years later (McIntosh 2005, 191). By the time of Thutmose III (1479–1425 BC) and Ramesse II (1290–1224 BC), the Egyptian Kindgom had regularly fielded an army of 20,000–25,000 strong, with sophisticated combinations of forces and weapons, well trained in tactics and combat (Ferrill 1985, ch. 2). During the late Warring Period in ancient China, the Kingdom of Qin had an army of between 200,000 and 500,000 strong (Hui 2005, 89–90).[89] And when their own army had proven to be insufficient, many major ancient states had also regularly employed mercenaries (e.g., Egypt, Greece, Persia), and mercenaries have certainly been a product of warfare (Keegan 1993, 221–34; Hamblin 2006, 381).

In addition to the standing army, all states have installed three key apparatuses that directly support the war machine. The first is a more sophisticated extraction apparatus: a centralized bureaucracy that symbolizes and underpins a centralized state (Yang 1991; Lin 1990; Kuhrt 1995, 53–5; McIntosh 2005, 173–83; see also Elias 1939[1994]). The second is the rise of three specialized professions: strategic studies, diplomacy, and espionage. In ancient China, Sun-Wu (Sun-Tzu, 孙武/孙子), Wu Qi (吴起), and Sun-bing (孙膑) all wrote classical texts on the strategic and tactical aspects of warfare during the Spring and Autumn period and the Warring State period (Sawyer 1993).[90] In ancient India, Kautilya's *Arthasastra* dealt mostly with governance, diplomacy, spying, and strategies, but also military tactics. In ancient Mesopotamia, China, and India, spies and diplomats roamed the land and played important roles in states' survival: diplomats were busy with making one's alliance and breaking others' alliance (these are two sides of the same coin) whereas spies were busy with subversion and espionage (Sawyer 1998).[91] The third supporting apparatus is a highly specialized and prized profession of weapon-making. All states had steadily poured tremendous amount of resources into developing more and more lethal weapons: indeed, some of the most epoch-making technological innovations had almost exclusively been driven by the search for better weapons, be it bronze, iron, steel, machine gun, tank, or the atomic bomb.

B. A Culture of War

The ideational (or "cultural") impact of war over human societies can be summarized in one sentence: all societies/states, after the transformation of their systems into an offensive realism system, had been pervasively and profoundly militarized and most have remained so. All states, ancient and modern, far apart in time and space, have independently developed the means of indoctrinating men into warriors with a doctrine/culture of crude offensive realism.

On this front, there is little difference between civilized civilizations and barbarian civilizations. The only difference between ancient/primitive states/societies and modern/"civilized" ones lies with their exact media of indoctrination. In ancient times, the spreading of war-making ideas had been accomplished via rituals, symbols, and story-telling. In modern times, while retaining and perfecting those traditional channels, the spreading of war-making ideas has been accomplished predominantly via (national) education and pop culture (literature, movies, and TVs). As a result, all surviving (and most perished) societies/states have ingrained a web of war-making ideas among their subjects. These interconnected ideas have become part of their collective memories, or simply, "(national) culture".[92]

Within this vast web of the culture of war, I shall merely single out two key dimensions: from the glorification of war to the notion of "just/sacred/holy war"; from organized religion and cosmology to the notion of "just/sacred/holy war".

Before I do that, however, I shall underscore that our languages present a strong, although largely neglected, piece of evidence indicating the prevalence of warfare in our culture. All surviving major languages today contain countless phrases and words that are connected to warfare, from eulogizing fallen heroes, courage, and victory to agonizing over defeat and suffering, and to despising cowardice and betrayal.

a. Glorification of War for the Sake of War-making

Crudely speaking, ideas that glorify war can be divided into three categories: glorification of warrior kings, glorification of warriors/heroes, and ethnocentrism, eventually culminating in the notion of Just/Sacred/Holy War and hence, self-sacrifice for the group. These ideas have been passed down to us generation after generation via vertical inheritance through epic, education, and pop culture.

In ancient Mesopotamia, Gilgamesh (reign c.2700–2680 BC), the great warrior king of Uruk who had supposedly overthrow the hegemony of Kish's king Agga (or Akka) over Uruk, had been the hero of the greatest epic in Mesopotamia since c.2700 BC (Hamblin 2006, 45–8). Likewise, King Sargon of the Akkaddian Empire had been depicted as the ideal warrior-king very early on (Hamblin 2006, 77–8). Later on, Assyrian king, Ashurnasirpal II (reign c.883–859 BC) glorified his conquest and atrocity to an unprecedented degree (Kaufman and Wohlforth 2007, 27).

In ancient Egypt, beginning with the Naqada II period (c.3500 BC) the latest, "legendary kings are associated with the falcon war-god Horus, emphasizing their military prowess: Horus fights, Horus seizes, and Horus decapitates" (Hamblin 2006, 312–21, quote from 313). Egyptians rulers were associated with violent smiting of enemies, and each new ruler had to start his reign with a war, ritualized it may be (Gnirs 1999, 73).[93] By the Old Kingdom period (c.2650–2150 BC) the latest, war had become a legitimate means for "expanding Egypt's borders", and foreign affairs had been reduced to suppression of the enemy and "smiting the foes" (Gnirs 1999, 71–3).

In China, the epic battle between the Yellow Emperor and his archrival Chi You had long underpinned the founding myth of ancient China (Lewis 1990, esp. ch. 5). In Republican Rome, imperiums who conquered would be welcomed via a *triumph* within the city (Roth 2009, 66–7; see also Rosenstein 1999; Eckstein 2006, ch. 6), aptly embodying Julius Caesar's famous boast "I come, I see, and I conquer."

Of course, once the idea that a ruler must smite the enemy and conquer new territory in order to secure a place in history has been inoculated among the ruling class, the "chiefly ambition" then easily becomes a force that comes back to increase warfare (Ferguson 2008, 44–6). The fact that the first archaic state arose not from preexisting complex chiefdoms in a less competitive system within today's eastern Shangdong province but from simple chiefdoms in a highly competitive (not even circumscribed, physically) region in central China (i.e., Er-li-tou in central Henan province) strongly points to the key roles played by ambitious chiefs as political entrepreneurs (Liu 2004, chs. 8 and 9). In the modern period, both the unification of Hawaiian Islands and the making of the Zulu Empire had been the work of ambitious chiefs (Marcus and Flannery 1996, 155–8; Keegan 1993).

The notion that males must demonstrate their military prowess inevitably makes warriors a distinguished class or strata.[94] Steles depicting warriors carrying multiple weapons (daggers, arrows, bows, axes) began to appear in numerous places and weapons began to accompany warriors in their burials since the very ancient (Guilaine and Zammit 2005, ch. 4). Eventually, this led to the notion of "hero" (Guilaine and Zammit 2005, ch. 5, esp. 217–28), as captured by Pericles' moving funeral oration to fallen Athenian heroes. Heroes had often been carved into stones (e.g., steles, monuments) and recorded in legends and eventually history textbooks.

Finally and most prominently, since ancient times, political units have taught ethnocentrism, manifesting as nationalism/patriotism, depending on who is talking about whom, as one of the key components within their (national) education.[95] An implicit, if not explicit (within many expansionist states), goal of this nationalistic education has always been to indoctrinate a willingness to wage war and sacrifice for one's group. Indeed, ancient states-men such as Lord Shang, Kautilya, and Han-Fei-Zi had been explicitly con-cerned with this question of overcoming subjects' reluctance to sacrifice via education, in addition to the threat and actual act of severe punishment. This is understandable: war is no easy lunch; you need to make people willing to fight (Carneiro 1994; Ferguson 1994; Gat 2006; Lebow 2008).

Without an exception, these ideas of war-making have pervaded all the societies today. In addition to the ancient civilizations and states mentioned above, other ancient or pre-modern civilizations and states that had these traits include: Azetc (Hassig 1992; 1999), ancient Greek States (Raaflaub 1999), Inca (Burger and Salazar 2004), Japan (Farris 1999), Maya (Webster 1999), and Persia (Briant 1999). Among modern states, almost all major European states before the First World War, Nazi Germany, Imperial Japan, Fascist Italy, attained an extreme war-making spirit (Schweller 2006; Lebow 2008). Even today, almost all the states still retain a powerful war-making culture, to a various degree.

b. Organized Religion and Cosmology: toward Just/Holy/Sacred War

Although religions may have originated before war and religions may not have been a major independent cause of war in history, all societies—without an exception, had adopted religion as the spiritual spear of war-making very early on.

Worshipping military gods appeared very early on (Hamblin 2006, 23–4). From Mesopotamia and Egypt to far away systems such as China, India, Peru, and Oaxaca Valley, divine/priestly kings had occupied the center of cult and organized religion very early on (Kemp 1989; Lewis 1990; Wilkinson 1999; McIntosh 2005; Hamblin 2006; Avari 2007, 88–90, 157–8). And one of the key, if not the vital, signs of kings' divination is his martial prowess and military conquests: In all these earlier civilizations, victory in war makes a particular King a king of god, and the King's brutality and cruelty in war had been invariably praised.

In the Sumerian King List, Sumerian kings had been proclaimed to descend from heaven, thus explicitly combining secular and religious power (Hamblin 2006, 37–9; van de Mieroop 2007, 42–51). In China, since ancient times, the Emperor had long been known as the "Son of Heaven", endowed with divine (military) power. In all the ancient systems, most, if not all, military campaigns had been preceded by seeking and obtaining gods' approval: "God is with you" (Bible, Deuteronomy 20.1; see also Lewis 1990; Liverani 2005, 116, 286–7).

The Romans thoroughly combined religious rituals with warfare. Not only did "the Campus Martius, the place where the army mustered, was named for the Roman god of war (Mars)", but elaborate rituals usually preceded actual march and fighting. More prominently, the *triumph*, one of the best known Roman rituals, would feature an *imperium* whose army had killed over 5000 foreign enemies parading through the streets of the city of Rome. The imperium would dress as the god Jupiter and ride on a chariot, followed by prisoners to be executed (usually immediately after the parade), plundered treasures, and other booties (Roth 2009, 61–2, 66–7). In terms of cosmology, "the Roman society was organized around a ritual calendar of which war was a key part" (Roth 2009, 60). Similarly, the cosmology and ethics of Israelite states had been thoroughly molded by their experience and understanding of war (Liverani 2005; Crouch 2009).

The rise of monotheistic religions eventually paved way for the missionary zeal via "just/holy/sacred war" against "no-believers", as a convenient cover for the less glorious goals of obtaining food, territory, women, prestige, and power, in addition to reinforcing the "us-versus-them" group identity and competition. "The obligation of a 'just war' was already evident in many of the older religions . . . With the new universal religious ideologies, the obligation of a 'just war' was reinforced, as was the ban on belligerency among the faithful . . . Some of the new salvation ideologies incorporated a strong missionary zeal that could be translated into holy belligerency against non-believers" (Gat 2006, 435).[96] Eventually, to a various degree, all major states, societies, and civilizations had developed the notion of "just/holy/sacred war", from Mesopotamia (Hamblin 2006, 73–101), Egypt (ibid. 353–4), Anatolia (ibid. 302), and Levant (ibid. 237–84), to China (Lewis 1990) and Europe (Keegan 1993). For Ibn-Khaldun ([1377]1967, 224), wars proclaimed by religions to be "holy" are "holy and just". For the Incas, war was a necessary instrument for enforcing a cosmos order: the Incas claimed that their deities— the Sun and the Moon, among others—had instructed them to conquer states/ societies around them (Salazar 2004, 33).

C. A Brief Recapitulation

Although Heraclitus might have overstated the power of war in making history when asserting "war is the father of all things", he could not have been more right when it comes to the relationship between war and state/ society/us. Without war, there would be no states (Wright 1984; Marcus and Flannery 1996, 157; Spencer 2003; Spencer and Redmond 2004; Ferguson 2008, 39–40; Redmond and Spencer 2006; 2012). With war, sooner or later, there would be states—providing the population within a system is large enough to produce a state, because warfare dictated a minimal group size below which a group becomes extremely vulnerable to raiding, not to mention other forms of aggression.[97] "Hence, war has been the principal means by which human societies . . . have been transformed into vast and complex states and empires . . . War is able to forge structural complexity in centralized polities because it has 'aggregative' effects" (Carneiro 1994, 18).[98]

If states have indeed been a product of repeated wars, then it should not be a surprise that states/societies have been thoroughly shaped by warfare. War-making by states/societies then profoundly comes back to shape every one of us by creating a highly integrated war machine physically and by producing war-fighting subjects psychologically and culturally: *There is a powerful feed-back mechanism between war, capabilities for making war, and socialization for aggression* (C. R. Ember and M. Ember 1994; Ross 1998, 138–9; Lebow 2008). War makes states/societies/us and states/societies/we make war (Tilly 1985; see also Elias 1939[1994]).[99]

Put it differently, war had gained a life of its own since its birth, and its vitality had not diminished a bit until the very recent: War tends to be self-reinforcing although not self-perpetuating (Ferguson 1994, 87; see also ch. 3 below). This is so because once a system is transformed into an offensive realism system, war becomes a powerful selection force over states within the system: you either expand and survive, or be expended and perish. States within the system had to innovate, imitate, and compete in order to stay alive within the system, be it reform by King Sargon in Akkad within the ancient Sumerian system or Lord Shang within the Kingdom of Qin in the Warring Period in ancient China (Hamblin 2006, ch. 3; Hui 2005, 81–4). "[T]he struggle for existence between neighboring tribes has had an important effect in culti-vating faculties of various kinds" (Spencer 1873, 193; see also ibid. ch. 8).

VI. PARADIGM GAINED: THE COMING OF OFFENSIVE REALISM DOCTRINE

Without an exception, all major civilizations have been the products (and victims) of conquest and expansion: war has been one of the most powerful forces shaping human history (Keegan 1993; Diamond 1997; Trigger 2003; Otterbein 2004; Hamblin 2006). As such, it should not have been a surprise that at least some of them had produced offensive realism doctrines: after all, men's thinking cannot be totally severed from the world in which they live (Marx and Engels 1846). In this section, I document the coming of offensive realism as a doctrine and the socialization of us (especially statesmen) into offensive realists (see Table 2.1 for a summary).

A. Ancient and Classical Texts from China, India, Europe, and the Near East

Three major civilizations, China, India, and Europe, had left definite texts on statecraft in the spirit of offensive realism (for an earlier discussion, see Tang 2008a; 2010a, ch. 6).[100] Shang Yang (c.390–339 BC), a key advisor to King Hui of the Kingdom of Qin (which eventually unified the heartland of today's China into the first Chinese empire in 221 BC), expounded the first explicit statement of the offensive realism position in his *Book of Lord Shang* (*Shang Jun Shu*/商君书).[101] For Shang Yang, states are inherently aggressive, and their aggressiveness is limited only by their capabilities: "In today's world, the powerful conquers, the weak defends... States with ten thousand chariots inevitably choose to conquer, and only states with merely one thousand chariots defend" (Shang Yang: book 7). In such a world, the only viable means of survival is war of conquest: "The only reason behind a state's prosperity and power is agriculture and war" (ibid. book 3). Hence, preventive war, the hallmark of offensive realism, is not only desirable but also just: "For the purpose of eliminating war, war is just" (ibid. book 18). All these statements staunchly reflect the doctrines of offensive realism (Tang 2008a; 2010b, ch. 6).

Writing after Shang Yang, Kautilya in ancient India promulgated the same doctrine of offensive realism in his *Arthasastra* (c.300 BC). For Kautilya, not assuming the worst over others' intentions is a grave sin: Hence, the famous Mandala dictum of "my neighbor is my enemy whereas my neighbor's neighbor is my friend" (Boesche 2003:18–19). Once other states are believed to be inherently malignant, all possible means should be deployed to weaken and eventually conquer them. Not surprisingly, the pages of *Arthasastra* are filled with prescriptions of conquering and holding lands via means such as poison, women, spy, and priests! Another ancient text from India, the *Law of Manu* (c.100–200 AD) preached similarly: "A king... should try to take possession of countries that he has not yet possessed and should protect those that he has" (quoted in Brenner 2007, 99).

The (Western) European civilization, traced back to classical Greece and Rome, too had produced texts bearing the hallmarks of offensive realism. Yet, compared to its splendid achievements in arts and philosophy, ancient Greek and Roman discourses on war had been much less developed, although traces of offensive realism were perhaps present in Aristotle's (1998, book I) notion of "natural slavery".[102] Not until Machiavelli did Europe produce an explicit statement of the offensive realism doctrine in *The Prince*. For Machiavelli, as long as a prince conquers and retains his conquest, "his methods will always be judged honorable and praised by all" ([1532]2005, book XVIII, 62). And Machiavelli explicitly warned those princes who might have dreamed of being kind and nice (or benign): "In our times we have not seen great deeds accomplished except by those who were considered miserly; the others were all wiped out" (ibid. book XVI, 54).

To some extent, it is a mystery that the great civilizations of the ancient Near East (i.e., Assyria, Babylon, Egypt, and Persia) had not left behind a single coherent text of offensive realism.[103] They had, however, left behind bits and pieces of thoughts that thoroughly reflect the doctrine of offensive realism. Mostly prominently, the *Old Testament* repeatedly praises wars that pleased God (Yahweh), from Moses to David to Solomon. God ordered Moses to enlist the Levites to slaughter the followers of the Golden Calf sect (Exodus 32:26–8). God also ordered Moses "[to] conquer them and utterly destroy them ['seven nations greater and mightier than you', i.e., the Hittites, the Girgashites, the Amorites, the Canaanites, the Perizzites, the Hivites and the Jebusites]. You shall make no covenant with them nor show mercy to them... You shall destroy their altars, and break down their sacred pillars, and cut down their wooden images, and burn their carved images with fire" (Deuteronomy 7: 11). God commanded Saul to "go and smite Amalek, and utterly destroy all that they have and spare them not; but slay both men and women, infant and sucking, ox and sheep, camel and ass". And when Saul carried most of the atrocities prescribed by God but spared Agag and the best of the cattle, God repented that he had made Saul the King of Israel (Samuel 15:1–3; see also 13:2; 12:31)! Throughout the Bible, butchery and mutilation are praised as the work of God through His followers. Words and phrase such as blood, blood-shedding, kill, destroy, and "punish/avenge with sword, famine, and pestilence" were littered within the Bible, literally. This should not be a surprise: the ancient Near East in which the Jewish/Judean states were living through had long been an utterly brutish and bloody (offensive realism) world.

B. Offensive Realism among Statesmen and Us

For much of our history, offensive realism had also been the guiding ideology among statesmen. Again, this should not have been surprise: unless a statesman becomes an offensive realist and makes his/her state an offensive realist state, his/her state is unlikely to last very long. Most of the estimated 100,000 independent political entities in 1000 BC did not make it into the near-modern period (c.1500 AD).

Assyrian King Ashurnasirpal II (883–859 BC) graphically depicted his brutality and atrocities in war, "fraying rebellion leaders , burning captured men and women alive, and displaying the corpses, decapitated heads, and skins of frayed leaders around the defeated cities" were inscribed in stones (Kaufman and Wohlforth 2007, 27).[104] Charlemagne, in his war against the Saxons, in one afternoon in 782 AD, "had 4,500 Saxons decapitated after they had peacefully surrendered". And he had joyous poems written to celebrate the accomplishments of murdering and enslaving thousands of Avars, women and children included (Lebow 2008, 231). For Ghengis Khan, "Man's greatest good fortune is to chase and defeat his enemy, seize his total possessions, leave his married women weeping and wailing, ride his gelding, [and] use the bodies of his women as nightshirt and support" (quoted in Sanderson 2001, 318). For one of Katherine's ministers, "that which stops growing begins to rot". For France in 1799, "that only a military offensive could enable the nation to achieve its defensive political objective" (both quoted in Jervis 1978, 185–6).

In the 19–20th centuries, the doctrine of offensive realism, often embodied in the supposedly more scientific Geopolitics and Social Darwinism-inspired racism, was widely believed by leading statesmen before and after First World War (Van Evera 1984; Schweller 1996). During the Second World War, all three archetypal offensive realist states, Nazi Germany, Fascist Italy, and Imperial Japan, fervently embraced offensive realism doctrines in the form of geopolitics and racism (Lebow 2008, ch. 8). Finally, for General Douglas MacArthur, "a warlike spirit, which alone can create and civilize a state, is absolutely essential to national defense and to a national perpetuity . . . Every man brought into existence should be taught from infancy that the military service of the Republic carries with it honor and distinction, and his very life should be permeated with the ideal that even death itself may become a boon when a man dies that a nation may live and fulfill its destiny" (quoted in Sanderson 2001, 318).

In contrast to the thriving of the offensive realism doctrine, defensive realism, not to mention "pacifist" doctrines, had been widely rejected by statesmen (and hence, states) for much of human history. During the Spring/Autumn and Warring period in ancient China, although there was a Confucian-Mencius doctrine of pacifism, it was the Legalist (offensive realism) doctrine advanced by Lord Shang and Han-Fei-Zi who advocated a ruthless struggle for power that eventually won the hearts and minds of the many kings within the system. Thus, when Menicus preached the idea of "governing by virtue rather than by force" and argued that "only a ruler who does not enjoy killing will be able to unify China" to the King of Wei (Menicus, book 2), his preaching fell on deaf ears. Indeed, the Confucian-Mencius doctrine did not find a single adherent among the states during the Spring-Autumn Period and the Warring Period (Hui 2005).[105] Similarly, Bernard Brodie (1973, ch. 6) noted that although an anti-war idea had been developed by Stoic philosophers (e.g., Cicero) in the Roman Empire (much later than the culture of glorifying war of conquest, which was developed by Homer, Plato, and Socrates in ancient Greece), the anti-war idea had little influence on actual state behavior for much of the Western history (see also Mueller 1989, 17–52; Lebow 2008). Indeed, some "anti-war" ideas were actually geared toward a world empire (e.g., *Pax Romana*, *Pax Ecclesiae*, and "Grand Design" of Henri IV), thoroughly reflecting the offensive realism doctrine of preventive war.

More importantly, as detailed above, states within those ancient offensive realism systems had indeed practiced the core offensive realism doctrine: "the best defense is a good offense." During the early dynasty period (c.3200–2575 BC), Egyptian armies "periodically invaded its neighbors, keeping them off guard, and dispersing enemy troop concentrations" so that Egypt could be spared of destruction (Wenke 2009, 243). Likewise, during the Warring Period of the ancient Chinese system, major states were in a constant cutthroat struggle for survival via hegemony (Hui 2005, ch. 2).

When much of the recorded human history had been an offensive realism world and the doctrine of offensive realism had been deeply ingrained into our cultural heritage, it should not be a mystery why modern and contemporary students of IR readily take the Hobbesian world as an inherent (natural) property of anarchy rather than something made by their ancestors (e.g., Waltz 1979, 66; Mearsheimer 2001, 2; cf. Wendt 1992). If the Hobbesian anarchy had been firmly in place long before Homer, Sun Tze, Thucydides, Lord Shang, and Kautilya, one simply cannot expect later students of IR to ignore the long shadow of history and the canonical insights of the founding fathers of their discipline. No wonder then that most of the early theorists of realism have been offensive realists: from Machiavelli's *ambizione*, to Cousin and Herder's "organic state", to Haushofer's Geopolitico and Social Darwinism, offensive realists had dominated the realism school before the two World Wars (Schweller 1996, 92–101).

Finally, I haste to add that the memory of war as part of our cultural heritage has thoroughly socialized most of us into "naïve/folk (offensive) realists" when it comes to international relations (Ross and Ward 1995; Robinson et al. 1995; Drezner 2008; Kertzer and McGraw 2012). For many of us, (offensive) realism comes *naturally*!

SUMMARY AND CONCLUSION

For adherents of sociobiology and evolutionary psychology (e.g., van der Dennen 1995; Thayer 2004; Gat 2006; Smith 2007), war originates from "human nature": men are inherently aggressive because our biological evolution has programmed us to be so. And when competition for resources becomes pressing, war naturally breaks out. Yet, the part of our human nature determined by our biological evolution is a necessary but insufficient cause of war, and even with competition for resources, war does not necessarily break out: war cannot be explained by biological or even material factors alone,[106] because war has an indispensable social (or cultural) component. Meanwhile, although archaeological anthropologists have produced overwhelming evidences on the origins of war, they have paid scant attention to the transformation of international systems into offensive realism systems by war (and the transformation of units within the system thereafter). Finally, for IR theorists who have bothered to explore the origin of war (e.g., Wendt 1992; Mercer 1995), it was mostly identity that does most of the explanation. Yet, a purely ideational explanation for the origin of war (or anything else) cannot possibly hold because material forces hold ontological priority over ideational forces (Tang 2011b; 2013).

Existing theories noted above capture something valid but not the complete picture. By synthesizing material and ideational forces organically via the central mechanism of social evolution (i.e., artificial variation–selection–inheritance), our theory provides a genuinely endogenous (hence complete) explanation for not only the origins of the offensive realist state and war but also the subsequent transformation of the system into an offensive realism world. Along the way, our theory also offers an endogenous sociology of knowledge of offensive realism in particular and realism in general.

To recap briefly, long before relative population pressure crossing a certain threshold, human beings had already possessed the tools and skills of warfare. As relative population pressure (or scarcity) set in, some groups, feeling the crunch from the relative population pressure, were then bound to think about deploying offensive realism tactics (e.g., raid, plunder, or outright, conquest) to survive: they became offensive realist states (as a kind of mutant). Of course, once one group did that, the first war soon broke out within a subsystem.

The first war would constitute a watershed event in the system. After the first war, selection began to operate powerfully upon groups and individuals (especially group leaders). Previously non-offensive realist states will learn to become offensive realist states: the former will fear that it will be the latter's next target, and it will be swallowed unless it swallows others. Meanwhile, victorious conquerors will impose their offensive realism doctrine and culture upon their new subjects. Both mechanisms, as forms of horizontal inheritance, reinforce the dynamics that transform the system into an offensive realism system. More critically, non-offensive realist stats will be wiped out, leaving only (strong) offensive realist states to survive. Eventually, only groups (and leaders) that have adopted and internalized offensive realism doctrine could have survived within the system. Socialization (as vertical inheritance) will then indoctrinate generations of states and individuals (especially leaders) with offensive realism as their code of conduct. As the ideas of offensive realism spread, the whole system became firmly entrenched as an offensive realism world. These two levels of selection and inheritance (i.e., individual and group) mutually reinforce each other.

Eventually, the whole system would be firmly transformed into an offensive realism system and states within it would be socialized into offensive realism states or absorbed by other offensive realism state. Within such a system, the only viable defense (in the long run) is a continuation of successful offense. Within such a system, a polity could only have survived with a war machine that is as effective as, if not more effective, than its neighboring polities (Otterbein 2004, 179). There would be few, if any, non-offensive realist states left in the system. As such, interactions among human communities will be firmly locked into a competitive path: the nature of international politics since then would remain thoroughly conflictual until the very recent (see Chapter 3 below). Because all major states and civilizations were fashioned in war and maintained by military force and war-making (Ferrill 1985, 34; Tilly 1985; Carneiro 1970; 1994; Diamond 1997), all of us, especially statesmen, had been thoroughly socialized into (offensive) realists.

Without the objective possibility and the necessity of competing for scarce resources, neither group identity nor tools/skills to kill alone or the two combined will make war necessary (hence inevitable). When juxtaposed with the other three conditions (frequent interaction, dwindling resources, and the necessity for defense), however, in-group identity and tools/skills to kill makes (vicious) competition inevitable because competition is now not only objectively possible but also objectively and logically necessary.

Although admitting biologically determined human nature and territoriality as a necessary condition of war, our theory improves upon sociobiological explanations (e.g., van de Berghe 1974, Wrangham 1999). The making of the offensive realism world is not in our genes or even within our biological evolution alone. Rather, it is a product of social evolution: both material forces and ideational forces had played essential roles in the coming of war and the subsequent transformation from paradise to the offensive realism world. Hence, once we adopt a social evolutionary approach toward human society, the need for inclusive fitness to explain "sacrifice" by individuals for their groups melts away although biological factors should be part of any theory of the origin of war (see also Thayer 2004; Gat 2006).

Our theory also subsumes the process-oriented neo-evolutionism in anthropology that emphasizes agent, action, and structure (e.g., Flannery 1999): our theory centers upon the central mechanism of social evolution, and the central mechanism implies roles for agent, action, and structure (see also Chapter 5 below). Our theory also improves upon more psychological and cultural explanations. Although Wendt correctly noted that a predatory state (as a "rotten" apple) can potentially turn an initially peaceful system into a Hobbesian one, he does not explain the origins of the predatory state.[107] More recently, Lebow (2008) argued that warriors are driven by spirit (or honor) and this in turn makes them especially prone to violence. Yet, he did not offer an explanation for the origins of the warrior class. By demonstrating that warriors and warrior societies too are products of social evolution, our explanation also goes deeper than that of Lebow. Finally, our theory achieves something that has not been achieved before: it explains why most (although not all) of us have been (offensive) realists for so long.

Altogether, by adopting SEP, we have provided a genuinely endogenous explanation for the transformation of the initial paradise-like system into the nasty and brutish offensive realism world (or the Hobbesian world). We also readily explain why most, if not all, states had come to believe in the offensive realism doctrine, field a standing army, and practice offensive realism. Finally, we also readily account for offensive realism's dominance in the discipline of IR for much of the history.

Interestingly, a social evolutionary understanding of war does not necessarily doom us to a "pessimistic" projection of human society. Because the international system (as part of the human society) has always been an evolutionary system, the offensive realism world cannot possibly last forever, just as the initial Eden paradise preceding it did not. Eventually, the offensive realism system would also be transformed into a system where war becomes less rampant (and absolute) than it used to be although war may not be eradicated from the earth any time soon. This is the story to be told in the next chapter.

3

From Mearsheimer to Jervis

INTRODUCTION

From the debates of grand theories of international politics, an important division inside the realism camp has also emerged.[1] Offensive realism and defensive realism, despite starting from the same set of bedrock assumptions of realism, arrive at fundamentally divergent conclusions about the nature of international politics (Glaser 1994–5; Mearsheimer 2001; Taliaferro 2000–1; Tang 2008a; 2010b).

In this chapter, I argue that the differences between the two realisms cannot be resolved by logic deduction: It can only be resolved empirically by bringing the dimension of time to the debate, with SEP. I underscore that an offensive realism world (Mearsheimer's world), which grew out of the paradise-like world, is a self-destructive system and it will *inevitably and irreversibly* self-transform into a defensive realism world (Jervis's world) over time exactly because of the imperative of an offensive realism world for state behavior.[2] In an offensive realism world, a state must either conquer or be conquered. This central mechanism of seeking security through conquest, together with three other auxiliary mechanisms, will eventually transform an offensive realism world into a defensive realism world.

Due to this transformation of the international system, offensive realism and defensive realism apply to two different worlds rather than a single world. In other words, each of these two theories explains a period of human history, but not the whole. Different grand theories of international politics are for different periods of international politics, and different epochs of international politics actually need different grand theories of international politics (see the concluding chapter for a more detailed discussion).

Before I proceed further, two caveats are in order.

First, although I focus on the evolution from Mearsheimer's world to Jervis's world and the debate between offensive realism and defensive realism, my exercise is *not* another effort to restate the realism case. My central goal, to repeat, is to advance a social evolution paradigm, or more precisely, a social evolution paradigm, toward international politics. I am *not* endorsing offensive realism or defensive realism, in the theoretical sense.[3] Rather, I am interested in offering a neat resolution of the debate between the two realisms.

Second, just because international politics has evolved from an offensive realism world to a defensive realism world does not mean that offensive realist states cannot exist in a defensive realism world (e.g., Iraq under Saddam Hussein, the United States under George W. Bush). It merely means that the system has been fundamentally transformed and it will not go backwards.

The rest of the chapter is structured as follows. Section I briefly introduces the debate between offensive realism and defensive realism, making it explicit that an implicit assumption that the fundamental nature of international politics has remained pretty much the same has been the critical cause why this debate could not be resolved. Sections II and III together present the case that international politics had evolved from an offensive realism world to a defensive realism world. Section III identifies "to-conquer-or-be-conquered"—the imperative for state behavior in an offensive realism world—as the fundamental mechanism behind the transformation. Section IV underscores selection against offensive realist states, negative learning that conquest is difficult, and the rise and spreading of sovereignty and nationalism as the three auxiliary mechanisms behind the transformation. A brief conclusion follows.

I. THE OFFENSIVE REALISM–DEFENSIVE REALISM DEBATE

The fundamental difference between offensive realism and defensive realism centers on the question whether there are genuine defensive realist (or benign) states out there or to what extent is international politics conflictual (Tang 2008a; 2010b, esp. chs. 1 and 4).[4]

Offensive realism believes that international politics has always been an offensive realism world—an anarchy populated mostly by offensive realist states. For offensive realism, there are few, if any, defensive realist states out there (Mearsheimer 2001, 29, 34).[5] Because an offensive realist state seeks security by intentionally decreasing others' security (Mearsheimer 1994, 11–12), *international politics is almost completely conflictual.*

In contrast, defensive realism believes that international politics has been a defensive realism world—an anarchy populated mostly by defensive realist states. While not denying there may be offensive realist states out there (e.g., Jervis 1999, 49; Waltz 1979, 118, 126; Wolfers 1952, 496), defensive realists believe that there are some, if not many, genuine defensive realism states out there (Glaser 1994–5, 60–72; Jervis 1999, 49).[6] Because a defensive realist state does not seek security by intentionally decreasing others' security (although they often decrease others' security unintentionally, through a spiral or a security dilemma), international politics is not completely conflictual despite being fundamentally conflictual.

As recognized by many, if the two realisms start from the same bedrock assumptions of realism yet arrive at fundamentally divergent conclusions about the nature of international politics, then there must be some auxiliary—although sometimes implicit—assumptions that make the differences (Brooks 1997, 455–63; Taliaferro 2000–1, 134–43). Because the two realisms' fundamental differences arise from their differences in assumptions, they cannot be resolved by logic deduction. Rather, these differences can only be resolved by "an empirical duel" that can determine which theory's assumptions fit better with empirical evidences: does history provide more justifications for offensive realism's assumptions or more justifications for defensive realism's assumptions (Brooks 1997, 473)?

Recognizing that the differences between them are differences in assumption that can only be resolved by an empirical duel, proponents of the two realisms have tried hard to prove their favored grand theory a better theory on the empirical battleground. Strikingly, they have self-consciously decided that if they are going to do a "duel", they are going to do it fair-and-square: They are going to do it on the same empirical battleground, or the same historical era. Thus, proponents of the two realisms have almost exclusively looked at the modern Great Power Era for supporting empirical evidences, with only passing mentioning of other historical periods.[7] Here, an assumption that different theories of international politics can resolve their differences *only* by looking at the same historical period is evident.

By assuming that different theories of international politics can resolve their differences *only* by looking at the same historical period, both camps have implicitly assumed that the fundamental nature of international politics has *not* changed that much since the beginning of human history. Consequently, both camps believe that the whole history of international politics *should and can* be adequately explained by a single (good) grand theory (i.e., their preferred grand theory). This belief is the ultimate cause why the debate between the two realisms could not be resolved.[8]

The next two sections offer a social evolutionary resolution of the debate between the two realisms: The two realisms are appropriate grand theories for two different historical eras or two different worlds because international politics had evolved from an offensive realism world to a defensive realism world.

II. FROM MEARSHEIMER TO JERVIS: THE FUNDAMENTAL MECHANISM

In an offensive realism world in which most, if not all, states are offensive realist states, a state can achieve its security only by reducing others' security. Consequently, other than internal growth and armament, a state has to expand and conquer in order to achieve its security (Mearsheimer 2001, ch. 2). This logic of the offensive realism world—"to conquer or be conquered"—is the fundamental mechanism that will drive the transformation of an offensive realism world into a defensive realism world. Because the central force behind it had been the imperatives for state behavior of an offensive realism world, the whole transformation process is endogenously driven.[9] Moreover, this fundamental mechanism has no viable replacement.

As states pursue conquests and some conquests succeed, two interrelated outcomes become inevitable: The number of states decreases, and the average size of states—in terms of land, population, and material wealth—increases.[10] These two interrelated outcomes dictate that all surviving states in the system will have accumulated more resources in terms of land, population, and wealth (Elias [1939] 1994, 269–70).[11] Because more land means more defense depth, more population means more men for fielding a larger army, and more wealth means more resources for improving military and buying allies when necessary, increase in these three factors contributes to an increase in a state's defense capability. Because defense is usually easier than offense, conquest overall becomes more difficult. This holds even a state's increased power may make it more likely to pursue conquest, because it will still have to face more powerful opponents.[12]

If so, as states act according to the central logic of offensive realism— seeking security through conquest—for a sustained period of time, their actions will gradually but inevitably make the central logic increasingly difficult to operate.

A cursory look at the macro-history of international politics easily confirms that the number of states had decreased greatly and the average size of states had increased greatly. According to one estimate, there were 600,000 independent political entities in 1000 BC (Carneiro 1978, 213). Today, there are only about 200. According to another estimate, human population had increased from 1 million in 1 million BC to 50 million in 1000 BC, and to 1.6 billion in 1900 (Kremer 1993, 683). Because the land surface on earth since the last Ice Age has remained largely unchanged, fewer states occupying the same surface area must mean more territory and more population for each state. Most importantly, conquest has been the *indispensable* mechanism behind this process of reducing the number of states and increasing the average size of states (Carneiro 1978; Tilly 1990; Diamond 1997).

Transformation of International Politics

To further substantiate my central claim, I offer a more detailed examination of two international subsystems—ancient China and post-Holy Roman Empire Europe.[13] I show that in both systems, the number of states had indeed decreased and the average size of states had indeed increased greatly due to wars of conquest. As a result, the rate of state death in both systems had decreased greatly, indicating that conquest had indeed become more and more difficult.[14]

Ancient China (1046/4 BC to 1759 AD)

Ancient Chinese history (recorded) has the unique feature of going through cycles of fragmentation to unification, and each episode of state death can be conveniently demarcated as the period between fragmentation and (re)unification. Ancient China thus experienced five major episodes of state death (Table 3.1).

The first episode lasted from 1046/4 to 221 BC.[15] Between 1046 and 1044 BC, the Zhou tribe, which was a major tribe within the Shang Kingdom, initiated the attack against Shang by commanding an alliance of more than 800 tribes (Sima 1997 [c.91–87 BC], 82).[16] In 221 BC, the state of Qin eliminated all other

Table 3.1. Pattern of State Death in Ancient China, 1045 BC to 1759 AD

Historical Period	Western Zhou/Spring-Autumn / Warring States to Qin	Post-Eastern Han to Western (Xi) Jin	Easter (Dong) Jin to Tang	Post-Tang to Yuan	Post-Yuan to Qing
Timeframe	1045 to 221 BC	190 to 280 AD	316 to 668 AD	907 to 1276 AD	1583–1759 AD
Number of states at the beginning	>800	>25	29[17]	21[18]	8[19]
Years to eliminate all other states in the system	825	91	353	370	177
Rate of state death (states eliminated per century)	>97	>26.7	7.9	5.4	3.9
Average time (years) needed to eliminate a state	c.1.03	c.3.79	c.12.6	c.18.5	c.25.3

states in the system and founded the first unified empire in Chinese history. In this episode of 825 years, more than 800 independent political entities were eliminated, and the rate of state death was more than 97 state deaths per century.

The Qin dynasty lasted barely twenty years and was replaced by the Han dynasty. The (Eastern) Han dynasty went into an implosion in 184 AD. In 190 AD, a major war between two rival fractions of warlords erupted and China entered its second episode of state death. At the beginning of this episode, there were about 25 major warlords (Luo [c.1330–1400] 1999). In 280 AD, the state of Jin, which replaced the state of Wei with a coup, eliminated the last remaining rival state Wu in the system. In this episode of 91 years, about 24 states were eliminated, and the rate of state death was about 26.7 state deaths per century.

In 316 AD, (Western) Jin was attacked by Xiong-Na and the Chinese core plunged into fragmentation again, and it was not until 589 AD that the Sui dynasty was able to unify the Chinese core again. The Sui dynasty was again short-lived (lasting from 581 to 618 AD), and a stable unification was not achieved until 668 AD under the Tang dynasty. In this episode of 353 years, 28 states were eliminated, and the rate of state death had decreased to 7.9 state deaths per century.[20]

The Tang dynasty imploded from 875 to 884 AD and finally collapsed in 907 AD, and China entered its fourth episode of state death. This episode of state death would last until 1276 AD when Genghis Khan's Mongol army finally conquered China. In this episode of 370 years, 20 states were eliminated and the rate of state death had decreased to 5.4 state deaths per century.

The Mongol Yuan dynasty was replaced by the Ming dynasty in 1368. In 1583, the Manchus, which would eventually found the Qing dynasty, began its long drive toward the conquest of China and finally eliminated all the other states in the system in 1759.[21] In this episode of 177 years, seven states were eliminated and the rate of state death had decreased to 3.9 state deaths per century.

Post-Holy Roman Empire Europe, 1450–1995 AD

For convenience, I focus on continental Europe and exclude the littoral states (e.g., Great Britain, Ireland, Iceland, Corsica, and Cyprus).[22] Thus, the European international system denotes the area between the British Channel in the west and the Urals in the east, and between Iberian Peninsula in the south and Norway in the north. With continental Europe, we also exclude mini-states (e.g., Monaco, Vatican). Excluding the littoral and mini-states has minimal influence on the results due to the overwhelming weight of the remaining continental states.

I chose 1450 AD as the starting point of my inquiry for two reasons. First, starting the mid-fourteenth century, the Holy Roman Empire began its long decline and became highly fragmented in the 15th century, and its domain began to resemble a genuine anarchy.[23] Second, states in the modern Weberian/ IR sense began to emerge around the mid-15th century and state deaths caused by war began to play a prominent role in shaping European politics.[24]

The whole time span from 1450 to 1995 is divided into five major phases: 1450–1648, 1648–1815, 1815–1919, 1919–1945, and 1945–1995. Except for the last phase, each phase contained at least one major war that had caused many state deaths (Table 3.2).

The first episode of state death in post-Holy Roman Empire Europe lasted from 1450 to 1648. At the beginning of this episode, there were more than 581 independent political entities. Major causes of state death in this episode included the unification of France and the Netherlands, the expansion of Sweden and the Austria-Habsburg Empire, the expansion of the Ottoman Empire into Southeast Europe, and the Thirty Years War. By the end of the Thirty Years War (1648), the number of states in the system was reduced to about 260. In this episode of 199 years, more than 321 states were eliminated, and the rate of state death was about 161 state deaths per century.

The second episode lasted from 1648 to 1815. Major causes of state death in this episode included the Napoleonic Wars, the expansion of Prussia, and the expansion of Austria. In this episode of 168 years, the number of states in the system was reduced from about 260 to 63, and the rate of state death in this episode was about 117 state deaths per century.

The third episode lasted from 1815 to 1919. Major causes of state death in this episode included the unification of Italy and Germany and the First World War. In this episode of 105 years, the number of states in the system was reduced from 63 to 30, and the rate of state death in this episode was about 31 state deaths per century.

Table 3.2 Pattern of State Death in post-Roman Europe, 1450–1995 AD

Period	1450–1648	1648–1815	1815–1919	1919–1945	1945–1995vf
Number of states at the beginning and the end of each period	c.581[25] c.260[26]	c.260 c.63[27]	c.63 30[28]	30 25[29]	25 35[30]
Years of the period	199	168	105	27	51
Number of states eliminated in the period	c.321	c.197	33	5	4[31]
Rate of state death (states eliminated per century)	c.161	c.117	c.31	c.19	N. D.
Average time (years) needed to eliminate a state	c.0.62	c.0.85	c.3.18	5.4	N. D.

The fourth episode lasted from 1919 to 1945. In this episode, the major cause of state death was Soviet Union's annexation of East European states after the Second World War. In this episode of 27 years, the number of states in the system was reduced from 30 to 25, and the rate of state death in this episode was about 19 state deaths per century.

The final episode lasted from 1945 to 1995. Major causes of state death in this episode included the (re)unification of Germany, the collapse of the former Soviet Union, and the disintegration of the former Yugoslavia Federation and the former Czechoslovakia Republic. Other than the case of Germany unification, however, state deaths in this episode actually led to the (re)birth of many states. Moreover, none of the four state deaths were caused by wars of conquest and expansion. As a result, the number of states in the system actually increased from 25 to 35.

Summary: State Death and the Evolution of International System

Although the two international systems examined above had evolved in different space and time,[32] they had gone through a similar evolutionary path. In both systems, the number of states had decreased greatly and the average size of states had increased significantly,[33] precisely because states in the two systems had been operating according to the logic of offensive realism (i.e., security through conquest and expansion). As a result, both systems eventually reached the same outcome that conquest had become increasingly difficult (although conquest did succeed from time to time), reflected in the steadily decreasing rate of state death.

The conclusion is also supported by evidences in the more recent history. As Mearsheimer (2001, 41) himself noted, no major attempts of empire-building on the European Continent had ever succeeded after Westphalia. Napoleon and Hitler came really close, but a powerful counter-alliance eventually overwhelmed them. Indeed, in the Great Power Era, only one attempt toward achieving regional hegemony through conquest—the continental expansion by the United States—had actually succeeded.[34] Arguably, the success of United States was largely due to its unique geographical environment: there was no crippling counter-alliance to counter the United States even though it behaved aggressively (Elman 2004).

The evidences strongly suggest that as states in an offensive realism operate according to the imperatives of an offensive realism system, they will also make the logic of offensive realism increasingly inoperable. The offensive realism world is a self-destructive system: exactly because states act according to the logic of an offensive realism world, the world will be transformed. The inherent dynamics of the offensive realism system eventually leads to the system's own demise.[35]

III. FROM MEARSHEIMER TO JERVIS: THREE AUXILIARY MECHANISMS

The last section highlights states' pursuit of conquest and expansion according to the logic of the offensive realism system as the fundamental mechanism behind the transformation of an offensive realism system into a defensive realism system. This section focuses on three auxiliary mechanisms—all of them depend on and build upon the outcome engineered by the fundamental mechanism—that will further cement the world into a defensive realism system.[36]

Selection against Offensive Realist States

At the beginning of an offensive realism world, there may be other types of states (e.g., defensive realist states) in the system. Yet, as the system evolves, only offensive realist states that have attempted and succeeded in conquests could have survived in the system, and other types of states will either be quickly eliminated or socialized into offensive realist states. Thus, for much of the time of an offensive realism world, only one type of state—the offensive realist type—can exist in the system.

By the time that the offensive realism system reaches its late stage—that is, after the number of states has been greatly reduced and the average size of each state has greatly increased, however, some states would have accumulated sufficient defensive power versus a potential aggressor. As a result, these states can survive mostly on defensive strategies, *if they choose to*. And if some of these states do choose to survive mostly on defensive strategies, then a new type of state—the defensive realist type—emerges in the offensive realism system.[37] Once the system becomes populated by two types of states—an offensive realist type and a defensive realist type—a new selection dynamics becomes possible within the system.

In this late stage of an offensive realist world in which most states have accumulated more power to defend themselves either alone or by forming alliances, conquest becomes more difficult. Moreover, if a state pursues expansion but fails, it will be severely punished by the victors.[38] As a result, more likely than not, offensive realist states will be punished—sometimes severely.

In contrast, while defensive realist states may have to fend off aggressions from time to time; they will more often end up in better positions than aggressors, not only because they are more likely to defend themselves successfully but also because they do not have to endure the punishment for losing a war of conquest.

Hence, as the offensive realism systems evolves to its late stage, selection within the system will increasingly go against offensive realist states and favor defensive realist states. The foundation of this shifting of selection pressure is the increased size of states through the elimination of states.

The Negative Spreading of Ideas: Conquest is Getting Difficult

If states are strategic actors, then they must also be learning actors: states will learn and adopt ideas that are deemed to be good for their interest and reject those that are deemed to be bad for their interest, *in the long run.*[39]

When conquest has become quite difficult in the late stage of the offensive realism world, a state that pursues conquest is more likely to be severely punished than to be rewarded. If so, one can expect that this state (and other states) will gradually learn the hard lesson that conquest is getting more difficult and rarely pays from its own and others states' experiences of having failed in pursuing conquest. Coupled with the selection pressure against offensive realist states, one can expect a majority of the states to eventually learn the lesson that conquest is getting more difficult at some point, even if the learning process may be slow and non-linear.[40]

As a result, the system of states will gradually become a system populated mostly by states that have largely given up the option of conquest as a means toward security because they have learned the lesson that conquest is difficult and no longer pays. Such a world does not preclude the possibility that some states may remain offensive realist states and some new offensive realist states may still pop up from time to time. Because even these offensive realist states will more often than not be severely punished, however, one should expect that most of them too will eventually learn the lesson and become defensive realist states.[41]

Further, after a period of time of spreading via negative learning, the idea that conquest is no longer easy can then spread via positive learning. The net result of this whole learning process is a change of belief among states—from one that conquest is easy and profitable to another that conquest is no longer easy and profitable.

Finally, after the idea that conquest is no longer easy and profitable is generally accepted among states, the notion that security via defensive strategies is superior to security via offensive strategies logically becomes the next idea to spread among states. This positive spreading of the idea that security via defensive strategies is superior to security via offensive strategies reinforces the change of beliefs among states—from a belief that conquest is easy and profitable and offensive strategy is a better way toward security to a new belief that conquest is no longer easy and profitable and defensive strategy is a better way toward security.[42]

This rise and spreading of ideas first through negative and then positive learning are *not* a purely ideational process. Instead, it has a firm foundation in the *objective* social reality, and this objective foundation was provided by the repeated failures of conquest and the selection against offensive realist states, which was in turn underpinned by the decreased number of states and increase average size of state.

Only with more and more objective cases of unsuccessful conquest will states gradually learn that conquest has indeed become more difficult and it hardly pays in a world of bigger and harder targets. Only after the idea that conquest is easy has been largely disproved (or the idea that conquest is difficult became somewhat proved) can the idea that conquest is difficult spread via positive learning.

The Rise and Spreading of Sovereignty and Nationalism

The third auxiliary mechanism behind the transformation from Mearsheimer's world to Jervis's world has been the rise and the spreading of sovereignty and nationalism, the twin ideational pillars of the defensive realism world.[43]

Many have argued that the gradual rise and spreading of sovereignty after the medieval time has played a critical role in transforming the offensive realism world into a more benign defensive realism world (e.g., Ruggie 1983, 273–81; Hinsley 1986; Wendt 1992, 412–15; Biersteker and Weber 1996; Krasner 1999; Osiander 2001; Spruyt 2006). Yet, none of them has explained why sovereignty rose and then spread after the medieval time, but not before.[44]

Sovereignty is essentially a judicial recognition of the norm of co-existence within the state system (Barkin and Cronin 1994, 111). Hence, acceptance of coexistence as a norm is the first step toward sovereignty. Acceptance of coexistence as a norm, however, critically depends on coexistence as a reality, and this reality can only be provided by the increasing difficulty of conquest and expansion. In a world in which conquest is easy, it will be impossible for the norm of coexistence to rise and then spread. As such, sovereignty can only rise after many states recognize the futility of conquest: Counterfactually, why would states respect each other's sovereignty if they can easily conquer each other? Indeed, before the First World War, the norm in international politics was the "right to conquest." The "right to conquest" became delegitimatized only after the Second World War, with respecting other states' sovereignty gradually becoming the new norm concurrently (Korman 1996; Fazal 2007, ch. 7).

The rise of sovereignty provides the objective foundation for nationalism to rise and then spread because nationalism critically depends on the occupation of a core territory (Anderson 1983; Murphy 1996, esp. 92–100).[45] The rise and spreading of nationalism further cement the system of states into a defensive realism system.

First, consistent with prospect theory (Levy 1997), a population that takes the state as its own cherished property will be more willing and determined to defend the state (than to grab somebody else's territory). Nationalism thus makes conquest less likely to succeed initially. Moreover, even if the conquest succeeded initially, occupation will be more difficult because a more nationalistic population will be less willing to obey the new master. The net result is to make the whole enterprise of conquest more difficult thus less rewarding (Edelstein 2004), despite the fact that nationalism might have indeed contributed to the outbreak of many wars and greatly increased the severity of wars (Van Evera 1994; Cederman et al. 2011).[46]

Second, because offensive alliances that are geared for conquest and expansion usually cannot form and sustain if parties in the alliance cannot first agree how to divide the potential spoils of conquest and yet nationalism makes dividing and trading territory more difficult (Jervis 1978, 205; Fearon 1995, 389–390), nationalism makes offensive alliances more difficult to form and sustain. Because an offensive realist state will be less likely to initiate conquest without allies, the net result from this interaction between nationalism and the dynamics of offensive alliance makes offensive alliance more difficult to form, thus again making conquest more difficult and less likely to be pursued in the first place.

Summary

The three auxiliary mechanisms, by building upon the outcome engineered by the fundamental mechanism outlined in the last section, have all played indispensable although auxiliary roles in transforming an offensive realism world into a defensive realism world.[47] Together with the fundamental mechanism, they have gradually but firmly transformed an offensive realism world into a defensive realism world. This conclusion is also supported by more recent developments.

After the Second World War violent state death virtually ceased: a phenomenon had no historical precedence (Fazal 2007; Zacher 2001). After the Second World War, the number of states in international system has not decreased, but has actually increased. Most evidently, many weak states and small buffer states that would have very little chance of survival in an offensive realism world (e.g., Bhutan, Luxembourg, Singapore) survived today (Jackson 1990; Strang 1991; Fazal 2007). After the Second World War, once a country has gained *de jure* independence and is recognized by the international community, respect for that country's territory integrity is the norm and to annex that country—or even part of it—will not be accepted by the international community (Zacher 2001). Thus, neither Indonesia's annexation of East Timor nor Iraq's invasion of Kuwait gained international recognition. The only exception might have been India's annexation of Sikkim in 1975.[48] Conquest has become not only more difficult, but also increasingly, if not fully, illegitimate in the international system.

For much of human history, most wars were wars of conquest. By eliminating conquest as a principal cause of war, the evolution from an offensive realism world into a defensive realism world has also eliminated many wars. To paraphrase John Mueller (1989), war of conquest and expansion has been becoming or already is obsolete.[49] All these developments suggest that international politics has firmly evolved from Mearsheimer's world into Jervis's world. Our world today is really a much less dangerous world for states' survival than it used to be.

Although some offensive realists may want to deny it, since the Second World War, many statesmen have indeed gradually come to recognize that they are now living in a world far less dangerous than it used to be. Whereas states in the offensive realism world had steadily expanded the size of their stand army, after the Second World War, we have two striking developments on that front. First, most (including all the major states) have now relied on an all-volunteer standing army. Second, compared to historical times, the size of the standing army has been greatly reduced from its historical high in the Second World War. Both developments can only be sensible when wars of conquest have become largely obsolete, even if we admit that military technologies have been a key cause of the second development.

CONCLUDING REMARKS

In this chapter, I offer a social evolutionary account for the transformation from an offensive realism world to a defensive realism world, underscoring the fundamental mechanism and three auxiliary mechanisms behind this transformation. I argue that international politics had firmly evolved from an offensive realism world in the past to a defensive realist world of today, and by doing so, I neatly resolve the debate between offensive realism and defensive realism.

I reject those theses that cannot imagine transformations in international politics and believe that international politics will be permanently stuck in the offensive realism world (e.g., Waltz 1979, 66; Mearsheimer 2001, 2). International politics has always been an evolutionary system and the fundamental nature of the system can be transformed even if some features of the system (e.g., anarchy) remain the same. My thesis improves upon those theses that seek to understand the making of the offensive realism world but say nothing about the possibility of its evolution into a different world (e.g., Mercer 1996; Thayer 2004). It also betters those theses that identify different types of anarchies but do not fully explain how one type of anarchy had been transformed to another type of anarchy (e.g., Wendt 1992).

Finally, my thesis improves upon those theses that offer no or only a partial explanation of the transformation from one type of international system to another type. Many have emphasized the prominence of norms and ideas (e.g., sovereignty) in governing international politics without explaining how those ideational forces originate and come to dominate international politics in the first place (e.g., Kratochwil 1989; Mueller 1989; Johnston 2001, 489–90; Spruyt 2006).[50] Others do say something about how those ideational forces arise and spread, but either do not include the objective/material world in their historical narrative or do not ground those ideational forces upon the object-ive/material world and thus do not offer an endogenous explanation for the origin and spreading of ideas (e.g., Ruggie 1983; Onuf 1989; Buzan 1993, 340–3; Wendt 1992, 419; 1999, chs. 6 and 7; Crawford 2002). For instance, Wendt argues that the three worlds can only be sustained by self-reinforcing behaviors, and thus can only be transformed by exogenous changes in ideas and practices: the cause of transformation was purely ideational, according to Wendt (1999, ch. 6). For Wendt (1992, 418–22), a specific precondition for the transformation from the Hobbesian world from a Lockeian world is that "there must be *a reason* to think of oneself in novel terms," (419; emphasis added), yet he never explained why states would want to change their ideas and practices, other than heeding exogenous (i.e., Wendt's) preaching.

In contrast, in our social evolutionary framework, states change their ideas and practices without having to heed exogenous teaching: the transformation of ideas and practices is endogenously driven. I show that the gradual reduc-tion in the number of states and increase in the average size of states provide the objective foundation for the rise and spread of several powerful ideas and that the rise and spread of those ideas in turn cement the transformation of the system from an offensive realism world into a defensive realism world.

4

A More Rule-based International System Unfolding

INTRODUCTION

There is no doubt that the international system has become more rule-based (or institutionalized), judged by the total numbers of rules and the general tendency of states in obeying some of the rules, for whatever reason (e.g., Simmons 2000; Guzman 2002; 2008). This fact has led to various optimistic projections that we are going to move from security communities to "a world state" and "a world society", however defined (Adler and Barnett 1998a; Wendt 2003; Buzan 2004; Suganami and Linklater 2006). But is this optimistic thinking warranted? This chapter addresses this question, not on any ideological terms, but on the ground of social evolution. My central thesis is that although human society in general (and the international system in particular) has become more rule-based, there will not be a harmoniously institutionalized "world state" or "world society".[1] The fundamental cause behind this is that institutions are usually made and backed by power. In other words, the very notion of institution entails conflict of interest, struggle (not always but often violent), and power (Tang 2011a). As such, although and precisely because the international system (and the broader human society) has become more rule-based, there will not be a world state, unless the term becomes an empty shell. My projection is based on two theoretical pillars: SEP and a general theory of institutional change that I have developed elsewhere with a social evolutionary approach (Tang 2011a).

The chapter is divided into five sections. The first section recalls a general theory of institutional change as one of the theoretical foundations and derives its implication for understanding the process of institutionalizing peace, especially at the regional level. The second section examines three cases of institutionalizing regional peace to illustrate the argument. Armed with our new empirical and theoretical understanding, the third section resolves several contentious issues regarding international institutions within the existing IR literature. The fourth section argues for a reorientation of the institutionalism approach toward international politics. The fifth section advances the thesis why a "world state" is impossible and desiring for such a utopia may be dangerous. A concluding section follows.

Three caveats are in order before I proceed further. First, although I consider neoliberalism a legitimate grand theory of international politics because it does capture some aspects of a more rule-based world ontologically, I do not label a more rule-based world as a neoliberalism world. Neoliberalism captures only a very limited part of a rule-based world and thus presents a misleading picture of our world. As such, neoliberlaism needs to *radically* transform itself in order to become a good grand theory of international politics, and such a radically transformed approach toward international institutions can no longer be called neoliberalism. Indeed, the approach toward institutions advocated here rejects some of the key propositions of neoliberalism. Moreover, institutionalism, a term that is now favored by leading neoliberalists (e.g., Keohane and Martin 2003), is more accommodating than neoliberalism. For instance, the English School is also an institutionalism approach (Evans and Wilson 1992; Suganami 2003). Second, although I do address some normative issues associated with the notion of a "world state (society)", the bulk of my critique of a "world state" is based on an empirical reading into the evolution of international politics. Third, I am mostly interested in the process of institutionalizing regional peace, and I do not address the other important question how institutions come back to shape agents' behavior and future institutional changes, unless absolutely necessary.

I. A NEW APPROACH TOWARD INTERNATIONAL INSTITUTION

Institutions are essentially embodiments of ideas. Because there is diversity of knowledge among agents (i.e., there will always be more than one idea about how a future institutional arrangement should look), the process of institutional changes is essentially about how to turn a very limited few of those numerous ideas into institutions. As such, we can take ideas (for a particular institutional arrangement) as genes and institutional arrangements as phenotypes, and then apply SEP—with the mechanism of *artificial* variation–selection–inheritance at its core—to institutional change. Based on this bedrock take on institutions and institutional change, I have developed a SEP-based general theory of institutional change (Tang 2011a). In this section, I introduce the general theory of institutional change and then underscore some of its most critical implications for understanding international institutions.[2]

The general theory of institutional change has the following key aspects.

First and foremost, the struggle for the power to make rules is at the heart of the matter. Institutions are often made by power (or under the shadow of power) and backed by overt or covert power (see also Elias [1939]1994; Knight 1992; Soltan 1998). Most of the time, *power and institutions are inseparable*.

Second, the process of institutional change consists of five distinct phases: (1) generation of ideas for specific institutional arrangements, (2) political mobilization by supporters of specific ideas, (3) struggle for power to design and dictate specific institutional arrangements (i.e., to set specific rules), (4) setting the rules, and (5) legitimatizing/stabilizing/reproducing. These five phases correspond to the three phases of mutation (variation), selection (reduction in variation), and inheritance (stabilization) in evolution: generation of ideas corresponds to mutation; political mobilization and struggle for power to selection; and setting the rules and legitimatizing/stabilizing to inheritance.

Third, the notion that institutions are usually welfare-improving public goods is misleading, inspired by the invalid harmony approach toward institutions, exemplified by functionalism (e.g., Parsons 1937; 1951) and neoclassical economics-inspired new institutional economics approach toward institutions (e.g., Coase 1937; North 1981; 1990; Williamson 1975; 1985). More often than not, institutions are private goods that serve private interests, and institutions that improve agents' collective welfare are products of power struggle in a long haul rather than instant gratification from rational design (for details, see Tang 2011a, ch. 2).

Fourth, "institutions matter", but why do institutions matter? The short answer is that institutions matter mostly—if not only—because they are made and backed by power (Tang 2011a, ch. 5). As a result, ultimately speaking, institutions usually cannot be truly autonomous actors, independent from power. Although some institutions seemingly work on agents without any external input because agents have internalized those rules, the process of internalization has always been a power-backed process, as Elias (1939[1994]) and Foucault (2000) had demonstrated beyond any reasonable doubt. The notion that institutions can be autonomous actors is profoundly misleading, and much of the past effort to prove it can only have been futile.

Fifth, "institutions matter", but how do institutions matter? Once created, institutions come back to shape agents' behavior: institution (backed by power) both enables and constrains (Giddens 1979; 1984). By shaping agents' behavior, institution in turn shapes social outcomes, including the evolution of social structure.[3]

From the general theory and SEP, we can draw some explicit implications for understanding institutions in international system.

First and foremost, like institutional change in domestic politics, the heart of institutional change in international politics too is the struggle for the power to make rules, and this process almost inevitably needs power. In international politics, most of the time, it has been states (rater than individuals) that have created international institutions, and the state (as the ultimate hierarchical organization) itself symbolizes the monopoly of power. Hence, at the very beginning, international institutions have been instruments and products of statecraft (Keohane 1984; Mearsheimer 1995; Jervis 1999; Schweller 2001). International institutions are also the product of power politics: most international institutions are backed by explicit or implicit power, just as are most domestic institutions (Tang 2011a).

Second, because power is the key for making and maintaining institutions (and thus order), an actor or a coalition of actors that won the struggle for power to impose rules will have more, sometimes decisive, effect over the exact nature of institutions. In international politics, this means that a hegemonic state or a coalition of states that won the last major war or major debate will have a more, sometimes decisive, effect over the exact nature of international institutions and thus order (e.g., Keohane 1984; Hurd 1999; Ikenberry 2000). This was indeed the case when it comes to peace after a major war (Gilpin 1981; Ikenberry 2000), sovereignty (Spruyt 1994b), territorial integrity (Zacher 2001), de-colonialization (Spruyt 2000), trade (Keohane 1984); abolition of slave trade and piracy (Clark 2007, ch. 2; de Nevers 2007), racial equality (Clark 2007, ch. 4; Suzuki 2009), and perhaps the whole international law apparatus (Anghie 2004).

Third, from a social evolutionary perspective, a more extensive institutionalizing of peace in international politics can only occur after peace based on a defensive realism world is in place, not before.

Fourth, once in place, institutions can come back to reinforce peace and transform the international system into a more rule-based system. Yet, this feedback loop is too operated through power, though not necessarily in the form of material power as narrowly defined in much of the IR literature (Foucault 1980; Digeser 1992; see also Tang, n.d.-a). *Consequently, most international institutions cannot be autonomous actors independent from power, just as most domestic institutions have never been autonomous actors independent from power.*

As becomes clear below, this framework of analysis will allow us to move beyond existing understandings about international institutions. For instance, although many have noted that the modern international system seems to possess a capacity for moving toward a more rule-based system (e.g., Wendt 1999; 2003; Linklater and Suganami 2006), they have yet to offer an adequate explanation how such a capacity comes into existence. Likewise, although many have asserted that it has been institutions that underpin peace, we show that such an interpretation is invalid: (shallow) peace comes before institutions (see Section II below). Finally, although existing interpretations have asserted (or wished for) the possibility of a "world state", we show that such a wish holds only false and dangerous promises.

II. "THREE" ROADS OF INSTITUTIONALIZING REGIONAL PEACE

In this section, I examine three cases of institutionalizing regional peace: Latin America, Western Europe, and Southeast Asia.[4] I show that all three cases are consistent with a social evolutionary interpretation of the transformation of international systems via institutionalizing peace after the coming of a defensive realism world (within a particular region).[5] Specifically, I show three things.

First, consistent with our overall social evolutionary approach toward the transformation of international system, institutionalization of regional peace often starts and can only succeed *after* the whole system or a fairly isolated subsystem has evolved into a defensive realism world. In other words, major attempts of institutionalizing peace really began *after* a defensive realism (or shallow) peace had been established, however tenuously, most prominently symbolized by the cessation of major state deaths within an isolated subsystem (and perhaps the overall international system too): defensive realism peace within a subsystem is a necessary though insufficient condition for institutionalizing regional peace. The way towards deep regional peace therefore is from shallow peace to deep peace via institutionalization, if a move from negative or precarious peace to shallow peace had taken place before.[6] Because this defensive realism peace only gradually solidified after 1648, but especially after 1945, largely due to the acceptance of sovereignty and territorial integrity (see Chapter 3 above), major projects of institutionalizing regional peace mostly began and/or accelerated after 1648, but especially after 1945.[7]

Second, consistent with the social evolutionary approach toward institutional change, this process of institutionalizing regional peace has often been led by *power and ideas that promote peace*, rather than either ideas or brutal power alone. Moreover, the source of power in the institutionalizing regional peace can come from inside (more often) and outside, with the former being more critical for and capable of pushing things forward (Acharya 2004; 2009; Frazier and Stewart-Ingersoll 2010). When this is the case, a harmony approach towards institutional change (e.g., functionalism, neoliberalism) that marginalizes the role of power or an approach towards institutional change that marginalizes the role of ideas (e.g., realism) has little to offer for understanding the real processes of institutionalizing regional peace (or other processes of institutional change). In contrast, the general theory of institutional change that organically synthesizes power and idea offers powerful explanation for the processes of institutionalizing regional peace.

Third, more often than not, institutionalization of peace spreads to economic integration, not the other way around.[8] In other words, institutionalization of peace has been mostly jumpstarted by security concerns (or realist concerns, if you want) rather than by prospects of immediate economic gains, or the presence of a common identity for that matter (for similar findings, see Kacowicz 1998; Adler and Barnett 1998a; Ripsman 2005; Kupchan 2010). This is easy to understand: for states that just came out of a defensive realism world, security (both internal and external) is their paramount concern. Economic interdependence itself therefore cannot produce institutions of peace, although institutions of peace, once in place, can come back to facilitate more economic interdependence as cooperation, as neo-institutionalism has long held (e.g., Axelrod and Keohane 1985; Russett and Oneal 2001).[9]

Before I proceed further, four caveats are in order. First, although the process of institutionalizing peace within a region is usually taken to be part of "regionalism", I shall refrain from engaging the vast literature on regionalism (for recent reviews on regionalism, see Vayrynen 2003, Mansfield and Milner 1999; and a special issue of *Review of International Studies* 2009). I am only interested in the conditions and the actual processes of institutionalizing peace in the domain of traditional security. By focusing on regions, however, I do concur with the emerging consensus that geography has a powerful impact on how order emerges (e.g., Solingen 1998; 2008; Buzan and Wæver 2003; Acharya 2007), without the earlier ethnocentric emphasis on civilizations or common identities (e.g., Bull 1977, 15; Bull and Watson 1984).[10]

Second, what follows in this section is not a detailed empirical survey or comparative cases studies of the three regions: that has been covered by many able scholars.[11] Rather, I am mostly interested in demonstrating that the institutionalizing of peace in all three regions has followed a general pattern that is consistent with the general theory of institutional change and the new approach toward international institutions in particular. I shall not engage with the question why states within a region choose to institutionalize peace at a particular time, since this has been addressed by many scholars (e.g., Acharya 2001; Adler and Barnett 1998; Hurrell 1998; Solingen 1998; 2008; Kacowicz 1998). Because I am mostly interested in the initiation of the institutionalizing process, I do not discuss the spreading/diffusing/expansion of regional peace either. Finally, although the interplay of domestic politics and international politics has been a key driver for such a process (Solingen 1998; 2008; Wæver 1998; Tang 2011c), I shall not engage with this issue either. Suffice to say that examining this interaction will further strengthen my thesis

Table 4.1. The Institutionalizing of Peace in Three Regions

Period \Regions	Latin America	European Union	Southeast Asia
1945–1959	1947: Inter-American Treaty of Reciprocal Assistance (Rio Treaty); 1948: Organization of American States (all 35 independent states of the Americas) focusing on democracy, human rights, security and development; 1951: Charter of OAS	Treaty of Paris, 1951, ECSC; Treaty of Rome, 1957, EEC	Failed attempts: SEATO, 1954
1960–1969	1959: Establishment of the Inter-American Development Bank; Latin America FTA (failed attempt); 1967: Treaty of Tlatelolco (Latin America Nuclear Weapons Free Zone Treaty)	1960, OECD Treaty (Paris); France-Germany reconciliation deepened (e.g., 1963 Franco-German Treaty); 1965, Treaty for a Single Council and a Single Commission of the European Communities (with French objections)	1961, failed project of ASA; 1967, founding of ASEAN (Bangkok Declaration)
1970–1979	Argentina-Brazil rapprochement 1979; Tripartite Agreement (Argentina-Brazil-Paraguay) on Itainpu-Corpus (hydroelectric)	1972–9, Expansion of the Community, 1979, European Monetary System (EMS) began to operate	1971, Zone of Peace, Freedom, and Neutrality; 1976, first ASEAN Summit and the Treaty of Amity and Cooperation, Declaration of ASEAN Concord
1980–1989	1982: Bahamas most recent country to enter Inter-American Treaty of Reciprocal Assistance; July 1986, November, 1988, August, 1989, three consecutive treaties between Argentina and Brazil (i.e., PICE; Treaty of Integration and Cooperation, Treaty of Integration, Cooperation, and Development) to consolidate the cooperation between the two core states.	1985–1987, The Single European Act; 1988–1989: Ending the Cold War	
1990–1999	1990–1991: nuclear free zone between Argentina and Brazil; 1991:	1991–1992, Maastricht Treaty (Treaty on European Union); EU	1992, ASEAN Free Trade Agreement; 1994, ASEAN regional forum;

Mercusor by the Treaty of Asunción (later amended by the 1994 Treaty of Ouro Preto); 1991, Mendonca Declaration on chemical and biological weapons by Argentina, Brazil, and Chile; April 1996, tripartite body for coordinating security policies between Argentina, Brazil, and Paraguay	expansion, all the way through today; 1997, Treaty of Amsterdam; 1999, Launching of the euro; NATO expansion	Expansion of ASEAN (1995, Vietnam, Laos, and Burma; 1997, Cambodia) 1998, first ASEAN plus Three (APT) meeting, Second protocol of Amity and Cooperation in Southeast Asia
2000–2010	2003: Brasilia Declaration on International law and security; 2004: Cusco Declaration, the Union of South American Nations (UNASUR); 2006: Cochabamba Declaration; 2008: South American Union of Nations Constitutive Treaty; 2010: Protocol to the Constitutive Treaty of the Union of South American Nations on Commitment to Democracy	2001, Treaty of Nice 2004, Constitutional Treaty (Rome) of the European Union Further expansion of EU	2002, Bali Concord (ASEAN Community by 2020); 2002, Declaration on the conduct of parties in the South China Sea; 2003, Bali Concord II (adoption of AEC, ASC, ASCC[12]); 2007, the ASEAN Charter

Sources: European data from Nugent (2006); ASEAN data from ASEAN official website, <www.asean.org>; Latin America data from <http://www.oas.org>; and <http://www.mercosur.int/>. We have ignored many inter-regional initiatives (such as ASEAN with China, Japan, South Korea, the so-called ASEAN plus Three or APT).

that institutionalizing of regional peace has been a power-backed process, as Wæver (1998, 98) put it succinctly when commenting on the European project: "this interaction of domestic struggles over the meaning of state, nation and Europe, is where the direction of [Europe's] developments will be decided".

Third, I shall not deal in detail with the complex relationships between institutionalizing peace, democratization, and peace, other than stating the following: (a) shallow peace facilitates the institutionalization of peace, and institutionalization of peace can come back to solidify shallow peace into deep peace, whether among democracies or non-democracies (Russett and Oneal 2001; Hasenclever and Weiffen 2006); (b) institutionalizing of peace can come back to strengthen democratization and democracies (Pevehouse 2005; Parish and Peceny 2002); (c) democratization and democracies can come back to propel states into building more inter-democratic institutions (via inter-governmental organizations) and further institutionalizing of peace.

In sum, there is a positive feedback loop between peace, institutionalizing of peace, and democratization (Hurrell 1998, 240–8; Hasenclever and Weiffen 2006, esp. 569–74; Weiffen et al. 2011; see also Russett and Oneal 2001).[13] Figure 4.1 summarizes the dynamics.

Fourth, I do not deal with the micro-level process of institutionalizing regional peace, that is, what happened in conferences of states' leaders, workshops at track I and II diplomacy. These processes are covered under the general theory of institutional change and well studied by more in-depth studies of institutionalizing regional peace (e.g., Kacowicz 1998; Acharya 2001; Oelsner 2005; Checkel 2007a). Instead, I focus on the more macro processes because I am mostly interested in the general dynamics of institutionalizing regional peace.

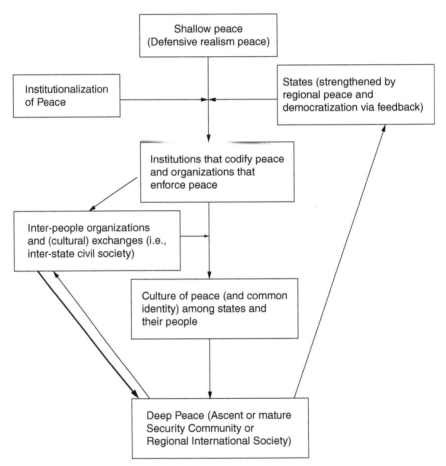

Figure 4.1. The Institutionalization of (Regional) Peace in a Defensive Realism World

A. The Coming of Institutionalized Peace: the Southern Cone[14]

The last major intra-regional conflict within the Southern Cone of Latin America subsystem, the Chaco war between Bolivia and Paraguay, ended in 1932–5. Yet, despite the presence of shallow peace (without democracy), the Southern Cone had been saddled by animosity, arms race, brinkmanship, and almost war until the 1980s (Kelly 1997; Hurrell 1998; Centeno 2002; Oelsner 2005). For a long period of time, there were no tangible attempts of codifying a regional peace within the subsystem. Between 1977 and 1981, however, a turning point "suddenly" descended (Hurrell 1998, 232–40). This turning point was the détente between Argentina and Brazil, symbolized by the agreement of Itainpu-Corpus, on hydroelectric power of River Parana. From then on, Argentina and Brazil increasingly began to work together on the institutionalizing of regional peace, notwithstanding their continuous competition on some other areas such as regional leadership and frictions on some other issues.[15]

The rapprochement between Argentina and Brazil was followed by the democratization of the six countries from military rule to civilian rule, followed by a sustained period of democratic consolidation. This wave of democratization eventually propelled these states into a regional agreement (i.e., Santiago Agreement 1991) that allows collective intervention by member states to protect democracies within member states (Parish and Peceny 2002).

On the front of institutionalizing regional peace, after the initial rapprochement, the reconciliation between Argentina and Brazil quickly gathered pace. In 1986, the two countries signed the "Economic Integration and Cooperation Program" (or PICE in Spanish and Portuguese), followed by the denuclearization agreement in 1990 (Velázquez 2004). In 1991, the *Treaty of Asuncion* officially launched the project of building a common market in the Southern Cone (i.e., MERCOSUR), building upon the foundation laid down by the 1986 PICE between Argentina and Brazil. By the late 1990s, although issues can still divide these countries, war has become unthinkable within the Southern Cone, or at least between Argentina and Brazil.

It is evident that the institutionalization of regional peace in the Southern Cone was initiated by the Argentina–Brazil rapprochement (Kelly 1997, 2; Resende-Santos 2002; Oelsner 2005, 7–8), the two most powerful actors within the subsystem. After their initial rapprochement in later 1970s and early 1980s, Argentina and Brazil began to work together on institutionalizing peace in the region in the 1990s, although they still compete against each other on other things (Resende-Santos 2002; Oelsner 2005, ch. 5; Solingen 1998; 2008). This two-state security cooperation was then reinforced by a similar process between Argentina and Chile a bit later (Oelsner 2005, ch. 5). Eventually, this ABC core was able to declare a nuclear-free zone and agree to full de-nuclearization in 1990–1991. Overall, "the creation of MERCUSOR in 1991 was the almost exclusive result of Argentina-Brazilian partnership. Under the lead of Argentina and Brazil, and fostered by the remarkable advances of Argentina and Chile, the Southern Cone moved away from negative peace in the direction of positive, stable peace" (Oelsner 2005, 195).

Institutionalization of regional peace in the Southern Cone has been achieved relatively free from external power (i.e., the United States). As long as the more important players within a subsystem can get together and work together, they can institutionalize peace. There is no need for an external (imperial) power, although the presence of an external (benign) imperial power may help (but it may also hinder) the process. Indeed, the joint effort to suppress mass insurgencies in the 1970–80s among the six countries (i.e., the Condor Plan), blessed by the U.S., had not been helpful at all for the project of institutionalizing regional peace (Oelsner 2005, 9).

Overall, the process of institutionalizing regional peace in the Southern Cone conforms to our social evolutionary approach toward international politics. In contrast, neo-institutionalism's functionalist approach toward institutional change simply cannot explain the paths traveled by the Southern Cone states. For instance, the Latin America Free Trade Area (LAFTA) project, launched in 1960, never got a life (Oelsner 2005, 10–11): when Argentina and Brazil, the two most powerful actors within the subsystem, were in the state of mutual animosity, the region could not institutionalize peace. Only after the two states reached an amicable *modus operandi* could they and the region move forward with institutionalizing regional peace. Institutionalizing peace has been achieved by backing (good) ideas with power rather than ideas alone, with powerful actors getting their way.

B. The Coming of Institutionalized Peace: Western Europe

The pacification of Western Europe, often known as the "European Project", has been undoubtedly the most studied project of institutionalizing regional peace (for a standard survey of the European Project, see Nugent 2006). Yet, even here, partially due to the misguided harmony approaches toward institutionalizing regional peace, many crucial points have been obscured in the all too unproductive realism versus utopianism debate that takes power and ideas to be mostly incompatible. Since the contour of the European Project has been clearly established, there is no need for me to elaborate on this front. Instead, I highlight some key facts, in light of our new approach toward the process of institutionalizing regional peace.

Foremost, institutionalization of peace came after a shallow peace had established: after the Second World War, state deaths too ceased within (Western) Europe. Moreover, the two key impetuses behind the European project had too been traditional security concerns: (1) to confront the Soviet

Union and its communist allies; (2) to prevent member states within West Europe from coming to blows against each other again, in the aftermath of yet another bloody war (Wæver 1998; Ripsman 2005; Kupchan 2010, 201–17).[16]

Second, the process of institutionalization regional peace in Europe has also been a thoroughly power-backed process. More specifically, power came from two sources. Initially, an external benign hegemon (i.e., the U.S.) provided the key pillar, with both political power and money (i.e., the Marshall Plan).[17] The project really began to quicken its pace, however, after France and West Germany, the two key states within the system, came to work together as a tandem. Moreover, although European states have created numerous regional organizations that became another source of power, these organizations themselves have been created and backed by sovereign power (Wæver 1998; Ripsman 2005; Kupchan 2010, ch. 5). Likewise, although the establishment of the (shallow) peace also coincided with the imposing of democracy, most prominently, in West Germany and Italy, the imposing of democracy itself was a power-backed process.

Third, security cooperation, which was driven by security concerns, had been the key driver behind the initiation of European economic integration. Indeed, some of the seemingly economic initiatives, such as the European Coal and Steel Community (ECSC, codified in the Treaty of Paris 1951) and the European Economic Community (EEC, codified in one of the Treaties of Rome 1957), were fundamentally propelled by political (and security) concerns, as both Jean Monnet and Konrad Adenauer, two key architects of the European Project, readily acknowledge (cited in Moravcsik 1998, 94; Nugent 2006, 37; for similar interpretations, see Wæver 1998; Ripsman 2005; Kupchan 2010, 201–8; cf. Moravcsik 1998).

Fourth, a common European identity came fairly late in the process. Moreover, this forging of a common European identity (more among the elite) too has been a power-backed process (see also Ikenberry and Kupchan 1990; Checkel 2007a).[18]

Hence, the real path of the European project had roughly progressed in three stages, namely, (1) political and security cooperation; (2) economic cooperation and integration, and (3) a common identity. By looking at the second stage without emphasizing the first, neoliberalism interpretation of the European project has neglected the crucial role of the first stage in which power had been paramount. By looking at the last stage of the project and mostly at the regional level, constructivist interpretation of the European Project has too painted an all-too-harmonious picture of the whole process. Altogether, by sticking with a harmony approach toward institutional change, neoliberalism and constructivism interpretations of the European project reify the later two stages of the European project and neglected the role of power, drawing "a too linear conjunction of 'we-identity', formal institution, polity and peace" (Wæver 1998, 92).

C. The Coming of Institutionalized Peace: Southeast Asia

Born out of the de-colonization movement (with the exception of Thailand), the original ASEAN five (Indonesia, Malaysia, the Philippines, Singapore, and Thailand) had not experienced a major conflict since the undeclared war between Indonesia Malaysia in 1962–1966 over the control of Borneo. Since then, the five countries have enjoyed a shallow peace, however tenuously (Acharya 2001).

Like many newly independent states, these five countries faced two inter-related security challenges: (1) domestic fragility (e.g., domestic communist insurgency); and (2) external threats (e.g., from each other but also from their former colonial masters, and more critically, from Communist China and Vietnam after 1949). The United States tried to impose a NATO-like treaty system upon the SEA states through SEATO in 1954. In 1961, Malaysia, the Philippines and Thailand formed the Association of Southeast Asia (ASA), facilitated by behind-screen maneuver from the British. Yet, SEATO never did take off and it dissolved after U.S. withdrawal from Vietnam. ASA atrophied even sooner.

A genuine institutionalizing regional peace among the five countries really began when the five countries formed the ASEAN in 1967, without U.S. (or British) involvement. From then on, ASEAN replaced SEATO and ASA as the true engine of institutionalizing peace. This process culminated in the 1971 Declaration on Zone of Peace, Freedom, and Neutrality (ZoPFN), and most importantly, the Treaty of Amity and Cooperation (TAC, originally in the form of Declaration of ASEAN Concord) in 1976 reached in the first ever ASEAN Summit. After the last major interstate conflict in SEA (the Vietnam-Cambodia conflict, 1979–1989), coincided with the end of the Cold War, ASEAN then began to integrate Burma, Laos, Vietnam, and finally Cambodia (much like the EU expansion after the collapse of the Eastern bloc). By this time, the original ASEAN five countries have already had institutionalized a fairly robust shallow peace, the four new member states had to accede to "the ASEAN Way".

Again, the overall contour of the process conforms to our interpretation of institutionalizing regional peace. Foremost, the process really began after a shallow peace had come to exist among key regional states, and this shallow peace had not been accompanied by democracy or democratization for a very long time.

Second, the process has been a power-backed process. Again, external hegemons had not been helpful in pushing the process ahead. Indeed, these countries' experiences of de-colonialization might have doomed initiatives imposed by external hegemons from the start. SEATO failed partly because there were only two regional states in the organization (i.e., the Philippines and Thailand), and many key regional states (e.g., Indonesia, Burma, and India) were vocally against it in the spirit of seeking independence from their former Western colonial masters (Acharya 2009, ch. 3). ASA too faltered because of the evident imprint of external powers. In contrast, once the five states got together, especially after a post-Sukarno Indonesia came on board, the process of institutionalizing peace gradually gained momentum.

Third, security and political concerns had again been the initial propeller behind the process (Acharya 2001). Regional economic integration came relatively late to these states' mind: indeed, for a long period, these states' interregional trade (with U.S., Japan, and Europe) dwarfed intraregional trade among them.[19] The goal of establishing a free-trade area across ASEAN was not set until 1992.

Finally, a common ASEAN identity, even among elites, has yet to firmly emerge (Roberts, unpublished manuscript). Once can perhaps say that "the ASEAN Way" is part of the ASEAN identity (Acharya 2001), but even this "ASEAN Way" has been a product rather than a cause of the process of institutionalizing regional peace. Moreover, this forging of a common ASEAN identity has too been a power-backed process.

Summary

All three major theses receive confirmatory evidences from the preceding survey of the three cases of institutionalizing regional peace. First, in all the three regions examined, institutionalization of regional peace began *after* shallow peace had been in place, with various time lags. Hence, a necessary but insufficient condition for institutionalizing regional peace is the existence of shallow peace itself.

Second, in all the three regions examined, the actual process of institutionalizing regional peace has been a thorough power-backed process. Under anarchy, institutions too are made and backed by power. Institutionalization of regional peace thus requires effective power (sometimes euphemistically called "leadership"), and the two sources of such power are major states within a region and/or external power, with the former being more crucial. Our discussion thus reinforces but goes further than some of the existing works that emphasize the role of power in institutionalizing regional peace (e.g., Solingen 1998; Wæver 1998; Buzan and Wæver 2003, Katzenstein 2005; Tang 2006; Frazier and Stewart-Ingersoll 2010; cf. Acharya 2007; 2009).[20]

Third and related to the second, in all the three regions examined, the process of institutionalizing regional peace has also been about *what ideas got backed by power*, rather than either merely ideas or brutal power.

Fourth, initially, all regional institutions had been made for a purpose, but the purpose has not been to facilitate or manage economic interdependence (Kacowicz 1998; Adler and Barnett 1998; Ripsman 2005; Solingen 2008,

288–9; Kupchan 2010). Rather, regional institutions had been made to cope with pressing (internal and external) security concerns.

With these generic conclusions in hand, we can even venture to project possible future outcomes for two regions: the Middle East and Central Asia.

By any measure, the Middle East has been the most war-prone region after the Second World War (Solingen 2007). According to our theory, there may be two key causes behind such a dismal state (for other explanations, see Solingen 2008). First, the region as a whole has yet to have firmly evolved into a defensive realism world: important states within the region still see each other as foes (e.g., Israel vs. Palestine and Syria). Second, no major states within the region have been powerful enough to push for institutionalizing regional peace (Nasser's Egypt came close), and no external power has been helping (Solingen 2007; 2008). Not surprisingly, the Middle East, despite having multiple regional organizations (e.g., the Arab League, the Gulf Co-operation Council), has been inept in constructing a deep regional peace.[21]

In contrast, although Central Asia has been painted as the ground for a new great game after the Cold War, it has progressed into a shallow peace in a remarkably short period of time. With the rapprochement and then strategic partnership between Russia and China in place, Central Asia had two key regional states that can and have worked together to institutionalize peace in this volatile region, most prominently embodied in the Shanghai Cooperation Organization (SCO). Although a deep peace is unlikely within Central Asia without deep democratization of the region (especially within the two major states and perhaps other members of the SCO), a shallow peace is likely to be maintained as long as Russia and China can stay on workable terms (Tang 2000). At this stage, the situation between Russia–China on the one hand and the whole Central Asia regional on the other can be taken to be in a similar state between the beginning of Argentina–Brazil rapprochement and the Southern Zone. A key difference between the two regions might be that without a process of democratization, SCO is unlikely to become another Southern Zone any time soon.

III. RESOLVING EXISTING DEBATES ABOUT INTERNATIONAL INSTITUTIONS

Debates on international institutions in the past decades have essentially centered around six key questions (e.g., Keohane 1984; Mearsheimer 1995; Keohane and Martin 1995; Wendt 1995; Ruggie 1995; Jervis 1999; Johnston 2001). Armed with the discussion above, we can now resolve these debates (for a summary of the stands by different IR schools on these debates, see

Table 4.2), thus paving the way for a proper approach toward (international) institutions to be outlined in the next section.

A. The Purpose of Institutions, or Institutions and Collective Welfare

A fundamental fallacy promulgated by the harmony approach toward institutions and institutional change—which includes variants such as neoclassical economics and the neoclassical economic-inspired new institutional economics

Table 4.2. Debating Institutions in International Politics

Questions about institutions	Defensive realism	Neoliberalism/ The Pluralist Strain of the English School	Constructivism/ The Solidarist Strain of the English School	Social Evolution of International Politics
Do Institutions come to advance collective welfare?	Not necessarily, perhaps only rarely	Yes	Yes	Not necessarily, perhaps only rarely, Those that do come from social selection
Institutions come from power politics or repeated cooperation?	Mostly power politics, rarely from repeated cooperation	Some power politics, but more often from repeated cooperation	Mostly often from repeated cooperation	Mostly power politics, rarely from repeated cooperation
Can institutions be autonomous actors?	No,	Yes, to some extent	Yes, to a great extent	No,
Institutions shape preferences over strategies	Yes	Yes	Yes	Yes
Institutions shape preferences over outcomes	No	Yes, but only weakly	Yes, powerfully	Yes, sometimes powerfully, but often only in the long run
Institutions shape identities (and then conceptualization of interests)	No	No	Yes	Yes, but only in the long run
Collective identities to institutions?	No	Ambiguous	Yes	Yes, but collective identities came from institutions and power, not the other way around

(NIE), structural functionalism in sociology, and the Austrian approach in economics—is that institutions are rules that have been designed to solve coordination problem (when interest converges) and cooperation problem (when interest collides). This harmony approach fallacy toward institutions has been the implicit mantra of the functionalism-inspired neoliberalism and the utopianism-inspired social constructivism and the solidarist strain of the English school in IR (Tang 2011a, chs. 1 and 2; see also Keeley 1990; Sterling-Folker 2000).

Indeed, many have explicitly or implicitly defined institutions to be welfare-improving arrangements. For instance, Keohane (1984, 79–80) repeatedly emphasized that institutions exist because of existing "common or complementary" and "shared" interests that are perceived by agents. Similarly, Krasner (1982a, 186) defined international regimes (the then label for institutions) as "implicit or explicit principles, norms, rules, and decision-making procedures around which actors' expectations converge in a given area of international relations". Likewise, Reus-Smit (1997, 557–78) defined "Fundamental institutions are those elementary rules of practice that states formulate to solve the coordination and collaboration problems associated with coexistence under anarchy" (see also Hasenclever et al. 2000, 3).[22]

Such a harmony approach-inspired definition of institution immediately points to a misguided theory of institutional origin or change: institutions arise to solve problems and therefore advance agents' collective welfare. When this is the case, institutions and welfare improvement are inherently linked, and the direction of any process of institutional change is preordained: institutional changes always move agents toward the Pareto superior or optimal outcomes (for details, see Tang 2011a, chs. 1 and 2). This harmony approach-based definition of institution marginalizes the role of power and actual conflict (based on real or perceived conflict of interest) among agents in the making of institutions, if not totally eliminates it. As a result, it paints a rosy picture of institutions and the society. As Dahrendorf sardonically put it: "everything [in a society] has been settled in the best possible way already: everybody, wherever he stands, is content with his place in society, and a common value system unites all men in a big happy, family" (Dahrendorf 1968, 176–7; see also Idem, 1958, 173–4; Coser 1967, 164; Collins 1994, 198–200).

By leaving out the conflict paradigm that holds ontological priority and thus epistemological priority over the harmony paradigm, the harmony approach toward institutions (and human society as a whole) is fundamentally invalid. As such, students of international institutions too should reject a purely harmony approach toward institutions (or a purely conflict approach toward institutions for that matter). Instead, we must bring the conflict paradigm and the harmony paradigm into an organic synthesis when understanding institutions and human society (Tang 2011a).

B. Power Politics or Repeated Cooperation?

Regarding whether power politics can produce institutions, neoliberalists and constructivists on the one side and realists on the other side have little disagreement. Both camps acknowledge that power politics can produce institutions: power can make rules (Keohane 1984; Mearsheimer 1995; Ikenberry 2000; Jervis 1999; Schweller 2001). After all, the title of the canonical text of neoliberalism aptly captures the idea that institutions are made by power, although it mistakenly believes that institutions can sustain without power (Keohane 1984; see the discussion below).

Neoliberalists and constructivists, much inspired by Axelrod's (1984) famous tournament of computer programs on achieving cooperation under the Prisoner's Dilemma, however also insist that many, if not most, international institutions are product of repeated cooperation/coordination and power only plays at most a marginal role in producing these institutions.[23] For neoliberalists and constructivists, therefore, institutions are both the cause and effect of international cooperation (Keohane 1984; Martin and Simmons 1998, 743; Wendt 1999, 219–20).[24]

Again, the gap between offensive realism's position on this question and that of neoliberalism and constructivism is insurmountable. For offensive realism, states are inherently aggressive, whether due to human nature or anarchy (Tang 2008a). As such, there will be no genuine cooperation unless states face a common threat (Mearsheimer 2001). For offensive realism, therefore, there is very little possibility that repeated cooperation will lead to institutions, simply because there is very little possibility of repeated cooperation. In an offensive realism world, there will be few, if any, institutions, if institutions are to be products of repeated cooperation.[25]

Defensive realism occupies a middle ground between neoliberalism and offensive realism. Defensive realism admits that institutions are part of social life and they may play important functions. Indeed, defensive realism emphasizes that states may eventually codify repeated cooperation into cooperation-promoting institutions (Jervis 1970; 1982; 1999; Tang 2010b, chs. 5 and 6). Yet, defensive realism insists that institutions are fundamentally a product of power politics, not repeated cooperation.

Neoliberalism's stand holds little for explaining the origins of international institutions. Most of the time, international institutions are product of power politics rather than repeated cooperation. Moreover, even if when agents produce institutions to codify repeated cooperation and to regulate repeated interactions, this process of making rules will still be a process pervaded by power. As such, it is difficult to sustain the claim that institutions are products of (voluntary) repeated cooperation without power (Tang 2011a, chs. 3 and 4).

Such a stand, again, is a typical harmony approach-based fallacy that should be rejected.

C. (Material) Power versus (Ideational) Institutions

The human society is made of both material forces and ideational forces, and material forces hold ontological priority over ideational forces, although material forces do not necessarily have more ontological weight than ideational forces when it comes to making every social fact (Tang 2011b; 2013). Thus, any social science must be based on both materialism and ideationalism. Obviously, pure materialism cannot adequately understand any social system, including international politics: Such an approach can only be adequate for understanding the physical world before the coming of *Homo sapiens*. Pure ideationalism will not do either, because even if one insists that an idea matters—and ideas do matter—one still needs to explain how that idea comes to exist and matter. And unless one is prepared to accept infinite regression, there is no alternative but to look at the material world for explaining how and why an idea comes to exist and matter (Searle 1995, 27–39; 34–5; 55–6, 120–5). Therefore, to adequately understand international politics (or any aspects of the social system), the unproductive enterprise of pitting materialism against ideationalism must give away to the more productive enterprise of synthesizing the two forces together. The challenge is how to synthesize these two forces organically (Tang 2011b).

The general theory of institutional change introduced above synthesizes material forces and ideational forces organically via a social evolutionary framework. The theory dictates that power and institutions are inherently inseparable in human society. Although institutions are ideas that have been solidified into rules, power—*part of being material*—is indispensable for making and sustaining rules. *Indeed, power and institutions are inseparable* (Tang 2011a, esp. ch. 5). When this is the case, there is not much point to debate whether it is material power or ideational institutions that have shaped human society as if (material) power and (ideational) institutions are incompatible: they do it together. "The tendency in international relations scholarship to view power and institutions as two opposing explanations of foreign policy is therefore misleading" (Wendt 1992, 401; idem., 1995, 74).

Moreover, within any social system, it is often difficult, if not impossible, to tell which factor has more weight in making a specific social fact (Jervis 1997). The real challenge is to understand how different factors interact with each other to make a specific social fact. To face this challenge, the right way forward is not to ask whether material power or ideational institutions matter or even which matters more (e.g., Glaser 1994–95; Jervis 1999; Mearsheimer 1994; 2001), but rather to organically synthesize material forces with ideational forces. Questions such as whether institutions can matter independently from power (we know they cannot, most of the time) or whether institutions (backed by power) can matter when confronted by opposing power (we know they do, sometimes) should be replaced by questions such as how institutions interact with power to shape outcomes. Won't the spreading of ideas (in the form of institutions or not) be difficult, if not totally impossible, without an objective foundation and the backing of power? Won't institutions matter much less, if they matter at all, without power?

In sum, we must study institutions closely, not because institutions can survive without material power: we know they cannot. Rather, we study institutions because institutions, backed by power, do shape agents' behaviors and in turn, social outcomes. *Studying how institutions shape agents' behavior and in turn social outcomes is thus studying power and ideas.* Indeed, power cannot be understood adequately, if we cannot grasp that institutions can hide, smooth, reproduce, sanitize, and transform power (Foucault 1980; 2000; Tang, n.d.-a). Hence, the task ahead is not to show institutions or power is more determinate in shaping outcomes, but to show how institutions are made, maintained, and then spread when being backed by power, and how institutions then come back to work with power, and how the interaction between institutions and power shapes outcomes.[26]

Finally, it should be briefly pointed out that much of the confusion regarding the role of power in the making and sustaining of international institutions has been underpinned by two key conceptual errors, with a detailed discussion to be offered elsewhere (Tang, n.d.-a). First, most IR theorists, whether realists or their opponents, have adopted a narrow and essentially outdated definition of power as *only* material power. This has resulted in a very restricted view of power (e.g., Baldwin 1978; 1979; 1980). This situation did not change until the very recent (see Barnett and Duval 2005; Guzzini 1993; 2000; 2005; Nye 2004). Meanwhile, the discourse on power in political theories itself has been rather muddled (Tang, n.d.-a). This has undoubtedly hindered IR theorists from coming to grips with the complexity of power adequately.

Second, realists and their opponents have had very different ideas about the *purpose* of power. On the one hand, realists, firmly with a conflict approach, have explicitly argued that power is exercised for self gains. On the other hand, opponents of realists (i.e., liberals, neoliberals, and constructivists), firmly with a harmony approach, have implicitly assumed that power will be exercised for the interest of constructing the community and for the welfare of the community. In fact, power can be exercised for both goals. In other words, power and conflict of interest are not inherently linked, although conflict often dominates (Giddens 1979, 88–94; 1984, 256–7). To move forward with our understanding of power (and institutions), we need to move beyond our narrow and outdated definition of power (Tang, n.d.-a).

D. Institutions as Autonomous Actors?

In the domestic arena, institutions have long been argued to not only shape but also sometimes dominate human behaviors—independently from (social) power, most prominently by the functionalist approach and institutional analysis in sociology (Parsons 1937; 1951; Merton 1968). As such, for a long time, the notion that institutions have "a life of their own" has been widely accepted (e.g., Commons 1934, 635–6; North 1981; 1990; cf. Nye and Keohane 1977[1989], 19).[27]

As economists, sociologists, and political scientists have increasingly recognized, however, the most critical reason why institutions shape or even dominate individual behavior has been that most, if not all, institutions are made and backed by explicit or implicit power (Tang 2011a; see also Elias 1939 [1994]; Foucault 1980; 2000; Knight 1992; Soltan 1998; Acemoglu, Johnson, and Robinson 2005). In this sense, most institutions cannot possibly be truly autonomous actors independent from power. Moreover, even if agents internalize those ideas embodied in institutions (or more accurately, these ideas as institutions penetrate our body and soul), this process of internalization has always been a process under power, and a key source of power is sovereign power (Elias 1939[1994]; Foucault 1980). As such, institutions cannot be autonomous actors even in domestic politics, strictly speaking. To take internalized institutions as autonomous actors is a gross simplification, if not an act of reification.

Adding the lack of a true sovereign in international politics and thus a key source of power to enforce and inoculate a common set of institutions and culture (Lebow 2007, 422–3), it should be clear that international institutions will have an even slimmer chance to evolve into autonomous actors than their domestic counterparts. The notion that institutions, once they are in place, can be autonomous actors in international politics as implied by some neoliberalists and constructivists has been thoroughly mistaken.

E. Institutions Shape What, and How?

There is no doubt that institutions (backed by power) matter: institutions do shape something in human society. The question is what institutions exactly shape? For much our discussion, the question has been underspecified. Without specifying the question adequately, existing discussion on this question suffers from much confusion.[28]

Institutions certainly shape history as social outcomes, through several channels. Foremost, institutions can soothe, legitimatize, and reinforce power, and power operates more seamlessly precisely because it has been encapsulated by institutions (Elias [1939]1994; Foucault 1980). In addition, institutions, as "carriers of history" (David 1994), play a key role in generating path dependence (Tang 2011a, ch. 4). Finally, at a more micro level, institutions can certainly shape social outcomes by shaping agents' preferences. All these have become conventional wisdom.

For IR theorists, a key issue regarding what institutions exactly shape has been whether institutions shape agents' preferences for strategies, agents' preferences for outcomes, or agents' individual identities and conceptualization of interests (Powell 1994, 328–31). The differences between defensive realism, neoliberalism/the pluralist strain of the English School, and constructivism/the solidarist strain of the English School can be summarized as the following (see Table 4.2).[29]

All three schools admit that institutions shape agents' preferences for strategies. Defensive realism, however, denies that that institutions can shape agents' preferences for outcomes (Mearsheimer, 1994; Glaser 1994–95, 83–5; Jervis 1999, 53–62; Schweller 2001, 163, 176–83; Schweller and Priess 1997; Waltz 2000),[30] whereas both neoliberalism and constructivism insist that institutions can shape agents' preferences for outcomes (e.g., from a concern for relative gains to a concern for absolute gains). Finally, constructivism emphasizes that institutions can shape agents' individual identities (and agents' collective identities and culture/common knowledge can then come back to shape institutions, see immediate below), whereas both defensive realism and neoliberalism deny this possibility.[31]

So far, the debate has not been productive, and a key reason has been that a key element—time—has been missing from the debate. Once we grasp that institutions are often made and backed by power, it becomes clear that institutions can potentially shape agents' identities and culture, and thus both preferences for strategies and preferences for outcomes, *given time* (Elias 1939 [1994]; Foucault 1980). After all, institutions are the main instruments of socialization, although socialization can never be complete (in other words, not all things can be socially constructed). The real question about whether institutions can shape agents' identity and their preferences over goals and strategies, therefore, is how, when, and for how long, not whether.

Defensive realism, consistent with its anti-evolutionary stand, essentially denies that institutions can change a lot of things even in the long run. In contrast, neoliberalism and (to a greater extent) constructivism, holding a more (but still quasi-) evolutionary stand, insists that institutions can change a lot of things in the long run.

Once we admit that the social system is an evolutionary system, we should come to the side of neoliberalism in the median run and constructivism in the long run, although defensive realism's position may be hard to disconfirm in the short run. In this sense, neoliberalism and constructivism have to expand the time horizon of their inquiries in order to gain an upper hand over defensive realism, following the examples of Elias and Foucault. At the same time, however, we have to keep in mind that not all things can be socially constructed, and there is an inherent limit to how far institutions can facilitate states' choice of seeking cooperation as a strategy, *even in the long run*.

A related issue has been IR theorists' differentiation of regulative rules from constitute rules. Non-social constructivists marginalize, if not essentially deny, that rules can constitute agents: all rules are regulative. In contrast, social constructivism, partially inspired by harmony approach-based functionalism (with a heavy dose of utopian thinking), emphasizes the constitutive side of institutions (e.g., Hollis 1988, 137–41; Porpora 1993; Adler and Barnett 1998, 35–6; Wendt 1999; Buzan 2004, 7; Johnston 2001; Duffield 2007). Again, once we add the dimension of time to the picture, this differentiation becomes false, if not somewhat dangerous.

To begin with, all regulative power/institutions regulate us, but only some power/institutions do so by constituting us. In other words, not all power/ institutions can penetrate into our body and soul, even given time. More importantly, Elias's (1939 [1994]) and Foucault's (1980; 2000) sociology of power/institutions had demonstrated that power/institutions can indeed constitute agents over the (very) long run. Yet, this process of constituting, or more precisely, the process through which power/institutions penetrate our body and soul, has too been backed by power. Hence, both regulative rules and constitutive rules are backed by power. As such, just because some rules have constituted us does not mean that these rules are necessarily good and the process of constituting has been just: they can be unjust, harmful, and even evil. Social constructivists, by emphasizing rules constituting us, tend to gloss over the fact that norms, even constitutive ones, constitute agents precisely they have backed by power over a long period of time. As a result, constructivists easily fall into the trap of utopianism toward social norms and foreclose the possibility of a critical approach toward social norms (see Section IV below).

Finally, there is the seemingly simple question whether institutions can shape cooperation. This question actually conflates two entirely different although related issues: *cooperation as a preferred social outcome versus seeking cooperation as a preferred strategy*. Existing discussions generally do not differentiate these two issues from each other (for a more detailed discussion, see Tang 2010a, chs. 4 and 5). As a result, much confusion reigns. There are two divergent points here.

First, both neoliberalism and constructivism insist that although institutions are machineries created by states, institutions—once in place—can stabilize existing cooperation and condition cooperative behavior in the future (Axelrod and Keohane 1984; Keohane 1984; 1989). For neoliberalism, therefore, forging and maintaining institutions as a strategy is *conducive and often critical* to achieve and sustain cooperation. Defensive realism does not deny that forging and maintaining institutions are *conducive* to achieve and sustain cooperation. What defensive realism denies is that institutions are *critical* in sustaining and facilitating cooperation. For defensive realism, institutions are merely tools of statecraft: Institutions are simply states' instruments of achieving states' interest and they are effective in so far as states believe to be in their interest (Jervis 1999, 55–62). Thus, when states see gains from cooperating with each other, they will cooperate with or without institutions. And when states do not see gains from cooperating, they will not cooperate even if institutions are already in place. Existing institutions, therefore, do not necessarily make states' choosing seeking cooperation as a strategy a more likely outcome.

Second and perhaps more critically, defensive realism does not see the possibility that cooperation-facilitating institutions can induce states to see cooperation as a more preferred outcome. For defensive realism, cooperation is a means, never an end, and means do not dictate ends. In contrast, neoliberalism and constructivism hold that institutions can induce states to see cooperation as a more preferred outcome.

Again, on both points, time may be a critical dimension to consider. For instance, in an offensive realism world, temporary cooperation is a means. As the world evolves into a defensive realism world firmly, however, states may come to hold respecting each other's territorial sovereignty as a desired outcome rather than merely a strategy for avoiding war (see Chapter 3 above). Most prominently, in today's Europe, it is hard to argue that some of the key EU members do not see the whole EU project as a desired outcome but merely a means for avoiding another bloody war. Hence, as time goes by, cooperation-facilitating institutions can be internalized by agents, and agents can come to see cooperation as a desired outcome no matter what in some cases. Once again, a social evolutionary approach offers a solution for the debate.

F. Common Identities to International Institutions?

Another key argument put forward by constructivists, often mixed with liberal theory of democratic peace, has been that a common/collective identity/ culture or common knowledge facilitates, if not entails, cooperative institutions (e.g., Risse-Kappen 1996; Adler 1998, 119; Lebow 1994, 268–73; Wendt 1994; 1999; Onuf 1998, 59; Checkel 2001; Johnston 2001; Hemmer and Katzenstein 2002).[32] More often than not, these theorists have pitted common identities against power-based and interest-based theses advanced by realists and neoliberalists (e.g., Keohane 1984), with Waltz's of-little-use neorealism theory as a convenient straw man (and now a dead horse). There are at least two major problems with this constructivism stand.

First, collective identities (or the "We-feeling") do not arise out of the blue, but are usually constructed with the backing of power. As such, power and common identities are not incompatible: indeed, they are often inseparable. This is not just true within a society (Elias 1939[1994]; Foucault 1980), but also, if not more so, in international politics (Wæver 1998; Acharya 2001; 2009). By falling back on common identities and knowledge, (holistic) constructivism reduces politics to a question of (common) knowledge (Sárváry 2006, 172–3), as functionalists such as Barnes (1988) has done regarding power before (for a critique, see Haugaard 1997; see also Tang, n.d.-a). Both acts create a partial, if not false, image of the real world.

Second, contra many constructivists (e.g., Risse-Kappen 1996),[33] common identities are neither necessary nor sufficient for initiating cooperation. As others have documented (Checkel 2007a; Kupchan 2010; Roberts, n.d.), and our brief case studies concur, a common (regional) identity among people within a regional community usually came (*very*) late in the processes of institutionalizing peace (see also Tang 2011c). In other words, common identities have been products rather than causes of existing cooperation (and conflict). To take common identities as a cause of cooperative institutions therefore is to reverse the causal chain. Indeed, this reflects another structural functionalist fallacy: the fallacy insists that individuals internalize social norms (thus come to share a "common identity") and then reifies this internalizing of social norms by relying on this internalization to assert that the society will indeed gel into a well functioning organism (Parsons 1937; 1951). The whole enterprise becomes tautological and circuitous.

Fundamentally, collective identity is mostly dictated by the degree of internalization of rules and other ideas by actors within a particular system. As such, institutionalization within the system is a key factor in shaping any collective identity. Because institutionalizing is process in which power has a central place, it is illogical to pit collective identity against power/institutions.[34]

In sum, identifying some identities as a key cause of cooperative institutions without addressing how these identities come to exist in the first place is an act of gross simplification, if not reification: *so far, few constructivists have explored first how identities form and only afterwards how these identities shape future interactions.* Also, how do we know that the identities picked are the more important ones for explaining certain social outcomes? Why not some other identities that may point to some totally different social outcomes? By banking on those identities that support their favored social outcomes, constructivists have committed a methodological error commonly known as "selection of cases based on outcomes" (Geddes 2003, ch. 3).

The practice of identifying some identities or cultural traits as key to cooperation or conflict reflects a lazy and invalid functionalism way of understanding social outcomes. Identity (or culture), when being tagged as ready facilitators of cooperation or conflict, is a dangerous liaison not just for constructivism, but for the broader IR and social sciences, to paraphrase Zehfuss (2001).

IV. REORIENT THE STUDY OF INSTITUTIONS AND ORDER IN IR

The preceding section makes it clear that many of the key debates on international institutions have been largely misconstrued. To better understand international institution, we therefore need to reorient our approach toward international institutions. This reorientation will eliminate, or more accurately, synthesize, many existing schools, approaches, or "-isms" in IR (and the broader social sciences) and lead us to a sounder approach toward institutions.[35] Most critically, we have to reject the unholy alliance of holism and the harmony approach that has been dominating the studying of institution in IR (and domestic politics). Instead, we shall adopt an issue-based and a more critical approach when studying institution—international or domestic (Tang 2011a).

A. In Praise of Issue-based Institutionalism: Rejecting Holism

After the Waltzian (1979) structuralism revolution, structuralism, as a form of collectivism, has remained a dominating approach in IR.[36] When it comes to international institutions, holism, which is an extreme form of collectivism (Tang 2011b),[37] has also been a dominating school (e.g., Cox 1981; Wendt 1999; 2004), partly because institutions underpin overarching concepts such as structure and order.

Yet, holism, as a form of extreme of collectivism, is an invalid approach toward human society. Because individuals hold ontological priority over collectives, holism, which marginalizes if not ignores individuals, is untenable because it reifies the collectives and its properties (e.g., structure, order): holism can only present a distorted picture of the human society (Tang 2011b; 2013a). We therefore have to reject a holism (or structuralism-) based approach toward (domestic or international) institutions and the broader human society. Only an issue-based institutionalism, that is, an approach that seeks to understand the origins and effects of specific institutions, in social sciences is defensible, theoretically and morally (see the next subsection).

Foremost, an issue-based institutionalism mandates a close-to-reality approach toward the origins and effects of institutions. This will allow, if not compel, us to see agents' struggle for power behind institutional changes and the power hidden behind or inside institutions. We simply cannot assume positive utilities and normative values for any existing institutions and norms. Moreover, just because institutions can socialize agents (including individuals within states) does not mean that socialization (and by implication, all existing institutions) is necessarily good (Foucault 1980). To equate institutions and socialization with being good (or normal) is a typical harmony approach (e.g., functionalism) fallacy (e.g., Parsons 1937; 1951; Merton 1968).

Worse yet, in international politics, this functionalism fallacy is often buttressed by our ethnocentrism, consciously or unconsciously. We tend to believe that our institutions and values are right and superior and others should submit to them. Submitting to our institutions and values is good, benign, and status quo-oriented whereas resisting them is unjust, undemocratic, uncivilized, and revisionist (e.g., Bull 1977; Johnston 2001; Johnston 2008; Ikenberry 2008; for a critique, see Anghie 2004; Keeley 1990). This may or may not be true, and the only way to find out is to study the origins and effects of specific institutions.

Second, only an issue-based institutionalism prevents us from idealizing (and reifying) institutions, and more importantly, big things such as system, order, structure, or architecture.[38] Rules are made for specific issues, and only parts make a system. As a system of institutions (or rules), structure can only be a product of a long historical process. Because an order is partly underpinned by the structure, order too can only be a product of a long historical process. Because institutions are made for specific issues and it is these issues-based rules that eventually form a system of institutions (i.e., structure) which partly underpins an order, neither the social system nor its order is preordained to be a well functioning organism, contra structural functionalism. If we start with order or structure without getting into the nitty-gritty of rule-making and rule-enforcing, however, we easily fall into the trap of idealizing and reifying order and structure, as structural functionalism had done. Only an issue-based institutionalism can allow us to see the possible injustice, domination, hegemony hidden under/behind and within power/institutions and values.

Third, an issue-based institutionalism is the only right approach for realizing a better, although always imperfect, rule-based world. The fundamental challenge of human society is about coping with emerging challenges rather than grand designing. As such, a proper institutionalism approach toward human society must be consistent with this spirit of "coping". A holistic (or structural) approach toward institutions, whether it is embodied in constructivism or the English School, is inconsistent with this spirit of "copying", empirically and morally (for earlier critiques, see Ringmar 1997, 285; Neumann 2004; Checkel 2007b, 7; see also ch. 5 below). Only an issue-based institutionalism is consistent with the spirit of "coping". Indeed, only an issue-based institutionalism is consistent with the spirit of preserving human freedom (Tang 2011a, ch. 5), because it is based on a social evolutionary approach toward institutions and the human society in general (for earlier expositions with less evolutionary flavor, see Popper [1945]1967; Hayek 1978).[39]

B. Needed: a Foucauldian or Critical Institutionalism

Once we grasp that power and institutions are inseparable, and power/institutions may entail injustice (Foucault 1980; Tang 2011a), it becomes clear that we need to adopt a more critical approach toward (international) institutions.[40] Put it rhetorically, whenever you study power, knowledge, institutions, you need to bear Foucault in mind because a Foucauldian approach toward power/institutions allows us to avoid some obvious analytical and normative pitfalls (Keeley 1990, 84).

First and foremost, a critical approach avoids the harmony approach toward institutions that has dominated the study of international institutions so far. For instance, neoliberalism believes that cooperation evolves from repeated interactions among egoists (Axelrod 1984), and repeated (coopera-tive) interactions then lead to institutionalization of (cooperative) ideas, norms, and code of conduct among states. Consequently, true to its harmony approach roots, neoliberalists often implicitly deny that institutions can be welfare-decreasing (for a brief and simplistic exception, see Barnett and Finnemore 1999, 701, 726–7). Instead, they implicitly or explicitly assume (and thus focus on) the "benevolent, voluntary, cooperative, and legitimate" side of international institutions and order (Keeley 1990, 85–90; quote from 90).

Because institutions are often made and backed by power, the possibility that institutions can reduce welfare is real and cannot be assumed way (Tang 2011a). For instance, the idea of sovereignty reflected the preferences of the winning coalition in European history, and the spreading of sovereignty had been powered first by colonization and by de-colonization only later on (Barkin and Cronin 1994; Hager and Lake 2000; Osiander 2001; Anghie 2004). Similarly, Western colonialism had been central to the making of "international law" (Keal 2003; Anghie 2004). Likewise, the notion of free trade has been a product of power politics backed by the leading commercial power in various time (Polanyi [1944]2001). The list can go on and on.

Unfortunately, although there have been some fine exceptions (Anghie 2004; Cox 1981; Keeley 1990; Nayak and Malone 2009; Meyer 2008; Said 1993; Shinko 2008; Schweller 2001; Worth 2011), most studies on existing institutions have been driven by an implicit or explicit desire to justify and legitimate existing institutions and order (e.g., Ikenberry 2000; Checkel 2001; Johnston 2001; 2008). By doing so, many students of international institutions have continued the sin of "serving the interest of the powerful" that had been severely criticized by their realist nemesis: (Carr 1939; Morgenthau 1978, 10–11; Waltz 1979, 201, 205; cf., Keeley 1990, 84). They continue to behave as "miserable comforters" (Koskenniemi 2009).

Hence, although more IR theorists are now taking the spirit of critique a bit more seriously (e.g., Keeley 1990; Jackson and Nexon 2004; Sterling-Folker 2004; Mattern 2004; Meyer 2008; Worth 2011), most IR theorists have yet to grasp the full implications of critique for understanding IR (cf. Brass 2000).

In light of a more critical approach toward institutions, the task of IR scholars is not to sing panegyrics by identifying justice and legitimacy in the existing international order (e.g., Keohane 1984; Ikenberry 2000; Clark 2004; 2007): politicians will do this job (and do it better, if you may). Rather, the task of IR scholars is to expose the hypocrisy, injustice, and illegitimacy within existing institutions/power and order in international politics in the spirit of Foucault (1980; 2000), Gramsci ([1926–1937] 1992–1996), Said (1978; 1993), and Morgenthau (1970), without denying that some institutions have indeed improved human welfare. In other words, we should focus on institutions that have reduced welfare, how they came to exist and stay, and how even good institutions have been corrupted and eventually replaced by bad ones.

Indeed, we should go further. We shall try to document the sometimes triumphant but often tragic resistances and struggles against hegemonic rules, values and norms. Rather than merely noting in passing that "[resistance] represents one of the more interesting axes of tension in contemporary world politics" and then leaving it there as Reus-Smit (1997, 568) has done, we need to look into these resistances and struggles, and understand the logic, power, and ideas behind them. Only by doing so, can we truly understand the inherently conflictual processes in the making of the international system/ society from a subaltern perspective, rather than touting the triumphs of the enlightened while pushing resistances and struggles aside.

Second, because all of us are egocentric and ethnocentric, we tend to take our own morals to be universal, and more importantly, have an impulse to universalize our morals (discussed immediately below). Yet, as Alasdair MacIntyre (1984, 265–6) incisively put it, "morality which is not particular society's morality is to be found nowhere". When this is the case, we shall guard against anything moral and ethical that claims to be universal—whether it is from "them" or "us". A critical approach toward power and institutions helps us minimize our egocentrism and ethnocentrism. Indeed, it calls for a constant self-criticism of our ethnocentric belief in our values and norms. We certainly need rules to regularize our interactions, but these rules must be constantly scrutinized, challenged, reformed, and overthrown if necessary, and we can only scrutinize, challenge, reform, and overthrow unjust rules when we have done our homework regarding those rules. In contrast, an approach that implicitly or explicitly embraces the possibility of universalizing values spells danger, as Foucault incisively observed (Paras 2006, 131).

Finally, it merits pointing out that it is on this critical ground that we have called for a more issue-based approach toward institutions: A critical or Foucauldian approach toward institutions thus necessitates an issue-based approach toward institutions. As long as we focus on big things such as the structure or system without ever looking into specific institutions/power relations when studying institutions, we cannot really uncover, not to mention redress, injustice and inequality. A mostly structural and yet critical approach toward power and institutions is thus an oxymoron, methodologically and normatively. We have to go down to specific institutions governing specific issues before we can make any normative judgment regarding a social system (or order): before we can judge the forest, we have to examine the trees. Otherwise, we inevitably reify.

C. Towards a Social Evolutionary Approach toward Institutions

For the past decades, the study of international institutions has been dominated by (American) neoliberalism, (liberal) constructivism, and the English School (both its pluralist and solidarist strains).[41] Yet, the preceding discussion implies that all three approaches suffer from fundamental deficiencies.

Most critically, at their birth in the 1970–80s, all three major approaches toward international institutions have been heavily inspired by structural functionalism (Parsons 1937; 1951; Merton 1968), even though functionalism had already been discredited in sociology and anthropology by then (e.g., Wrong 1961; Dahrendorf 1968), leaving perhaps (neoclassical institutional) economics and IR as the only two fields in which such structural functionalism still retains a significant audience.

Functionalism was the original unholy alliance between holism and the harmony approach (Tang 2011a; 2011b). Although functionalism has little to say about the actual process how institutions come to exist (hence, it does not really have a theory of institutional change), nor does it have a theory of institutional system (as part of asocial order), functionalism strongly implies a misguided theory of institutional change and of the institutional system. For functionalism, every institution exists to improve collective welfare and such institutions form an organic whole as part of a harmonious social order.

Functionalism's influence on neoliberalism is beyond dispute (Sterling-Folker 2000; see also Keohane 1984; Martin and Simmons 1998). Although neoliberalism departed from the holism of structural functionalism by looking into the actual processes of institutional change and the actual effect of institutions, neoliberalism retains the harmony approach toward institutions from functionalism.[42] Most prominently, according to neoliberalism, although there may be conflict of interest and power (narrowly understood) involved, there is no actual conflict in the making of institutions: Institutions are the product of repeated bargaining toward cooperation and coordination.

The English School, since its very beginning, has primarily focused on institutions and order (Bull 1977; Little 2000; Buzan 2004; Linklater and Suganami 2006), so much so that it can be fittingly labeled as "British Institutionalism" (Evans and Wilson 1992; Suganami 2003). Within the English school, there have been two strains: pluralist and solidarist. Although there are important differences between the two strains, they are fundamentally similar when it comes to the two pillars of structural functionalism. Overall, the English School has been a more exact replica of structural functionalism than neoliberalism.

To begin with, despite their differences, the two strains of the English School talk mostly about the three "big things" (i.e., international system, international society, and world society) and do not really get their hands dirty with the empirical task of understanding the dirty business of making institutions and order (Copeland 2003; for exceptions, see Clark 2005; 2007). Both strains are thus firmly within the holism approach. Meanwhile, both strains are also firmly within the harmony approach by emphasizing the possibility of cooperation, coordination, and harmony.

As such, the pluralist strain is an essentially truncated form of neoliberalism: the key difference between the two has been that the pluralist strain emphasizes both formal rules (e.g., treaties) and informal rules (e.g., norms) whereas neoliberalism focuses exclusively on formal rules.[43] Meanwhile, the solidarist strain is a truncated form of normative Kantian social constructivism (Adler and Barnett 1998, 9–15; Buzan 2004, 10–15; Copeland 2003, 430). The solidarist strain argues that as long as we do this and that, a common culture and value system will emerge from the international system and propel us into a world society in which individuals share similar laws and moral concerns.

Within the constructivism camp, the main divergent line has been the difference between holism (or, "structuralism") strain and the non-holism strain. Holists (e.g., Onuf, Wendt) have increasingly converged to the solidarist strain of the English School, talking about only big things with mostly philosophical languages (e.g., Onuf 1989; Wendt 1999; 2003; Linklater and Suganami 2006). Non-holists (e.g., Adler 1991; 2005, Crawford 2002; Checkel 2007a; Johnston 2008), to their credit, have retained their focuses on the real processes of social construction, thus avoiding the holism trap.[44] Despite their differences, however, both holists and non-holists submit to a harmony approach toward the process of social construction, whether institutions or culture. Few constructivists have squared with the fact that ideas mostly spread via power, thus conveniently ignoring the often bloody processes of spreading ideas via power. They readily believe that good ideas (e.g., liberalism and democracy) come to exist and spread via peaceful means. Yet, even good ideas cannot spread without power, often brutal power (Keal 2003; Anghie 2004).

A reorienting of the study of international institution thus demands a whole new approach. Our discussion suggests that only a social evolutionary approach is a valid approach toward institutions. A social evolutionary approach rejects the various approaches toward institutions inspired by functionalism while insisting a more issue-based and critical approach toward international institutions that organically synthesizes the various foundational paradigms in social sciences when looking at concrete social facts such as processes of institutional change (Tang 2011a; 2011b).

V. A WORLD STATE AS AN IMPOSSIBLE AND DANGEROUS UTOPIA

The fact that our world has become a more rule-based system both regionally (to a great extent) and globally (to a lesser extent) poses the interesting question how far this process of institutionalized peace can go. Many IR theorists of institutions and culture (i.e., Kantian constructivists, the solidarists within the English School), true to their utopian roots, wish for and believe in the possibility of a "world state" or "world society" (e.g., Wendt 2003; Linklater and Suganami 2006, ch. 4; Clark 2007).[45] Our evolutionary understanding of human society resolutely rejects the possibility of a world state or world society as utopian, while admitting the fact that our world has become a more rule-based system and the real possibility that our world may move further toward a more rule-based system. Indeed, a world state is a dangerous utopia.

A. A World State as an Impossible Utopia

There is no doubt that our world has become a more rule-based system. But will this lead to a world state? The answer is no, for the following three reasons.[46]

First, there is no possibility of imposing a universal order over the whole international system, because there is now an inherent physical and moral limit to the reach of power in today's international system. In domestic politics, the state (or an actor who won the struggle of power to impose rules) can impose its preferred rules, to a great extent. In contrast, with territory integrity and sovereignty as two foundational institutions within the international system enshrined in international politics after the Second World War (which was, without doubt, a major progress in international life), no country or international organization can impose an order through military force upon another country without causing enormous international uproar. America's imposing an order in Western Europe and in Japan and the Soviet Union's imposing an order in Eastern Europe have been two long exceptions, and in both cases, the order was imposed and backed by supreme power. Even within these two cases, however, the imposing of order had never been thorough. The record of enforcing rules by the United Nations since the Second World War has been even more dismal. All in all, "in world politics, rules and procedures will be neither so complete nor so well enforced as in well-ordered domestic political systems . . . " (Keohane and Nye 1977[1989], 19; see also Mearsheimer 1994–95).

Second, violating rules will always be part of social reality. Human beings tend to violate rules when profitable and facing no foreseen punishment. Saidemen and Ayers (2007a; 2007b) found that international organizations (which supposedly make and enforce rules) have only limited restraining effect over states' behavior. Even within the EU, the supposed prototype of a world state, member states do not always comply with within-community rules (Börzel et al. 2010). These violations expose the weakness of enforcing rules within a system, and this exposed weakness undermines furthering institutionalizing within the system as a form of feedback.

Third and more fundamental, there is an inherent limit to the internal ization of rules and norms in international politics (or the socialization of agents with rules and values), for a host of reasons. I shall list only three.

To begin with, internalization, or more precisely, the penetration of agents' body and soul by power, inherently requires brutal and longstanding power (Elias 1939 [1994]; Foucault 1980; 2000). Because there is little possibility of imposing a whole institutional order in post-Second World War international politics by brutal power, internalization in IR will be inherently more limited than that in domestic politics.

An equally insurmountable barrier against complete internalization is human nature. Human nature is composed of three parts: the part determined by biological evolution, socialization, and anti-socialization (Tang 2011b; see also Chapter 5 below). This fact essentially denies that socialization can ever be complete, even in domestic politics. Socialization certainly cannot completely socialize the part of human nature determined by biological evolution. And when it comes to identity-related issues, socialization tends to become very difficult.

Worse, socialization almost inevitably invites anti-socialization (or resist-ance).[47] Thus, Reus-Smit (1997, 566) admitted that "foundational constitu-tions" often contain "hegemonic beliefs", whereas "alternative conceptions have historically assumed an oppositional quality [i.e., anti-ideology], their proponents often decrying the way in which prevailing beliefs condition admission to international society and shape its basic institutional practice". As such, "It is not uncommon for states and nonstate actors to oppose the dominant interpretation of what constitutes a legitimate state or appropriate state behavior" (ibid. 568). More recently, Acharya (2009) documented that Asian leaders had strenuously resisted certain norms and rules from the West.

Moreover, we survive on material stuff, and survival on scarce material sources inevitably entails some conflict of interest and thus the possibility of actual conflict. And even if our minimal material need is satisfied, there is a status competition that cannot satisfy all agents because status and recognition tend to be zero-sum: Unlike material goods that can be potentially unlimited, positional goods such as higher status and recognition that are inherently limited in supply (Tang 2010d; see also Veblen 1898; Hirsch 1977; Frank 1985). And yet, the drive for higher status and recognition is a product of socialization, or part of the socialized aspect of human nature (Lebow 2008; Tang 2010d). Because institutions often create winners and losers, both materially and positionally (Knight 1992; for evidences in international relations, see Barnett and Finnemore 2004), institutions seldom harmonize interests among agents. This again limits agents' internalization of institutions.

Finally, ethnocentrism, manifesting as nationalism, patriotism, and racism, limits the possibility of a world state at a more fundamental level. Ethnocentrism plays upon groups' concern for relative power, honor, and status. Because obeying others' rules jeopardizes our ethno (LeVine and Campbell 1972), we resist internalization of other groups' norms and rules, even if other groups' norms and values may improve our welfare. In other words, we are deeply concerned with the question of ownership when it comes to ideas, norms, rules, and institutions.

Together, these mechanisms suggest that there is an inherent limit to internalization of rules and norms in international politics, even if many institutions can be installed. To put it in Foucouldian terms, there will be few docile bodies in IR (Joseph 2010; see also Koskenniemi 2009). As such, a world state is impossible.

B. A World State as a Dangerous Utopia

Not only is a world state an impossible utopia, it is also a dangerous utopia, partially because it is an impossible utopia.

The making of a world state critically depends on the spreading of a set of common rules and norms, assuming that the material foundation for such a world state embodied in the globalization of technology and capital sustains itself (in all likelihood, it will).[48] And it is precisely this critical dependence on the spreading of a set of common rules and norms that spells danger.

All common (or in our case, global) rules and norms start as local ones.[49] Thus, regarding international institutions, Reus-Smit (1997, 668) noted that "the values that constitutional structures comprise originate within the domestic political cultures of dominant states, and coalitions of such states generally exert a disproportionate influence on their international institutionalization" (See also Keohane 1984; Barkin and Cronin 1994; Keal 2003; Anghie 2004; Clark 2007). This is not surprising, "morality which is not particular society's morality is to be found nowhere" (MacIntyre 1984, 265–6).

Because common rules and norms start as local ones, the spreading of rules and norms inevitably require the backing of power, sometimes longstanding and brutal power. This is true in domestic politics (Elias 1939[1994]; Foucault 1980; 1990), but even more so in international politics (Barkin and Cronin 1994; Ikenberry 2000; Keal 2003; Anghie 2004; Clark 2007). The fact that the world as a whole system has evolved into a defensive realism world and in some places a more rule-based world does not nullify this key dynamics.

When the spreading of rules and norms in the international system often requires the backing of longstanding and brutal power, pursuing the spreading of rules and norms, even without violent power, spells danger. Although (non-violent) power does not always entail injustice, the possibility that it will cannot be neglected. After all, when we allow our impulse of universal proselytizing to drive our behaviors, we have usually done more harm than good. Here is MacIntyre (1984, 221) again, "when men and women identify what are in fact their partial and particular causes too easily and too completely with the cause of some universal principle, they usually behave worse than they would otherwise do".

The rise of monotheistic (and thus universalizing) religions, most prominently, Christianity and Islam, exemplified this danger perfectly (Foucault, quoted in Paras 2006, 131). Monotheistic religions sanctioned our missionary zeal by endorsing the so-called "just war" against no-believers as a cover for the less glorious goals of food, territory, sex, power, and bloody vanity. Monotheistic religions also reinforced the "us-versus-them" group identity and competition: "The obligation of a just war was already evident in many of the older religions. With the new universal ideologies, this obligation was reinforced, as was the ban on belligerency among the faithful" (Gat 2006, 435). Only Buddhism and Confucianism were able to escape from this trap.

The rise of international law serves perhaps a more pertinent illustration. Keal (2003) and Anghie (2004) have documented that the rise of international laws had been propelled by the "mission" to "civilize" the non-Western people, by force if necessary. The path traveled by international laws had thus been paved by blood from the non-Western people, *even if* these laws may now serve the interest of the mankind. And much of the talking about global governance today might have been just another attempt to assert power for the sake of maintaining one's power (this time, U.S.), conveniently ignoring the possible injustice entailed by the spreading of international laws yesterday and today (Bartelson 2006; Koskenniemi 2009; see also the forum on liberal peace in *Millennium,* vol. 38, no. 3, 2010).

In sum, because the spreading of rules and norms is inseparable from power, it cannot be guaranteed to be just (and often it is not). Because all of us can be fallible, none of us can claim that our moral and ethical codes are universal and they should be applied and enforced everywhere, as Antony Anghie (2004, 4) put it forcefully when criticizing the European/colonial origins of international law: "How could it be claimed the European civilization, in all its avowed specificity, was somehow universal and binding on non-European states?"

Moral absolutism is thus a dangerous trap (MacIntyre 1984, 220), and we shall resolutely reject it. Only moral relativism (or pluralism) is consistent with an evolutionary approach toward knowledge and thus an open society: moral relativism produces less evil because and it guards against the possible tyranny of local/ethnocentric ideas backed by power that pretend universality (Tang 2011a, ch. 5). Indeed, only moral relativism is consistent with a critical approach toward institutions, and only a critical approach toward institutions is consistent with an evolutionary approach toward knowledge and thus an open society. Thus, although we should not deny that human groups share certain common rules and norms, we have to critically scrutinize these rules and norms and preserve the possibility of changing toward the better. After all, if history is any guide, too often, hidden behind the noble aura of world state, "just" war, and universal principles is an insidious desire and actual practice of subjugating other "uncivilized" and "barbarous" peoples, since the ancient (Anghie 2004; 2009). And the fact that many contemporary advocates of international law and world order who may or may not consider them to be imperialists are not shy about pronouncing explicitly and implicitly imperialist principles should at least give us a pause in believing in the possibility of a world state (for examples, see the references cited in Anghie 2004, ch. 6; 2009; Craig 2004; Koskenniemi 2009).

Finally, a world state attracts us precisely because it is a dangerous utopia. Because men cannot live without dreams or hopes, some utopian thinking may be a necessary evil. But we must not forget the possible danger of actually pursuing a utopia. All utopias thrive on ideologies, thus inevitably imposing a limit on critique: critique has to stop somewhere. Yet, because critique is the key driver of knowledge process and social changes (Popper [1937]1959; [1945]1967, Foucault [1984]1997; Connolly 1993), suffocating the spirit of critique essentially means that all utopias demand us to remain stuck in a static society. This is not only untenable, but also dangerous, as Popper ([1945]) said a long time ago, and we still cannot afford to ignore him. We therefore shall firmly resist the temptation to universalize our morals (especially through power) that lurks behind the utopian notion of "a world state".

TOWARDS A BETTER BUT ALWAYS IMPERFECT WORLD

In this chapter, I have outlined a thesis that although a world state is impossible, the international system has indeed moved and will continue to move toward a better but always imperfect and thus open society, due to the powerful but always imperfect mechanism of artificial selection by human agents in social evolution. Such a thesis holds important implications for our future.

To begin with, because the world has evolved from an offensive realism world to a defensive realist world, the possibility that the world evolves into a more rule-based world is real. When most states come to learn the rules of the defensive realism world, and understand that conquest is no longer a viable option in both the material and ideational sense, states can and will resort more and more to cooperation for gaining security. And as states move toward more cooperation in security and economic affairs, the rules that codify and facilitate more cooperation may eventually become more extensive and internalized.

Second, regions are going to be more institutionalized than the whole system. Geography is still important, despite (or because of) globalization. Geography facilitates intra-regional interaction and limits inter-regional interaction. States within a particular region may well gel into a regional security community, and arrive at a common identity, but this identity will be very limited in scope. More importantly, this regional identity is unlikely to extend to other states outside the regional security community, due to the power of ethnocentrism and geography. There is an inherent limit to the institutionalizing of peace at the global level.

Third, because states tend to resist institutions and norms dictated by others, a more institutionalized world is destined to be pluralistic and thus democratic. While hegemons can claim that the institutional system they established is the best possible world that all other states can live with and thus demand other states to accept and respect the system (e.g., Ikenberry 2000), other states will not be easily fooled (Schweller 2001; see also Carr 1939).

Finally, we have to remind ourselves that the United States will remain an odd actor within the international system. The United States will remain the leading hegemon in the international system for some years to come. As such, when the United States wield its power wisely, it will be a blessing for the world. When it wields its power unwisely, however, it will be a curse for the world. Yet, the United States will likely remain an under-socialized actor in the international system, due to its uniquely blessed geographical location and enormous power advantage over other states (Tang and Long 2012). Since the possibility that the United States will be the bull in the china shop can never be eliminated, other states within the system will always hesitate to let down their guard against the United States. This will also limit the institutionalization of peace within the whole system.

In sum, the spreading of rules and norms has gradually propelled our world into a better world. If so, we should look forward to a world in which some of the ideas of defensive realism may no longer apply, even though defensive realism is the fitting theory for much of the world today. A more rule-based world might have been unfolding before our eyes, and such a world may bring more institutionalized peace in the future. A more rule-based world is also less likely to be a world dominated by the United States (or other hegemons), although the United States would retain considerable influences globally for the foreseeable future.[50]

Part III

Implications and Conclusion

5

International Politics as an Evolutionary System

INTRODUCTION

After expounding SEP as a foundational paradigm of social sciences and applying it to address the transformation of international system in history, I am now ready to address some broader issues regarding the transformation of social systems. I underscore that the interaction among agents and the interaction between agents and *the system* (of which structure is only one component) through time and across space ultimately drives the dynamics within the system, and in turn, the transformation of the system. As such, social sciences' (including IR) "structuralism" obsession with (agent-)structure (and things related to it) has been a disastrous and illicit affair, and it is time to end it.[1] Instead, social scientists should embrace a genuinely systemic approach if they desire to adequately understand the dynamics within a system and a social evolutionary approach if they desire to adequately understand the transformation of a system (Tang 2011b; idem, 2014–15).

The rest of the chapter is divided into three major sections. In the first section, I deal with the all-too-prominent agent-structure problem, stressing its inadequacy for understanding the system. I emphasize that structure alone dictates very little, and even a focus on the interaction between agents and structure (as defined in IR and other fields of social sciences) with a "structuration" (e.g., Giddens 1979; 1984) or a "emergentist (or morphogenetic)" approach (e.g., Archer 1995) is inadequate for understanding the dynamics within and the transformation of a system (see also Kontopoulos 1993; Porpora 1993; for discussion in IR, see Dessler 1989; Wendt 1987; Carlsnaes 1992; Buzan et al. 1993; Doty 1997; Wendt 1999; Wight 2006; Sørensen 2008; for critical reviews of the agent-structure debate in IR, see Gould 1998; Wight 2006, ch. 4).[2] This is so simply because the so-called agent-structure problem still leaves out a large chunk of human society. As such, any further playing within the agent-structure problematique is doomed to fail.

Building on the first section, the second section reinforces the notion that structure alone does little and we in social sciences need to do away our long-standing "structuralism" obsession with structure (and the agent-structure problematique) by examining two debates about the "logic of anarchy". I show that there is no such thing called "the logic of anarchy", only a logic of system.

The third section addresses the reach of system upon agents. I first identify the five major channels through which the system impact units. I then discuss the implications for theorizing state behavior of our new understanding about agents and system, illustrating with a major debate. A brief conclusion follows.

Before that, it is important to recall our definition of a society (or a social system) from the introduction. Statically speaking, society is a system comprising of agents or actors (i.e., individuals and collectives of individuals), an institutional system (i.e., the structure), and the physical environment. Hence, society as a system is more than just a structure and interacting units. Dynamically, society contains all possible processes within the system (e.g., behaviors, interactions, institutionalization, socialization, and internalization etc.). Moreover, processes within the system are more than interactions among units (including their behaviors) and those between agents and the structure (however defined) alone: *certainly, units' interactions with the physical environment constitute key processes within the system* (cf. Keohane and Nye 1977/[1989], esp. 260–4; Buzan et al. 1993, 18; Wendt 1999, 145–7). Further, interactions within the system produce "emergent" *trends* within the system (e.g., industrialization, colonization, decolonization, globalization, global warming, and democratization) and these major trends are critical properties within the system (cf. Wendt 1999, 145–7). In sum, as a system, society exhibits systemic (or "emergent") properties that cannot be reduced to the sum of the individuals and components within the system (Jervis 1997), but the fact that a society has a system of institutions (i.e., a structure, see below) is one of, but not the only, fundamental reasons why society cannot be reduced to a sum of individuals (Giddens 1976[1993], 128; 2006, 106–7). This is summarized schematically in Figure 5.1.

With our complete definition of a social system (i.e., the "society"), it becomes clear that most existing definitions of society are incomplete. Most prominently, following Waltz (1979, 79; 1986, 327), most authors have left out the physical environment as part of the definition of a social system. Thus, Buzan et al. (1993, 18), define system as comprising "units, interactions, and structure". Although their definition contains both the static aspects and the dynamics aspects of a system, it still leaves out the physical environment. The same problem bedevils Wendt's (1999) discussion, which is based on an implicitly similar definition of the social system as that of Waltz.[3] As becomes clear below, such an incomplete definition of the system can only lead to misleading understandings.

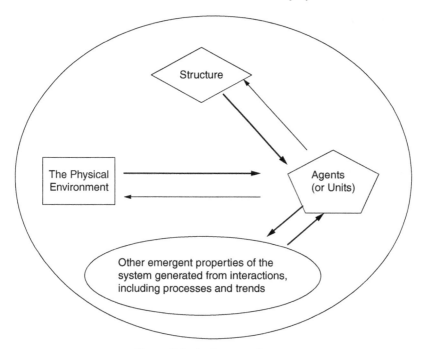

Figure 5.1. Society as a System

I. (INTERNATIONAL) SYSTEM, NOT (INTERNATIONAL) STRUCTURE!

In this section, I first sort out the various notions of international structure and then underscore that structural theories, however sophisticated, are inherently inadequate for understanding the international system simply because structure, however defined, is only a part of the system but never the whole system.[4] For understanding IR (and the broader human society), systemic and evolutionary theories rather than structural ones are the way to go.

A. What Is Structure Anyway? (And Does It Matter?)

The rise of Waltzian structural realism (neorealism) brought the structure of international politics to the center of IR. Yet, just what is structure? For Waltz, the structure of international politics has three dimensions: the principle of organizing (in the case of international politics, anarchy as lacking a central authority),[5] the differentiation of units, and distribution of power.[6] Since anarchy remains constant and there is no differentiation among units, the only variable that can truly vary in Waltz's structure is distribution of power, or "how they [units] stand in relation to one another (how they are arranged or positioned)" (Waltz 1979, 80).[7]

Apparently, Waltz's definition of structure is a purely materialism one (for similar definitions, see Mearsheimer 1995, 91).[8] Since Waltz, IR theorists have advanced other notions of structure, usually by adding things to Waltz's sparse definition of structure.[9] Other realists have attempted to add technology (e.g., offense-defense balance, nuclear weapon) to this materialism definition of structure (Jervis 1978; idem 1997, ch. 3; Nye 1988; Glaser 1994–95; 2010). For neoliberalists, however, structure definitely includes interdependence and international institutions that govern interactions as part of interdependence (Keohane and Nye 1987; 1977[1989]). Interdependence is both material and ideational but more the former. Since institutions are codified ideas (Tang 2011a), however, neoliberalists' definition of structure is more ideational than that of Waltz (Wendt 1999, 160). For constructivists, consistent with constructivism's overall ideationalism stand, international structure is mostly ideational: the most critical component of international structure is culture, which may include norm, institution, (common) identity, and shared knowledge (Adler 1991; 2005; Wendt 1992; 1999, ch. 3; see also Adler and Barnett 1998a, 10).

Apparently, when it comes to defining structure, Waltz and Wendt are the two poles along the continuum from materialism to ideationalism, with Keohane and Nye occupying a somewhat middle ground. Anyhow, there has not been a consensus on what exactly structure (of international politics) is. This is hardly surprising. In other fields of social sciences, structure too remains a "contested concept" (for critical reviews, see Porpora 1989 [1998]; López and Scott 2000; Wight 2006, esp. ch. 4).

From a social systemic perspective, however, even if we have a consensus on structure, we cannot possibly arrive at an adequate understanding of international politics and the broader human society. This is so simply because structure is only one part, not the whole, of the international system: system and structure are not the same.

Waltz essentially takes systemic theories and structural theories to be interchangeable, thus implicitly conflating structure and system.[10] In his words, "structural realism presents a *systemic* portrait of international politics depicting component units according to the manner of their arrangement . . . Changes of structure and hence of system occur with variations in the number of great powers . . . Systems theories, whether political or economic, are theories that explain how *the organization of a realm* acts as a constraining and disposing force on the interacting units within it" (Waltz 1988, 618; see also Waltz 1979, ch. 5). Apparently, for Waltz (1979, 100–1), the paramount dimension in a system is its structure (i.e., "the organization of a realm") and only a structural change can qualify as a systemic change. Most realists have accepted Waltz's claim that his structural theory is a *systemic* theory (e.g., Schweller 1996; Mearsheimer 2001), and only perhaps Buzan et al. (1993, ch. 2), Spirtas (1996, 292), and Jervis (1997, 107–10, see, however, ibid. 124) have explicitly pointed out that Waltz's theory is more structural than systemic. Indeed, even many of Waltz's non-realist critics have conflated structure with system (e.g., Hollis and Smith 1991, esp. 110–18; Wendt 1999, 11).

This practice of equating structure with system is seriously mistaken. Although structure can only exist within a system and is a critical dimension of a social system, *structure plus units is still not the system: system is far more than the structure and the units,* contra Waltz (1979, 79). A human society as a system has at least three components: agents, a social structure, and the physical environment (foremost, time and space). More importantly, not only units interact with each other, but also the three components of the system interact with each other, and these interactions generate properties that cannot be understood by simply adding them together or admitting parts of them.[11] As a result, only a system theory can adequately understand the dynamics within a social system. A structural theory, no matter how elaborate, cannot possibly be up to the task. Structure alone explains little: as such, a purely structural theory makes little sense (Powell 1994).

A (purely) structural theory merely has to state what the structure is and how the structure shapes certain social outcomes. Waltz's theory, by emphasizing how anarchy (which is constant) and polarity (as the other dimension of structure) shape units' behaviors (e.g., balancing) and the possible outcomes from their interactions (e.g., de facto balance of power), is a structural theory, not a full-blown system theory by any measure. Although Waltz was correct to argue "that international politics can be understood only if the effects of structure are added to the unit-level explanations of traditional realism", he was mistaken in claiming that "if an approach allows the consideration of both unit-level and structural-level causes, then it can cope with both the changes and the continuities that occur in a system" (Waltz 1988, 617–8). Contra Waltz, such a theory cannot possibly be adequate for understanding "the changes and the continuities" within a system (Lebow 2007, 418–21), because the system is more than units and the structure. Like other structural theorists before him (e.g., Parsons), Waltz too vastly exaggerates the explanatory power of structural theories (see below).

A systemic theory certainly admits that units and structure cannot be separated in reality and considers both unit-level and structural-level factors and the interactions between them (Waltz 1988, 617–18; see also Buzan et al. 1993; Powell 1994, 321–4; Wendt 1999). A systemic theory, however, is much more than putting units and structure together via "structuration" (cf. Giddens 1979; 1984; Buzan et al. 1993), "morphogenesis" (cf. Archer 1995), or interaction/constitution (cf. Wendt 1999). A systemic theory subsumes structure and the so-called agent/agency-structure problem.

At the real minimum, a system theory must deal with how units interact with each other within the system (with the structure being only one source of systemic constraints), how units interact with other parts of the system, and how these interactions together drive the change of system. A systemic theory, when properly constructed along the line of SSP (Tang 2011b; see also Jervis 1997, esp. ch. 3), is thus vastly more complex and potent than a structural theory can ever hope to be.

B. Some Properties of the International System

In this section, I single out some key properties of the international system that are critical for understanding the system, without pretending that we can exhaust the list. By doing so, I reinforce the notion that structural theories can never be adequate simply because these *systemic* properties cannot be accommodated by structure, however defined. I shall leave out the distribution of material capability among units because it has been much emphasized by realists (e.g., Waltz 1979; Mearsheimer 2001). I also leave out "collective identity", "(common) culture" among units because it has been much emphasized by constructivists (e.g., Adler and Barnett 1998; Wendt 1999; Lebow 2008).[12]

The geographical environment of a (sub)system

Social interactions unfold in real (and now virtual) space, and geography is the key dimension of space. Geography has been one of the most crucial factors in shaping human history, especially the early years (Carneiro 1970; Diamond 1997), although it certainly did not determine human destiny as Geopolitics had maintained.

Most prominently, for much of human history, geography had decisively shaped the amount and scope of interactions among units. The coming of sea voyaging, air travel, intercontinental missile, and finally telecommunication and internet has greatly reduced geography's shielding and restraining power, but geography's impact over human interaction remains powerful (Mearsheimer 2001).

Geography's impact is perhaps most visible at the level of region. Region has been a critical force in shaping the interaction among states within it (Solingen 1998; Katzenstein 2005; see also Acharya 2007), resulting in "regional security complexes (RSCs)" (Buzan 1986; 1991; Buzan and Wæver 2004).[13] Most of the time, external forces (e.g., an extra-regional state) can impact the dynamics within a RSC *only if* they can penetrate the geographical barrier encircling the RSC (Tang 2004). Hence, for much of our history, there were only regional international systems: a genuinely global international system emerged only after the 18–19th centuries, and this global system has remained only partially so (see Chapters 2, 3, and 4 above).

The number of units within a system

The total number of units within a particular system is an important property of the system. Within a system within only great powers, the number of units is the number of poles. As Waltz (1979) implied, change in the number of units within a great power system constitutes a structural change.[14] By logic extension, then, any change in the number of units within a system constitutes a systemic change. Indeed, quantitative change in the number of units within a system can lead to a qualitative transformation of the system (Carneiro 2000; see also Jervis 1997 and Chapter 2 above).

The nature of most units within the system

The *objective* nature of most units within the system is a critical property of an international system.[15] As becomes clear in the proceeding chapters, whether most states within the system are offensive realist ones or non-offensive realist ones has powerful effect on states' behavior. This property is different from the identity of each individual unit or the collective identity among a group of units. Existing discussions have vastly underappreciated this dimension and its impact (see also Tang 2008a).

The amount and scope of interaction among the units

Because interactions among the units (as processes) are inherently part of the system (Jervis 1997; Rescher 1997), many have emphasized interactions, to a various degree and on different aspects. Realism emphasizes competition for power and war, liberalism commerce, neoliberalism institutional change (and organizations), and constructivism social learning and constituting. Evidently, interactions can generate both conflict and cooperation (i.e., outcomes from this process are under-determined) and some key divergences of major IR theories are due to their different emphases on these different interactions and their consequences.

Even if interactions per se are unit-level things (e.g., Waltz 1979, 80), the amount and the scope of interactions (among units and beyond) is a systemic property (Wendt 1999, 145–50).[16] Amount is the total sum of interactions (and frequency is the total amount divided by time). Scope is the number of domains in which units interact with each other (e.g., economic, political, social). Evidently, interdependence (among units) is subsumed under amount. Understood as such, it is no wonder that interdependence (as an outcome of interaction) can come back to shape further interactions, as most major IR theories have recognized.

Finally, it is important to note that whereas social theorists tend to emphasize the more intentional and regular kind of interactions (e.g., Waltz 1979; Nye and Keohane [1977]1989; Wendt 1999), a systemic approach insists that all interactions, whether intentional or intentional, regular or irregular, impact a system. Surely our instinctive behaviors, without much intentional input such as seeking safety, eating food, and having sex, have shaped our history no less profoundly than our intentional behaviors, and some episodes of irregular interaction (e.g., the Mongol invasion) had a far more profound effect upon the whole system than many regular ones.

The amount and scope of interaction between units and the physical environment[17]

As noted above, processes within the system are more than interactions among units (including their behaviors) and those between agents and the structure (however defined) alone. Certainly, units' interactions with the physical environment constitute key processes within the system. Anyone with the slightest knowledge of human history would admit that this interaction has had a profound impact over the history of human society (Diamond 1997). One only needs to recall the coming of settled agriculture, ocean voyaging, Black Death, and the discovery of the Americas.

The degree of institutionalization

This dimension has received a lot of attention from IR theorists, with the notable exceptions of (offensive) realists (e.g., Waltz 1986, 336; Mearsheimer 1994–95; Glaser 1994–95). This dimension can be measured along three dimensions: density, rigidity, and internalization. The different takes on international institutions by realism, neoliberalism, and constructivism/the solidarist strain of the English School can be plotted along these three dimensions (for details, see Tang, n.d.-b; for earlier discussions, see Mearsheimer 1994–95; 1995; Keohane and Martin 1995; Ruggie 1995; Wendt 1995; Jervis 1999; Tang 2010b, ch. 6).

Put somewhat crudely, realism (both offensive and defensive) denies that international politics can have a lot of institutions (i.e., density low) whereas both neoliberalism and constructivism believe that international politics can have a lot of institutions (i.e., density high). Moreover, realism believes that institutions do not have much of a bite (i.e., rigidity low) whereas neoliberalism, the English School, and constructivism believe do have quite a bit of bite (i.e., rigidity high). Finally, defensive realism, neoliberalism, and the pluralist strain of the English School deny that states will internalize those ideas dictated by international rules (i.e., internalization low), constructivism and the solidarist strain of the English School emphasize that states often do internalize those ideas (as rules) to be part of their value system and self-identity (i.e., internalization high).

Here, it is important to emphasize that interdependence does not automatically lead to institutionalization, at least not formally, although institutions most likely need interdependence to exist: Unless agents are in regular contact with each other, there is little need for institutions. In other words, although some interactions are regulated, many are not, formally or informally. Of course, the more interaction (or the more interdependent agents are), the denser the institutional system that governs the interaction is likely to become. Moreover, because the institutional system of a society constitutes the bulk of the society's structure for most sociologists and social scientists (Tang 2011a; see also López and Scott 2000), the more interdependent agents are, the more pervasive the reach of the structure becomes.

The amount of agents' knowledge about the system

The amount of agents' knowledge about the nature of each other and the nature of the system is another critical property of a social system. The amount of agents' knowledge about each other and the system captures how much knowledge agents have about each other and the system, and it says nothing about the exact content (e.g., whether their knowledge is true or false) of their knowledge. Apparently, the larger the amount of agents' knowledge about each other and the system, the greater agents' actions will be shaped by each other and the system. This means that states can still re-make the system even if they do not get the nature of the system right: there are more than just self-fulfilling and self-negating tendencies operating within a system (see Chapters 2 and 3 above; cf. Jervis 1997; Wendt 1999; Houghton 2009).

The commonality of agents' knowledge about the system

The commonality of agents' knowledge about the nature of each other and the nature of the system constitutes another critical property of a social system. Here, it is important to differentiate the commonality (or convergence) of knowledge from constructivism's notion of "culture", which covers everything from taboo, norm, collective identities, to (common) knowledge (e.g., Adler 1992; Wendt 1999, esp. 141–2). First, commonality of knowledge here is even thinner than the rational choice/game theory-based notion of "common knowledge" (i.e., "something is common knowledge if all actors know it, all know that all others know it, and so on ad infinitum": Morrow 1994, 349) As such, commonality of knowledge here is much thinner than constructivism's notion of "collective knowledge" (Wendt 1999, 157–65).[18] Commonality of knowledge here merely says that agents' knowledge of each other and the system overlap with each other somewhat. Second, although both knowledge and culture can be attained, inherited, transformed, rejected or discarded, knowledge is something to be tested whereas culture is something to be enforced, believed, and internalized.

Perhaps the most critical component of this dimension is states' awareness of the overall nature of the system. From the chapters above, it is clear that there have been at least four broader conceptualizations of the international system: (1) the international system is a peaceful paradise; (2) the system is an offensive realism world; (3) the system is a defensive realism world; (4) the system is a rule-based (or post-defensive realism/neo-liberalism) world. Because states' behavior can be profoundly shaped by their conceptualization of the whole system,[19] whether their conceptualizations converge or diverge has important effect over the dynamics within the system.

Apparently, this sub-dimension is at least partially underpinned by the objective nature of the system as captured by "the nature of (most states within) the system". As such, this dimension overlaps with the objective side of the dimension "the nature of most units of the system": objective reality and agents' (subjective) understanding of the objective reality interact with each other to re-shape each other. When most states see each other as offensive realist states (correctly or incorrectly), they tend to behave as offensive realist states and thus (re)make the world into an offensive realism world while laying the foundation for the coming of the defensive realism world. By the same token, when most states see each other as non-offensive realist states (correctly or incorrectly), they tend to behave as non-offensive realist states and thus (re) make the world into a non-offensive realism world while laying the foundation for the coming of a more rule-based world. There are indeed self-fulfilling and self-negating tendencies operating within the system (Jervis 1997; Wendt 1999; Houghton 2009).

Another important sub-dimension within this dimension is states' memories of their past, singled out first by Schweller (1996) and developed further by He (2009).[20] Schweller noted that past memory of predatory states is a necessary condition for security dilemma: "In a world that has never experienced crime, the concept of security is meaningless" (1996, 91). Apparently, if there is no memory of violent past, defensive realist states may totally forget the possibility that there may be greedy states out there (or other states can become aggressive now or in the future). In so doing, states can firmly believe that all their fellow states are just like themselves (that is, peace-loving) and eliminate much of the uncertainty about each other's intentions and greatly diminish the power of the security dilemma (Tang 2009b).[21]

Examining reconciliation as a process of building peace, He (2009) noted that national myths of two states who used to be enemies—which at least partly contain memories of their past—can diverge or converge. When they diverge, they are likely to end up in a vicious cycle of increasing tensions. When they converge, they are likely to end up in a virtuous cycle of building deep peace (see also Tang 2011c).

Major trend(s) in the system

Finally, major trends in the system, which have been greatly underappreciated by major grand theories of IR (with the exception of neoliberalism on inter-dependence perhaps), constitute another major property of the system. These trends, ranging from colonization to de-colonization, globalization (of the world economy), and democratization, are what we called "processes" or "processesual variables". These trends, often with a strong positive feedback dynamics, constitute a key property of the international system that units have to reckon with. All else being equal, states that recognize these trends and adapt to them quickly and efficiently tend to do better than states that recognize them slowly (if at all) and adapt them clumsily.

Summary

In summary, a social system possesses many critical properties that cannot be easily accommodated by "structure", however defined. Fundamentally, without taking units, structure, and the physical environment together as a system, it is impossible to adequately understand the dynamics within the system, much less the transformation of the system. By singularly focusing on agent-structure, pitting structure against units, or even attempting to transcend the agent-structure divide, students of IR have missed a great deal of what has been going on within the international system for a long time. For a summary of the different approaches towards structure and system, see Table 5.1.

II. STRUCTURE ALONE DICTATES LITTLE[22]

The preceding discussion suggests something obvious yet extraordinarily important: structure alone, whether or not taken to be equivalent to be anarchy by IR theorists, does not dictate a whole lot of international politics. When this is the case, all IR (and the broader social science) theories in the structuralism tradition have committed the sin of exaggerating structure's impact upon the dynamics within the system, including units' behavior. Structure, however defined by IR theorists and social scientists, leaves many key properties of the system out of our purview, thus cannot possibly offer an adequate understanding of IR and the broader human society. I shall illustrate my case against structuralism with two cases. With the debate

Table 5.1. Conceptualizations of System (and Structure) Compared

Aspects \Approaches	Waltz/Mearsheimer (structural realism)	Keohane (structural neoliberalism)	Adler/Wendt (structural constructivism)	Tang (social evolution)
Notion about the nature of structure	Mostly material. Extremely incomplete	Mostly material, with some ideational stuff (i.e., institutions).	Mostly ideational: (i.e., cultures, identity) Extremely incomplete	System, not structure. Beyond structuralism
Evolution of the System	Anti-evolutionary. The nature of the system remains roughly the same.	Semi-evolutionary. System can evolve, but mechanisms not adequately identified.	Semi-evolutionary. System can evolve, but mechanisms not adequately identified.	Genuinely Evolutionary. Mechanisms adequately identified.
The reach of the system: the five channels	Incomplete. Mostly selection via unit survival, with only limited social learning. No constituting. No anti-socialization.	Incomplete. Selection of ideas, rational learning. No selection at the level of state survival. No constituting. No anti-socialization.	Incomplete. Social learning, construction, and constituting. No selection at the level of state survival. No anti-socialization.	Complete. All five channels as a system.
System (including structure) vs. State (as agents)	There is no possibility that agents can fundamentally re-make the system. System (or structure) dominates	Agents can re-make the system somewhat (via institutions). No possibility of changing states' identities. System (or structure) dominates, but less than what structural realism holds.	Agents can transform the system (by adopting new cultures). System (or structure) dominates, but less than what structural realism and structural neo-liberalism hold.	Agents' behaviors are shaped by the system, and agents' interaction with the structure and other components of the system can transform the system. Agents, structure, and the system co-evolve.

between structural offensive realism and structural defensive realism, I shall demonstrate that both sides in the debate have exaggerated structure impact upon states. With Wendt's structural constructivism, I shall show that constructivism simply cannot be structural: structural constructivism is an oxymoron.

A. Offensive Realism vs. Defensive Realism on the Meaning of Anarchy

Following Waltz's (1979) structuralism revolution, both offensive realists and defensive realists, regardless whether they are hardcore structuralists themselves, have embraced structuralism wholeheartedly. Most prominently, both offensive realists and defensive realists have admitted that anarchy is the linchpin component of the structure. Seeking to bolster their cases, both offensive realists and defensive realists thus argue that it has been the structure that ultimately decides why their favored theory is a more accurate theory of international politics and thus should be the more appropriate theory for guiding states' policies (e.g., Mearsheimer 2001; Glaser 2010).

Because anarchy remains a constant for both strains of structural realism, each of the two realisms must insist that anarchy favors (or induces) only the type of behavior that it emphasizes and deny that anarchy can also favor the type of behavior that the other side emphasizes: both camps have thus sought to monopolize the meaning of anarchy. Defensive realists argue that anarchy favors mostly (but not only) *defensive* strategies (e.g., Waltz 1979; Jervis 1978; Walt 1987a; 1987b; Glaser 1994–95)[23]; whereas offensive realists argue that anarchy favors only *offensive* strategies (Copeland 2000a; Labs 1997; Mearsheimer 1994–95; 2001). Seeking the moral high ground, each side also charges the other side for introducing a normative bias to the "logic of anarchy". Offensive realists correctly charge that defensive realists for introducing a normative bias for defensive measures into the "logic of anarchy" (e.g., Schweller 1996, 90–2; Zakaria 1992, 196; 1998, 26–31),[24] without admitting that they have committed the same sin (just the opposite way around). Like a mirror image, defensive realists too can charge offensive realists for misreading the "logic of anarchy" and introducing an offensive bias to it because for defensive realists, structural imperatives and factors such as nuclear deterrence and offense-defense balance strongly favor defensive strategies (Jervis 1978; Walt 1987b; Glaser 1994–95; Van Evera 1999; see also Snyder 1991. For earlier reviews of the debate, see Brooks 1997; Jervis 1999; Taliaferro 2000–1; Tang 2008a).

In reality, structure does not dictate many things that it can supposedly dictate: both sides in this debate have thus exaggerated the impact of structure. As a result, both sides have greatly difficulties in admitting transformational changes in international politics. Offensive realists, by introducing an offensive security-seeking bias into their theory, have had great difficulties in explaining the drastic reduction of war in our more recent history, not to mention of the essential elimination war as an option of statecraft in some key regions of the world (Mueller 1989; Lebow 1994; Jervis 2002; see chs. 3 and 4 above). In contrast, defensive realists, by introducing a defensive security-seeking bias into their theory, have had great difficulty in explaining the prevalence of (successful) wars of conquest in much of our history (see Chapters 2 and 3; see also Mearsheimer 2001; Hui 2005; Hamblin 2006).

To put it differently, the two structural realisms cannot cope with the possibility that the nature of international politics has undergone fundamental changes because anarchy is constant (Lebow 1994, 277–8; Fettweis 2004, 99). The two realisms can only attempt to deny that any transformational change has taken place or can ever take place (e.g., Waltz, 1979: 66; idem, 2000, 5; Mearsheimer, 2001: 2), because such changes, if true, fundamentally unravel their logic (cf. Wendt 1999, 248). Indeed, Mearsheimer (1990) had to wish for (or predicate) that Europe will be back to its future (of violent struggles) now that the stabilizing bipolarity had collapsed in order to save (structural) offensive realism. Not surprisingly, (structural) defensive theorists strongly object to Mearsheimer's predictions (Van Evera 1990–91; Jervis 1991–92; 2002; see also Jervis 1997, 103n.38 and references cited there).

Worse, being overzealous in stressing the primacy of structure (or anarchy) and then monopolizing the logic of anarchy, many (structural) realists have twisted things to fit with their structuralism logic. For instance, Grieco (1990, 49–50, also 10) asserted: "An absolute necessary effect of anarchy is the danger states perceive that others might seek to destroy or enslave them." Similarly, Glaser (1992, 502) asserted, "these motivations [i.e., greed and insecurity] arise from different sources, and are therefore essentially independent of each other". For Glaser, insecurity comes from anarchy (i.e., structure) whereas greed from states within (see also Waltz 1979).

Yet, anarchy alone does not dictate insecurity or fear for one's survival. On the one hand, individuals' and groups' insecurity or fear for one's survival was already apparent in most vertebrates, long before *Homo sapiens* came along (Wilson and Wrangham 2003). On the other hand, for much of the early human history, anarchy (among groups) was a free-wandering paradise for our ancestors, and human groups feared each other little (see Chapter 2 above). Hence, anarchy per se does not dictate insecurity. Rather, "the acuteness of states' insecurity varies substantially as a function of conditions other than a lack of common government" (Milner 1992, 483; see also Wendt 1992; 1999; Schweller 1996, 90–2; Lebow 2008).

In addition, all structural theorists, whether realists or not, believe that structure dictates our uncertainty over others' intentions (Keohane 1984; Glaser 1994–95; Copeland 2000; 2003). Yet, our uncertainty over others' intentions and the fear derived from it has nothing to do with anarchy: it is everywhere, even in our daily life under hierarchy.[25] After all, calling 911 after being hurt by somebody else provides only marginal comfort to victims, and sometimes victims do not get to call 911.

In sum, both realisms have staked a position that anarchy (or structure) dictates a lot of things within a system thus have greatly exaggerated the power of structure (or anarchy). In reality, structure, not to mention anarchy (however defined) as part of structure, does not dictate a whole lot: structure or anarchy has little logic by itself (Powell 1994, 324–6; Wendt 1999, 146, 247; cf. Buzan et al. 1993). Surely, anarchy alone cannot lead states to war, peace, uncertainty over others' intentions, fear of one's survival, evil, or tragedy (e.g., Schweller 1996; Kydd 1997; Tang 2010a), contra Waltz (1979; 1988), Spirtas (1996), and Mearsheimer (2001).

Rhetorically, if anarchy remains mostly constant, how can we explain the variations in international politics across time and space (Powell 1994, 332)? If we admit there have been some variations, this can only mean that anarchy has never been that determinate even for states' most important behavior.

B. Structural Constructivism?

The exaggeration of structure's impact is not limited to post-Waltz realisms: almost every major structural IR theory has committed the sin. Most prominently, despite aspiring to challenge Waltz's structural (neo-)realism, Alex Wendt (1999) remains firmly with structuralism. In Wendt's words, "... social constructivism is not just about idealism, it is also about structuralism or holism" (1999, 139; see also 142–4). Concurring with Waltz (1979), Wendt insists that "structural theorizing is likely to yield a high rate of explanatory return" (1999, 184).

To be sure, Wendt's structural constructivism is a vast improvement over Waltz's structural realism when it comes to structure. Not only Wendt correctly adds ideational forces to structure, he also correctly notes that interactions can be understood to have structure thus as part of the structure, though at a micro level rather than the more macro level (Wendt 1999, esp. 145–57; cf. Waltz 1979; Buzan et al. 1993).[26] Wendt also brings the agent-structure problem under the light of mutual constructing and constituting. As a result, whereas Waltz (1979) can only see the nature of structure (i.e., anarchy) as enduring, Wendt (1999) can project that the nature of structure has changed and is still changing (see also Powell 1994, 321).[27]

Unfortunately, a structural approach is even less suitable for constructivism than for (structural) realism. Structural constructivism is an oxymoron.

Ontologically, even after including the interaction among agents as part of the processes-based structure, Wendt still leaves many processes that many not have well defined structures out of the picture. Most prominently, it still leaves the physical environment of human societies and the interaction between agents and the physical environment out of the picture. Most likely, this omission allows Wendt to claim that ideational forces "constitute" most material forces while paying lip service to a "rump materialism" (Wendt 1999, 109–13). Because material forces hold ontological priority over ideational forces, however, Wendt's stand is simply invalid (for a more detailed critique, see Tang 2013).

Epistemologically and methodologically, whereas realism is mostly a materialism approach and can thus somewhat afford to ignore the real processes of ideational change and the transformational power of ideas in human society, constructivism, as an ideationalism approach, cannot afford to ignore the real processes of ideational change while preaching the transformational power of ideas. In order to have much a say on ideational change at all, constructivism needs to look at real processes of ideational change at the individual, state-level, and inter-state level (e.g., Adler 1991[2005]; Lebow and Risse-Kappen 1995; Katzenstein 1996; Acharya 2001; Checkel 2007a; Johnston 2008). To understand the real process of ideational change in international politics, constructivism has to not only bring international politics and domestic politics together as neoclassical realism has been striving to accomplish (e.g., Lobell et al. 2009), but also to bring social psychology into the picture (cf. Jervis 2004; Lebow 2008; Tang 2011c; 2012).[28]

Failing on both fronts, Wendt's theory is at most quasi-evolutionary and almost purely utopian. Without micro processes of ideational change, Wendt simply has no endogenous forces to drive systemic changes despite noting systemic changes. As a result, Wendt could only foresee the possibility of international systems being transformed by (three) "cultures as self-fulfilling prophecy", or "desires all the way down" as Doty (2000) puts it: the four master variables and key processes as singled out by Wendt (1999, Chapters 6 and 7) simply cannot have driven the transformation from a Hobbesian system to a Lockean system and then to a Kantian system. Most devastatingly, Wendt has no explanation for the following question: how did the three "cultures" or anarchies come to exist in the first place? Certainly, before a culture can constitute and constrain agents (whether via internalization or not), it has to be *there*. Wendt's charge that Waltz reifies structure thus equally sticks with Wendt himself (1999, 146–7): *by singularly focusing on structure, Wendt reifies the system*! Wendt has to go further than what he has done (Wendt 1999, 247, 249), there is no such thing as "a logic of structure" (however defined): there is only "a logic of system"![29]

Fundamentally, constructivism in IR needs to bridge the gap between macro social (material and ideational) changes and psychological changes.[30] By staying with structuralism, structural constructivism can only provide a superficial thus a distorting picture of human society.

III. SYSTEM UPON STATES: FIVE CHANNELS

The preceding discussion makes it clear that although structure presumes the existence of units and a system, it is misleading to single out structure (versus units) if we want to understand how states' behaviors are shaped by the international system.[31] Rather than the reach of the structure, we should talk about the reach of the system. This section underscores the five channels through which the international system can impact states (as key units), critically building upon existing discussions on system, structure, and the agent-structure problematique (e.g., Parsons 1937; 1951; Giddens 1979; 1984; Waltz 1979; Jervis 1997; Wendt 1999; Wight 2006; Lebow 2008).

A. The Five Channels

There are essentially five channels through which the system—in which structure is only a component—impacts units' behavior and units' nature. The first four channels, *constraining/enabling, learning, selection, and constituting/constructing* make of what we usually mean by "socialization", broadly speaking.[32] The fifth channel, which most IR theorists (and perhaps most social scientists) do not recognize, is "anti-socialization" (for exceptions, see Scott 1985; 1990; for two recent discussions of anti-socialization in IR, see Schweller and Pu 2011; Epstein 2012).[33]

Constraining/Enabling

The first channel, constraining/enabling, has been singled out by Giddens's (1979; 1984) structuration theory toward the agent-structure problematique. Giddens restricted his discussion to how the structure shapes agents. Yet, the channel of constraining/enabling can be extended to understand how the physical environment shapes agents' behavior and how agents shape each other's behavior, which in turn, will reproduce and shape the whole system. Indeed, constraining/enabling must be extended to cover the interaction between the physical environment and agents and the interaction among agents: only by doing so can we avoid the implicit or explicit pitfall of extreme ideationalism in much of the discourse on the agent-structure problematique, from Parsons (1951) via Giddens (1979; 1984) to Wendt (1999).

The physical environment certainly constrains what we can do physically and mentally. A group who resides in a desert is unlikely to imagine and produce boat, not to mention sea voyaging. By the same token, the group is unlikely to invent rice cultivation. At the same time, the physical environment also enables what we can do physically and mentally. Air, water, and other things allow us to live on. More critically, the physical environment stimulates our mental capacities to overcome certain physical barriers, and once our mental capacities invent things that can utilize the energy resided within the physical environment, the physical environment enables a lot of things. Thus, the oceans around us make long-distance trade, colonial expansion, and eventually, globalization possible after the coming of sea voyaging. Likewise, the sun makes the solar energy industry possible after we have developed the know-how to harness solar energy more efficiently and effectively.

Agents also constrain and enable each other. For instance, having allies enables one to behave in certain ways (e.g., standing firm against an opponent). At the same time, however, allies also constrain: allies may prevent one from doing certain things (e.g., being too provocative). Likewise, having opponents certainly prevents one from doing certain things (e.g., being too provocative). Yet, at the same time, having opponents may also enable one to manipulate allies.

Learning

Because learning is the key for units to understand the system and then adjust their behaviors accordingly, learning is the second foundational channel for the system to impact units. Unless units can comprehend the system (i.e., its properties) somewhat, units' behaviors will have to be driven exclusively by instincts.

Learning, when broadly defined, is the process of generating and selecting new ideas and retaining/reinforcing old ideas by agents (e.g., individuals within states) (cf. Levy 1994, 283). Learning therefore embodies a social evolutionary process within the ideational dimension of social evolution, as pointed out by Campbell (1960; [1965]1998; 1974a; 1974b; see also Popper [1937]1959; [1963]1991). Learning does not necessarily lead to change in ideas: it may merely reinforce existing ideas. Learning certainly does not necessarily lead to a change of behavior, although a change of behavior usually comes after and thus reflects some kind of learning. To equate learning with change in behavior is to fall into the positivism trap (Levy 1994, 289–91). Finally, because what we learn may not be objectively correct, learning does not necessarily lead to improvement of welfare, at least not in the short run.

Learning can be divided into several categories along different dimensions, and these different learning processes overlap with each other (e.g., Levy 1994; Adler and Barnett 1998, 43–5; Bar-Siman-Tov 2004, 69–71). Foremost, learning can be divided into negative learning and positive learning. Negative learning means learning from one's own and others' negative experiences that are generated from interactions with other units but also other components within the system (i.e., the structure and the physical environment). Positive learning, also known as emulation or imitation (Schweller and

Wohlforth 2000, 78–80), means adopting one's own and others' "successful" ideas, behaviors, culture, and institutions (as codified ideas).

Evidently, negative learning contains an explicit selection element. Moreover, because we tend to learn more from negative experiences, it is highly probable that negative learning plays an equally, if not more, critical role in our learning than positive learning. The folk wisdom that "failure is the mother of success (and success is the mother of failure)" speaks of the power of negative learning loud and clear.[34]

It is also possible to talk about individual learning versus collective learning (that is, learning by a collective entity). *Strictly speaking, however, collectives do not learn*: only individuals within them learn. Collective learning thus ultimately depends on individual learning. When all individuals accept and/or internalize an idea invented or imported by an individual (or at least conform to the idea without openly challenging it), collective learning is complete. Of course, because there will always be some individuals within a collective who may question and refuse to accept and/or internalize others' ideas, collective learning is often incomplete.

Positive learning within a collective setting overlaps with constructivists' notions of "social learning" (Adler and Barnett 1998b) and "socialization" (e.g., Johnston 2001; Checkel 2007, 5–14). Constructivists' notions of "social learning" and "socialization", however, are sloppy concepts to be avoided. Foremost, "social learning" is a misnomer, if not an oxymoron, because all our learning is social: for our species, there is no possibility of asocial learning. Meanwhile, constructivists' notion of "socialization" covers at least two processes. The first is to conform to others' ideas (including social norms) without internationalizing them, whereas the second depends on internalizing others' ideas (Adler and Barnett 1998b; Johnston 2001; Checkel 2007, 5–14). Apparently, the first notion of socialization is better captured by (positive) learning whereas the second is better captured under constituting or construction: When an idea is internalized by an agent, the agent can be understood to have been "constituted" or "constructed" by the idea.

Learning can be from one's own experiences but also from others' experiences (i.e., vicarious learning). Although learning from others' experiences (especially negative ones) is often less costly than learning from our own experiences,[35] we likely learn more efficiently from our own (negative) experiences than from others' experiences due to the heuristic and egoistic nature of our daily thinking.

Finally, the differentiation of learning into tactic learning (sometimes also called imitation or emulation) and adaptation/strategic learning (e.g., Lebow 1994, 273–6; Levy 1994) should be rejected. This scheme is misleading because learning of any kind is potentially strategic and adaptive. Moreover, this categorizing scheme can only be operationalized *ex post*, thus easily becoming tautological when it is deployed to explain change of agents' idea and behavior.

Selection

We can differentiate two kinds (or levels) of selection in social evolution (Wendt 1999, 100–1). The first is the elimination and retaining of specific ideas (and behaviors entailed by ideas) via our mental exercise. Apparently, the first kind, which is nearly constant and can often be instantaneous, is covered under negative learning (see above). Since the first kind of selection is covered under negative learning, selection below means the second kind of selection.

The second kind of selection is the eliminating and retaining of some units within a system, a process that often simultaneously eliminates some of the ideas and behaviors possessed by those eliminated units. A weaker form of the second type of selection is that a unit is punished if it: (1) misreads the physical environment; (2) behaves without learning the proper lessons from its own or others' experiences within the system; and (3) violates the rules (normative or not) with a system. This second kind of selection is what Waltz meant by selection, although he may well deny that violating normative rules carries much of a cost in international politics (1979, 73–7, 118–19; 1986, 330–1; 1988, 618).[36] Most IR theorists have also forgotten that units' misreading of their physical environment constitutes a key cause of being punished in any biological and social systems.

Overall, this second kind of selection tends to be irregular and slow. Moreover, this kind of selection does not necessarily entail a complete elimination of a particular behavior or unit: Within a particular system, several types of behavior and units can exist side by side.[37] Finally, this selection via eliminating (and retaining) some units within a system has become rare in the post-offensive realism world, although it had been a powerful (but never instantaneous) force in shaping international politics for much of our history (see Chapters 2 and 3 above). As such, units in today's international system can now afford to commit more errors!

Constituting

We can broadly define *constituting* or *constructing* of agents as the process through which agents' *consciously* internalize ideas (norms, ideas, institutions, memories, code of conduct, self-identity, etc.) and the process through which agents are *unconsciously* penetrated by ideas within the international system, in the Foucauldian sense. Of course, conscious internalization and unconscious penetration often mutually reinforce each other within a social system

(Elias [1939]1994; Foucault 1980; 2000), and it is not easy to clearly separate these two processes.

Here, it is important to differentiate this process of constituting agents from the process through which a system is constituted or constructed. The latter is the process through which agents' behaviors and their interaction with the system construct (or remake) the system. In contrast, the former is the process through which agents' ideas and behaviors are shaped by the system. There is no doubt that the two processes constantly interact with and thus "mutually constitute" each other. Agents, through their behaviors and their interaction with the system, construct (or make) the system, and the constantly-being-constructed system then comes back to re-shape agents' behaviors. Yet, collapsing the two processes altogether runs the risk of falling into logical circularity.

Anti-socialization (or ideational resistance)

Anti-socialization is inherent in any social system with a minimal degree of socialization, usually through institutionalization, indoctrination, and penetration that are almost always backed by power.[38] Essentially, anti-socialization is the process through which, agents consciously resist the socializing pressure from the system. Anti-socialization is thus a (dialectical) consequence of socialization: without socialization, there is no anti-socialization (Tang 2011b).

At the beginning of our group living, the institutional structure was sparse. As such, socialization was relatively weak and anti-socialization was perhaps even weaker. As a society's institutional structure becomes denser and more rigid, however, socialization becomes more pervasive and suffocating (Elias 1939[1994]; Freud 1961).[39] This increasing institutionalization (or "rationalization") of a society and indoctrination and penetration of agents, invariably backed by power, inevitably drives some units to anti-socialization: there is a dialectic relationship between socialization and anti-socialization (Tang 2011a; 2011b). As Foucault (1988, 123) put it, "As soon as there is a power relation, there is a possibility of resistance. We can never be ensnared by power: we can always modify its grip in determinate conditions and according to a precise strategy."

In international politics in particular, "South–South Cooperation" reflects developing states' attempt to rebel against the reigning Western-centric order (whether they have succeeded in their endeavor is another matter). The call for (and possible coming of) non-Western perspectives and even "non-Western IR theories" signals an all too apparent revolt against the Anglo-Saxon hegemony in IR theories (e.g., Ayoob 2002; Kang 2003; Amitav and Buzan 2009; Ringmar 2012). "Dependency theories" (Smith 1979) and Edward Said's (1978) great polemic *Orientalism* are resisting attempts on the intellectual front in the broad and supposedly value-neutral social sciences that have long been dominated by Western ideas and biases (see also Said 1993).

Here, it is also important to recognize that anti-socialization does not necessarily have to be driven by agents' urge to re-shape a system (not to mention overthrow the system and erect a new system). Acts of anti-socialization, even if successful, do not necessarily lead to a transformation of the system. Finally, anti-socialization is different from realists' notion of balancing. Whereas anti-socialization is mostly a form of ideational resistance or struggle against the dominant/dominating ideas within a system, an agent's balancing is mostly a "physical" exercise against a particular agent and its targets do not have to be the dominant hegemon.

B. Implications for Theorizing State Behavior: the Five Channels as a System

Among the five channels, constraining/enabling is evidently the most foundational.[40] Learning comes next: Ideas do not grow out of nowhere, and they can only be generated by some kind of learning. Selection, by itself alone, cannot possibly generate an idea or behavior: it merely selects the things out there. Selection of units in social system operates upon units that have been shaped by learning, not upon a blank slate. Constituting too depends on learning although learning does not necessarily lead to constituting: it is impossible to constitute an agent without learning. Anti-socialization too depends on learning: unless agents learn something about (the nature of) the dominant ideas, agents cannot resist those ideas.

Yet, the most critical point here is that the five channels constitute a system—they work together rather than independently to shape units' ideas, identity, behavior, and thus, the nature of the system (including structure). As such, it is profoundly misleading to single out one or two channels while neglecting the rest or to merely admit the five channels but take them to be independent of each other. Unfortunately, all major grand theories of IR have committed this error, one way or another: each of them accuses others for neglecting the channel(s) it favors while forgiving its own sin. Thus, neoliberalists rightly fault realists for marginalizing learning (e.g., Keohane 1986), whereas constructivists rightly fault realists and neoliberalists for neglecting constituting (e.g., Wendt 1999), and realists rightly accuse neoliberalists and constructivists for forgetting selection (e.g., Waltz 1986, 330–2; Feaver et al. 2000, 166–7).

Waltz singles out selection via elimination of units and other less punishment but denies learning (and constituting/constructing) any role in shaping states' behavior.[41] Most prominently, Waltz (1979, 74–8, 127–8) insists that selection (of balancing behavior) can operate without learning. Yet, as correctly pointed out by many (Keohane 1986, 164–5, 173; Levy 1994; Elman 1996, 42–4; Taliaferro 2000–1, 138), Waltz's scheme of balancing (against capability) fundamentally depends upon learning: unless states can learn about others' capabilities, states cannot know against whom to balance.[42] Inevitably, Waltz later on had to admit that learning is essential for his theory of balancing-of-power, although he used "imitation" (1986, 331)!

As constructivists like to point out (e.g., Wendt 1999; Johnston 2001, 488–94), scholars in the more rational choice approach—both realists and neoliberalists are adherents of rational choice—emphasize selection and learning but downgrade constituting.[43] Yet, constituting does occur, perhaps far more frequently and pervasively than its proponents and opponents recognized. Waltz (1979) was certainly constituted by his concern for the stability and peacefulness of Cold War bipolarity whereas Keohane (1984) by his concern for the stability of the post-the Second World War U.S.-centric international system (Ayoob 2002, esp. 32–7; Craig 2003).

Hence, it is untenable for realists, neoliberalists, and other rational choice theorists to deny constituting a role in shaping states' behavior (and in turn, in shaping the international system). Ideas do spread and some ideas do penetrate deeply into our body and soul, to paraphrase Foucault (1980). When we internalize some ideas, these ideas can indeed come to shape our behavior, often unconsciously (Elias 1939[1994]; Foucault 2000). Although it is often difficult to assess the exact weight of constituting versus learning/selection/anti-socialization in shaping a particular behavior (and thus social outcome) in a given condition (Jervis 1997; Tang 2011b), it is wrong to deny that we do internalize ideas. Certainly, the spreading of ideas such as sovereignty and nationalism and their internalizations by states and IR theorists has played a critical role in shaping modern international politics and IR as a science (Bull and Watson 1984; Spruyt 2000; Anghie 2004; see Chapter 3 above).

Meanwhile, most constructivists emphasize positive learning and constituting (e.g., Adler 1997a; Adler and Barnett 1998, 43–5; Wendt 1999, esp. 324–36; Checkel 2001; Johnston 2001; Acharya 2004), but neglects negative learning (as a form of selection) and especially the selection of units in history.[44] Yet, at the unit level, negative learning is indispensable for positive learning: without the former, the latter has no foundation. Many of the ideas that are there for positive learning are first put into firmer place via negative learning: without some kind of negative learning, units simply cannot judge which idea is good and which is bad. Constituting also demands some selection pressure upon units (i.e., there is some kind of sanction against violation), although not necessarily by eliminating units. Unless units are punished somewhat regularly when they depart from the (normative) culture of a system, the culture has little bite and thus at most a weak foundation to last. Moreover, consistent with constructivism's functionalism and idealism/utopian origin (Sterling-Folker 2000), constructivists tend to emphasize the internationalization of the dominant good ideas (e.g., Checkel 2001; Johnston 2001), but generally ignore the possibility that units can internalize bad ideas (e.g., accepting a misleading conceptualization of the system, following a misleading code of conduct, and acquiring a false consciousness). Yet, European powers' internalization of Geopolitics/Social Darwinism and modern Imperial Japan's internalization of the dominant ideas of "civilized nations" brought only disasters to others and eventually themselves (Schweller 2006; Suzuki 2009).

Lastly, almost all major grand theories of IR have neglected anti-socialization as a key channel through which a system affects units. As such, they easily fall into the Parsonian functionalism fallacy of "over-socialized men (or units)" and then use "over-socialized" units to explain the stability of a social system (Wrong 1961; see also Sterling-Folker 2000; Goddard and Nexon 2005). Only by recognizing anti-socialization as a key channel can we avoid this typical fallacy of Parsonian functionalism (Tang 2011a; 2011b).

In sum, within any social system, agents' behaviors are shaped by the five channels as a system, underpinned by the various forces and dimensions in human society. As such, it is profoundly misleading to single out one or two channels, or admit the five channels but think they work independently to shape units' behaviors. Instead, we have to take the five channels as a system and admit that it is through systemic effects that units' behaviors are eventually shaped by the five channels.

C. Wanting Debates: An Illustration

Because major grand theories of IR tend to emphasize one or two channels while neglecting others or treat the five channels as independent, many existing debates on state behaviors in IR have been misleading: they reflect a lack of systemic understanding of how the system drives state behavior. I illustrate with one case.

On the one hand, many critics of realism contend that realism is invalidated whenever states behave differently from realism's selection-based predictions/prescriptions for states' behavior (e.g., Keohane 1986, 182–3; Lebow 1994, 274; Schroeder 1994a, esp. 116–23). This reflects a lack of appreciation of the centrality of (negative) selection of units through punishment (sometimes by death) in realism on the part of realism's critics.

Realists since Waltz have explicitly emphasized the channel of (negative) selection of units through punishment in shaping states' behavior (Waltz 1979; 1986; Jervis 1997, 118–9). Hence, realism is "as much about the *consequences* of behavior as about the *determinants* of behavior" (Feaver 2000, 166; emphasis original). As such, the fact that a state has not acted according to realism's prescriptions (i.e., realism failed to predict the state's behavior) does not automatically disprove realism per se.[45] This is so not only because realism does allow the possibility that a state may act in violation of realism's pre-scriptions for whatever reason, but more importantly because realism also asserts that the state will pay a price—sometimes a heavy price—for doing so (Waltz 1979; 1986; Feaver 2000, 166–7). In other words, realism not only prescribes (or preaches) certain behaviors, it also asserts that failing to heed those prescriptions will bring losses if not ruins. *As a result, if a state violates realism's prescriptions but then gets punished, realism is actually validated.*

Thus, the fact that Britain and France (and many other European states) failed to robustly balance the looming threat from Hitler's Germany does not disprove realism per se, as many critics of realism believed (e.g., Lebow 1994, 274; Schroeder 1994a). *In fact, it strongly vindicates the case of realism* because Britain and France were heavily punished for "betraying" realism. Likewise, just because Gorbachev did not behave according to realism's preaching does not invalidate realism either, contra to realism's critics (e.g., Lebow 1994, 259–68): realists can simply counter that Gorbachev and his country were severely punished by some of his un-realism or even anti-realism policies! Similarly, if over-expansion is inconsistent with the specific prescription of defensive real-ism, then the fact that most major attempts of over-expansion after the 19th century had failed strongly supports defensive realism (Jervis 1997, 106; see also Snyder 1991; Tang 2010a)![46]

Realism is thus actually much more difficult to disprove than many of its critics and proponents have believed. To disprove realism, it is not enough to simply show that some states did not act according to realism's rules: *one must also show that those states actually benefited (or prospered) from their viola-tions of realism.*

On the other hand, realists are not entirely off the hook either. Because many realists too have failed to adequately appreciate realism's critical reliance on selection pressure to explain and predict states behavior (e.g., Waltz 1986, 330–2; Elman and Elman 1995),[47] they often amend their theories and thus risk being "degenerative" in the Lakatosian sense, when facing counter evi-dences that certain states did not behave according to what realism preaches (e.g., Schroeder 1994a).[48]

For one thing, many realists have been busy in trying to explaining devi-ations from realism's prescriptions by adding state-level and even psycho-logical variables or adding all kinds of states' behavior to the list of "self-help" or "balancing" (e.g., Elman and Elman 1995; Brooks and Wohlforth 2000–1; Taliaferro 2004). This certainly does not make realism a "progressive" para-digm because it makes realism water-proof from challenges. Indeed, Elman and Elman (1995, 184–6) essentially insisted that states remain consistent with realism as long as they are reacting to external threats, without grasping that this would have reduced realism to minimal rational choice or "minimally strategic" actors. Of course, this will make everybody and nobody a realist (Legro and Moravcsik 1999; see also the pointed rebuttal to Elman and Elman 1995 by Schroeder 1995, 193–5).[49]

Similarly, realists can simply insist that whereas some specific measures that Gorbachev deployed to rescue the Soviet Union from its perilous situation in the mid-1980s may be inconsistent with realism's prescriptions, the outcome of the Cold War in which the United States and its allies came out as the winning side is perfectly consistent with realism's key assumption that material powers determine the outcome of conflictual confrontations. Yet, few realists have explicitly pointed this out but have instead worked hard to label all of Gorbachev's policies as consistent with realism or to repeat/reinforce the argument that the material pressure upon Gorbachev and his colleagues had been so immense that there were only very few choices (e.g., Brooks and Wohlforth 2000–1; see also Schweller and Wohlforth 2000). Yet, as Lebow (1994, 259–68) forcefully pointed out, one is hard pressed to squeeze at least some of Gorbachev's behaviors into the realism straitjacket. And certainly, Gorbachev could have taken several roads not taken (e.g., North Korea, Cuba).

Realists failed to grasp that a far more convincing and productive way to counter their critics is to show that those states that did not act according to realism's prescriptions were indeed (heavily) punished afterwards. More critically, as Feaver (2000, 166–7) forcefully pointed out, realists have yet to operationalize "punishment." To do so, realists have to state explicitly what behaviors are consistent with realism and what are not, and then show that those states that depart from realism's prescriptions have been (severely) punished. This requires realists to go beyond the balance-versus-bandwagon dichotomy and provide a much more nuanced "ladder of choices" for states (e.g., Tang 2010a, ch. 4).

Marginalizing selection as a key channel through which system impacts states also brings perils to constructivism. So far, constructivism has made mostly normative arguments for why states should behave in a certain way, but gives no clue on whether states will be punished if they do not (e.g., Wendt 1999; Adler 2005). Without a selection mechanism, constructivism cannot predict state behavior, but can only preach certain behaviors and hope states heed all its prescriptions.[50] When this is the case, constructivism is extremely vulnerable: all its opponents need to show is that states are not thoroughly socialized. Because anti-socialization is inherent in any social system, this outcome is virtually guaranteed: no social system can completely socialize all the units within it.

In contrast, as noted just above, although realists too prescribe behaviors, realists have a fall back position: selection will eventually drive state into certain behaviors. If constructivism is to have more bite, constructivism, like realism, must specify when it expects states to behave in a certain way, and equally important, whether states will be punished if they fail to do so. Selection must be part of the logic for all major theories of international politics, including constructivism.

CONCLUDING REMARKS: SYSTEM, NOT AGENT-STRUCTURE!

In our century-old obsession with structure, generations of scholars have failed to grasp that structure has never been that forceful in shaping the real world as we have believed. Contra Waltz (1959, 231–2) and many other structuralists before and after him (e.g., Parsons 1937; 1951; Giddens 1979; 1984; Wendt 1999), a structural explanation cannot possibly be a final explanation for anything in society.[51] By exaggerating the impact of structure, structural theories inevitably marginalize, if not totally obscure, the impact of other forces (not just agents) within the social system. Our long obsession with structure and the agent-structure problem has been profoundly misplaced (Loyal and Barnes 2001).

IR's obsession with structure (or more narrowly, anarchy) has been equally fatal. Structure certainly is a key component of any social system, but it is not the whole system, or even the heart of the system: much of the real politics is not dictated by structure alone. By exaggerating the impact of structure, structuralism inevitably obscures, if not eliminates, much real politics from international politics.

Waltz (1979) was certainly correct to argue that structure, as part of the system, has a role in selecting (or shaping) state behavior. Yet, the selection process and its outcome depend on the whole system rather than the structure alone: the system, rather than the structure (not to mention anarchy) alone, selects.[52] The same logic applies to outcomes within systems that are derived from interactions within the system even more powerfully. As such, there is no "logic of anarchy" or even "a logic of structure" (however defined): there is only "a logic of system" (cf. Buzan et al. 1993; Wendt 1999, 247, 249)! Structural theories—with or without agents, thus cannot take us far toward an adequate understanding of international politics, such as conflict and cooperation (e.g., Jervis 1978; Glaser 1994–95; 2010; Van Evera 1999; Wendt 1999; Montgomery 2006; Wight 2006; Sørensen 2008), not to mention the transformation of the international system.

The human society, a system populated by human agents, has always an evolutionary system. The central dynamics within the system and therefore the driving force behind systemic change has always been the interaction between components of the system (structure being only one of them) across time and space. Within the system, components of the system (and therefore the system itself) co-evolve with each other rather than one dictating another.[53] To adequately understand the human society (including international politics), structuralism thus will never do: only SEP (which subsumes SSP and other foundational paradigms) is up for the task. As such, it is high time for social scientists and students of IR to bid adieu to structuralism and embrace

SEP. IR, just like other social sciences, has to become an evolutionary science, rather than merely a structural or even a systemic one. And when we do so, the agent–structure problem, which most reflects our egocentrism or anthropocentrism (Elias [1970] 1978),[54] will be dissolved.

For all structural theories—with or without agent–structure is more or less a straitjacket and agents are essentially zombies under its spell (e.g., Waltz 1979; Keohane 1984; Wendt 1999; Mearsheimer 2001; for a classical critique, see Wrong 1961).[55] This notion is the core assumption (or preaching) of structural functionalism in sociology of the Parsons–Merton kind,[56] which had long since fallen from grace in sociology. IR and other social sciences should follow the suit and say goodbye to structuralism. Structuralism, a "Parsonian nightmare", has haunted social sciences for way too long.[57]

Fundamentally, because structure, however defined, reflects a collectivism (or for Wendt, holism) stand, one commits the grave error of neglecting the paradigm with ontological priority (which is individualism), whenever one starts and then ends with structuralism. To understand human society adequately, we have to start with individualism (states, even individuals) and then synthesize individualism and collectivism organically (for a more detailed discussion, see Tang 2013).

Conclusion

By deploying the social evolution paradigm (SEP), I have been able to offer an endogenous account for the transformation of international politics from the initial paradise-like (but still self-help) anarchy to the "nasty, brutish, and short" Hobbesian (Mearsheimer's) offensive realism world, then to a Lockeian (Jervis's) defensive realism world, and then to a more rule-based world. My exercise thus demonstrates the power of SEP: only (social) evolutionary explanations of human society can be genuinely endogenous and thus complete. In this concluding chapter, I elaborate on the theoretical and policy implications of our social evolutionary interpretation of international politics.

I. SEP AND IR AS AN EVOLUTIONARY SCIENCE

In the preceding chapters, by uncovering the dynamics behind the transformation from a paradise-like world to an offensive realism world and then the transformation from the offensive realism world to a defensive realism world, and then from a defensive realism world to a more rule-based world, I show that the international system has always been an evolutionary system and the fundamental nature of the system can be transformed, even if some features of the system (e.g., anarchy) remain the same. As such, theories that cannot imagine transformations in international politics and believe that international politics will be permanently stuck in a single type of world must be firmly rejected, and theories that admit transformations yet cannot provide endogenous explanations of the transformations must be pushed aside.

Consequently, international politics must be a genuine evolutionary science, and students of international politics must "give Darwin his due".[1] To paraphrase Hermann Muller (1959) (although with a more hopeful note), 150 years without Darwinism in the science of international politics are enough. This demand for an evolutionary perspective has important implications for our understanding the history of international politics at both the micro and the macro levels.[2]

Since the Waltzian structural revolution as a quasi-systemic revolution, students of IR have embraced systemic theories wholeheartedly, and all major grand theories of international politics are quasi or incomplete systemic theories.[3] Yet, systemic theories are merely dynamic theories (i.e., things are constantly interacting with each other within the system, and things do change but the system tends to reproduce itself), but not evolutionary theories. Systemic theories do not specify the condition under which a system can evolve into a different system without an exogenous push. To paraphrase Ruggie (1983, 285), these theories contain only a reproductive logic, but no, or at most a weak, transformational logic.[4] Without an evolutionary element embedded in, a systemic theory of international politics can only hope to understand how a particular system (or the structure as part of a system) shapes state behavior, but cannot possibly understand how a system can evolve into a different system in which the original theory may no longer apply (Cox 1981, 133).[5] Because the system of international politics has been an evolutionary system that has undergone fundamental changes, systemic theories—no matter how sophisticated—can only be adequate for understanding a particular system within a specific time frame, but are inherently incapable of understanding the whole history of international politics. We simply cannot hope to understand the whole history of international politics by imposing a non-evolutionary theory (one or the other) upon an evolutionary system, pretending that the system is not evolutionary.

Our attempt to impose a non-evolutionary theory upon an evolutionary system, I contend, has been the key reason why existing debates between the three major grand theories of international politics (offensive realism, defensive realism, and neoliberalism) could not be resolved.[6] In these debates, proponents of the three major grand theories all strive to prove that their favored theory is the better, if not the best, theory for understanding international politics, thus implicitly striving toward the goal of explaining the whole history of international politics with a single grand theory (e.g., Keohane 1986; Glaser 1994–95; Brooks 1997; Jervis 1999; Wendt 1999; Copeland 2000a; Mearsheimer 1994; idem 2001; Taliaferro 2000-1). This belief in a better or best grand theory of international politics for the whole history of international politics is underpinned by the (implicit) assumption that the fundamental nature of international politics has remained roughly the same. By striving toward the vaulted goal of explaining the whole history of international politics with a single grand theory, we have been implicitly trying to impose non-evolutionary theories upon an evolutionary system. Yet international politics has always been an evolutionary system, and its fundamental nature has undergone transformational changes although some of its properties (e.g., anarchy) persist. As such, to impose a single grand theory on the whole history of international politics cannot but be doomed from the start:

explaining the whole history of international politics with a single grand theory is a mission impossible.

Once we grasp the ultimate reason why the debates among the three grand theories have not been resolved is that the system of international politics has always been an evolutionary system and yet IR has not been an evolutionary science, a neat resolution of the debates becomes evident: *different epochs of international politics may require different grand theories of international politics.* In other words, the three different grand theories may be from and for three different epochs of international politics.[7]

To begin with, offensive realism does not seem to fit well with the historical facts of the Great Power Era. Offensive realism predicts that every great power will seek expansion and conquest until achieving regional hegemony because expansion and conquest are conducive to security. Yet, as Mearsheimer himself admitted, all but one major attempts of expansion in the Great Power Era had failed miserably and their perpetrators were severely punished. If so, then to predict (and recommend) that great powers will continue to pursue expansion is to demand great powers to strive toward the impossible and act against their own interests, thus violating realism's assumption that states are strategic actors. Indeed, states might have known better: offensive realist states have become increasingly rare since the late 19th century (Schweller 2006, 104).

In contrast, defensive realism seems to fit with the history of the Great Power Era much better: Defensive realism predicts that conquest will be difficult and empire will not last, and the history of the Great Power Era seems to show that it had indeed been the case (Kupchan 1984; Snyder 1991; Walt 1987a; 1987b).

From the preceding discussion, it becomes abundantly clear that the reason why defensive realism fits with the historical record of the Great Power Era better than offensive realism does is simply that international politics had begun to evolve toward a defensive realism world by the time of the Great Power Era. By then, the number of states had decreased significantly and the average size of states had increased significantly. Thus, defensive realists happened to look at the right period of history for their theory. In contrast, because international politics had begun to evolve out of the offensive realism world and toward a defensive realism world by the time of the Great Power Era, offensive realists have been looking at the wrong period of history for their theory when focusing on the Great Power Era.

If so, then while both offensive realists and defensive realists strive to draw from and explain the history of the Great Power Era; they should actually focus on two different periods of history for supporting evidence. Offensive realists should look at the pre-Great Power Era for offensive realism whereas defensive realists should look at the Great Power Era for defensive realism. Consequently, although the two strains of realism can be unified methodologically, with defensive realism subsuming offensive realism because possibility is the extreme form of probability, they should not be unified.[8] These two theories are incompatible ontologically——they are from and for two different periods of international politics.

The relationship between neoliberalism and defensive realism is a bit more complex.[9] Robert Jervis (1999, 45, 47) rightly pointed out that "the disagreements between neoliberalism and [defensive] realism have not only been exaggerated, but they have also been misunderstood, . . . and their differences have been at least partly due to they tend to focus on two different domains: Neoliberalism tends to focus issues of international political economy and environment, whereas realism is more interested in international security."[10]

There has, however, been an even more outstanding contrast that Jervis failed to notice. Whereas defensive realism (and realism in general) has tried to examine a long period of history of international politics (post Westphalia or even the whole post-1495 Great Power Era), neoliberalism has rarely ventured into the terrain of international politics before the Second World War: Almost all of the empirical cases that neoliberals claim to support their cases have been from the post-Second World War period, mostly Europe.

Neoliberalism's self-consciously imposed temporal restriction is fundamental—it speaks of something critical about neoliberalism loud and clear. Although neoliberalists have also implicitly strived toward proving that neoliberalism is valid across the entire history of international politics, they have long conceded the temporal limit of neoliberalism: Neoliberalists have known it all along that while their theory is useful for understanding the post-Second World War world, it is largely irrelevant for understanding the pre-Second World War period.

Neoliberalists are right to concede the temporal limit of their theory. A neoliberalism world can only evolve from a defensive realism world, but cannot possibly evolve directly from an offensive realism world. In an offensive realism world in which the logic is to-kill-or-be killed, attempts to pursue cooperation will be generally suicidal, and there will be few, if any, repeated cooperative interactions (Tang 2008a; 2010b, ch. 4).[11]

In contrast, in a defensive realism world in which the logic is to live and let live, cooperation finally becomes a viable means of self-help and repeated cooperation becomes a real possibility (Axelrod 1984; Glaser 1994–95).[12] Moreover, only in a defensive realism world can ideas and norms that evolve from repeated cooperative interactions have a chance of being solidified into institutions. In other words, cooperation as self-help must have a firm objective foundation, and that objective foundation could only be provided by the transformation of an offensive realism world into a defensive realism world. Because the transformation was not firmly completed until after the Second World War, it is no wonder that neoliberalists have self-consciously restricted their cases to the post-Second World War era: what happened before the Second World War is largely irrelevant to neoliberalism!

To summarize, no single grand theory of international politics can cover the entire history of international politics because the nature of international politics has undergone transformational and systemic changes. If so, we must give up the noble but impossible goal of explaining the entire history of international politics with a single grand theory: this is dictated by the ontology of international politics.[13] Instead, a more modest goal of explaining a particular period of international politics with a well-specified grand theory will be more rewarding. In other words, the now increasingly unproductive enterprise pursued by major grand theories of international politics to prove that one's own theory is a "scientifically" superior theory than another should give away to the more productive enterprise of refining individual theories within different historical eras. Indeed, it is impossible to know which grand theory is a scientifically superior theory without first specifying the specific historical epoch that the theory claims to explain: theories of international politics are not timeless.

Finally, the social evolutionary interpretation of international politics also holds some interesting implications for other research programs. For instance, temporally, the emergence of a tenuous "democratic peace (DP)" in history coincided with the evolution from an offensive world to a defensive realism world.[14] As such, a legitimate question will be: what is the relationship, if any, between the evolution from an offensive realism world to a defensive realism world and the making of DP? There are essentially three possibilities. First, the transformation has no relationship with the emergence of DP and DP has its unique origin. Second, the transformation explains much of the increased peace among states, and DP is merely a secondary outcome of the transformation. Third, the transformation underpins the rise of DP: DP is real, but we have missed its more fundamental cause. The same questions can be raised regarding the so-called "dictatorial peace" (Peceny et al. 2002).

II. POLICY IMPLICATIONS: SECURITY-SEEKING, PAST, PRESENT, AND FUTURE

Our recognition that international politics had firmly evolved a paradise-like world to an offensive realism world around 4,000–3,500 BC and then from an offensive realism world into a defensive realism world by the Second World War the latest and that it has been moving toward a world of institutionalized peace in some major regions since 1945 has not only important implications for theorizing international politics, but also important implications for states' seeking security in the present and the future.

Immediately after the Cold War, there was a mini-debate about the future of Europe between Mearsheimer on the one side and Jervis/Van Evera on the other (Mearsheimer 1990; Van Evera 1990–91; Jervis 1991–92). As an offensive realist, Mearsheimer boldly predicted that Europe's past would be its future now that the stabilizing bipolarity had collapsed. In contrast, as defensive realists, Van Evera argued that Europe would not go back to the future, while Jervis cautioned that one cannot predict with much confidence that the future will resemble the present or the past.[15]

Such debates among the major grand theories of international politics about the nature of international politics are not just meaningless and egoistic quarrels among scholars. Instead, these debates bear great relevance for the real world because each grand theory carries implicit and explicit message for states' security strategies.[16] Understanding what kind of world we are live in, therefore, is of crucial importance to how we live the world today and what kind of world we are going to live in the future.

Underscoring the evolutionary nature of international politics, our discussion has firmly established that different theories of international politics are from and thus *for* different epochs of international politics. More specifically, Mearsheimer was right, but is wrong and will be wrong: his policy prescriptions will produce disasters in today's and tomorrow's world. In contrast, Jervis was wrong—his policy prescriptions would be suicidal in an offensive realism world—but he has been right and may remain right for a while. Finally, Keohane was wrong—his policy prescription too would be suicidal in an offensive realism world—but he might have become more right after the Second World War and may become more right in the future. Put it differently, whereas offensive realism is a theory for the past, defensive realism is a theory for the present and a limited future and neoliberalism is a theory for a limited present and more the future.

Because different theories of international politics are from and for different epochs of international politics, explaining a past epoch of international politics well should not automatically give a theory the claim that it is the better or the best theory for guiding states' security policies in the present or the future. A theory that can explain our past well may well be a good theory "scientifically", but it may not be a good guide to our present or future: indeed, it may be the exact opposite! If so, when a state is to decide on a particular grand theory of international politics for guiding its policies, the state cannot decide solely on the theory's scientific merit, but must first determine what kind of world we are living in and whether a theory is the right theory for our world.[17] It will be a grave mistake to guide policies for one epoch with a grand theory from and for anther epoch *even if* the chosen grand theory is a good theory "scientifically".

In an offensive realism world, a defensive realism state will be a sucker, and it will be either eliminated or socialized into an offensive realist. In contrast, in a defensive realism world, an offensive realism state (an atavistic predator state) will be severely punished. In a world that has been becoming more rule-based (especially after the Cold War?), an offensive realism strategy will be utterly dangerous, whereas a defensive realism strategy will be less productive than a neoliberalism one but much less dangerous than an offensive realism one.

To return to the Mearsheimer versus Van Evera and Jervis debate, our discussion should have firmly put the debate to rest. By establishing that international politics has always been an evolutionary system and uncovering the dynamics of the evolutionary process, our discussion strongly suggests that international politics had firmly evolved from an offensive realism world into a defensive realism world and beyond. If so, then although we cannot teleologically predict the future,[18] we can confidently proclaim that international politics will not go back to the "nasty, brutish, and short" world of offensive realism or go through (long) cycles, because an evolutionary system simply does not go backwards or through cycles. As a result, offensive realism cannot possibly be a good guide for states' security strategies today.

Most states are still living in defensive realism subsystems. As a result, defensive realism should be a better guide for most states' security strategies today (Tang 2010b). Cooperation in such a world will still be hard to come by: the road to cooperation is usually more tortuous than the road to conflict. Yet, cooperation is inherently possible in such a world (Jervis 1999; Kydd 2005; Tang 2008a; 2010b). Moreover, the defensive realism world contains the seeds for a more rule-based world as states increasingly institutionalize rules that facilitate peace and cooperation.

So how are we to behave in such a world? I suggest four key measures. Foremost, (defensive realist) states should reach for cooperation whenever possible, according to the operational code of defensive realism (Tang 2010a). Second, states should regularize cooperation with institutions (or rules) whenever possible. Third, states should socialize each other with welfare-improving rules and further hope that each of them can internalize these formal and informal rules and eventually take those welfare-improving rules as part of their value system and thus identity. Fourth, we have to be mindful that even in such an increasingly rule-based world, some actors will still break some rules. The key to this problem is to enforce rules without violence, whenever possible. All these measures will make our world more rule-based and better.

For states already in more mature rule-based systems (e.g., the European Union and perhaps MERCOSUR too), their tasks are less demanding: all they need to do is to follow the rules of their rule-based world, in a much more conducive environment.

APPENDIX I

Evidences from Ethnographic Anthropology

As noted in Chapter 2, ethnographic anthropology has contributed critical knowledge to our understanding of the origin of war. This short appendix summarizes some key evidences from ethnographic anthropology that support our theory, in addition to the evidences cited in the main text. For more information, interested readers should consult excellent surveys of the vast literature by Keeley (1996), Kelly (2000), and Ferguson (2006), but especially the more critical surveys by van der Dennen (1995; 2007) and Fry (2006).

Relative Population Pressure and Competition for Resources as a Necessary (if Not Sufficient) Cause of War

Our theory suggests that a high relative population pressure (rather than absolute population density per se) that crosses a certain threshold level and hence the necessity of competing for scare resources within a circumscribed ecosystem is a necessary, if not sufficient, cause for the outbreak of war within the system. Important evidences that support our theory came from Keeley (1988; 1996, 117–21): he found that relative population pressure is closely correlated with warfare. Additionally, Keeley (1996, 138–41) noted that "hard times" tend to coincide with more wars among groups. The tragedy unfolded on the Eastern Island in Polynesia also supports the notion that the necessary competition for resources as dictated by a high relative population pressure is a necessary and sufficient cause of war (Keegan 1993, 25–30; Diamond 1997).[1]

Becoming sedentary tends to thrust groups into a more profound sense of territoriality, and this in turn entails a more profound appreciation of the necessity of defense. Mobile hunter-and-gathering groups have experienced few, if any, wars. In contrast, even semi-nomadic groups with a more heightened sense of territoriality tend to experience wars (Kelly 2000). Indeed, Soltis, Boyd and Richerson (1995) found that more than half of the wars in Irian Jaya Papa New Guinea recorded in their dataset were caused by competition for territory. More interestingly, newly sedentary foragers tend to become associated with more hierarchical social organizations (Kent 1989; cf. Knauft 1990b), and as Kelly (2000) argued, segmented groups tend to associate with warfare.

Indirect supporting evidences come from Chagnon (1968[1997]), showing that war among the Yąnomamös has not been as intense and brutal as the major subsystems detailed in Chapter 2 above. Among the Yąnomamös, war exists but usually in the form of raiding rather than outright conquest for the sake of occupying territory. Because the Yąnomamös have a relatively small population over a vast (but rapidly shrinking!) territory and thus a low relative population pressure, the fact that they exhibit less intense and brutal warfare supports our thesis that high relative population pressure has been a key driver behind the outbreak and intensification of warfare.

Warfare among Primitive Peoples Could Be Very Frequent, Brutal, and Total

Keeley (1996) provided the broadest and finest survey on this front. More specifically, his many tables showed that (1) primitive wars among smaller groups can mobilize a similar proportion of the whole male population as modern states in modern wars (as high as 40 per cent); (2) the casualty rate in primitive warfare tends to be much higher than wars between modern states, sometimes reaching 100 per cent; (3) the percentage of death due to warfare in primitive warfare can be as high as 40 per cent of the total population (33–6, 63–6, 83–97, 173–7, 189, 194–7). Likewise, Ember and Ember (1998, 5, table 1.1) showed that among the 90 primitive groups that were not pacified by Western colonial power, war was constant in a full 56.66 per cent of these communities and only 9 per cent of groups had not experienced war or only rarely.

Some subsystems degenerated into systems of brutal warfare after the coming of the West: their developments unfolded before the eyes of Western ethnographers. These systems have come from Africa (e.g., the Zulu empire), Oceania (Maori versus Marooi), and Hawaii (Keegan 1993, 24–32; 103–6; Diamond 1997; Flannery 1999). For additional evidences from other parts of the world, see Keeley 1996; Martin and Frayer 1998. These evidences testify the similar path taken by different subsystems.

Before the Standing Army: Training and Tactics

As noted in Chapter 2, small communities cannot afford to field a standing army. As a result, training in combat skills and tactics within these communities generally cannot reach the same level of training for standing armies in the past and today. This explains why Turney-High (1949[1991]) found many deficiencies in primitive warfare such as lack of discipline, lack of concentration, and deficiencies in modern formation and formal tactics. Yet, none of these "shortcomings" suggests that primitive warriors were less capable than their modern counterparts: indeed, the exact opposite may be true (Keeley 1996, 42–8, 173–6). Also, some small communities have managed to adopt some of the key measures for grooming warriors and training them in skills and tactics. For instance, both the Kayapó of central Brazil and the Masai of East Africa developed the system of dividing males into age groups that would eventually turn young males into a warrior caste/class, in striking similarity to the Spartan system in ancient Greece (Carneiro 2000, 12929).

War Tends to Spread

Citing Jorgen Jorgensen's study of Indian warfare, Keeley (1996, 127–8) noted that wars tended to be clustered rather than uniformly distributed and speculated that one factor that intensifies warfare is an aggressive neighbor (i.e., a "rotten apple").

Kelly's (2000, esp. ch. 3) study of the Andaman Islanders also strongly points to the possibility that the ancestors of Andaman Islanders had experienced war and they had also learned war from more recent intruders. Unfortunately, Kelly does not appreciate the profound implication of this fact for his theory of the origin of war.

Supplementary Tables for Chapter 2

Table S2.1. The Origin and Spread of War in Ancient Mesopotamia and Egypt (all years in BC)

Mesopotamia, including northern Syria Zagros and Taurus Mtns.	Egypt
Akkadian Empire: 2350–2100. War became rampant and total, and remained so for a long period of time. Evidences: the establishment a 5000 strong standing army by King Sargon, the Stele of Naram-Sin (reign 2254–2218), and other martial arts.[1]	Middle Kingdom: 2061/2055/2040 to 1730/1650/1569. War stayed total whenever occurred, as in the preceding period.[2]
Sumerian Early Dynastic Period: 2900–2350. War became extremely rampant, some well recorded (i.e., the Lagash-Umma conflict): The "Standard of Ur" (c.2550) and the "Stele of the Vultures" (c.2425).[3] Other evidences: weapons (including war chariots), many arts depicting siege, burials with weapons, monuments with sacrifices, scalping of skulls/ sacrifices, and mass graves.	Intermediate years: 2190/2160 to 2061/2055/2040. Old Kingdom, III–VIII: 2770/2686/2650 to 2190/2160. War stayed total whenever occurred. War, however, usually only occurred when the hegemonic Egyptian kingdom weakened or when the kingdom campaigned against external enemies. Abundant evidences of warfare: steles, monuments, Pyramid texts, martial arts.[4]
Jemdet Nasr period: 3100–2900. Fortified cities, some evidences of warfare?	Early Dynastic Period, O, I–II: 3200/ 3150–2770/2686/2650. War stayed rampant and total. Abundant evidences of warfare: e.g., the famous "Narmer palette" (c.3040) showing killing of captives and execution, massive fortification, naval battle.[5]
Uruk phase (late, middle, early): 4000–3100. Uruk emerged as the first city around 4000. Fortified cities, some evidences of warfare?	Naqada I–III period (i.e., Predynastic): 4000–3150/3200. Warfare appeared and quickly became rampant and brutal: fortification, mace, war-gods, martial arts (e.g., the "Battlefield Palette"), sacrifice of captives.[6] The transition period between Late Neolithic and Predynastic (c.5000–4000): Villages appeared. Few, if any, evidences of warfare.
Ubaid Phase: 5500–4000 (Ubaid replacing Halaf, around 4500 in northern and central Mesopotamia). Eridu (southern Mesopotamia): 5700–4750. Few signs of warfare.	6000/5500–5000 (Early and Middle Neolithic): Badarian culture. Agriculture appeared. No sign of warfare.
Halaf replacing Hassuna and Samarra culture around 5000.	10000/9000–6000/5500: Epipaleolithic (or Mesolithic).

(Continued)

Table S2.1. Continued

Mesopotamia, including northern Syria Zagros and Taurus Mtns.	Egypt
Hassuna Culture (North), Samarra (Central). Evidence of war (rare): Fortification at Samarra (6000–5000).[7]	Domestication of plants and animals began. No sign of warfare.
Late Paleolithic (13000–10000): Natufian Culture (early and late).	Late Paleolithic (22000–10000/9000) No sign of warfare, other than Gebel Sahaba or Site 117 as a unique site of war, dated around 12,000–10,000.

The chronology of Mesopotamia combines Cryer 1995, 660–1; Van De Mieroop 2007, p. 14, and McIntosh 2005, appendix 1, "Chronology", 349–60; and Gnira 1999, 71 2.

The chronology of Egypt combines Khurt 1995, table 10 (p. 128), table 11 (p. 136); Shaw 2000, 479–80; Wenke 2009, table 5.1 (pp. 197–8); and Hamblin 2006, table 12.1 (p. 310). These authors use roughly the same chronology. See also Wilkinson 1999, 27.

For a discussion on the chronology of the Near East, see Cryer, Federick, 1995. "Chronology: Issues and Problems." In Jack M. Sasson et al. (eds.) *Civilizations of the Ancient Near East*, New York, NY: Charles Scribner's Sons, 651–64.

For introductory and in-depth discussion on the archaeology of ancient Near East, especially Mesopotamia, see:

Maisels, Charles Keith. 1993. *The Near East: Archaeology in the Cradle of Civilization.* London: Routledge.

Matthews, Roger. 2003. *The Archaeology of Mesopotamia: Theories and Approaches.* London: Routledge.

For general introduction to the Great Near East, see Redman, Charles. 1978. *The Rise of Civilization: From Early Farmers to Urban Society in the Ancient Near East.* San Francisco, C. A.: W. H. Freeman and Company. This is a somewhat dated survey but it is excellent in terms of its attempt to synthesize the available evidence into a more or less evolutionary interpretation of the ancient Near East. Unfortunately, as most "evolutionary" literature in anthropology of this time, its evolutionary flavor mostly rests on getting the stages and time sequences right, and the central mechanism of social evolution has no place within it.

Other excellent general survey is Maisels, Charles Keith. 1990. *The Emergence of Civilizations: From hunting and gathering to agriculture, cities, and the state in the Near East.* London: Routledge.

Also useful is Kuhrt, Amelie, 1995. *The Ancient Near East, c. 3000–330 BC.* 2 vols. London: Routledge.

For a collective of anthropological perspectives on the formation of states in the ancient Near East based on archaeological evidences, see Stein, Gil and Mitchell Rothman (eds.) 1994. *Chiefdoms and Early States in the Near East: The Organizational Dynamics of Complexity.* Madison, WI: Prehistory Press.

Two general texts are extremely informative:

Sasson, Jack M., et al. (eds.) 1995. *Civilizations of the Ancient Near East.* New York, NY: Charles Scribner's Sons.

Myers, Eric M. (ed.). 1997. *The Oxford Encyclopedia of Archaeology of the Near East.* Oxford: Oxford University Press.

On Ancient Mesopotamia in particular, see:

Pollock, Susan.1999. *Ancient Mesopotamia: The Eden That Never War.* Cambridge: Cambridge University Press.

McIntosh, Jane R. 2005. *Ancient Mesopotamia: New Perspectives.* Santa Barbara, CA: ABC Clio Press.

Van De Mieroop, Marc. 2007. *A History of the Ancient Near East, ca. 2000–323 BC.* 2nd edn., Malden, MA: Blackwell. (The title of the book is misleading, because the book really only focuses on Mesopotamia rather than the entire Ancient Near East.)

On Ancient Egypt in general, see:

Kemp, Barry J. 1993. *Ancient Egypt: The Anatomy of a Civilization.* London: Routledge.

Shaw, Ian. (eds.) 2000. *The Oxford History of Ancient Egypt.* Oxford: Oxford University Press.

Wenke, Robert J. 2009. *The Ancient Egyptian State: The Origins of Egyptian Culture, c. 8000–2000 BC.* Cambridge: Cambridge University Press, esp. chs. 4, 5, and 6.

See also the chapters on Egypt in Kuhrt 1995; Hamblin 2006; and entries in Sasson et al. 1995.

For more specialized topics on Egypt, see:

Wilkinson, Toby A. H. 1999. *Early Dynastic Egypt.* London: Routledge.

Spalinger, Anthony J. 2005. *War in Ancient Egypt: The New Kingdom.* Malden, MA: Blackwell.

For warfare in the Ancient Near East, see Hamblin, William J. 2006. *Warfare in the Ancient Near East to 1600 BC: Holy Warriors at the Dawn of History.* London: Routledge. This is a comprehensive treatment on warfare in the Ancient Near East, containing a wealth of information.

Table S2.2. The Origin and Spread of War in Ancient China (all dates in BC)

Time Period	Name of Culture/Major Sites	Evidences of Warfare
Eastern Zhou (Spring and Autumn/Warring States, 771–221BC) Western Zhou (1046–771BC) Late Bronze age to Iron age	Numerous cites Numerous cites	War became extremely rampant and well recorded; wars were first recorded in texts on oracles (especially conquests) and then on bronze, bamboo pieces, and silk. Very sophisticated weapons; All cities were protected by walls and moats.
Shang (c.1700–1046BC): middle to late Bronze age	Yin Xu (安阳殷墟), late Shang Er-li-gang (二里岗), middle Shang Er-li-tou (二里头/late phases), early Shan (with residues of late Xia?).	War became extremely rampant, some well recorded; Most, if not all, cities were protected with walls with stamped earth, moats, and fortress. Burials with weapons (e.g., chariots, *ge*) became standard for noble

(Continued)

Table S2.2. Continued

Time Period	Name of Culture/Major Sites	Evidences of Warfare
		males. Scalping of skulls, sacrifices, mass graves with signs of violent death.[8] Well developed ancient states (Shang): more hierarchical, with more elaborate rituals. Other symbols of power appeared (e.g., chariot, bronze).
Xia (c.2200–1700BC): early to middle Bronze age	Er-li-tou (二里头/early phases): archaic state (late Xia?) Xin-zha/新砦 (transition between Lung-shan and Er-li-tou (early Xia?) Lung-shan/龙山(later phases)	War became rampant, but not well recorded. New weapons introduced: chariots, light bronze weaponry. Many cited had walls made from stamped earth, moats, and fortress. Burials with weapons rare and few in number and type. Scalping of skulls/sacrifices, mass graves.[9] More symbols of power appeared (e.g., bronze, *ge*).
Pre-three dynasties period (c.3000–2200 BC): Late Long-shan phase, age of legendary kings (i.e., Huang Ti; Zhuan Xu; Rao; Xun; Yu)[10] Late Neolithic age and copper/ early Bronze age	Long-shan/龙山 (Yellow River Basin)[11] Liang-zhu/良渚 (Yangtze Delta), archaic state[12] [Hung-shan/红山 (Northeastern China)	War became frequent, but not well recorded. Some cites already had wall made from stamped earth, moats, and other fortification. (e.g., stone citadels). Villages protected by ditches/fence, Burials with stone weapons rare/few in number and types. Scalping of skulls/ sacrifices, mass graves. Symbols of power (jade, and weapons "yue") appeared.[13] The first archaic state in the ancient Chinese system formed: the Liang-zhu state
4000–3000BC (Late Neolithic Age): late Yan-shao period and early Long-shan (Lung-shan) Period	Northern China: Yan-shao/ 仰韶(late); Ta-wen-kou/大汶口(late) Southern China(Yangtze Delta and Lake Tai area): Ho-mu-tu/河姆渡(late); Ma-chia-pang/马家浜(late) Northeastern China: Hung-shan/红山 Northwest China: Ma-jia-yao/马家窑	War definitely existed then. War became more frequent, than previous period?[14] Some walled cities with stamped earth/ditches appeared. Many village protected by ditches and fence. Some symbols of power (jade, pottery) appeared?

5000–4000 BC (Late Neolithic Age): early Yang Shao period	Northern China: Yan-shao/仰韶(early)/Pan-Po(半坡); Ta- wen-kou/大汶口 (early) Southern China(Yangtze Delta and Lake Tai area): Ho-mu-tu/He-mu-du/河姆渡; Ma-chia-pang/马家浜 (early)	Settlements spreading to large areas, more settlements. Settled agriculture became common. Rice cultivation appeared. Forensic evidences of war are rare, but war most likely had originated: villages with palisade with baffled gates and moats, several fortified sites.[15]
Middle Neolithic Age (c.7000–5000BC): Pei-li-gang period; Ho-mu-tu period.	Northern China: Pei-li-gang/裴李岗 Southern China: Pengtoushang/彭头山	Settlements sporadic, initial appearance of settled agriculture. Rice cultivation appeared (Pengtoushang/彭头山). Virtually no evidence of war. Moat appeared, but mostly for the sake of protection from beasts (Pengtoushang/彭头山).
Early Neolithic Period (c.9000–7000 BC)	Northern China: Nanzhuantou/南庄头, Dong Hulin/东胡林, Yujiagou/于家沟etc Southern China: Yuchanyan/玉蟾岩, Diaotunghuan/吊桶环, Xiangren Cave/仙人洞, 甑皮岩/Zengpiyan etc.,	No evidence of warfare. No signs of settled agriculture. Pottery appeared. Confirmed sites: >10

Main sources of evidences from Chang 1986, esp. chs. 3, 4, and 5; Chang 2005; Chang and Xu 2005; Du 2007, esp. 14–27; Liu 2004; Liu 2010; Zheng 2005; Zhou and Wu 2004. Kwang-chih Chang's (1986) fabulous *The Archaeology of Ancient China* remains a standard but dated introduction. For more recent authoritative surveys of the archaeological evidences from China, see Liu 2004; Zheng 2005; and entries by Zhu and Tang in Liu 2010. I also draw from Cioffi-Revilla (2000), table 1 and Otterbein (2004, 160, table 6.4).

Table S2.3. The Origin and Spread of War in North Coastal Peru and Valley of Oaxaca

North Coastal Peru: Chavin/Moche	*Valley of Oaxaca/Zapotec*
600–1470 AD (the late horizon), war continued to be brutal and rampant. Rival kingdoms/empires (e.g., Wari empire) fought each other for conquest and prestige.	100BC–100 AD, war stayed brutal and rampant. Zapotec expanded outside the valley, erected a skull rack. Competitions between Zapotec, Mixtec, and Teotihuacan intensified.
200 BC–600 AD (the early intermediate and middle horizon"), war stayed brutal and rampant. Rival states/kingdoms (Chavin and Moche) fought each other.	500–100 BC, war stayed brutal and rampant. Conquest of the whole valley by Monte Alban I (originally the people at San Jose Mogote), and the Zapotec state formed. Evidences: numerous monuments with execution,

(Continued)

Table S2.3. Continued

North Coastal Peru: Chavin/Moche	Valley of Oaxaca/Zapotec
	hieroglyphic evidences of sacrifice and conquest, elite warrior classes.
900–200 BC (the early horizon/period). War stayed brutal and rampant. States existed. Evidences: Chavin expansion, fortification, sacrifice, trophy heads, monuments in the form of pyramid.	850–500 BC, war became brutal and rampant. Evidence: escalating of raiding, fortified villages/towns, extensively burnt village remains and villages, burials with weapons, monuments with execution and other hieroglyphic evidences of sacrifice and conquest (i.e., Monument 3).
2000/1800–900 BC ("the initial period"). War became brutal and perhaps rampant. Evidences: weapons abundant, warrior class emerged, iconographic evidences (e.g., decapitations, trophy heads, and body parts).[16]	1600–850 BC: raiding/war became more frequent. Evidences: villages expanded and their numbers increased, raiding intensified, palisade appeared and burned.[17]
3000–2000/1800 BC (late pre-ceramic period). Permanent settlements became normal. Public space with monuments appeared. War appeared in the late part of this period. Evidences: weapons (including club, spear, and slings), headless skeletons and mutilated skulls.	2050–1600 BC: villages appeared, raiding appeared shortly?
4500–3000 BC (early Preceramic period). Hunting and gathering groups, semi-permanent settlements most. No war.	8050–2050 BC: Hunting and gathering groups. No war

On Peru, chronology and evidences are drawn from Haas et al. 1987; Burger 1989; 1995, 230–1; Cioffi-Revilla 2000; Stanish 2001; Otterbein 2004, 130–42; Pozorski and Pozorski 1987, chart 1; and Pozorski and Pozorski 2006.

On Zapotec, chronology and evidences are drawn from Marcus and Flannery 1996; Blanton et al. 1999; Cioffi-Revilla 2000; Spencer 2003; Spencer and Redmond 2001; 2004; Flannery and Marcus 2003; Otterbein 2004, 121–30, and Joyce 2010.

Table S2.4. The Origin and Spread of War in Ancient Anatolia (all dates in BC)

Middle to late Bronze Age (2000–12000)	The rise of Old Hittite state (1c.1650–1500) and New Hittite states (c.1400–1200) versus Assyrian colonies. War was rampant and brutal. Abundant evidences: sophisticated fortifications weapons, written records in Hittite and Assyrian.[18]
Early Bronze age (3000–2000)	Age of warring city states (e.g., Troy, Hattusas). War became widespread. Abundant evidences: sophisticated fortifications, symbols of power, weapons, and mass graves (e.g., Titrish Huyuk). Mersin (c.4500): strong fortification with numerous weapons.

Chalcolithic age (c.5500–3000)	Arslantete (3300–3000): fortifications and ruins, weapons, site of the Uruk expansion Korucutepe (c.3500–3000): warrior burials with weapons (dagger and mace).[19]
Late Neolithic (c.6500–5500)	War might have originated. Hacilar (c.5700–4800): fortifications and destructions. Catal Huyuk (c.6500–5500): especially the late phase, fortified villages, wall paintings, and weapons.[20]
Early Neolithic (c.21,000–6,500)	Farming villages appeared, plants and animals domesticated, pottery invented.[21] Sites: Cayonu (c.8250–5000); Nevali Cori (c.8300–500). No evidences of war, although possible weapon (a triangular stone mace) might had appeared?

Sources: Kuhrt 1995, 225–82; Meyers 1997, 122–31, Macqueen 1995; Zimansky 1995; Hamblin 2006, 285–307; Sagona and Zimansky 2009, esp. chs.7, 8, and 9.

The Coming of Warfare to Secondary Systems

Our theory insists that exodus of losers in conflicts within the pristine systems to areas around them and the subsequent learning by groups in those secondary systems when encountering the intruders would eventually transform the secondary systems into offensive realism systems. By the age of written texts the latest (c.1,500 BC), if not earlier, war had engulfed most secondary systems. Since evidences from the secondary systems are extensive, I shall elaborate on them only briefly and list secondary sources that readers can refer to later on.

A. Levant/Canaan

The ancient Levant covers today's Israel, Palestine, Jordan, Lebanon, and coastal Syria.[1] Levant is a secondary system: it borders (northern) Mesopotamia on the east and ancient Egypt on the southwest respectively. As the two pristine systems being transformed into offensive realism worlds, they also came to penetrate Levant and eventually transformed (and absorbed) Levant into an offensive realism world: Indeed, the two pristine systems came to blows against each other via the Levant.

One of the most famous archaeological sites in Levant has been the imposing fortification at Jericho (dated to around 8000–7500 BC): it had a massive fortress with a circuitous wall and an observation/defending tower built from stone, with a deep V-bottomed ditch. Roper (1975) initially identified the structure as a signature of warfare. After Bar-Yosef's (1986) meticulous reinterpretation, however, most archae-ologists now hold that this structure most likely served the purpose of defending against flood and beasts, or at most, occasional raids by other human groups (e.g., Ferguson 2006, 483; Hamblin 2006, 29–30; but see Watkins 1989, 16–17). As such, the structure at Jericho does not support the notion that warfare had already been frequent back then. With Jericho gone as the key evidence of warfare, firm evidences of warfare within the ancient Levant before 5000–4000 BC have been lacking.

By the middle fourth millennium (3500–3000 BC), however, warfare might have already become frequent. By then, the Uruk civilization from southern Mesopotamia had expanded into Levant, and it is highly likely that war had played an important role in this expansion (Hamblin 2006, 40–2). This interpretation is supported the fact the important Sumerian colony in Habuba Kabira (dated to around 3500–3200 BC) and other smaller colonies (dated to around the same period) had often been protected by strong fortification (ibid. 238–9).

After the unification of northern (i.e., lower) Egypt around 3100–3000 BC (Kemp 1989, ch. 1; Kuhrt 1995, 125–34; Wilkinson 1999, ch. 2), Egyptian armies began to frequently campaign for conquest and plundering in Egypt's surrounding regions, including southern Canaan: Not surprisingly, at Arad in southern Canaan, a massive fortification was erected around 3000–2800 BC to defend against Egyptian aggressions (Hamblin 2006, 318–20).

With all these memories (and legends) of past conflict, it is no wonder that the Hebrew Bible (the *Old Testament*) had documented wars between Akkad/Sumner, Babylon, Egypt, and Assyria extensively. Indeed, the *Old Testament* can be understood as not only a history of bloody war and conquest within the Israelite people but also a history of Israel's bloody interactions with its victims and more powerful neighbors (Kuhrt 1995, ch. 8; Liverani 2005). The following sentence from the *Old Testament* perhaps summarized it all: "All kingdoms designated by the name of Assyria are so called because they enrich themselves at Israel's expense . . . all kingdoms designated by the name of Egypt are so called because they persecute Israel" (*Genesis Rabbah* 16.4, as quoted in Leverani 2005, vi).[2]

For more on the coming of warfare in ancient Levant, see Kuhrt 1995; Sasson et al. 1995; Liverani 2005; Hamblin 2006; and Sagona and Zimansky 2009.

B. Europe (pre-Greek Europe, Ancient Greece to the Rome Empire)

Before 5500 BC, very few evidences of warfare existed in the European system (Ferguson 2006, 480–90). One exceptional site during this period is the Ofnet Cave in today's Bavaria, Germany, dated to around 7500 BC (i.e., the Mesolithic period). Within this site, several skulls have evidences of being struck across the back of the head with an axe, strongly indicating violent death (Keeley 2004, 111; Guilaine and Zammit 2005, 80–1).

By 5000–4500 BC, indisputable evidences of warfare appeared (Vencl 1984; Keeley and Cahen 1989; Keeley 1997, 2004; Christensen 2004; Ferguson 2006; Guilaine and Zammit 2005). In the Talheim site (in today's Bade-Wurttemberg, Germany), dated to around 5000 BC, 34 individuals (mostly males) were buried with extensive evidences of violent death (e.g., skulls smashed behind, wounds by projectiles and axes). In the Asparn-Schletz site (in today's Lower Austria), dared to the same time as Talheim and surrounded by a ditch, 67 bodies were buried with extensive evidences of violent death. Finally, in Herxheim, more than 300 individuals were buried in a mass grave, again with extensive evidences of violent death. These three sites strongly indicated that war had come to dawn in Europe (Keeley 1996, 38; Guilaine and Zammit 2005, 86–101).

In Southern France, before 3500 BC, skeletons with injuries by projectiles were rare. After 3500 BC and between 3000–2200 BC, there was a dramatic increase of skeletons with injuries by projectiles, strongly indicating that war had engulfed the region between 3500 and 3000 BC (Guilaine and Zammit 2005, 127–33, 240–51).

Before 3000 BC, male burials with weapons (i.e., warriors or even heroes) were rare. After 3000 BC, male burials with weapons became common. Likewise, before 3000 BC, fortifications were rare but became extremely common after 3000 BC (Keeley and Cahen 1989; Christensen 2004; Guilaine and Zammit 2005, ch. 4).[3]

In Neolithic time, the most well-known iconographic evidences of warfare in Europe came from rock paintings in the Spanish Levante. These paintings graphically depicted battle scenes by two groups of archers (Guilaine and Zammit 2005, 103–19). Most significantly, combat and maneuvering tactics such as formation, command, marching, and flanking/encirclement were already evident in these paintings, unambiguously pointing to the presence of warfare (ibid. 110; see also Ferrill 1985, 21–2). Overall, by 3000–2000 BC, warfare had come to pervade the European system (Keeley 2004; Guilaine and Zammit 2005, chs. 4 and 5).

By the classical age, many states within the ancient Greek system had developed a highly militarist culture.[4] The best known of them had been Sparta: Sparta practiced stringent eugenics by killing imperfect infants and separating men from women during men's most fertile years to guarantee effective birth control, all for the purpose of maintaining a fierce fighting force (de Souza et al. 2004, 82–7).

For an excellent overview of warfare in the Neolithic Age and Bronze Age in Europe, particularly today's France, Germany, and Spain, see Guilaine and Zammit 2005. On warfare in ancient and classic Greece, a good introduction is de Souza et al. (2004). For more detailed evidences on warfare in ancient and classic Greece, good sources include William K. Pritchett's (1971–1991) monumental *The Greek States at War* (5 vols.), Sage's (1996) *Warfare in Ancient Greece: A Sourcebook*, and Hanson's (2009) *The Western Way of War: infantry battle in classical Greece*, 2nd edn.

On warfare in the age of Rome (republic and imperial), a good introduction is Roth's (2009) *Roman Warfare*. For more in-depth treatment, see Harris's (1979) *War and Imperialism in Republican Rome, 327–70 BC* and Eckstein's (2006). *Mediterranean Anarchy, Interstate War, and the Rise of Rome*.

For more detailed treatments on both ancient Greece and Rome, see Sabin, Philip, Hans van Wees, and Michael Whitby eds., 2007. *The Cambridge History of Greek and Roman Warfare* (2 vols.). Cambridge: Cambridge Univeristy Press.

C. Ancient India

Fortification first appeared in the ancient India subsystem around 3600–2700 BC (the early Harappan period) and became common after 2600 BC (the mature Harappan period, see Avari 2007, 32, 41–4). Around 1700 BC, Aryan tribes from today's Iran began to migrate to India (via today's Afghanistan and Pakistan) and eventually merged with indigenous culture to form the Indo-Aryan culture (also known as the Vedic culture),[5] and there should be little doubt that this inflow of external groups had involved extensive conflict (Avari 2007, 66–9).

By about 700 BC, numerous clan states and kingdoms were constantly at war with each other: war had come to dominate the subcontinent. During this pre-Mauryan era (600–320 BC), Darius I of Persia and Alexander the Great invaded India (Avari 2007, ch. 5). The establishment of the Mauryan Empire (321–185 BC) had been especially violent (Thapar 2003, ch. 6; Avari 2007, ch. 6).

Mahabharata and *Ramayana*, the two great epics in ancient India, both captured legends of heroic warriors with royal heritages (Thapar 2003, 98–104; Avari 2007, 99–100). The notion of divine king had been highly developed in ancient India by the formative period of the pre-Mauryan era (c.600–320 BC; see Thapar 2003, 117–22; Avari 2007, 88–90, 157–8).

A concise introductory text to ancient India is Avari 2007. A more in-depth treatise, with a flavor of archeological anthropology, is Thapar 2003. Also useful are Kulke and Rothermund's (1998) *A History of India* (3rd edn.) and Stein's (2010) *A History of India* (2nd edn.). Unfortunately, although D. K. Chakrabarti's (1999) *India: An Archaeological History* is informative, it does not address warfare.

D. Other Less Secondary Systems:
North America and Africa

For an overview of warfare in pre-colonial North American system, see Keeley 1996; Ferguson 2006, 490–5. On the Tennessee Valley, see Smith 1998. On Northwest Coast of North America, see Maschner 1998; Maschner and Maschner 1998. On the Mississippi River valley, see Redmond and Spencer (2012).

On warfare between the Nuer and the Dinka (Africa), between the Zulus and the Ngunis (Africa), and between Iroquois and Huron (Lake Ontario, North America), see Otterbein (2004, ch. 8) and references cited there. In all three cases, competition for scarce resources (e.g., land, games, and women) had been a critical cause of war.

E. Warfare by Nomads

An obvious challenge that can be posed against our theory on the origins of war is that the theory can only explain the origins of war in sedentary agrarian societies, yet it seems to be that some of the most ferocious war-making societies have been nomads (the Hsiung Nun, the Huns, and of course, the Mongols). Can the same theory explain the rise of these war-making nomadic societies? The answer is an affirmative yes. Depletion of readily supplied food underpinned by population growth, natural disasters (e.g., drought, snowstorm), and allure of wealth, mild climate, and fertile land from settled agricultural lands readily explain the origins of these war-making nomads. In other words, nomadic societies relying on horse chariots (originated in Mesopotamia around c.1500 BC, see Hamblin 2006, ch. 5; van de Mieroop 2007, 122–5) and horse-raiding based on cavalry (developed around 900–800 BC; see Barfield 1989, 28–30) developed much later than the origins of war in those pristine systems. Hence, more likely than not, nomadic societies learned to be nomadic warriors after the origins of war in those sedentary pristine systems.

Of course, once nomadic peoples became fearsome warriors by mastering cavalry, they could overwhelm their sedentary opponents from time to time. Hence, the Amorites might have played a key role in the collapse of the Third Dynasty of Ur (Charpin 1995; Whiting 1995; cf. Kuhrt 1995, 70–2; Van De Mieroop 2007, 82–5). Likewise, the Han Dynasty of China battled against the Hsing-nu's for almost two centuries (Si-Ma, 1997[c.87 BC]). Indeed, through the long history of ancient China, empires, kingdoms, and warlords at the heartland of the ancient Chinese system had battled nomadic powers for millenniums (Barfield 1989; Di Cosmo 2004). In the European system, the Germanic tribes and the Huns might have played a key role in the eventual collapse of the Rome Empire (Heather 2006).

Endnotes

INTRODUCTION

1. I take the pluralist strain of the English School to be a truncated form of neoliberalism whereas its solidarist strain is a close sibling of constructivism. See Chapter 4 below.
2. I consider these three theories legitimate grand theories of international politics because they roughly capture three distinctive eras of international politics: a world that we had experienced; a world that we have been experiencing; and a world that we may be making (see Chapters 2, 3, and 4 below). Many scholars now believe that constructivism does not constitute an independent grand theory of IR because it is more an epistemological position (e.g., Barkin 2003; Booth 2005, 272). My reason for denying that constructivism constitutes an independent grand theory of IR is different: constructivism captures only some key processes in the social world, but not a "world", ontologically speaking. This is evident in constructivists' defenders and critics (e.g., Keohane 1989; Wendt 1999). Moreover, constructivism is almost purely ideational. Other important strands of theorizing IR include critical security theory of Robert Cox, Ken Booth and their followers (Booth 2005). Here, I shall not be too concerned with the exact content and individuals of these debates. For other takes on these debates, see Keohane 1986; Baldwin 1993; Powell 1994; Frankel 1996; Jervis 1999; Copeland 2000b; and Tang 2008a.
3. As Ruggie (1983, 271) pointed out, in Waltz's model, there can only be changes of structure (i.e., polarity), but not changes of system, because anarchy cannot be transformed into hierarchy. In reality, a system can be fundamentally transformed even if only one of its dimension experiences changes initially while other dimensions remain the same (Jervis 1997).
4. Our definition of the physical environment is thus more than "time and space" or "place and moment" in Giddens's and Bourdieu's definitions of society (Bourdieu 1998, 32).

CHAPTER 1

1. From a different angle, Sterling-Folker (2002: 78n17) also denies that the work of Modelski and his collaborator (e.g., William Thompson) is really evolutionary.
2. Because evolution can only operate within a system, systemic approach is an integral part of evolutionary approach, and the latter subsumes the former. See Section III below.
3. Hodgson and Knudsen (2010b, 32-7) call such a system "complex population system".
4. Hence, if a system has never experienced changes through time (i.e., it is frozen in time), then there is no point in applying the evolutionary approach for understanding the system.

5. This section draws heavily from a standard introduction to the modern synthesis (Futuyma 1998, chs. 1–3, esp. 17–49).

6. Phenotypes depend on the expression of genes; whereas genotype is an organism's genetic makeup. I am presenting a very simplified picture of selection here. For details, see Tang 2014, 165.

7. See immediately below on Neo-Darwinian and various notion of Lamarckian. Genotype is an organism's genetic makeup. I refrain from using the more conventional term "gene" here because gene is actually not easy to define (Futuyma 1998, ch. 3). Briefly, gene is a segment of genetic material that carries information that can be expressed. While Darwin (1859) emphasized natural selection as the central mechanism of his theory, it is also apparent that natural selection was not the whole of his theory. As such, it is misleading to treat Darwinism or Neo-Darwinism as merely a theory of natural selection, as Futuyma (1998, 19–23) noted.

8. For a while after the modern synthesis, most biologists accepted that selection operates primarily on individual organism, although there were debates whether selection also operates on groups or even species (Williams 1996[1966]; Dennett 1995). Today, the notion of multi-level selection has increasingly been accepted (for a detailed discussion, see Okasha 2006).

9. Ronald A. Fisher (c.1919–1930), J. B. S. Haldane (c.1924–1934), and S. G. Wright (c.1920–1932) all made important contributions from the field of theoretical population genetics, but Dobzhansky (and Mayr) never read them (mostly due to the heavy dose of math in those papers). Julian Huxley (1973 [1942]) popularized the notion of "the modern synthesis", but contributed no fundamental ideas to it.

10. A good short story about the episode of the Modern Synthesis is Gould (1982).

11. RNA viruses replicate via RNA replicase (RNA-dependent RNA polymerase, a specific kind of enzyme). Retroviruses too are RNA viruses, but they replicate via a DNA intermediate, with the aid of reverse transcriptase (i.e., RNA-dependent DNA polymerase).

12. RNA viruses replicate via RNA replicase (RNA-dependent RNA polymerase, a specific kind of enzyme). Retroviruses too are RNA viruses, but they replicate via a DNA intermediate, with the aid of reverse transcriptase (i.e., RNA-dependent DNA polymerase).

13. Partly because little was known about the genetic material and other fundamental mechanisms in biological evolution during Darwin's time, the possibility of direct inheritance of acquired characteristics (i.e., often known as Lamarckian inheritance) was widely accepted then and even Darwin himself was unwilling (or unable) to rule it out. To differentiate the modern understanding of evolution from Darwin's original position, the former is called Neo-Darwinism. In the literature, there are actually five notions of "Lamarckian" process. Many authors have discussed Lamarck and Lamarckism by conflating these five notions, resulting in serious confusion. The ideational evolution in social evolution is somewhat Lamarckian, but more than that (hence, Super-Lamarckian). I address these notions in details in Tang 2014–15, ch. 2. For a brief discussion, see Table 1.1 below.

14. This characteristic of the evolutionary approach makes it more akin to theories in social sciences than to theories in natural sciences where the power to predict is more important (Richards 1992; see also Scriven 1959). Earlier, Mayr (1969) noted that the then dominant philosophy of physics, Popperian or otherwise, does not really apply to biological sciences.

15. On the centrality of mechanism in scientific explanations, see Bhaskar [1978]2008; Bunge 1997.

16. For instance, a creationism explanation of the diversity of the biological world must use numerous designs to explain why birds have feathers and why chameleons can camouflage.

17. The most prominent external force or factor, of course, has been God or "the Creator".

18. For a succinct rebuttal of creationism, see Futuyma (1998), appendix II. For a more thorough dismantling of creationism and "intelligent design", see Kitcher 1982; 2007.

19. Genetic code is the code for translating stretches of DNA into proteins, via messenger RNAs.

20. As detailed elsewhere, the notion of "survival of the fittest" is *the* bedrock assumption of Social Darwinism, which found in its extreme form in Geopolitics and Nazism. Indeed, "survival of the fittest" was not even coined by Darwin, but by Herbert Spencer, and Darwin only adopted it in the fourth edition of his book (unfortunately), with important reservations.

21. For instance, whereas sickle blood cells confer some advantages to people in Africa where malaria has been rampant because sickle blood cells provide some resistance to malaria; sickle blood cells would be fatal in a place of high altitude because they are deficient in transporting oxygen.

22. Darwin, however, should not be completely excused. He also talked about "as natural selection works solely by and for the good of each being, all corporeal and mental endowments will tend to progress toward perfection" (1859, 489). Such a stand, of course, contradicts his admission that evolution via natural selection is "clumsy, wasteful, blundering, low and horribly cruel". When it comes to human evolution, Darwin's belief in progress was even more apparent (e.g., 1874, 132). For a brief discussion of Darwin's thinking on progress in evolution, see Kaye (1986, 11–22).

23. Gould's tireless self-promotion has made the notion of "punctuated equilibrium" popular among social scientists. For an application of the concept in political science, see Krasner (1984).

24. This does not mean that different stretches of DNA do not have different susceptibility to changes. By "blind mutation" in biological evolution, we merely mean that mutations are *un-directed*.

25. It is important to emphasize that the equivalent of a mutant is a new idea only *at the most fundamental level* because variations such as invention or new institution can be taken as mutations when looking at a different level (see above).

26. Fracchia and Lewinton (1999, 61) charged that selection is the explanatory law in earlier Darwinian theories of cultural evolution. *Here, I shall state categorically that selection is not the explanatory law in my framework, but only part of the*

explanatory framework. For earlier discussions that are generally less rigorous (if not wholly confusing), see Stuart-Fox (1999), 42–4; Carneiro (2003), 171–79.

27. Hence, both Veblen (1898) and Campbell (1960; 1965[1998]) were wrong in insisting on a natural selection approach toward social evolution. John Commons (1934) was the first to explicitly emphasize the force of artificial selection in social evolution although many had noted the role of artificial selection in biology before him (e.g., Darwin 1871; Spencer [1898] 2003). For details, see Tang 2014–15.

28. Power is undoubtedly a contested concept, with a huge literature. I offer a unified analytical framework toward power and a review of the literature elsewhere (Tang, n.d.-b). Some evolutionary anthropologists came extremely close to admitting power as a selection force in social evolution (e.g., Cavalli-Sforza and Feldman 1981, 64–5; Richerson and Boyd 2005, ch. 5), and perhaps only too much admiration for biological evolution has prevented them from doing so.

29. This means that path dependence is much broader and prevalent in social systems (Tang 2011a).

30. Although culture as a whole is an adaptation by our species, it is counterproductive to talk about whether a whole cultural system is an adaptation or not, even at a given time and space. We need to get down to specific cultural traits.

31. This is why kinship selection theory is essential for theorists who defend individual selection but reject group selection: Kinship selection renders group selection unnecessary. Many have used "levels of selection" and "units of selection" interchangeably. As Mayr (1997) pointed out, this practice is misleading. "Levels of selection" refer to the *target* or *object* of selection; whereas "units of selection" must mean a measurable entity that selection can operate on. In many cases, however, we can only talk about level, but not unit. For instance, selection may operate on multiple phenotypes, not a single isolated phenotype.

32. Hayek emphasized the role of group selection in social evolution most forcefully, going as far as asserting that "cultural evolution is founded wholly on group selection" (cited in Angner 2002, 698-9; see also Sober 1984, 280).

33. This is the core of the so-called "agency-structure" problem (for a detailed discussion, see Tang 2011a and Chapter 5 below). Durham (1991, esp. 207–10) was a rare exception among evolutionary theorists by addressing this problem, however briefly.

34. Many authors have suggested that ideational evolution within the human society has been Lamarckian. For a recent discussion, see Jablonka and Lamb 2006, esp. 220–31.

35. Note that Lamarckian evolution cannot explain why individuals and groups retain both ideational impairments and ideal improvements (Hodgson 2001, 98-9), and only a Darwinian mechanism can.

36. Obviously, stages and directionality are inherently linked to the notion of progress (physical and moral) in (social) evolution. Progress is a very tricky term, and I can only address it in detail elsewhere.

37. The Stone Age can be further divided into three sub-stages: Paleolithic, Mesolithic, and Neolithic.

38. Another scheme of labeling stages, savagery, barbarism, and civilized, first espoused by Edward B. Taylor (1871), should be rejected due to its heavy dose of ethnocentrism-tainted moral superiority.

39. Carneiro (2003, 161–9) insisted that social evolution is both directional and reversible, without grasping that directionality and reversibility do not go along with each other.

40. This statement makes those worries on how to strictly apply biological evolution to social evolution unnecessary and unproductive (e.g., Papkin 2001).

41. Since I deal exclusively with systemic social change here, I shall state only the operational principles for taking on this task here. For the operational principles for understanding state behaviors, see Tang and Long (2012). For the operational principles for understanding human psychology and individual behaviors, see Tang n.d.-c. For more detailed discussion, see Tang 2014–15.

42. Carnerio (2003, 171–3) expounded a similar argument. Unfortunately, his understanding of social evolution is firmly Spencerian (Tang 2014–15).

43. Most forms of determinism require some kind of reductionism. Biological evolution-determinism subsumes all forms of genetic determinism, biological determinism, and (ecological) environment determinism. "Biological evolution-determinism" is slightly better than "genetic determinism", but no much better for explaining human behavior, not to mention the whole human society.

44. Unfortunately, many have taken any evolutionary approach to mean *functionalism*/adaptationism. This is perhaps most evident in the study of institutions. For a more thorough critique of this functionalism approach toward social institutions, see Tang 2011a.

45. For a collection of essays with supposedly evolutionary interpretations of world politics, see Thompson (20001). Unfortunately, many chapters in this volume were influenced by Modelski and Thomson's pseudo-evolutionary long-cycle approach or by sociobiological/EP approach. Sterling-Folker (2002) demonstrated good grasp of biological determinism versus socialization (within human nature), individual versus group, and material versus ideational. Unfortunately, she has not developed those themes systematically.

46. Neoliberalism focuses on institutions whereas constructivism on norms (as informal rules). Norms are "standards of behaviors" or "collective expectations for the proper behavior of actors with a given identity" (Florini 1996, 364; Katzenstein 1996, 5). Theories that take institution as independent variable (i.e., institutions matter) cannot have a genuine theory of institutional change: any theory of change within this literature must be *ad hoc* (Calvert 1995, 59).

47. To some extent, Adler's 1991 paper and Wendt's 1992 paper (discussed below) nicely complement each other: Whereas Adler focuses on the process of ideational changes, Wendt focuses on the impact of new ideas upon the nature of the international system. Yet, this also means that both frameworks suffer from similar deficiencies. See Chapter 4 below for a more detailed discussion.

48. Huntley (1996) articulated the origin idea of understanding democratic peace as an evolutionary outcome within the international system.

49. As Palan (2000, 589–590) points out, Wendt (1999) makes a surreptitious effort to advance his extreme ideationalistic position. Wendt (1999) starts by admitting that "brute facts have ontological priority over institutional facts (110)", then imports the argument that "ideas constitute those ostensibly material causes (94, emphasis original)", and arrives at the extreme ideationalistic position that "the

most fundamental factor in international politics is the 'distribution of ideas' in the system (96, see also 137–8, 309)". Here, Wendt conflated priority with weight. For details, see Tang 2013.

50. I thus challenge my thesis's critics to identify alternative explanations that do not have to rely on the fundamental mechanisms uncovered here to drive the systemic transformation international politics.

51. For instance, in my framework, the evolution of military technology is a natural outcome from the competition among states: the demand to kill and defend drives the evolution of military technology (see Chapter 2 below; see also Diamond 1997; Thayer 2004, ch. 4). Likewise, my framework also neatly explains the coming of territorial sovereignty (see Chapter 3 below, see also Spruyt 1994b).

CHAPTER 2

1. It is important to emphasize that it is the "*relative population pressure*" relative to key eco-capacities of the land rather than absolute population density per se that makes the difference (Keeley 1988; idem 1996, 118–20; Ferguson 1989). Not surprisingly, earlier attempts to link absolute population density with war had produced inconclusive findings.

2. An international system is defined as a system that consists of all the individuals and collectives (e.g., tribes, states) within the system, the structure of the system (if any), and the physical environment. For much of human history, geography tends to divide the earth into regional international systems, or subsystems. These subsystems can be understood to be equivalent to Buzan's (1986) "regional security complexes (RSCs)". RSC, however, is too restrictive a label: it limits itself to security matters. A system can exist between actors (e.g., between the Roman Empire and the Han Empire) that are not geographically adjacent as long as they are linked together somehow.

3. Obviously, this also means that war has a strong cultural component within it (see Section V below).

4. I prefer more recent surveys because they are generally more reliable than earlier ones: more recent surveys tend to piece together archaeological discoveries from many sites and use more reliable dating methods, whereas some earlier treatises tended to be based on scanty evidences and speculations.

5. As becomes clear below, the increasing sophistication in organization, technology, and intensity of warfare after the first outbreak of war can be taken to be a "natural" product of warfare.

6. In this sense, war has been one of the prime movers in the evolution of human society, contra Ferguson 1994. As van der Dennen (1995, 59) noted, the thesis that war of conquest makes states can be traced back to Ibn-Khaldun's *Introduction of History* (originally published in 1377 AD).

7. For a well-immersed survey of the vast literature on the origins of war, see van der Dennen (1995).

8. It is of critical importance that we differentiate these two puzzles. Whereas causes of specific war can be numerous, the very first war within different systems may have only a few valid combinations of specific factors and mechanisms as its cause.

After the first war and socialization by warfare settled in, however, war can be fought for different combinations of causal factors. As such, a general theory for the causes of war may be an unrealistic goal (cf. van Evera 1999; Betts 1999).

9. As becomes clear in Section V below, these two questions are inherently intertwined. Most importantly, without war, there would be no states.

10. By doing so, I am thus implying that although the first war within a system had its unique combination of causal factors and mechanisms, there might have been great similarities in the origins of war in different (independent) subsystems and a general theory of the origins of war is possible.

11. Regardless of which school, all theorists on the origins of war at least tacitly accept that anarchy, defined simply as a lack of central authority among *political units*, is a permissive (thus necessary) condition for the origin of war, since Hobbes. This notion will be admitted here without elaboration.

12. Of course, this does not mean that Hobbes told us nothing about IR.

13. Hobbes was more explicit (both want the same thing and they cannot have it at the same time, see Hobbes [1651]1985, ch. 13, 184). Rousseau used Hunger.

14. After sociobiology has been blunted by waves of criticism (some justified, some unjustified; see Kitcher 1985; Buller 2005a; 2005b; Richardson 2007), sociobiology changed into EP. Some (e.g., van der Dennen 1995, ch. 4; Dawson 1996a, 8–11) have taken Malthus ([1798]1951), Spencer (1857), and Darwin (1871) to be the second generation of theorists or the first generation of sociobiologist to speculate on the origins of war. This is a misunderstanding: these authors had merely commented on a possible (unintended) outcome (hence, function) of war—most prominently, the survival of the fitter [not the fittest] based on group competition. They did not argue that the survival of the fitter is a causal factor behind the origin of war. In contrast, sociobiologists contend that war *originates* because war serves these functions (see below). For a good survey of the vast sociobiological literature on the origin and evolution of war, see van der Dennen 1995, ch. 4.

15. Human nature is a loosely defined term. I have argued that human nature has three parts: the part determined by biological evolution, the part determined by socialization, and the part called anti-socialization (Tang 2011b). Sociobiology focuses on the first part, whereas most sociologists (and anthropologists) concenetrate on the second part. Neither practice grasps the whole picture.

16. For a critique of Gat's earlier work (Gat 2000a; 2000b), see Ferguson (2000). For a devastating critique of Gat (2006), see van der Dennen 2007, 77–81.

17. For instance, Buss's (2008) textbook on EP puts war as a small section within the chapter on aggression. Ironically, it was van der Dennen (1995, 68–94), a prominent sociobioloigst, who advocated a clear delineation of these terms. For a briefer discussion, see van der Dennen 2007, 77–81.

18. Raid remains the most favored tactic among primitive groups (e.g., Chagnon [1968]1997).

19. Wrangham's (1999, 13) admission that "the high frequency of intense aggression seen at Gombe and suggested by the other eastern chimpanzee populations may be unusual for the species as a whole" certainly does not strengthen his thesis that human warfare has robust connection with coalitionary killing among chimpanzees. Moreover, his theory of chimpanzee violence theory based on "imbalance of

power" has two key components: hostility and imbalance of power. Yet, one must ask how hostility comes into existence in the first place. Otherwise, the theory becomes utterly tautological! Interestingly, Wilson and Wrangham (2003, esp. 382–7) have become less forceful in advocating a sociobiology explanation of the origin of war. We do not know whether this has been a change of heart.

20. Indeed, in one of his most famous passages, Darwin (1871[1874], 138) had recognized that conflict between human groups poses a very thorny problem for his theory of natural selection: why would individuals fight against another group? (See also Alexander 1979, 377–8.) "Inclusive-fitness" only marginally solves "group selection." For a brief discussion, see van der Dennen 1995, 18–21.

21. As Collins (2012) noted, (news of) potential conflict generates fear rather than excitement. This is so even among Yanamamos who do raid for women (Chagnon [1968]1997, ch. 6). Thayer (2004, 100–1) went so far as to make competition for resources (perhaps other than females as mates) the least important factor for explaining the origin of war, although he had to repeatedly smuggle this explanation into his narratives (cf. van den Berghe 1974 and below). As I show in Section VI below, the notion that men fight for fitness as an offensive realism idea is a product of social evolution, based on a misunderstanding of our past.

22. By conflating war with intra-group violence, sociobiologists have explicitly implied that you can simply add individuals together to make groups. Elsewhere (Tang 2011b; 2013), I show that such a stand commits the blunder of conflating ontological priority with ontological weight.

23. Some key capacities for war that might have already been evolved in our ancestors may include: territoriality, hunting via ambush (i.e., "coalitional killing" for Wrangham and his colleagues), and primitive group identity/cohesion.

24. A somewhat modified version of the Rousseau thesis has been that primitive humans were engaged in "ritual warfare" rather than "real" warfare (for a critique, see Otterbein 2004, 34–8).

25. In other words, archaeological anthropology has been occupied more with the origin of state than with the origin of war. In contrast, although I admit that war and the making of states are inherently connected, I am not interested in the making of states per se, but really the origin of war within a system and its subsequent transformation of the system (with the state being one of the outcomes).

26. For instance, Reyna (1994) discussed that two states or empires (Bagirmi and Wadai) in the Chad Basin came to blows in the early 19th century. By then, both states were Islamic states (hence, little wonder then that the two states came to blows based on some kind of religious principles). Likewise, although the peoples of the Polynesian islands might have experienced both peace and war, one could not be certain that they did not have knowledge of warfare before they came to occupy those islands, if they were really migrants from the Asian continent (Diamond 1997). The same logic applies to Andaman Islanders (Kelly 2000, 78), although Kelly does not seem to recognize this.

27. As Ferguson (1995) noted, competition for access to Western technologies and goods might have been a key cause of some of the Yanomamo wars.

28. For example, Otterbein (2004), offering a critical synthesis of his earlier work, contends that there had been two paths toward the origins of war: a hunter-based

path and a gathering-settled agriculture-based path. Otterbein asserts that warfare cannot be the cause of pristine state formation: these pristine states were direct and peaceful outcomes of settled agriculture (ibid. 10–15, 41–3, 177–80). For hunters, warfare decreased sharply after the big game (e.g., buffalos) disappeared, and came back only after city states came to exist. Otterbein thus essentially argues that "maximal chiefdoms" (or complex chiefdoms) predated war in most settled societies, whereas war remained important among hunter societies. Mostly likely, however, Otterbein got the causal relationship the wrong way: war makes chiefdoms (and states) and only later on states make war (Ferguson 2006, 473).

29. Wendt used a very broad definition of institution. Despite the fact that Glaser (1994–95) has already argued persuasively that cooperation is an important means of self-help, Wendt adopted the offensive realism position that self-help is equivalent to competition (Wendt 1992, 400; 1999). As such, Wendt did not explicitly state that even self-help anarchy can have many kinds: at the very least, both the Hobbesian anarchy and the Lockeian anarchy are self-help ones but they differ from each other fundamentally. To avoid confusion, I use Hobbesian anarchy to denote what Wendt meant by "self-help anarchy". Gat (2006; 2009) did not mention Wendt and Mercer.

30. Indeed, Wendt (1999, 264) needs a group of states to characterize each other as enemies to get the Hobbesian anarchy rolling. See Schweller 1996 for another discussion of the role of predator state and memory of predatory state in driving the security dilemma within a system.

31. Wendt admitted that he was employing a narrower definition of material forces, and he gave more weight to material forces more recently (e.g., Wendt 2004; Wendt, personal communication February 2006). Wendt gave away his inability to account for the formation of the competitive self-help anarchy when stating that "explaining the emergence of Hobbesian identities 3,000 years ago" is "of only marginal relevance to explaining state identity today" even though he admitted that explaining the making of the competitive self-help anarchy is of critical importance for IR theory earlier (e.g., Wendt 1992, 396; 1999, 323). Snyder (2002, 19) questioned the compatibility between Wendt's culture theory and social identity theory.

32. Mercer seemed to forget the fact that distribution of implicit resources was involved in *all* of the SIT minimal-group identity experiments, and this reification has caused him to come so close yet eventually fail to offer a compelling explanation for the making of the competitive self-help anarchy. Indeed, even the formation of in-group identity must have a material base (see immediately below).

33. In the context of Sino-American relations, Gries (2005) too argued that competition and cooperation under anarchy are much more contingent than Mercer suggested: you need more than anarchy and in-group bias to drive competition or cooperation among nations.

34. Indeed, Ember and Ember (1992) found that intergroup mistrust, which is inherently tied to group identity, is a secondary factor in explaining war, compared to scarcity of resources. Such a finding is consistent with our thesis that group identity is a necessary but insufficient cause of warfare among groups (see the next section for details). It should be noted, however, that Ember and Ember

(1992) conflated feud, brawling with warfare. For a critique, see van der Dennen (2007, 86).

35. Not surprisingly, even today, isolated groups still do not maintain military organizations and have rarely experienced war even if they had experienced war before (Otterbein 1989, 20–1; 2004, 81–2). In a different context, Waltz (2000, 15) put the logic succinctly: "With zero interdependence, neither conflict nor war is possible."

36. Both traits, though primitive, are already present in our closest relatives, the chimpanzees.

37. Because most small bands of humans were originally an extended family or consisted of closely related families, kinship had been a prominent factor in shaping in-group identity. Hence, in-group identity developed over the course of history was perhaps much stronger than can be captured by modern SIT experiments. Also, within the egalitarian stage of human society, selection is usually for cooperative individuals and against those who are aggressive toward its fellow members within a community (Bohem 1999). Hence, while there are biological foundation for generating aggressive individuals (most prominently, the XYY individual, with a chance of about one in a thousand male births), these individuals are unlikely to prosper or even survive (Miller and Cook 1998, 72–82).

38. More dedicated weapons such as mace, sword, and composite bow would come later.

39. Although population increase and depletion of readily available resources are not identical, these two things are usually tightly linked. An area can be physically (or naturally) circumscribed by rivers, mountains, deserts, and frozen terrains. An area can also be socially circumscribed by human activities (e.g., irrigation necessitated by settled agriculture, as noted by Dickson 1987) and availability of mates.

40. The origin of agriculture remains a key question for anthropologists. For a recent discussion, see *Current Anthropology*, Vol. 52, No. S4, "The Origins of Agriculture: New Data, New Ideas" (2011).

41. Keeley (1996, table 7.2) documents the relationship between population density and the size of the buffer zone between groups.

42. This is a key conclusion of endogenous growth theory in economics (Jones 2005). A key mechanism behind this is that as population increases, the rate of technological innovation also increases.

43. One of the earliest villages has been Abu Hureyra, in today's Syria, dated around 9500 BC.

44. In contrast, even today, in the Amazon plain in which fertile and arable land is abundant, war is sporadic and does not normally aim for conquest of others' land (Carneiro 1970; Ferguson 1989).

45. Most prominently, settled agriculture is usually supported by extensive and elaborate irrigation system, which requires huge investment to build.

46. See van der Dennen 1995, 46–9 for a brief discussion on the relationship between territoriality, being sedentary, and defense.

47. Ember and Ember (1992) have shown that resources unpredictability often triggers violent conflict among adjacent groups. The fact that victors usually plunder their victims may partly reflect groups' concern for resources (M. Ember and C. R. Ember 1994, 190, 194; Keeley 1996, 106–8). Wrangham (1999, 13–14) also

noted that "harsh conditions of food availability" might have been a key cause of intergroup aggression among chimpanzee groups in Tanzania. See also the next section.

48. Again, it is critical to differentiate the origin of war within a system (i.e., the causes of the first war) from causes of wars within the system *after* the first war. Otterbein (2004, ch. 7) failed to single out the spreading of fear as a powerful driver of the diffusion of warfare. Gat (2006, 138–9) merely noted the fact that a conflict in the recent past usually comes back to reinforce competition and inoculate a new cause for the outbreak of conflict.

49. For example, in the ancient Chinese system, the Hsiung-nu (Xiong-nu) people, who might have been driven out from Iran or Siberia, would later on come to have almost four centuries of continuous warfare with kingdoms located in the heartland of China (Barfield 1989; Di Cosmo 2004).

50. Wendt, however, did not explain how the first "bad apple" (or predatory state) came into existence. The theory presented here does.

51. For simplicity, in most places, I use "states" to denote all independent political entities (e.g., tribes, chiefdoms, states, empires, and warlords).

52. Quite evidently, such a fact testifies to the power of our social evolutionary explanation for the making of the offensive realism world.

53. A cautionary note for interpreting presence of hunting tools or weapons as firm evidences of warfare is in order. Because many weapons were initially hunting tools, one cannot straightforwardly take presence of weapons to be evidences of warfare. Yet, certain weapons with exclusively military purposes constitute firm evidences of warfare. For example, tomahawk, mace, lance, sling, dagger (short sword), sword, and improved spear (javelin) are strong evidences of warfare because their usage is almost exclusively for combat and execution. Maces are only useful for shattering skull and bones (Hamblin 2006, 20–1). Dagger is only useful for close combat, not for killing animals (Ferrill 1985, 18–26): To strip meat from animal bodies, axes and knifes will do. Slings are key weapons for open field battle, but more importantly, for siege. Finally, metal weapons (after the appearance of metallurgy) constitute firm evidences of war: because metal weapons are expensive, they are dedicated weapons for warfare, not hunting (Hamblin 2006, 21–2; see also Otterbein 2004, ch. 4).

54. For earlier discussions of what constitute evidences of warfare, see Maschner 1998; Keeley 1998; Ferguson 1998 (all in Martin and Frayer 1998), Keeley 1996, ch. 3; idem, 2004; and Cioffi-Revilla 2000, 64–70. I leave out legends and stories of warfare, victory, conquest, heroes because these are almost universal among groups and so widely known. Keeley (2004, 110) used a similar typology as here. Cioffi-Revilla (2000) listed six kinds: forensic, locational, structural, artifactual (i.e., weapons), iconographic, and epigraphic. The first type here corresponds to Cioffi-Revilla's "forensic", the second type to his "artifactual", the third type to his "structural". My fourth type combines iconographic and epigraphic. I leave out "locational", which Cioffi-Revilla also considered to be "weak". It should also be noted that forensic and structural evidences of warfare existed long before iconographic and epigraphic evidences, by more than a millennium, if not more. All subsystems eventually came to have iconographic evidences, but some subsystems (i.e., Peru and Mexico) lacked writing (epigraphic).

55. Intra-species killing was already present in the chimpanzees.

56. For a more recent and full survey of the cave/rock art in Iberia peninsula, see Bicho et al. (2007). Dating these arts has not been an easy task. For a survey, see Pettitt and Pike (2007).

57. Unfortunately, "site 117" had already provided us with a glimpse into the horrifying world to come. "It [i.e., site 117] contained remains of fifty-nine individuals of whom twenty-four (40.7 per cent) show evidence of being killed with weapons" (Otterbein 2004, 74; see also Hamblin 2006, 32–3).

58. For more evidences of the increased population in other subsystems, see the individual chapters in Bocquet-Appel and Bar-Yosef 2008.

59. Interestingly, Wenke's estimation noted that there was a steady increase in population within Egypt up until 2500 BC, and then there was a drop before it grew again. This may be due to the spreading of warfare. Our ABM-based modeling of population growth and conquest indicated that there should have been a drop in population when warfare began to engulf the system (Tang et al. n.d.).

60. The conflict or competition between *Homo sapiens* and *Homo neanderthalensis*, which lasted until around 20,000 BP, was perhaps the first "war". In the end, the former wiped out the latter almost entirely. Unfortunately, few concrete evidences of this conflict have been discovered so far.

61. A wooden spear, found in a cave in Germany, has been dated to around 400,000 BP. From the diet of "Peking Man" (*Homo erectus*), dated to around 500,000–350,000 BP, one can also be fairly certain that these early hominoids had already mastered hunting tools such as spears (Kelly 2005).

62. Another piece of evidence may be that the soil in the "Fertile Crescent" (a misnomer, in fact) is anything but fertile: it is a dry and often barren field, without capacity to support a growing large population (Dickson 1987). This might partly explain why war first broke out in this region.

63. Another more widely known case, the case of Easter Island's collapse, however, might have been caused by contact with the Europeans rather than ecological degradation alone (Hunt 2006; Hunt and Lipo 2009; cf. Diamond 2005; Flenley and Bahn 2002).

64. Cioffi-Revilla (1996, 11) noted that wars in the ancient worlds had been less frequent than wars in the modern period (1495 AD on). Such an interpretation is imprecise, if not incorrect. Not all the wars in the ancient worlds had been recorded and many left not much trace. More likely than not, war within ancient systems after their transformation into offensive realism worlds might have been very rampant for a very long period of time, as Otterbein (2004, 11, fig. 1.1) seems to suggest (see also below).

65. Only after conquests had become more difficult, could the system be transformed into a defensive realism world, as Chapter 3 will show.

66. For the sake of flow, supporting materials for this section have been put into Appendix II. The first five systems have been generally accepted as the quintessential pristine systems (Cioffi-Revilla 1996; 2000; Trigger 2003). Otterbein (2004) excluded Egypt because he was also mostly interested in the endogenous origin of state within a system. Because there have been strong (yet insufficient) evidences that ancient Anatolia might have been a pristine system in which war originated

early on (Meyers 1997, 122; Hamblin 2006, 285–6), I include Anatolia as a possible pristine system. If the hypothesis that *Homo sapiens sapiens* (the modern) displaced *Homo neanderthalensis* (the archaic) via competitive and violent means, then the conflict between the two species was perhaps the first true war. Moreover, if the displacement occurred in the middle to late Paleolithic age somewhere between 130,000 and 30–50,000 years ago in the Levant, then we may need to take Levant as the pristine system where war originated. Unfortunately, although some kind of competitive displacement might have occurred (Shea 2001; 2003), there is no conclusive evidence on this front so far. I thus count Levant/Canaan as a secondary system (see Appendix II).

67. As noted above, natural and social "circumscription" is a precondition for the birth of states with a region via conquest and coercion (Carneiro 1970; Chagnon (1968[1997], 75; Dickson 1987).

68. For discussion on the difficulties on reconstructing the past of the ancient Near East, see Khurt 1995, introduction; van De Mieroop 2007, introduction, Wenke 2009, ch. 3; Maisels 1993; Matthews 2003.

69. According to Marcus and Flannery's (1996, 12–13) estimation, the maximum population of Zapotec civilization within the Valley of Oaxaca at the time of Spanish conquest was only between 350,000 and 500,000.

70. In its broadest terms, the ancient Near East covers Mesopotamia (e.g., Assyria, Babylonia, Elam), Egypt, Anatolia, Levant (e.g., Kuhrt 1995; Hamblin 2006), and even the Arabian Peninsula (e.g., Sasson et al. 1995). A narrower definition, which is what I adopt here, excludes the Arabian Peninsula, Egypt, and even Levant (e.g., Van de Mieroop 2007).

71. Major ecological events in Mesopotamia that preceded the coming of settled agriculture included the gradual rise in sealevel, starting around 14,000 BC until around 5–4000 BC. And then there was also a great flooding, around 2900 BC, perhaps gave birth to the stories of the great flood in the Bible. All these events might have impacted the evolutionary paths of the region. For a succinct introduction, see McIntosh 2005, chs. 1 and 2.

72. Algaze ([1993]2005) contended that the expansion of the Uruk culture from Southern Mesopotamia to the larger Syro-Mesopotamia region represented the first recognizable imperial expansion around 3800–3100 BC, almost one millennium before the Akkadian imperial expansion. Yet he did not touch upon the role of warfare in the Uruk expansion, although he did note that there were heavily fortified outposts (e.g., Habuba Kabira in today's Syria) that guarded the Uruk heartland (Algaze [1993]2005, 53–7). Most likely, the late half of the Uruk expansion (c.3500–3100 BC) was at least partly supported by military means and warfare (Hamblin 2006, 40–2), and certainly warfare had played a key role in the collapsing of the Uruk expansion (i.e., the rise of internal conflict within Sumer itself). Algaze now admitted that his neglect of the possible role of war in the Uruk expansion was a major omission. Personal communication with Guillermo Algaze, November 19, 2011. See also Algaze 2008.

73. With bronze arrowheads, the composite bow greatly increases the range and penetration of missiles.

74. In this context, it is highly plausible that northern Mesopotamia had cities no later, if not earlier, than southern Mesopotamia (Oates et al. 2007). Of course, the fact that no earlier evidences of warfare had been discovered in southern Mesopotamia may simply reflect the possibility that southern Mesopotamia had experienced more flooding than northern Mesopotamia, in addition to the essential haphazardness of archaeological discoveries.

75. Naram-Sin also had a rock cut relief at Darband-i-Gawr, essentially depicting a similar scene (ibid.).

76. Because writing had been perfected by the second millennium, wars since then had been better recorded (van de Mieroop 2007, chs. 5–10; Hamblin 2006, ch. 6). In Mesopotamia, writing was invented in the late early dynastic period, i.e., between the Akkadian empire and the third dynasty of Ur/Sumer, or around 2500–2100 BC (McIntosh 2005, 191–5; van de Mieroop 2007, 266–8).

77. Nadada II and III are also known as middle and late pre-Dynastic periods.

78. After the unification of southern Egypt, Egyptian armies frequently campaigned for conquest and plundering in regions surrounding regions, including southern Canaan. In response, Arad in southern Canaan had a massive fortification erected (Hamblin 2006, 318–21). See Appendix II below.

79. Wenke (2009, 181–8), following Kemp (1989, 50, fig. 16), interpreted the Tjehenu Palette depicting conquests by the Hierakonpolis kingdom before the reign of Narmer.

80. Structurally, *yue* is similar to stone axe, but it is larger than stone axe. More importantly, *yue* is a weapon for kill, not for grinding. Late, *yue* made from copper became a symbol of political power in the Xia dynasty (Zheng 2005, 424–6).

81. One estimate puts the population density at the heartland of the ancient Chinese system by the time of Xia (2200–1700 BC) at 600 inhabitants per square km (Song 1991). Another estimate puts the density at 2472.1 inhabitants per square km (cited in Cioffi-Revilla and Lai 1995, 472). This number is simply too high to be credible.

82. Astoundingly, Burger (1995, 78) held that these sculptures were only indicating "small-scale raiding"! Burger consistently understated the role of warfare in the making of the Chavin civilizations because he wanted to treat this civilization as a ritual not a physical one!

83. The chronology here draws heavily from table 3 in Marcus and Flannery 1996, 25.

84. As Marcus and Flannery (1996, 130) noted, writing might have been invented because writing is critical for keeping record of troops and rations.

85. Joyce (2010, 151–4) questioned whether it was Monte Albán that conquered Cuicatlán Cañada, but he did not deny that the skull rack was a signature of warfare.

86. Anatolia did produce the old and new Hittite Empires (c.2000 BC on). But this was much later than ancient Mesopotamia and ancient Egypt. A possible cause behind Anatolia's failure to reach the stage of state much earlier might have been it forbidding terrain that prevents consolidation of power (Macqueen 1995, 1085).

87. Since evidences came from all the pristine systems and secondary systems, I do not cite them specifically here. Readers who are interested in specific evidences from specific civilizations can refer to works cited in the previous section. For general discussions on the glorification of war and conquest in other civilizations and groups, ranging from ancient Mesopotamia to Persia, Greece, Egypt, and China, readers can refer to O'Connell (1989), Keegan (1993), and Hamblin (2006).

88. The maximum population of a complex chiefdom may go up to ten thousand (Earle 1987, 288). Carneiro (1987) noted that the maximum population of a village is about 2000.
89. In contrast, only after the Second World War did we see all-volunteer armies and reduction in the size of armed forces. These two developments are only possible when states are living in a non-offensive realism world in which wars of conquest have become mostly obsolete. See Chapter 3 below.
90. The famed *Seven Military Classics* (武经七书 *Wu Jing Qi Shu*) is a collection of some of the important Chinese classic writings on (military) strategies. Somewhat surprisingly, ancient Egypt and the Mesopotamia civilizations did not produce books of strategies.
91. Both Sun Tzu and Kautilya explicitly emphasized the value of spying and spies.
92. The fact that Johnston (1995) intended to show that China might have had a strategic culture that is different from (offensive) realism but ended up in finding that ancient China's strategic culture has been *parabellum* realism is especially telling (see also Wang 2011). When it comes to survival within offensive realism systems, there is really not much cultural dimension to it.
93. As Gnirs noted, this practice bears a striking resemblance to the Aztec world (cf. Hassig 1999).
94. Male military prowess also increases interpersonal conflict within a group (C. R. Ember and M. Ember 1994; Ferguson 2008).
95. Hence, our training for war started at a very young age. Indeed, for many civilizations without writing, the first formal kind of schooling was about combat rather than about literary learning.
96. Since warfare might have been a key cause of primitive religion, there is a feedback relationship between warfare and organized religion (as a key part of culture).
97. Hence, small bands are only found in zones of relative peace in the Amazon (Ferguson 1989, 186).
98. Georg Simmel's (1964) profound thesis that conflict increases cohesion with a group is another variant of this thesis (Coser 1956; for a more recent synthesis, see Collins 2012). Indeed, conflict demands instruments for maintaining and strengthening ingroup cohesion (Spencer 1873, ch. 8).
99. In other words, subjects' socialization in the culture of war is a product of war rather than an original cause of war, although the socializing process does come back to enhance war-making thereafter (C. R. Ember and M. Ember 1994, 492). The need to produce warriors via socialization also tends to increase interpersonal violence within groups (ibid.). Hence, the prevalence of interpersonal violence within groups does not point to a possible cause of war but an outcome of (intergroup) war.
100. For the proper differentiation of offensive realism from defensive realism (and other non-offensive realism theories), see Tang 2008a; idem, 2010b, chs. 4 and 6. Military strategists or theorists such as Sun Tzu or Clausewitz cannot be easily classified as offensive realists because they mostly address the art of war rather than war as part of statecraft (Tang 2010b, ch. 6).
101. As Hui (2005) has ably demonstrated, reform guided by Shang Yang's ideas was instrumental in making Qin a powerful state that eventually unified China. This should not be a surprise, only a hard-core offensive realist state like the state of

Qin could have accomplished the feat. All translations of the work of Shang Yang (*Shang Jun Shu* or *The Books of Lord Shang*) are mine. An earlier translation of *The Books of Lord Shang* by J. J. L Duyvendak (London: Probsthain, 1928) is available electronically from: classiques.uqac.ca/classiques/duyvendak_jjl/B25_book_of_lord_shang/duyvlord.rtf->. While Thucydides (c.400 BC) wrote before Shang Yang and conveyed the same message through an Athenian's voice (Thucydides: 5.89), it is difficult to classify Thucydides. For an interesting discussion on reading Thucydides, see Welch (2003).

102. Aristotle's defense of (natural) slavery, however, has been the subject of much debate, and I shall refrain from engaging with it.

103. The fact that ancient Peru and Mesoamerica did not leave behind texts of offensive realism before their paths were cut off by the Spaniards is easy to explain: even at the height of their power, their population was not large enough and their political centralization was not wide and long enough.

104. As Kaufman and Wohlforth noted, "these grisly details clarify the choices facing neighboring leaders threatened by Assyrian expansions" (ibid.).

105. Later on, when ancient China had been unified first under Qin and then solidified under the Han dynasty, a modified doctrine of Confucian-Mencius did become the official ideology of imperial China. But this adoption had been mostly for governance *within* a state. To some extent, this was a disciplining of bodies for the sake of maintaining order, as Elias (1939[1994]) had observed in medieval Europe.

106. In other words, even biology-determined human nature and competition for sources together will not constitute a sufficient explanation for the origin of war.

107. Wendt did not offer an account for the transformation of the system after the first offensive realist (or predatory) state came to the scene either. His theory is thus incomplete and exogenous.

CHAPTER 3

1. Brooks (1997) first made explicit the fundamental differences between the two realisms, and Taliaferro (2000–1) advanced a more systematic differentiation of the two realisms. Both Brooks and Taliaferro, however, erred in a several places. For a more coherent and systematic demarcation of the two realisms, see Tang 2008a; 2010b. Other useful discussions of the two realisms include Snyder 1991; Glaser 1994–95; Zakaria 1998, ch. 2; Jervis 1999; and G. Snyder 2002.

2. Offensive realism world and defensive realism world are heuristics labels for denoting the two different historical epochs. The two worlds roughly correspond to Wendt's (1999) Hobbesian anarchy and Lockeian anarchy. By "inevitably", I merely mean that *given all the things in place*, the transformation would have been inevitable. By irreversibly, I mean that the system will not go backwards, although some actors may retain outdated ideas and practices.

3. Elsewhere, I show that both realisms are incomplete and need more coherent and consistent restatements (Tang 2008a; 2010b).

4. Elsewhere (Tang 2008a; 2010b), I show that the fundamental difference between the two realisms can be alternatively understood to center on their differences on how to cope with our uncertainty over others' intentions and the fear derived from this uncertainty. The difference can also be framed as whether genuine cooperation other than temporary alliance when facing a common adversary is possible in international politics. I prefer the dichotomy of offensive realist state vs. defensive realist state because it is more rigorous than other commonly used dichotomies (e.g., revisionist state vs. status quo state, power-seeker vs. security-seeker). I also explicitly argue that the right yardstick to differentiate offensive realist states from defensive realist states is their different preferences on strategies rather than their different preferences over outcomes or goals. I define the two types of state, provide the rationales for adopting this dichotomy, and address other differences between the two realisms in great detail elsewhere (Tang 2010b). For the distinction of preference on strategies versus preferences over outcomes, see Powell (1994). For earlier and often misleading discussion on the differences between the two realisms, see Brooks (1997); Taliaferro (2000–1); and Rathbun (2007).

5. Here, it is worth noting that by arguing that all states are offensive realism states, Mearsheimer actually eliminates the uncertainty about other states' intention, thus nullifies one of the five bedrock assumptions he emphasizes. As such, there is no uncertainty about other states' intention in an offensive realism world: The only uncertainty is about when war will break out. Note, however, that the logic of offensive realism still holds and actually strengthens when there is no uncertainty about the aggressive nature of states. For a more detailed discussion, see Tang (2008a).

6. This assumption that there may be both defensive realist states and offensive realist states out there is crucial for maintaining the uncertainty about states' intentions under anarchy within the defensive realism framework: without this uncertainty, there will be no security dilemma, and defensive realism's logic collapses (Tang 2008a; 2010b; see also Schweller 1996; Kydd 1997, 126–7).

7. Levy (1983) puts the beginning of modern Great Power Era around 1495.

8. This is so despite that the historical facts in the modern Great Power Era generally support defensive realism's interpretation of history (G. Snyder 2002). To some extent, this chapter is to lay bare the reason why defensive realism fits with the specific historical record of the Great Power Era better than offensive realism did: Defensive realism looked at the right period of history for it, while offensive realism looked at the wrong period of history. See the concluding chapter below.

9. Also note that this process of self-transformation does not depend on anyone of the three mechanisms (i.e., democracy peace, interdependence, and international organizations or institutions) that have been commonly invoked by non-realists to support the thesis that the world has become more peaceful. For a realist's critique of the three non-realist mechanisms, see Waltz (2000).

10. Cederman and his colleagues (e.g., Cederman and Gleditsch 2004; Cederman and Girardin 2010) have provided similar simulated results based on agent-based modeling (ABM).

11. Although Elias uncovered the same outcome, he did not focus on its implication for transforming the system of international politics. Rather, he was most interested in its domestic impact.

12. Conquest becoming more difficult does not mean that conquest cannot succeed.

13. These two systems are selected for their (relatively) complete historical record. For two recent studies of the two systems that emphasizes the differences between the two systems, see Hui (2005); and Kang (2005). The differences between Hui's finding and mine are partially due to the fact that she examines a shorter time frame and focuses on "great powers." The dynamics uncovered here should also apply to other parts of the world (i.e., Africa, South and North America, the South Asia subcontinent): if their evolution had not been cut off by European colonialism, these parts of the world would have experienced the same evolutionary path as the two systems examined here had experienced. A comparative study that tests the balance-of-power theory at the global level with a very long timeframe (from 900 BC to 1600 AD) indirectly supports my claim here (Wohlforth et al. 2007). The study shows that in most ancient international subsystems, empire and hegemony were not only possible but also often robust, thus implying that conquest was relatively easy. The study also suggests that the prevalence of *de facto* balance-of-power among states might have arisen only fairly recently (i.e., post-1600). Such a result also is consistent with my argument that the defensive realism world did not come into existence until fairly recent (e.g., after the 17–18th centuries), perhaps first in the European system.

14. More recently, there have been several empirical studies of state death in international systems with the quantitative approach (e.g., Adams 2003; Fazal 2004; Zacher 2001). While these works are related to my work (especially those of Fazal and Zacher because they explicitly tie the changing rate of state death to the evolution of the international system), they differ from our work in two important aspects. First, they examine a relative short period of history. Second, they explain the changing rate of state death either with ideational changes (Zacher 2001) or materials factors (Adams 2003; Fazal 2004), *but not together.* Fazal (2004, 339–41) briefly touched upon both the material dimension and the ideational dimension without integrating them together. In contrast, my SEP approach explicitly seeks to organically integrate material forces and ideational forces through social evolution. My approach thus provides an explanation for how ideational forces come into play, whereas a purely ideational explanation will still have to explain how those ideas come into existence.

15. State death actually started much earlier. I choose 1046/4 BC as the starting point because the war between Zhou and Shang was clearly recorded in written history and its timing was firmly established by recent archeological research (Shaughnessy 1985–87; Jiang and Niu 1999).

16. During the spring–autumn period which followed the war between Zhou and Shang (770–476 BC), more than 180 tribes were recorded in historical texts. I thus take Si-Ma Qian's record of more 800 tribes at the beginning of Zhou as quite credible. The number of states eliminated in this episode can only go up if those tribes that were loyal to the Shang Kingdom are also counted. Another ancient historical text, *Lu Shi Chun Qiu* [Lu's Annals], put the number of states at the

beginning of Shang at 3,000, and the number of states at the beginning of Zhou at 1,800. For an earlier discussion, see Cioffi-Revilla and Lai (1995).

17. The period after Western Jin is usually called "wuhu shiliu guo" in Chinese historiography, literally "five nomadic tribes, sixteen states". In reality, in addition to the sixteen states, there were eight additional states in the system. The Tang dynasty was built upon the Sui dynasty, by incorporating five additional nomadic states into its territory. If we only calculate the rate of state death only up to Sui's unification of the Chinese core, it would be 8.4 state deaths per century.

18. The period after Tang's collapse is usually called "wudai shiguo", literally "five dynasties and ten states". There were actually twelve independent political entities because in addition to the ten states in the Chinese core, there were two tribal states, Kunming and Yanke, located in today's Guizhou province and Yunnan province. The Song dynasty (Northern and later Southern Song, 960–1276 AD) was formed by eliminating the other eleven states. Other than Song, the rest of the nine independent states include: Xi-xia (1038–1227), Liao (916–1125, later to become Western Liao after being attacked by Jin in 1125), Jin (1125–1234), Mongols (established in 1206), Tu-fang (today's Tibet and part of today's Qinghai and Sichuan), Da-li (today's Yunan province), Huangtou Huihu (occupying part of today's Gansu and Qinghai province), Xizhou Huihu (occupying today's Western Xinjiang), Heihan (occupying part of today's Western Qinghai, Xinjiang, and Central Asia). In 1276 AD, the Mongols eliminated the last independent state (Southern Song) in the system.

19. In 1584, other than Qing (Manchu), there were five other states in the system: four nomadic states (in the Western part of today's China, especially Xinjiang and Gangsu) and Ming. Ming was overthrown and replaced by a rebel. In addition, there was another rebel controlling today's Sichuan province and a loyalist to Ming controlling Taiwan. Therefore, the Manchu eliminated a total of seven states (political entities) in the whole process.

20. From this episode on, the number of states in the system is calculated from Tan et al. 1991.

21. The seven states eliminated include Ming, which was briefly replaced by a rebel in 1644.

22. I include Sardin and Sicily because they were eventually absorbed into modern Italy. Within Continental Europe, I exclude several mini-states that remain constant in the system (e.g., Monaco). I calculate the number of states in the system from three primary resources: Barraclough, *The Times Atlas of World History* (*TAWH*), Braubach et al. *Gebhardt Handbuch der Deutschen Geschichte* [Gebhardt Handbook of German History, or *GHGH*]), and Euratlas (<http:\\www.euratlas.com>). See Table 2.1.

23. In contrast, for much of the medieval time, the Holy Roman Empire was the only legitimate secular polity in Europe, indicated by the fact that the Holy Roman Empire was simply identified as "the Empire" and its ruler as "the Emperor", reflecting the Empire's universal stature. Under the reign of Innocent III (1198–1216 AD), the Papacy was at the zenith of its power, and most feudal lords were officially and factually under the rule of the Pope: feudal lords had only physical rights over their subjects, but their legal rights depended upon the

higher authority of the Pope. Hence, Europe at that time cannot be understood as a genuine anarchy.

24. Jack S. Levy (1983) thus put the beginning of the modern Power Great Era in Europe at 1495. If we extend our inquiry into pre-1450 but post-900 era, we would find that roughly the same dynamics reigned within the western Frankish Empire. For a very social evolutionary discussion, see Elias ([1939]1994, part III, esp. pp. 263–4, 269–71, 277–89). See also Tilly 1990.

25. We calculate the number of states in 1450 as the following. In 1450, today's Spain contained five states: Aragon, Castile (these two merged in 1479), Granada (conquered by Aragon-Castile in 1492), Roussillon (conquered by Aragon-Castile in 1493), and Navarre (conquered by Aragon-Castile in 1512). There were around 30 independent or semi-independent political entities within today's France (*TAWH*, 151, also see <http://historymedren.about.com/library/atlas/blatmapfrance1453. htm>). There were 31 independent or semi-independent political entities in the lower land area. There were about 100 independent political entities within today's Italy (*TAWH*, 150), and about 389 within today's Germany in 1450 (GHDG/GHGH, 769–70). In addition, there were about 26 other states in the system: Austria, Bohemia, Bosnia, Bulgaria, Byzantine, Croatia, Denmark, Dominion of the Teutonic Order, Finland, Lithuania, Livonia, Moldavia, Moravia, Mozovia, Norway, Poland, Portugal, Poskov, Russia, Serbia, Slovenia, Sweden, Tartary, Transylvania, Union of Switzerland, and Wallachia (<http://www.euroaltas.com>). Denmark, Finland, Norway, and Sweden formed the Kalmar Union between 1397 and 1523 AD.

26. For 1648, we counted those states that were under the Spanish monarch's suzerainty at that time but later emerged again as independent actors as semi-independent states. Within today's Germany, excluding free cities, or there were about 234 independent political entities according to TAWH (p. 191) or 243 according to our calculation from GHDG/GHGH. We chose the lower number (using the large number will not significantly influence the rate of state death). Within today's Italy, there were about 14 independent political entities (<http://www.lib.utexas. edu/maps/historical/ward_1912/europe_1648.jpg>). In addition, there were 12 other actors in the system: Austria-Bohemia, Denmark, France, Holland, Poland, Portugal, the Ottoman Empire, Russia, the Spanish Monarchy, Sweden, Switzerland, and Tataria.

27. The total number of states within the system in 1815 was estimated to be 63. In Germany, the number of independent political entities had been reduced to 41 (Fulbrook 1997, 2; Gooch 1970, 64); while that within Italy to 9 (Clough and Saladino 1968, 29). The other 13 actors in the system included Austria, Denmark, France, Holland, Moldavia, the Ottoman Empire, Portugal, Russia, Serbia, Spain, Sweden, Switzerland, and Wallachia (*TAWH*, 204–5).

28. The 30 states in 1919 were: Albania, Austria, Basque, Belarus, Belgium, Bulgaria, Catalonia, Czechoslovakia, Denmark, Estonia, Finland, France, Germany, Greece, Holland, Hungary, Italy, Latvia, Lithuania, Luxembourg, Norway, Poland, Portugal, Romania, the Soviet Union, Spain, Sweden, Switzerland, Turkey, and Yugoslavia.

29. The 25 states in 1945 were: Albania, Austria, Belgium, Bulgaria, Czechoslovakia, Denmark, E. Germany, Finland, France, Greece, Holland, Hungary, Italy, Luxembourg, Norway, Poland, Portugal, Romania, the Soviet Union, Spain, Sweden, Switzerland, Turkey, W. Germany, and the former Yugoslavia.

30. The 35 states in 2005 are: Albania, Austria, Belarus, Belgium, Bosnia-Herzegovina, Bulgaria, Croatia, Czech, Denmark, Estonia, Finland, France, Germany, Greece, Holland, Hungary, Italy, Latvia, Lithuania, Luxembourg, Macedonia, Moldavia, Norway, Poland, Portugal, Romania, Russia, Serbia-Montenegro, Slovakia, Slovenia, Spain, Sweden, Switzerland, Turkey, and Ukraine.

31. These state deaths have actually led to an increase in the number of the states in the system. As such, it is not really meaningful to calculate rate of state death for this period.

32. Hence, there have been spatial and temporal differences in the evolution of different systems: time and space are essential for social evolution to operate. Arguably, Africa and America (North and South) would have experienced a similar evolutionary process and eventually evolved into a similar state if they were not colonized by Western powers (hence, their "natural" evolutionary courses were abruptly interrupted). See Chapter 2 above.

33. I do not argue that the evolution of the two systems had been linear (i.e., the number of states had steadily decreased and the average size of states steadily increased). Indeed, the two systems had experienced periods of reversal (i.e., the number of states increased in some period of time). The recent increase in the number of states in the European system supports the argument that it had evolved from an offensive realism world into a defensive realism world (see below).

34. The five attempts of conquest toward regional hegemony identified by Mearsheimer (2001) include Imperial Japan, Napoleonic France, Wilhelmine Germany, Nazi Germany, and the United States. Other major failed attempts of continental conquest in Europe include Spain's expansion under Philip II and France's expansion under Louis XIV.

35. This is a negative feedback process on a grand scale: it had extended from the very early period of human history to the not so distant past. For negative feedbacks, see Jervis (1997). For an underdeveloped statement that "the logic of anarchy leads to its own demise", see Wendt 2003, 494.

36. While the third auxiliary mechanism (sovereignty and nationalism) has been singled out before (e.g., Ruggie 1983), it was not presented as part of an overarching explanation. More importantly, an objective foundation for the rise of sovereignty and nationalism was missing (see below). By listing the three mechanisms as auxiliary mechanisms, I am not suggesting that they are dispensable or minor but merely that they cannot operate without the results engineered by the fundamental mechanisms. One can enlist additional mechanisms (e.g., military technology) that have played a role in the transformation, but they are secondary and can be subsumed by the social evolutionary framework. For instance, military technology can be understood as a product of the evolution of warfare in human societies: The demand to kill drives the evolution of technologies of killing. Our

explanation therefore subsumes a purely technology-based explanation of the evolution of the system and explains a much longer period of human history.

37. These defensive realist states can be treated as mutants in the biological sense. At the late stage of the offensive realism world, some states can choose to become defensive realist states (see below).

38. For instance, expansionist France under Louis XIV and Napoleon, Nazi Germany, Fascist Italy, and Imperial Japan were all severely punished after losing their attempts at conquest: All of them were occupied for a significant period of time after losing their attempts toward conquest. Selection does not have to mean the elimination of actors (states), this is true even in natural selection.

39. Being strategic depends on learning because being strategic means making decisions after acquiring and processing information, and acquiring and processing information is a learning process. The small literature on learning in international politics has largely focused on the process and consequences of learning within a relatively short timeframe. For a good review, see Levy (1994).

40. Such a learning process is negative learning. Negative learning means learning from one's own and others' failures, while positive learning means just the opposite. After the rise of constructivism, positive learning has received most attention in the literature. Yet, because human beings tend to continue to do what used to work due to inertia, negative learning may have played an equally important role as positive learning has in the accumulation of knowledge. Learning first through negative and then positive learning itself is a social evolutionary process (Campbell 1960; 1974a; 1974b; see also Popper [1939]1959; 1972, 261–5). Levy (1994, 304) also noted that individuals and organizations tend to learn more from failure than success. Legro examined the process of ideational changes through collapse of old ideas and consolidation of new ideas without using the phrase of negative learning (Legro, 2005). Hence, in our formulation, selection and learning (which includes rationality) actually work together in the evolution of the system. In contrast, Waltz suggested that the selection of balancing behavior does not need rationality, even though he explicitly stated that "if some do relatively well, others will emulate them or fall by the wayside" (Waltz, 1979, p. 118), and emulation is a form of learning. A similar argument has been advanced by Alchian (1950) in the context of the emergence of optimal outcomes in economic competition. Both Waltz and Alchian denied that rationality (or learning) is needed in generating desirable outcome: But how can one know a particular behavior or technology is desirable or optimal and then adopt it without learning? Meanwhile, constructivism tends to emphasize (positive) learning while neglecting selection. Thus, pitting learning against selection or vice versa is therefore on the wrong footing for understanding human society. For details, see the discussion in Chapter 5 below.

41. Many great powers have become defensive realists after losing wars of conquest and then being severely punished. France after Napoleon, post-Second World War Germany, Japan, and Italy all became defensive realists. Most of the culturalist (constructivist) explanations of Germany and Japan's security policy emphasized only (political) culture (as learned ideas) (Berger, 1998; Duffield, 1995; Katzenstein, 1996). For a balanced critique of a purely cultural (or learning) explanation

of state behavior, see Sagan (1997). China had also gone from an offensive realist to a defensive realist partly because of the punishments it received when it pursued an offensive realism (or revolutionary) policy under Mao Tse-tong during the 1950–70s (Goldstein 2001; Tang and Gries 2002; Tang 2008a). Arguably, the United States might have been the only great power that has yet to be firmly socialized into a defensive realism state, mostly due to its unique geographical location. We develop this argument in greater detail in Tang and Long 2012.

42. A good indicator for this auxiliary mechanism may be the frequency of war in the two systems through time. Such a calculation, however, will require a major undertaking. Claudio Cioffi-Revilla and his colleagues were perhaps moving toward building a dataset for wars in ancient systems (e.g., Cioffi-Revilla 1996; Cioffi-Revilla and Lai, 1995), but not much progress has been reported in the literature since the mid-1990s.

43. One must note, however, that sovereign and sovereignty really predated 1648 and even Francisco Vitoria and Hugo Grotius (Anghie 2004). Indeed, my argument here also points to the possibility that the idea of sovereign and sovereignty can arise and might have arisen independently many times in subsystems in which the idea that conquest has become more difficult.

44. I do not deal with the diffusion of the sovereignty norm from Europe to other parts of the world. The large literature on state formation in Europe mostly focuses on why and how a particular form of state (i.e., sovereign territorial state) eventually came to dominate in the system (e.g., Tilly 1990; Spruyt 1994a; 1994b). This literature assigns an important role to competition among units (e.g., war, regulating and profiting from internal and international trade) for driving the evolutionary process. My interpretation complements this literature by providing a foundation for this process to operate.

45. Thus, nationalism came after sovereignty, although there have been continuous tensions between sovereignty and nationalism as these two ideas co-evolved (Barkin and Cronin 1994). The literature on the origin and spreading of nationalism and its impact is voluminous. For some of the most important works, see Anderson 1983; Gellner 1983; Smith 1986; Hobsbawn 1990.

46. Indeed, the fact that nationalism had made war much more severe can be understood to support the argument here, although at a different level: because war has become more brutal and total, citizens eventually came to dislike war and limit states' capacity and willingness to make war.

47. I offer two possible demarcation lines for delineating the two worlds: The Second World War (a conservative take) and Westphalia (an optimistic take). Alternatively, one can take Westphalia to symbolize the budding, while the Second World War is the maturation of Jervis's world.

48. For a more detailed discussion, see Korman (1996), esp. ch. 7. Obviously, my explanation easily explains the existence of small buffer states in recent human history, a phenomenon that a purely technology-based explanation cannot explain well (Fazal 2007). Both Wendt (1995, 78–9; idem 1999, 323–4) and Johnston (2001, 489–90) correctly noted that the survival of these states pose a challenge for a purely materialistic (realist) explanation of international politics.

49. Indeed, after 1989, very few wars have been inter-state wars [data from the ongoing project on armed conflict project at Peace Research Institute Oslo (PRIO), <http:\\www.prio.no>]. My thesis is less sweeping than Mueller's thesis that major war is becoming obsolete because I only claim that war of conquest has been becoming obsolete. I do not exclude the possibility that major war is also becoming obsolete. Mueller's thesis is of course a purely ideationalistic thesis, and he did not provide any material/objective foundation for why states now "dislike" wars. For a more recent discussion on the waning of major wars, see the collection of essays in Vayrynen (2006). My thesis also means a lesser role for peace among democracies in the overall pacifying of the international system, as captured by "democratic peace" (see the "Conclusion" chapter below).

50. Cox did not uncover the mechanisms that had been responsible for transforming the offensive realism world into a defensive realism world, although he came closer than others because he argues that material capabilities, ideas, and institutions work together to shape the course of history.

CHAPTER 4

1. The dichotomy of state versus society may be invalid, reflecting our desire to escape from power (Tang 2011a, ch. 5). Society has always been made by power, and the state as a source of power has always been a central actor in this process (Elias [1939]1994; Foucault 1980).

2. Although talking about institutions almost inevitably leads us to talk something about order, order is notoriously difficult to define and even more difficult to measure. I refrain from engaging order here but develop a more rigorous definition of order and a framework for measuring it (Tang, n.d.-b).

3. Hence, institutions (and structure as the overall international system within a society) and agents have a duality relationship (that is, institutions and agents mutually constitute each other). For details, see Tang 2011a, ch. 5. See also Giddens 1979; 1984.

4. I have put Latin America first among the three cases, partially because EU-centrism that that has been so prevalent in regionalism literature has been unhealthy (Solingen 2008, 288; see also Acharya 2000). The earliest security community, though, might have been the Nordic countries (Wæver 1998, 72–4). As many have now recognized, focusing on regions (or subsystems) is a more promising way for theorizing international society (and world society). See, for example, Buzan 1991; 2004, 16–18; 2011; Lake and Morgan 1997; Mansfield and Milner 1997; Adler and Barnett 1998a; 1998b; Buzan and Wæver 2003; Katzenstein 2005, and Acharya 2007.

5. Hence, I am mostly interested in the commonalities rather than the differences or the uniqueness of the three cases. For studies focusing on the differences, see, for example, Risse-Kappen 1996; Lake and Morgan 1997; Mansfield and Milner 1997; Hemmer and Katzenstein 2002; Fort and Webber 2006; Acharya 2009; He and Feng 2012. For earlier studies focusing on the former, see Adler and Barnett 1998a; Kacowicz 1998; Kupchan 2010. Adler and Barnett (1998, 32–3) noted that security communities can exist between states without geographical proximity, but they

are exceptions (e.g., Australia as part of the West, and U.S.-Israel). Geography remains important even in the age of globalization. Of course, geographical proximity does not entail amicable interactions.

6. On this front, I also venture to argue that once deep peace is in place, it is unlikely to unravel. For clarification of concepts such as shallow and deep peace, see Tang 2011c and the references cited there.

7. This dynamic also explains why many "negative zones of peace" (in Kacowicz's terminology) emerged after 1648 but then collapsed back into zones of war before 1945 (e.g., the Concert of Europe). Hence, the fact that attempts of institutionalizing peace before the coming of the defensive realism world had ultimately failed does not disconfirm my theses (for examples, see Kupchan 2010). Indeed, it strengthens my theses: it shows that institutionalization of regional peace really can only succeed *after* the whole system or a fairly isolated subsystem has evolved into a defensive realism world. Contra Kacowicz 1998, it is ultimately unsatisfactory to explain zone of peace with acceptance of territorial status quo: this acceptance as an idea is something to be explained.

8. In addition to the three cases presented here, the economic integration between China, Russia, and the five Central Asian states has followed the same pattern. For an earlier discussion, see Tang 2000.

9. Hence, we shall predict that notwithstanding the economic and financial difficulties of the European project, (West) Europe will not go "back to the future", contra Mearsheimer (1990).

10. It is unclear whether a common civilization or identity is a necessary, sufficient, facilitating, or even hindering factor to the formation of a regional order.

11. For a brief sketch of the exact processes of institutional peace in the three regions, see Table 4.1.

12. ASEAN Security Community (ASC), ASEAN economic community (AEC), ASEAN Socio-Cultural Community (ASCC).

13. Unfortunately, some of these authors have conflated organizations with institutions (i.e., rules), and most of those they talk about were organizations. Because institutions underpin organizations and organizations build and enforce institutions, however, the discussion cited above does hold positive implications for understanding institutionalizing peace. Russett and Oneal (2001) emphasized the tripod of peace: interdependence, international organization, and democratization. Adler and Barnett (1998, 45–6) also emphasized the role of positive feedbacks (self-reinforcing changes) in constructing a security community. Mature democracy may be a necessary condition for reaching and sustaining deep peace because only mature democracies can come to terms with their (unhappy) past (Tang 2011c).

14. Following Oelsner (2005), the Southern Cone includes members of MERCOSUR (Argentina, Bolivia, Brazil, Chile, Paraguay, and Uruguay), while excluding Central America and Mexico.

15. For instance, when Brazil and then Argentina experienced a financial crisis in 1998–2002, they again resorted to the measures of "begging your neighbor" by imposing non-tariff obstacles on trade.

16. There should not be any doubt that the two World Wars had given countries ample reason to treasure peace, thus creating the incentives and pressure for institutionalizing peace.

17. Not surprisingly, drawing from the European experience, many have emphasized a hegemon's role in the institutionalizing and maintaining of peace (e.g., Gilpin 1981; Ikenberry 2000; Lake 2001). For a similar thesis drawn from the ancient East Asian experience, see Kang 2005.

18. Most authors in the Checkel edited volume did not differentiate organizations from institutions. Most strikingly, even in EU as the most likely case for finding strong internalization, internalization of other's ideas has been extremely limited (Checkel 2007a, viii; 2007b; 16, 21).

19. When Sukarno's model of self-reliance was overthrown by Suharto's export-led growth, Indonesia, as the most powerful state within ASEAN, had incentives and power to propel ASEAN into a more peace-building organization and then institutionalizing peace through ASEAN. Equally important, SEA countries had pursued a strategy of export-driven economic growth as part of an overall strategy to confront domestic political challenges, contra Middle East states (Solingen 2007).

20. Of course, potential leader states within a region can deliberately refrain from exercising positive leadership (e.g., Indonesia in ASEAN; see Anwar 2006). Alternatively, potential leader states simply get distracted by domestic instabilities (e.g., Nigeria in West Africa, see Kacowicz 1998).

21. Indeed, the Arab League, founded in 1945, has been the oldest post-Second World War regional organization.

22. For a fine critical discussion regarding the definition of institutions, see Duffield 2007.

23. Unfortunately, Axelrod's experiments do not really capture much of the reality in international politics, contra Axelrod's claim. For a more detailed critique, see Tang (2008a). See also Gowa (1986).

24. Martin and Simmons's original statement is: "Institutions are *simultaneously causes and effects*" (Emphasis original). This statement is misleading: Institutions have to be created first, and then come back to shape actors' behaviors.

25. Hence, in an offensive realism world in which very few international institutions exist, offensive realism's stand that international institutions cannot shape international outcomes is easily supported.

26. Deutsch et al. (1957, 38) and Adler and Barnett (1998, esp. 39–40) did emphasize the role of power in constructing a security community, so did Ikenberry and Kupchan (1990). See also Kupchan 2010.

27. Of course, some of institutions' effects might have been unintended consequences (Jervis 1997, 81–7; 1999, 53–5).

28. I address whether institutions can shape agents' *collective* identities and the common knowledge among agents in the next section.

29. Again, the gap between offensive realism's position on this question and that of neoliberalism and constructivism is too much to be bridged.

30. This point has to be understood in light of realists' concern for relative gains. Jervis differentiates three types of institutions: institutions as standard tools of statecraft, institutions as innovative tools, and institutions as causes of changes in

preferences over outcomes (Jervis 1999, 55–62). He then points out that it is only the third type that can truly differentiate defensive realism from neoliberalism because defensive realism acknowledges the utility of the first two types of institutions (ibid. 55). The first two types can be understood as one type: institutions as tools or instruments of statecraft.

31. Hence, when a neoliberalist argues that institutions can change states' preference over outcomes via states' identities, he or she has already moved closer to a constructivism position.

32. Admittedly, some constructivists have been careful to note that common identities (or other cultural factors) do not necessarily entail cooperation (e.g., Jepperson et al. 1996, 39; Wendt 1999, 160). Our arguments here apply to both cooperative and conflictual situations: to rely exclusively on identities to explain cooperation and conflict as social outcomes is one-sided, to say the least. For mostly culturalist theories of conflict and cooperation, see Berger 1998 among many others.

33. Risse-Kappen (1996, 398) noted that the Japan–US alliance is an anomaly for his thesis: it should not be, as long as the U.S. could maintain a relatively benign domination over Japan.

34. Our understanding of institutionalization is thus broader than what neoliberalism (e.g., Keohane 1984; Keohane and Martin 1995) has in mind so far: institutionalization contains not only formal processes but also informal processes (i.e., culturalization).

35. For an overview of institutional approaches in economics, sociology, and politics, see Tang 2011a, esp. chs. 2 and 3 and references cited there.

36. Waltz (1979), of course, was inspired by functionalism, especially that of Durkheim. On this connection, see Goddard and Nexon 2005; and Buzan and Albert 2010.

37. See also Bunge 1997, ch. 9. Bunge uses systemism to denote a synthesis of individualism and holism (ibid. ch. 10). Neumann (2004) uses "organicism" to denote holism.

38. Notably, all these big concepts are ill-defined. I venture to define them vigorously and sort out the relationships between them elsewhere (Tang, n.d.-b).

39. Of course, an issue-based approach toward institution does not exclude a synthesis of the different approaches toward institutions: In fact, only such an approach can provide such a sound synthesis.

40. Although realism might have been quite "critical" among major IR schools (e.g., Morgenthau 1970, Schweller 2001; Cozette 2008) and "critical IR theory" explicitly claims to be "critical" (Booth 2005), I do not privilege a particular IR school here because none of the IR schools (including the so-called "critical theory" school) have been critical enough, according to the standards set here.

41. Although defensive realism does not deny that institutions have roles to play in international politics, it does not pay much attention to this question. My discussion here thus ignores defensive realism. The international law approach (i.e., the Grotian-Pudendorf kind) has often been a key component of the English School, and increasingly, the normative strain of social constructivism.

42. Initially, neoliberalism differed from functionalism in another aspect: neoliberalism generally takes organizations to be institutions. For why organizations should

not be taken as institutions, see North 1990; Duffield 2007; and Tang 2011a, ch. 1. Of course, organizations must have rules to operate.

43. For instance, the pluralist strain of the English School reifies the post-1648 Westphalian system without looking into the actual process of the making the Westphalian system. In contrast, although neoliberalism praises the post-1945 U.S.-centric structure of international political economy, it does look into real processes of institutional change.

44. Not surprisingly, there have been increasing calls for a dialogue and synthesis between the English School and social constructivism (e.g., Reus-Smit 2002).

45. Here, we adopt a minimalist definition of a "world state" or "world society": a world state is a world in which individuals within it adopt a similar set of basic rules and values and thus have a sense of "community" or "society". Adopting a maximalist definition of a world state can only strengthen our argument. It does not make much sense to differentiate "world state" or "world society". The practice of separating society from state mostly reflects our desire to escape from power (Tang 2011a, ch. 5).

46. On this account, I admit my siding with the English School (its pluralist strain) and neoliberalism, while rejecting Kantian idealism. For a discussion, see Linklater and Suganami (2006), ch. 4.

47. These constructivists (e.g., Reus-Smit 1997, 566–8; Johnston 2001, 492–3; Acharya 2009) who have acknowledged the possibility of resistance have been exceptions. Johnston provided a fine-grained discussion on the micro aspects of socialization and internalization.

48. One cannot fail to notice that globalization, the key process of bringing about an international society or a world society, has been critically driven by actors with power, be it leading states or non-state actors from these leading states (Woods 2000, 9; Buzan 2004, 12).

49. And local ones have too been imposed and backed by power (Tang 2011a).

50. Buzan (2011) also projected a world without superpowers to become more regionalized.

CHAPTER 5

1. In the same spirit, Loyal and Barnes (2001) called agency a red herring in social theory. Of course, I am not suggesting that "structure" per se should be eliminated from social sciences. Rather, I am suggesting system (with structure being part of it) is a far more promising starting point.

2. I do think that Archer's "emergentist" approach is more useful than Giddens's structuration approach because the former has a closer affinity with a systemic approach. Fortunately, the agent-structure debate has quieted down in IR, perhaps reflecting its sterility.

3. As far as I can tell, Wendt (1999) does not define "society" or "the social system".

4. In other words, structural theories can only be quasi-systemic theories (Jervis 1997). See also Ruggie 1983, 271; Waltz 1979, 79; Spirtas 1996, 392.

5. There have been many definitions of anarchy. For discussions, see Milner 1991. Here, I used the sparest definition: anarchy is a lack of central authority.

6. As becomes clear in Chapters 2 and 3 above, there is indeed differentiation among units within the international system, mostly critically, the differentiation of offensive realist states versus non-offensive realist states (see also Tang 2008a). Moreover, whether there is some kind of differentiation among units is not a part of structure, but a property of the system (see also Buzan and Albert 2010).

7. From a methodological point of view, Waltz's theory thus operates upon a single independent (explanatory) variable. Almost without an exception, theories centered upon a single explanatory variable are misleading and wrong, simply because social systems are too complex. Hence, we often find that proponents of such theories defend themselves on the ground of parsimony and not much else.

8. Wendt (1999, ch. 3) contends that (distribution of) power and interests are constituted by ideas. This is wrong: although interests and the meaning of (the distribution of) power are inherently constituted by ideas, distribution of material power itself is not constituted by ideas. Distribution of material power stands alone. Wendt thus committed the error of conceptual sloppiness.

9. For earlier reviews of notions of structure, see Powell 1994, 320–6; Adler and Barnett 1998a, 9–10.

10. For a summary of the criticism leveled against Waltz on this front, see Buzan et al. 1993, ch. 2. In sociology, Parsons (1951) also prominently took system and structure to be essentially equivalent. For similarities between Waltz and Parsons, see Goddard and Nexon (2005). Kaplan's (1957) earlier discussion of the international system was even more muddled and is now justly forgotten.

11. Hence, contrary Waltz (1979, 80), interactions can take place beyond the unit level.

12. For Wendt (1999), the key is what collective culture (i.e., Hobbesian, Lockeian, and Kantian) drives states. For Lebow (2008), the key is what kind of collective mixture of major motives (interest, spirit, and reason) drives states. I favor a broader conceptualization than Wendt and Lebow. For instance, units can be driven by prevailing institutions, social norms (including honor), and internal motives. Wendt's deploying culture/collective identity to explain the nature of most units can easily become tautological. See the discussion in Chapter 4.

13. A "regional security complex" is perhaps more appropriately called a "regional security system".

14. Although poles (i.e., great power or regional great powers) within a (sub)system can have more impact on the system, smaller players sometimes can have disproportional, impact upon the system. The impact of the two Koreas upon the post-1945 Northeast Asia subsystem is an instructive example. A similar case can be made for Israel (for the Middle East) and Pakistan (for South Asia). Waltz's focus on great powers reflects a selection/cognitive bias: we tend to focus on big things because we believe that only great powers can have important impact over the system (or structure). This is a typical non-systemic (or linear) thinking (Jervis 1997, ch. 2).

15. Here, it is important to note that the nature of most units in the system too is a product of social evolution (which is more than socialization), rather than socialization alone as advocated by constructivists today and functionalists yesterday.

16. Wendt may want to label these properties of interactions as part of "structure", partly because interactions (as micro) have a "micro structure" (1999, 147–50). Wendt's move is a hard squeeze and unnecessary: it is far more convenient to treat them as properties of the system rather than part of the structure. Apparently, for much of our history, this dimension was greatly conditioned by geography. Buzan et al. (1993, ch. 4) emphasize that the amount and the scope of interaction are underpinned by "interactive capacities", of which they single out transportation/communication technologies and norms and organizations. The notion of "interactive capacities" mixes too many things together to be useful.

17. This is very important because all too often social scientists merely focus on interactions among units and those between agents and structure while totally forgetting the interactions between agents and the physical environment (e.g., Archer 1995; Wendt 1999, ch. 4). This easily leads us to the pitfall of extreme ideationalism (e.g., social constructivism) and overemphasis of agent-structure.

18. Wendt (1999, 251) correctly noted that a culture does not necessarily entail cooperation or conflict.

19. Here, it is also important to emphasize that while states' perception of the system can be wrong at any given time, in the long run it tends to match social reality, due to selection and learning.

20. Memory is now a critical field of inquiry in anthropology, cultural studies, sociology, and political theory. For a discussion of memory in interstate reconciliation, see Tang 2011c and the citations there.

21. For similar arguments, see Copeland 2000a, 25, Kydd 2005, 18. Unfortunately, the human society had plenty of bad memories. Schweller (ibid.) also pointed out: "What triggers security dilemmas under anarchy is the *possibility* of predatory states existing among the ranks of the units the system comprises." Altogether, *in order for states to fear each other, they need both memories of past predators and the possibility that today's benign states can become predators tomorrow.*

22. Here, structuralism merely denotes theories that overemphasize structural constraints rather than a particular school of social theories called "Structuralism", heavily influenced by Saussure's structural linguistics. For a good discussion on Structuralism and notions of structure, see Wight 2006, ch. 4.

23. Although Waltz's neorealism is closer to defensive realism, it straddles offensive and defensive realism. For a more detailed discussion, see Tang (2010a, ch. 6). See also Spirtas (1996); Zakaria (1998), and Kydd (2005).

24. Mostly likely, the coming of defensive realism's stand has something to do with the necessity of limiting power politics after the coming of the "ultimate weapon" (Craig 2003).

25. Another negative consequence of this overemphasizing uncertainty over others' intentions is that we have greatly marginalized the role of other dimensions within uncertainty in IR (see Tang 2012 for a more detailed discussion).

26. One can even register a stricture against Wendt on this front: his move is a hard and unnecessary squeeze, and it is far more convenient to treat interactions as a property of the system even if interactions have a "structure". The same argument applies to his making distribution of interests as part of structure (Wendt 1999, 103–9).

27. This is why Wendt's structural constructivism is semi-evolutionary, or more evolutionary than Waltz's structural realism. Wendt (1999, 147) also correctly recognizes that individualism does not have to be atomism (which insists on the properties of units alone) whereas individualism can examine interactions among units. Hence, atomism is an even narrower form of individualism.

28. Wendt actually insists that constructivism actually "suggests a program of empirical research for studying the content of real world state interests [and many other things]" (1999, 133). What he does not appreciate is that his structuralism stand will essentially preclude such a research program.

29. Wendt's inability to account for the evolutionary changes of international systems cannot be pushed aside by merely defending "pragmatism (or ecumenism)" in explaining social changes and rejecting reductionism (Wendt 1999, 150–7).

30. On this front, Norbert Elias's (1939[1994]) magnum opus *The Civilizing Process,* which masterfully weaves together psychological changes and macro social changes (both material and ideational), should be a constant source of inspiration. For a more detailed discussion, see Tang 2013.

31. In the agent-structure discourse, agency or action (which is driven by human will) is often singled out to differentiate it from behaviors (which may or may not be driven by human will). By using behavior, I hold that agents' behaviors—whether willing, coerced, or random—all contribute to the dynamics within and the possible transformation of a social system.

32. Although socialization is useful for broader purposes, I refrain from employing it here because it is too blunt an instrument for understanding exactly how a system shapes agents. Elsewhere (Tang 2011b), I use socialization to denote part of human nature as drivers of human behavior. Both positive learning and constituting (via internalization) are mechanisms of social inheritance. See immediately below.

33. I refrain from using the term "resistance" that has been more in use because "resistance" can mean both *physical* resistance and *ideational* resistance, and only ideational resistance is anti-socialization. Political theorists in the Marxism/critical theory and Foucauldian tradition (e.g., Gramsci, Foucault), of course, have persistently advocated for "resistance," but this is different from documenting actual resistance or anti-socialization (e.g., Scott 1985; 1990). Physical resistance is roughly equivalent to realist's term "balancing". Anti-socialization is thus also different from realism's notion of balancing. Of course, anti-socialization (as ideational resistance) must have a material foundation. Also, anti-socialization should be differentiated from "anomie": anti-socialization as a channel is indispensable to anomie as an outcome; but anomie is often caused by a combination of the various channels. For a classical statement on anomie, see Merton 1968, 131–94. I thank Xiayu Pu for making me differentiate these terms more explicitly.

34. This is also supported by the fact that we often do counterfactuals after negative experiences but rarely after positive experiences, and counterfactuals are a powerful tool for learning and adjusting our behaviors to avoid similar mistakes in the future (Roese 1997; Epstude and Roese 2008).

35. Hence, Bismarck famously bragged that "fools learn by experience, wise men by other people's experience" (quoted in Jervis 1976, 239).

36. As Johnston (2001, 489) noted, in Waltz's framework, socialization is the same as selection through competition (see also Wendt 1999, 100–2; Schweller and Wohlforth 2000, 78–80). Wendt's (1999, 324–36) "cultural selection" is really inheritance or transmission via imitation and (social) learning, following Boyd and Richerson's (1980, 102) misguided discussion.

37. For example, in a late-state offensive realism world, defensive realist states can already prosper. In a defensive realism world, an offensive realist state can still exist although not necessarily flourish.

38. Indeed, even structural functionalists such as Durkheim, Parsons, and Merton admitted outcomes of anti-socialization (i.e., deviance, anomie, abnormal): their problem has been their inability or unwillingness to admit anti-socialization to be "normal"!

39. Kant (1784[1991], 44–5) captured it with "unsocial sociability" (see also Elias 1939 [1994], 440). Freud alerted us to the possibility that biological instincts can be part of the anti-socialization drive.

40. Because existing discussions tend to ignore the channel of constraining/enabling, I shall illustrate my points with them, although I insist that constraining/enabling is a foundational channel.

41. Waltz might have denied learning a role because he takes learning as equivalent to rationality and believes that his framework does not require rationality. This is unfortunate because rationality has several meanings and is not equivalent to learning. Of course, rationality critically depends on learning.

42. Waltz (1986, 331) also noted that states are "sensitive to costs". Thus, one should not take some of Waltz's inconsistent statements on learning vs. selection at face value (e.g., Taliaferro 2000–1, 156–7).

43. This partly explains the sense of comradeship between the two camps when facing the assault from (radical) constructivism (e.g., Keohane 1993; Keohane and Martin 1995; Jervis 1999).

44. Indeed, Wendt (1999, 157) has an illustration (i.e., a hotel fire) without admitting that his illustration perfectly captures "selection". As noted above, Wendt's (ibid. 323–36) notion of "cultural selection" is really inheritance or transmission, not selection per se.

45. I shall state explicitly that my discussion here is not a defense of realism per se, and I am not a realist.

46. Here, it is also important to note that the fact that a state tried to balance another state but did not succeed in achieve a de facto balance of power does not invalidate realism either because balancing effort can fail for a variety of reasons. For the distinction of de facto balance of power versus (actual) balancing (of power) behavior, see Ruggie 1983, 267.

47. Hence, even Waltz failed to appreciate how central the selection mechanism is for realism.

48. I shall also point out that much of the IR community has remained stuck in a Popper/Kuhn/Lakatosian positivism philosophy of social sciences while ignoring the more sophisticated doctrine of "scientific realism". On this front, see Monteiro and Ruby (2009).

49. The other defense of neorealism by Elman and Elman (1995, 192) approaches intellectual charlatanism: they insist that a theory can only be replaced by a better theory yet refuse to admit that any theory is better than neorealism. For counterpoints, see Schroeder 1995, 194–6; Fettweis 2004, 99.

50. Putting it differently, constructivism can only depend on self-fulfilling prophecy whereas realism can depend on both self-fulfilling and self-denying prophecy (Houghton 2009).

51. Waltz (1986, 343–4), of course, later on admitted that structure can only "shape and constrain".

52. Equally devastating for Waltz is the fact states' behaviors are not dictated by selection alone, but also by constraining/enabling, learning, constituting, and anti-socialization, as noted above.

53. In other words, SEP insists that all components within the system (including the system itself, holistically speaking) contribute to the systemic change and stability: we cannot assign more relative weight to some component than to other components before we perform our empirical inquiries. For a more detailed discussion, see Tang 2013.

54. Elias (1939[1991]; 1939[1994]) might have come close to transcending the problem, but not dissolving it.

55. Marx's historical materialism and his general approach are also a collectivism or holism/totalism approach. As such, the same kind of criticism has been leveled against historical materialism and Marxism-inspired "dependence theory" (e.g., Popper 1945[1967], chs. 13–17; Smith 1979).

56. Thus, one detects a striking similarity between structural realism and structural functionalism, although the former preaches conflict whereas the later harmony (Goddard and Nexon 2005).

57. I thank Dwayne Woods for coining this colorful phrase of "Parsonian nightmare" when commenting on a draft of another article of mine (Tang 2013).

CONCLUSION

1. Kitcher (2003) coined the phrase of "giving Darwin his due".

2. Although I have mostly focused on the macro level in this book, I have applied SEP to both the state level (Tang 2008b; Tang and Long 2012) and the psychological level (Tang 2009a; 2012).

3. As noted in Chapter 5 above, structural theories can only be quasi-systemic theories because structure is part of system but never the whole system.

4. Waltz (1986, 342–3) himself admitted that "a system's structure works against transformation," and "changes in, and transformation of, systems, originate not in the structure of a system but in its parts".

5. Kahler (1999, 191–2) made a similar point implicitly, noting that IR theorists "have been fixated on the post-1945 international system and immediate policies arising from the Cold War".

6. This is not to deny that debates among the grand theories, with an implicit goal of achieving theoretical unification, have advanced our understanding of

international politics significantly even though unification eventually proves to be impossible.

7. Our argument that different theories of international politics are from and for different epochs of international politics does not imply that different theories can only be formulated in different epochs. In fact, different (proto-)theories can arise in the same epoch because different individuals can have quite different interpretations of international politics.

8. Many (e.g., Brooks, 1997, 473; Snyder 2002, 151; Taliaferro, 2000–1, 161; see also Spirtas 1996, 387) have called for a methodological unification. Mearsheimer (2006, 110) also rejects the possibility of unifying the two realisms, without justifying his position.

9. The differences between neoliberalism and offensive realism will be too far apart to be bridged, and we do not explore them here. See Mearsheimer 1994; 2001; Jervis 1999, 48–9, 51; Tang 2008a.

10. Of course, neoliberalists have persistently attempted to invade the security domain, although not with significant difficulties (e.g., Wallander, Haftendorn, and Keohane 1999; Lake 2001).

11. Mearsheimer (2001, 51–3) emphatically denies that cooperation is a viable means of self-help in his offensive realism world, barring temporary alliances when facing a common threat. Both Jervis (1999, 50) and Glaser (1994–95, 60, 67, 71–2) implicitly or explicitly acknowledged that a state should seek cooperation to alleviate the security dilemma *only* when facing a like-minded security-seeking state (i.e., a status-quo or non-expansionist state). One cannot pursue cooperation with an offensive realism (revisionist) state. Elsewhere, I show that whether cooperation other than temporary alliance when facing a common threat is a fundamental divergent point between offensive realism theories on the one side and all non-offensive realism theories on the other side (Tang 2008a).

12. Although Axelrod did not explicitly state that his anarchy is a defensive realism one, his assumptions on the environment in which states interact with each other suggest an anarchy that is even more benign than a defensive realism one. For a detailed discussion, see Tang 2008a, 497–8.

13. Holsti (1998) made a similar point from an epistemological perspective.

14. The literature on democratic peace is voluminous. For a recent forum, see the special issue of *International Politics*, vol. 41 (2004). For an evidently evolutionary approach toward democratic peace, see Huntley (1996); Cederman (2001a; 2001b).

15. Events followed, of course, tend to support defensive realism's more optimistic predictions. For a good stock-taking of this debate, see Fettweis 2004.

16. While Waltz argued that theories of international politics should not intend to be theories of foreign policy; most theorists have an implicit goal of influencing states' policies with their theories. See the exchange between Waltz (1996) and Elman (1996).

17. These two questions are so closely intertwined that they are inseparable. Moreover, security experts in different states have indeed engaged in this kind of debate. In the United States, after George Bush Jr. took power, many analysts wondered whether Mr. Bush thought the Cold War was yet over (Daalder and Hill, 2001).

Likewise, in China, there was also a debate explicitly about what kind of world China is living in (Goldstein, 2001; Tang and Gries 2002; Tang 2008b).

18. An evolutionary approach cannot be teleological because evolution allows (exogenous) accidents. Thus, we do not provide a teleological prediction for the exact future of international politics, although we can argue that the endogenous dynamics of the system do suggest that any fundamental change in the system in the future will be "historically progressive" (Wendt 1999, 312). See also Chapter 4 above.

APPENDIX I

1. Ember and Ember (1992) also found that wars tend to break out in years with a severe uncertainty over available resources (e.g., after a drought, flood). Unfortunately, Ember and Ember (1992) conflated feud, brawling with warfare, as van der Dennen (2007, 86) pointed out.

APPENDIX II

1. Kuhrt 1995, 48–55; Van de Mieroop 2007, 63–73; Hamblin 2006, 73–101.
2. Kuhrt 1995, 118–84; Hamblin 2006, 382–455.
3. Hamblin 2006, 49–50; 55–9.
4. Kuhrt 1995, 118–84; Hamblin 2006, 321–58. As Hamblin noted, "the cultural magnificence of the Pyramid Age is based in part on the absolute military predominance Egypt had achieved during the Early Dynastic Period over any potential military power" (quote from p. 329).
5. Bard 2000, 77–80; Wenke 2009, 181–8; Hamblin 2006, 315–27.
6. Hamblin 2006, esp. 312–15.
7. Wilkinson 1999, 266–7; Hamblin 2006, 33–4.
8. Chang 1986, 317–38.
9. Chang 1986, 317–38; idem., 2005; Zheng 2005; Zhang 2008.
10. For a good introduction, see Zheng 2005, chs. 4, 5, and 6.
11. Long-Shan culture is an outgrowth from earlier Yan-shao cultures and Ta-wen-kou cultures, across the whole Yellow River valley (in at least three phases), Northern China. For a more in-depth survey of the Long-Shan culture, see Liu 1996. Hence, although the Xia-Shang-Zhou lineage in the Yellow River valley has dominated archaeological thinking on China, the first archaic state within the ancient Chinese system had appeared earlier elsewhere.
12. Liang-zhu culture is an outgrowth from Ma-chia-pang culture in Yangtze Delta and Lake Tai region. For evidences that Liang-zhu might have reached the stage of state earlier than the Yellow River valley, see Zhu Nai-Cheng (朱乃诚) 2010, 180–6.
13. Chang 1986, 262–7; 270; Liu 2004, 105, 109–11, 170–6; Zheng 2005, 295–305; Shao 2005; Zhu 2010; Tang 2010, 200–12.
14. Zheng 2005, 196–209; Zhang 2005.
15. Chang 1986, 116; Liu 2004, 93–5.

16. Burger 1995, 77–9; Stanish 2001, 48–9. See also the survey of *Las Haldas* by Pozorski an Pozorski 2006.
17. Flannery and Marcus (2003) dated the outbreak of war in Oaxaca/Zapotec to 1260 BC at the latest, based on the oldest defensive palisade discovered so far.
18. Many Assyrian texts referred to warfare between Assyria and the Hittite kingdom known as Urartu (Kuhrt 1995, 547–562; Macqueen 1995; Sagona and Zimansky 2009, ch. 9).
19. Hamblin 2006, 265–6; Sagona and Zimansky 2009, 160, Figure 5.7, daggers with arsenical copper.
20. Meyers 1997, 448–9; Hamblin 2006, 25–6.
21. Meyers 1997, 122–31; Hamblin 2006, 24; see also Sagona and Zimansky 2009, ch. 2, esp. 88–99.

APPENDIX III

1. In geographical terms, Levant and Canaan overlap with each other greatly, with Canaan being slightly larger. Canaan included today's Israel, Palestine, Jordan, Lebanon, (coastal) Syria, but sometimes also a bit of Cyprus and even Northern Iraq. Here, I use Levant to denote a narrower region.
2. *The Old Testament* also recorded the use of a sling by David versus Goliath in I, Samuel 17, 49–50.
3. For evidences of fortification in Eurasia, see figure 57 in Guilaine and Zammit 2005, 210–11 for a partial list of sites, see also ibid. 188–91.
4. For a brief compilation of scatted evidences from this period, see van der Dennen 1995, 53–8.
5. The fact that Aryans were originally from Iran has been firmly established (see Avari 2007, ch. 3; Kulke and Rothermund 1998, 48). It may be speculated that Aryans were really driven out from Iran by other groups such as the Elmans and Hittites.

References

Abler, Thomas S. 1991. "Comments on Knauft." *Current Anthropology* 32 (4): 409–10.

Acemoglu, Daron, Simon Johnson, and James A. Robinson. 2005. "Institutions as a Fundamental Cause of Long-Run Growth." In *Handbook of Economic Growth*. Vol. 1A, eds. Philippe Aghion and Steven N. Durlauf. North-Holland: Elsevier, 385–472.

Acharya, Amitav. 2000. "Ethnocentrism and Emancipatory IR Theory." In *(Dis) Placing Security: Critical Evaluations of the Boundaries of Security Theory*, eds. Samantha Arnold and J. Marsha Beier. Toronto: Center for International and Security Studies, 1–18.

Acharya, Amitav. 2001. *Constructing a Security Community in Southeast Asia: ASEAN and the Problem of Regional Order*. London: Routledge.

Acharya, Amitav. 2004. "How Ideas Spread: Whose Norms Matter? Norm Localization and Institutional Change in Asian Regionalism." *International Organization* 58 (2): 239–75.

Acharya, Amitav. 2007. "The Emerging Regional Architecture of World Politics." *World Politics* 59 (4): 629–52.

Acharya, Amitav. 2009. *Whose Ideas Matter? Agency and Power in Asian Regionalism*. Ithaca, NY: Cornell Univeristy Press.

Acharya, Amitav, and Barry Buzan, eds. 2009. *Non-Western International Relations Theory: Perspectives on and beyond Asia*. London: Routledge.

Adams, Karen Ruth. 2003. "Attack and Conquer? International Anarchy and the Offense-Defense-Deterrence Balance." *International Organization* 28 (3): 45–83.

Adams, Robert McCormick. 1981. *Heartland of Cities: Surveys of Ancient Settlement and Land Use on the Central Floodplain of the Euphrates*. Chicago, IL: University of Chicago Press.

Adler, Emanuel. 1991. "Cognitive Evolution: A Dynamic Approach for the study of International Relations and Their Progress," reprinted in Emanuel Adler, 2005. *Communitarian International Relations: The Epistemic Foundations of International Relations*. London: Routledge, 65–88.

Adler, Emmanuel. 1992. "The Emergence of Cooperation: National Epistemic Communities and the International Evolution of the Idea of Nuclear Arms Control." *International Organization* 46 (1): 101–45.

Adler, Emanuel. 1997a. "Seizing the middle ground: constructivism in world politics." *European Journal of International Relations* 3 (3): 319–63.

Adler, Emanuel. 1997b. "Imagined (Security) Communities: Cognitive Regions in International Relations." *Millennium* 26 (2): 249–77.

Adler, Emanuel. 1998. "Seeds of Peaceful Change: the OSCE's Security Community-Building Model." In *Security Communities*, eds. Emanuel Adler and Michael Barnett. Cambridge: Cambridge University Press, 119–60.

Adler, Emanuel 2005. *Communitarian International Relations: The Epistemic Foundations of International Relations*. London: Routledge.

Adler, Emanuel, and Michael Barnett eds. 1998a. *Security Communities*. Cambridge: Cambridge University Press.

Adler, Emmanuel, and Michael Barnett. 1998b. "A Framework for Studying Security Community." In *Security Communities*, eds. Emmanuel Adler and Michael Barnett. Cambridge: Cambridge University Press, 29–65.

Alchian, Armen A. 1950. "Uncertainty, Evolution, and Economic Theory." *Journal of Political Economy* 58 (3): 211–21.

Alexander, Richard D. 1979. *Darwinism and Human Affairs*. Seattle, WA: University of Washington Press.

Algaze, Guillermo. [1993] 2005. *The Uruk World System: The Dynamics of Expansion of Early Mesopotamian Civilization*. 2nd ed. Chicago, IL: University of Chicago Press.

Algaze, Guillermo. 2008. *Ancient Mesopotamia at the Dawn of Civilization: The Evolution of an Urban Landscape*. Chicago, IL: University of Chicago Press.

Anderson, Benedict. 1983. *Imagined Communities. Reflections on the Origins and Spread of Nationalism*. London: Verso.

Anderson, James. 1985. "Nationalism and Geography." In *The Rise of the Modern State*, ed. James Anderson. Brighton, Sussex: Wheatsheaf.

Anghie, Antony. 2004. *Imperialism, Sovereignty and the Making of International Law*. Cambridge: Cambridge University Press.

Anghie, Antony. 2009. "Rethinking Sovereignty in International Law." *Annual Review of Law and Social Science* 5: 291–310.

Angner, Erik. 2002. "The History of Hayek's Theory of Cultural Evolution." *Studies in History and Philosophy of Biological and Biomedical Sciences* 33 (4). 695–718.

Anonymous-A. [c.400 BC] 1988. *Zuo Zhuan.*[左传/Chronicles of Zuo]. Changsha, China: Yue Lue Publishing House.

Anonymous-B. [c.70BC] 1992. *Zhan Guo Ce* [战国策/Compiled Stories of the Warring Period], trans. and eds. Jianzhan He. Changsha, China: Yue-lu Publishing House.

Anwar, Dewi Fortuna. 2006. "Leadership in the History of Southeast Asia Integration: the Role of Indonesia in ASEAN." In *Regional Integration in East Asia and Europe: Convergence or Divergence*, eds., Bertrand Fort and Douglas Webber. London: Routledge, 59–68.

Archer, Margaret S. 1995. *Realist Social Theory: the Morphogenetic Approach*. Cambridge: Cambridge Univeristy Press.

Aristotle. 1998. *Politics*. Trans. C.D.C. Reeves. Indianapolis, IN: Hackett Publishing Company.

Arkush, Elizabeth N., and Mark W. Allen eds., 2006. *The Archaeology of Warfare: Prehistories of Raiding and Conquest*. Gainesville, FL: University Press of Florida.

Avari, Burjor. 2007. *India: The Ancient Past: A History of the Indian-Subcontinent from 7000 BC to AD 1200*. London: Routledge.

Axelrod, Robert. 1984. *The Evolution of Cooperation*. New York, NY: Basic Books.

Axelrod, Robert, and Robert O. Keohane. 1985. "Achieving Cooperation under Anarchy: Strategies and Institutions." *World Politics* 38 (1): 226–54.

Ayoob, Mohammed. 2002. "Inequality and Theorizing in International Relations: The Case for Subaltern Realism." *International Studies Review* 4 (3): 27–48.

Baldwin, David A. 1978. "Power and Social Exchange." *American Political Science Review* 72 (4): 1229–42.

Baldwin, David A. 1979. "Power Analysis and World Politics: New Trends versus Old Tendencies." *World Politics* 31 (2): 161–94.

Baldwin, David A. 1980. "Interdependence and Power: A Conceptual Analysis." *International Organization* 34 (4): 471–506.

Baldwin, David A., ed. 1993. *Neorealism and Neoliberalism: The Contemporary Debate.* New York, NY: Columbia University Press.

Bard, Kathryn A. 2000. "The Emergence of the Egyptian State (c. 3200–2686 BC)," in *The Oxford History of Ancient Egypt*, ed., Ian Shaw. Oxford: Oxford University Press, 61–88.

Barfield, Thomas J. 1989. *The Perilous Frontier: Nomadic Empires and China.* Malden, MA: Blackwell.

Barkin, J. Samuel. 2003. "Realist Constructivism." *International Studies Review* 5 (3): 325–42.

Barkin, J. Samuel, and Bruce Cronin. 1994. "The State and the Nation: Changing Norms and the Rules of Sovereignty in International Relations." *International Organization* 48: 107–30.

Barnes, Barry. 1988. *The Nature of Power.* Cambridge: Polity.

Barnett, Michael N., and Raymond Duvall. 2005. "Power in International Politics." *International Organization* 59 (1): 39–75.

Barnett, Michael, N., and Martha Finnemore. 1999. "The Politics, Power, and Pathologies of International Organizations." *International Organization* 53 (4): 699–732.

Barnett, Michael N., and Martha Finnemore. 2004. *Rules for the World: International Organizations in Global Politics.* Ithaca, NY: Cornell University Press.

Barraclough, Geoffrey (ed.). 1978. *The Times Atlas of World History.* London: Times Books Limited.

Bar-Siman-Tov, Yaacov. 2004. "Dialectics between Stable Peace and Reconciliation." In *From Conflict Resolution to Reconciliation*, ed. Yaacov Bar-Siman-Tov. Oxford, UK: Oxford University Press, 61–80.

Bartelson, Jens. 2006. "Making Sense of Global Civil Society." *European Journal of International Relations* 12 (3): 371–95.

Bar-Yosef, Ofer. 1986. "The Walls of Jericho: An Alternative Interpretation." *Current Anthropology* 27 (2): 157–62.

Beitz, Charles R. 1979[1999]. *Political Theory and International Relations.* Princeton, NJ: Princeton University Press.

Bell, Duncan S. A., Paul K. MacDonald, and Bradley A. Thayer. 2001. "Correspondence: Start the Evolution without Us." *International Security* 26 (1): 187–98.

Berger, Peter, and Thomas Luckmann. 1966. *The Social Construction of Reality: A Treatise in the Sociology of Knowledge.* New York, NY: Anchor Books.

Berger, Thomas U. 1998. *Cultures of Antimilitarism: National Security in Germany and Japan.* Baltimore, MD: John Hopkins University Press.

Berlin, Isaiah. [1960] 2002. *Liberty: Incorporating Four Essays on Liberty.* Oxford: Oxford University Press.

Betts, Richard K. 1999. "Must War Find a Way?: A Review Essay." *International Security* 24 (2): 166–98.

Bhaskar, Roy. 1986. *Scientific Realism and Human Emancipation*. London: Verso.

Bhaskar, Roy. [1978]2008. *A Realist Theory of Sciences*. London: Routledge.

Bible (The Holy Bible). King James Version.

Bicho, Nuno, et al. 2007. "The Upper Paleolithic Rock Art of Iberia." *Journal of Archaeological Method and Theory* 14 (1): 81–151.

Biersteker, Thomas J., and Cynthia Weber eds. 1996. *State Sovereignty as Social Construct*. Cambridge: Cambridge University Press.

Blackmore, Susan. 1999. *The Meme Machine*. Oxford: Oxford University Press.

Blainey, Geoffrey. 1988. *Causes of War*. 3rd ed. Basingstoke, UK: Macmillan.

Blanton, Richard E, Gary M. Feinman, Stephen A. Kowalewski, and Linda M. Nicholas. 1999. *Ancient Oaxaca: The Monte Alban State*. Cambridge: Cambridge University Press.

Blute, Marion. 2006. "Gene-Culture Coevolutionary Games." *Social Forces* 85 (1): 151–66.

Blute, Marion. 2010. *Darwinian Sociocultural Evolution: Solutions to Dilemmas in Cultural and Social Theory*. Cambridge: Cambridge University Press.

Bocquet-Appel, Jean-Pierre and Ofer Bar-Yosef, eds. 2008. *The Neolithic Demographic Transition and its Consequences*. Berlin: Springer.

Boehm, Christopher. 1999. *Hierarchy in the Forest: The Evolution of Egalitarian Behavior*. Cambridge, MA: Harvard University Press.

Boesche, Roger. 2003. "Kautilya's Arthasastra on War and Diplomacy in Ancient India." *Journal of Military History* 67 (1): 9–37.

Boland, Lawrence A. 1979. "Knowledge and the Role of Institutions in Economic Theory." *Journal of Economic Issues* 13 (4): 957–72.

Booth, Ken, ed. 2005. *Critical Security Studies and World Politics*. Boulder, CO: Lynne Rienner.

Börzel, Tanja A., Tobias Hofmann, Diana Panke and Carina Sprungk. 2010. "Obstinate and Inefficient: Why Member States Do Not Comply With European Law." *Comparative Political Studies* 43 (11): 1363–90.

Boucher, David. 1990. "Inter-Community & International Relations in the Political Philosophy of Hobbes." *Polity* 23 (2): 207–32.

Bourdieu, Pierre. [1980] 1990. *The Logic of Practice*. Stanford, CA: Stanford University Press.

Bourdieu, Pierre. 1998. *Practical Reason: On the Theory of Action*. Stanford, CA: Stanford University Press.

Boyd, Robert, and Peter J. Richerson. 1980. "Sociobiology, Culture and Economic Theory." *Journal of Economic Behavior and Organization* 1(2): 97–121.

Boyd, Robert, and Peter J. Richerson. 1985. *Culture and the Evolutionary Process*. Chicago, IL: University of Chicago Press.

Bradford, Alfred S. 2001. *With Arrow, Sword, and Spear: A History of Warfare in the Ancient World*. Westport, CT: Praeger.

Brandon, Robert N. 1982. "The Levels of Selection." *PSA: Proceedings of the Biennial Meeting of the Philosophy of Science Association* 1982 (1): 315–23.

Brandon, Robert N. 1998. "The Levels of Selection: A Hierarchy of Interactors." In *The Philosophy of Biology*, eds. David L. Hull and Michael Ruse. Oxford: Oxford Univeristy Press, 176–97.

Brandon, Robert N. 1999. "The Units of Selection Revisited: The Modules of Selection." *Biology and Philosophy* 14 (2): 167–80.

Brass, Paul. 2000. "Foucault Steals Political Science." *Annual Review of Political Science* 3: 305–30.

Braubach, Max et al. 1978. *Gebhardt Handbuch der Deutschen Geschichte* [Gebhardt Handbook of German History]. Stuttgart: Gebhardt.

Brenner, William J. 2007. "The Forest and the King of Beasts: Hierarchy and Opposition in Ancient India (c. 600–232 BCE)." In *The Balance of Power in World History*, eds. Stuart J. Kaufman, Richard Little, and William C. Wohlforth. New York, NY: Palgrave Macmillan, 99–121.

Brewer, Marilynn B. 1999. "The Psychology of Prejudice: Ingroup Love or Outgroup Hate." *Journal of Social Issues* 55 (3): 429–44.

Briant, Pierre. 1999. "The Achaemenid Empire." In *War and Society in the Ancient and Medieval Worlds: Asia, the Mediterranean, Europe, and Mesoamerica*, eds. Kurt A. Raaflaub and Nathan Stewart Rosenstein. Cambridge, MA: Harvard University Press, 105–28.

Brodie, Bernard. 1973. *War and Politics*. New York, NY: Macmillan.

Brooks, Stephen G. 1997. "Dueling Realisms." *International Organization* 51(3): 445–77.

Brooks, Stephen G., and William C. Wohlforth. 2000–2001. "Power, Globalization, and the End of the Cold War: Reevaluating a Landmark Case for Ideas." *International Security* 25 (3): 5–53.

Bull, Hedley. 1977. *The Anarchical Society: A Study of Order in World Politics*. New York, NY: Columbia University Press.

Bull, Hedley, and Adam Watson, eds. 1984. *The Expansion of International Society*. New York, NY: Oxford University Press.

Buller, David J. 2005a. "Evolutionary Psychology: The Emperor's New Paradigm." *Trends in Cognitive Sciences* 9 (6): 277–83.

Buller, David J. 2005b. *Adapting Minds: Evolutionary Psychology and the Persistent Quest for Human Nature*. Cambridge, MA: MIT Press.

Bunge, Mario. 1997. "Mechanism and Explanation." *Philosophy of the Social Sciences* 27 (4): 410–65.

Burger, Richard. 1989. "An Overview of Peruvian Archaeology (1976–1986)." *Annual Review of Anthropology* 18: 37–69.

Burger, Richard L. 1995. *Chavin and the Origins of Andean Civilization*. New York, NY: Thames and Hudson.

Burger, Richard L. and Lucy C. Salazar, eds. 2004. *Machu Picchu: Unveiling the Mystery of the Incas*. New Haven, CT: Yale University Press.

Buss, David M. 1995. "Evolutionary Psychology: A New Paradigm for Psychological Sciences." *Psychological Inquiry* 6: 1–30.

Buss, Leo. W. 1983. "Evolution, Development, and the Units of Selection." *Proceedings of the National Academy of Science of U.S.A.* 80 (5): 1387–91.

Buss, David M. 2008. *Evolutionary Psychology: the New Science of the Mind*. Boston, MA: Pearson.

Buzan, Barry. 1986. "A Framework for Regional Security Analysis." In *South Asian Insecurity and the Great Powers*, eds. Barry Buzan and Gowher Rizvi. London: Macmillan, 3–33.

Buzan, Barry. 1991. *People, States, and Fear*. 2nd ed. Boulder, CO: Lynne Rienner.

Buzan, Barry. 1993. "From International System to International Society: Structural Realism and Regime Theory Meet the English School." *International Organization* 47 (2): 327–52.

Buzan, Barry. 2004. *From International to World Society?: English School Theory and the Social Structure of Globalisation*. Cambridge: Cambridge University Press.

Buzan, Barry. 2011. "The Inaugural Kenneth A. Waltz lecture: A World without Superpowers: Decentralized Globalism." *International Relations* 25(1): 3–25.

Buzan, Barry, and Mathias Albert. 2010. "Differentiation: A Sociological Approach to International Relations Theory." *European Journal of International Relations* 16 (3): 315–37.

Buzan, Barry, Charles Jones, and Richard Little. 1993. *The Logic of Anarchy. Neorealism to Structural Realism*. New York, NY: Columbia University Press.

Buzan, Barry, Gowher Rizvi and Rosemary Foot. 1986. *South Asian Insecurity and the Great Powers*. New York, NY: St. Martin's.

Buzan, Barry, and Ole Wæver. 2003. *Regions and Powers: The Structure of International Security*. Cambridge: Cambridge University Press.

Buzan, Barry, Ole Wæver, and Jaap de Wilde. 1998. *Security: A New Framework for Analysis*. Boulder, CO: Lynne Rienner.

Calvert, Randall L. 1995. "Rational Actors, Equilibrium, and Social Institutions." In *Explaining Social Institution*, ed. Jack Night and Itai Sened. Ann Arbor, MI: University of Michigan Press, 57–93.

Campbell, Brian. 1999. "The Roman Empire." In *War and Society in the Ancient and Medieval Worlds: Asia, the Mediterranean, Europe, and Mesoamerica*, eds. Kurt A. Raaflaub and Nathan Stewart Rosenstein. Cambridge, MA: Harvard University Press, 217–41.

Campbell, Donald T. 1960. "Blind Variation and Selective Retention in Creative Thought as in Other Knowledge Processes." *Psychological Review* 67(6): 380–400.

Campbell, Donald T. [1965]1998. "Variation and Selective Retention in Socio-Cultural Evolution." In *Socio Changes in Developing Areas*, eds. Herbert R. Barringer, George I. Blanksten, and Raymond W. Mack. Cambridge, MA: Schenkman Publishing Company, 19–49. Reprinted in Geoffrey Hodgson, ed., *The Foundations of Evolutionary Economics*, Cheltenham, UK: Edward Elgar, 354–70.

Campbell, Donald T. 1974a. "Evolutionary Epistemology." In *The Philosophy of Karl Popper*, ed. Paul Arthur Schilpp. La Salle, IL: Open Court, 413–63.

Campbell, Donald T. 1974b. "Unjustified Variation and Selective Retention in Scientific Discovery." In *Studies in the Philosophy of Biology: Reduction and Related Problems*, eds. Fancisco J. Ayala and Theodosius Dobzhansky. Berkeley, CA: University of California Press, 139–61.

Campbell, Donald T. 1975. "The Conflict between Social and Biological Evolution and the Concept of Original Sin." *Zygon: Journal of Religion and Science* 10 (3): 234–49.

Campbell, Donald T. 1976. "On the Conflicts Between Biological and Social Evolution and Between Psychology and Moral Tradition." *Zygon: Journal of Religion and Science* 11 (3): 167–208.

Campbell, Donald T. 1991. "A Naturalistic Theory of Archaic Moral Orders." *Zygon: Journal of Religion and Science* 26 (1): 91–114.

Campbell, John L. 2002. "Ideas, Politics and Public Policy." *Annual Review of Sociology* 28: 21–38.

Caporael, Linnda R., and Marilyn B. Brewer. 1995. "Hierarchical Evolutionary Theory: There Is an Alternative, and It's Not Creationism." *Psychological Inquiry* 6 (1): 31–4.

Carlsnaes, Walter. 1992. "The Agency-Structure Problem in Foreign Policy Analysis." *International Studies Quarterly* 36 (3): 245–70.

Carneiro, Robert L. 1970. "A Theory of the Origin of the State." *Science*, new series 169 (3947): 733–8.

Carneiro, Robert L. 1978. "Political Expansion as an Expression of the Principle of Competitive Exclusion." In *Origins of the State: The Anthropology of Political Evolution*, eds. R. Cohen and E. R. Service. Philadelphia, PA: Institute for the Study of Human Issues, 205–23.

Carneiro, Robert L. 1987. "The Evolution of Complexity in Human Societies and its Mathematical Expression." *International Journal of Comparative Sociology* 28 (3/4): 111–28.

Carneiro, Robert L. 1994. "War and Peace: Alternating Realities in Human History." In *Studying War: Anthropological Perspectives*, eds. Stephan P. Reyna and R. E. Downs. Langhorne, PA: Gordon and Breach, 3–27.

Carneiro, Robert L. 2000. "The Transition from Quantity to Quality: A Neglected Causal Mechanism in Accounting for Social Evolution." *Proceedings of the National Academy of Sciences of U.S.A.* 97 (23): 12926–31.

Carneiro, Robert L. 2003. *Evolution in Cultural Anthropology: A Critical History*. Boulder, CO: Westview.

Carr, Edward Hallett. 1939. *The Twenty Years' Crisis 1919–1939: An Introduction to the Study of International Relations*. London: Macmillan.

Cavalli-Sforza, L. L. 1971. "Similarities and Dissmililarties of social, cultural and biological evolution." In *Mathematics in the Archaeological and Historical Sciences*, eds. F. R. Hodgson, et al. Edinburgh, Scott: Edinburgh University Press, 535–41.

Cavalli-Sforza, L. L., and M. W. Feldman. 1981. *Cultural Transmission and Evolution: A Quantitative Approach*. Princeton, NJ: Princeton University Press.

Cederman, Lars-Erik. 1997. *Emergent Actors in World Politics: How States and Nations Develop and Dissolve*. Princeton, NJ: Princeton University Press.

Cederman, Lars-Erik. 2001a. "Back to Kant: Reinterpreting the Democratic Peace as a Macrohistorical Learning Process." *American Political Science Review* 95 (1): 15–31.

Cederman, Lars-Erik. 2001b. "Modeling the Democratic Peace as a Kantian Selection Process." *Journal of Conflict Resolution* 45 (4): 470–502.

Cederman, Lars-Erik. 2002. "Endogenizing Geopolitical Boundaries with Agent-Based Modeling." *Proceedings of the National Academy of Sciences of U.S.A.* 99 (3): 7296–303.

Cederman, Lars-Erik, T. Camber Warren, and Didier Sornette. 2011. "Testing Clausewitz: Nationalism, Mass Mobilization, and the Severity of War." *International Organization* 65 (3): 605–38.

Cederman, Lars-Erik, and Luc Girardin. 2010. "Growing Sovereignty: Modeling the Shift from Indirect to Direct Rule." *International Studies Quarterly* 54 (1): 27–48.

Cederman, Lars-Erik, and Kristinan Skrede Gleditsch. 2004. "Conquest and Regime Change: An Evolutionary Model of the Spread of Democracy and Peace." *International Studies Quarterly* 48 (3): 603–29.

Centeno, Miguel Angel. 2002. *Blood and Debt: War and the Nation-State in Latin America*. University Park, PA: Penn State University Press.

Chagnon, Napoleon A. [1968] 1997. *Yąnomamö*. Orlando, FL: Harcourt College.

Chakrabarti Dilip K. 1999. *India: An Archaeological History: Palaeolithic Beginnings to Early History Foundations*. New Delhi: Oxford University Press.

Chang, Kwang-chih. 1986. *The Archaeology of Ancient China*. 4th ed. New Haven, CT: Yale University Press.

Chang, Kwang-chih. 2005. "The Rise of Kings and the Formation of City-States." In *The Formation of Chinese Civilization: An Archeological Perspective, eds.* Kwang-chih Chang and Pingfang Xu . New Haven, CT: Yale University Press, 125–39.

Charpin, Dominique. 1995. "The History of Ancient Mesopotamia: An Overview." In *Civilizations of the Ancient Near East*, vol. II, eds. Jack M. Sasson et al. New York, NY: Charles Scribner's Sons, 807–39.

Chaudhry, Azam, and Phillip Garner. 2006. "Political Competition between Countries and Economic Growth." *Review of Development Economics* 10 (4): 666–82.

Checkel, Jeffrey T. 2001. "Why Comply? Social Learning and European Identity Change." *International Organization* 55 (3): 553–88.

Checkel, Jeffrey T., ed. 2007a. *International Institutions and Socialization in Europe*. Cambridge: Cambridge University Press.

Checkel, Jeffrey T. 2007b. "Introduction." In *International Organization and Socialization in Europe*, ed. Jeffrey T. Checkel. Cambridge: Cambridge University Press, 3–27.

Chick, Garry. 1999. "What's in a Meme? The Development of the Meme as a Unit of Culture." Presented at the Annual Meeting of the American Anthropological Association. http://www.personal.psu.edu/gec7/ (Accessed January 2011).

Childe, Gordon V. 1941. "War in Prehistoric Societies." *Sociological Review* 33 (3–4): 126–38.

Childe, Gordon V. 1951. *Social Evolution*. London: Watts & Co.

Christensen, Jonas. 2004. "Warfare in the European Neolithic." *Acta Archaeologica* 75 (2): 129–56.

Cioffi-Revilla, Claudio. 1996. "Origins and Evolutions of War and Politics." *International Studies Quarterly* 40 (1): 1–22.

Cioffi-Revilla, Claudio. 2000. "Ancient Warfare: Origins and Systems." In *Handbook of War Studies II*, ed. Manus I. Midlarsky. Ann Arbor, MI: University of Michigan Press, 59–89.

Cioffi-Revilla, Claudio, and David Lai. 1995. "War and Politics in Ancient China, 2700 B.C. to 722 B.C." *Journal of Conflict Resolution* 39 (3): 467–94.

Cioffi-Revilla, Claudio, and Thomas Landman. 1999. "Evolution of Maya Polities in the Ancient Mesoamerican System." *International Studies Quarterly* 43 (4): 559–98.

Clare, Lee, Eelco J. Rohling, Bernhard Weninger, and Johanna Hilpert. 2008. "Warfare in Late Neolithic\Early Chalcolithic Pisidia, Southwestern Turkey: Climate Induced

Social Unrest in the Late 7th Millennium Cal BC." *Documenta Praehistorica* 35 (1): 65–92.

Clark, Gregory. 2007. *A Farewell to Alms: A Brief Economic History of the World.* Princeton, NJ: Princeton University Press.

Clark, Ian. 2005. *Legitimacy in International Society.* Oxford: Oxford University Press.

Clark, Ian. 2007. *International Legitimacy and World Society.* Oxford: Oxford University Press.

Clough, Shepard B., and Salvatore Saladino. 1968. *A History of Modern Italy.* New York, NY: Columbia University Press.

Coase, Ronald H. 1937. "The Nature of the Firm." *Economica,* New Series 4 (16): 386–405.

Cohen, Raymond, and Raymond Westbrook, eds. 2002. *Amarna Diplomacy: The Beginnings of International Relations.* Baltimore, MD: John Hopkins University Press.

Collins, Randall. 1994. *Four Sociological Traditions: Selected Readings.* Oxford: Oxford University Press.

Collins, Randall. 2012. "C-Escalation and D-Escalation: A Theory of the Time-Dynamics of Conflict." *American Sociological Review* 77 (1): 1–20.

Commons, John R. 1934. *Institutional Economics: Its Place in Political Economy.* New York, NY: Macmillan.

Connolly, William E. 1993. "Beyond Good and Evil: The Ethical Sensibility of Michel Foucault." *Political Theory* 21(3): 365–89.

Copeland, Dale. 2000a. *The Origins of Major War.* Ithaca, NY: Cornell University Press.

Copeland, Dale. 2000b. "The Constructivist Challenge to Structural Realism." *International Security* 25 (2): 187–212.

Copeland, Dale. 2003. "A Realist Critique of the English School." *Review of International Studies* 29 (3): 427–41.

Coser, Lewis A. 1956. *The Functions of Social Conflict.* Glencoe, IL: Free Press

Coser, Lewis A. 1967. *Continuities in the Study of Social Conflict.* New York, NY: Free Press.

Cosmides, Leda, and John Tooby. 1995. "From Evolution to Adaptations to Behavior: Toward an Integrated Evolutionary Psychology." In *Biological Perspectives on Motivated Activities,* ed. R. Wong. Norwood. NJ: Ablex, 11–74.

Cosmides, Leda, John Tooby, and Jerome H. Barkow. 1992. "Introduction: Evolutionary Psychology and Conceptual Integration." In *The Adapted Mind: Evolutionary Psychology and the Generation of Culture,* eds. Jerome H. Barkow, Leda Cosmides and John Tooby. New York, NY: Columbia University Press, 3–15.

Cox, Robert W. 1981. "Social Forces, States and World Orders: Beyond International Relations Theory." *Millennium: Journal of International Studies* 10 (2): 126–55. Reprinted in *Neorealism and Its Critics,* edited Robert O. Keohane, 1986. New York, NY: Columbia University Press, 204–254.

Cozette, Murielle. 2008. "Reclaiming the Critical Dimension of Realism: Hans J. Morgenthau on the Ethics of Scholarship." *Review of International Studies* 34 (1): 5–27.

Craig, Campbell. 2003. *Glimmer of a New Leviathan: Total War in the Realism of Niebuhr, Morgenthau, and Waltz.* New York, NY: Columbia University Press.

Craig, Campbell. 2004. "Review Article: American Realism versus American Imperialism," *World Politics* 57 (1): 143–71.

Crawford, Neta C. 2002. *Argument and Change in World Politics: Ethics, Decoloniza- tion, and Humanitarian Intervention*. Cambridge: Cambridge University Press.

Crick, Francis H. 1970. "Central Dogma of Molecular Biology." *Nature* 227: 561–3.

Crouch, Caryl L. 2009. *War and Ethics in the Ancient Near East: Military Violence in Light of Cosmology and History*. Berlin & New York: Walter de Gruyter.

Cryer, Frederick. 1995. "Chronology: Issues and Problems," In *Civilizations of the Ancient Near East*, vol. II, eds. Jack M. Sasson et al. New York, NY: Charles Scribner's Sons, 807–39.

Daalder, Ivo H., and Fiona Hill. 2001. "Get over It, Mr. Bush- The Cold War Has Finished." *International Herald Tribune*. March 24. <http://www.nytimes.com/ 2001/03/24/opinion/24iht-eddaal_ed2_.html>

Daggett, Richard. 1987. "Toward the Development of the State on the North Central Coast of Peru." In *The Origins and Development of the Andean State, eds.* Jonathan Haas, Shelia Pozorski, and Thomas Pozorski. Cambridge: Cambridge University Press, 70–82.

Dahrendorf, Ralf. 1958. "Toward a Theory of Social Conflict." *Journal of Conflict Resolution* 2 (2): 170–83.

Dahrendorf, Ralf. 1968. *Essays in the Theory of Society*. Stanford, CA: Stanford University Press.

Daly, Martin, and Margo Wilson. 1995. "Evolutionary Psychology: Adaptationist, Selectionist, and Comparative." *Psychological Inquiry* 6 (1): 34–8.

Darwin, Charles. [1871] 1874. *The Descent of Man and Selection in Relation to Sex.* 2nd. London: John Murray (E-book version from Powell Books).

Darwin, Charles. 1859. *On The Origin of Species by Means of Natural Selection, or The Preservation of Favored Races in The Struggle for Life*. London: John Murray.

David, Paul A. 1994. "Why are Institutions the 'Carriers of History'?: Path Dependence and the Evolution of Conventions, Organizations and Institutions." *Structural Change and Economic Dynamics* 5 (2): 205–20.

Dawkins, Richard. 1976. *The Selfish Gene*. Oxford: Oxford University Press.

Dawkins, Richard. 1986. *The Blind Watchmaker: Why the Evidence of Evolution Reveals a Universe Without Design*. New York, NY: W. W. Norton.

Dawson, Doyne. 1996a. "The Origins of War: Biological and Anthropological Theor- ies." *History and Theory* 35 (1): 1–28.

Dawson, Doyne. 1996b. *The Origins of Western Warfare: Militarism and Morality in the Ancient World*. Boulder, CO: Westview.

Dawson, Doyne. 1999. "Evolutionary Theory and Group Selection: The Question of Warfare." *History and Theory* 38 (4): 79–100.

De Nevers, Renee. 2007. "Imposing International Norms: Great Powers and Norm Enforcement." *International Studies Review* 9 (1): 53–80.

Dennett, Daniel. 1995. *Darwin's Dangerous Idea: Evolution and the Meanings of Life*. New York, NY: Simon & Schuster.

de Souza, Philip, Waldemar Heckel, and Lloyd Llewellyn-Jones. 2004. *The Greeks at War: From Athens to Alexander*. UK: Osprey.

Dessler, David. 1989. "What's at Stake in the Agent-Structure Debate?" *International Organization* 43 (3): 441–73.

Deutsch, Karl Wolfgang, et al. 1957. *Political Community and the North Atlantic Area: International Organization in Light of Historical Experience*. Princeton, NY: Princeton University Press.

Diamond, Jared M. 1997. *Guns, Germs, and Steel: The Fates of Human Societies*. New York, NY: Norton.

Diamond, Jared. 2005. *Collapse: How Societies Choose to Fail or Survive*. New York, NY: Viking.

Dickson, D. Bruce. 1987. "Circumscription by Anthropogenic Environmental Destruction: An Expansion of Carneiro's (1970) Theory of the Origin of the State." *American Antiquity* 52 (4): 709–16.

Di Cosmo, Nicola. 2004. *Ancient China and Its Enemies: The Rise of Nomadic Power in East Asian History*. Cambridge: Cambridge University Press.

Digeser, Peter. 1992. "The Fourth Face of Power." *Journal of Politics* 54 (4): 977–1007.

Dobzhansky, Theodosius. 1973. "Nothing In Biology Makes Sense Except in the Light of Evolution." *American Biology Teacher* 35 (3): 125–9.

Dopfer, Kurt. 2001. "Evolutionary Economics: Framework for Analysis." In *Evolutionary Economics: Program and Scope*, ed. Kurt Dopfer. Boston, MA: Kluwer, 1–44.

Doty, Roxanne Lynn. 1997. "Aporia: A Critical Exploration of the Agent-Structure Problematique in International Relations Theory." *European Journal of International Relations* 3 (3): 365–92.

Doty, Roxanne Lynn. 2000. "Desire All the Way Down." *Review of International Studies* 26 (1): 137–9.

Drezner, Daniel W. 2008. "The Realist Tradition in American Public Opinion." *Perspectives on Politics* 6 (1): 51–70.

Du, Jin-peng [杜金平]. 2007. *Xia-Shan-Zhou Kao Gu Yan Jiu* [夏商周考古研究/ *Studies in the Archaeology of Xia, Shan, and Zhou*]. Beijing, China: Science Press.

Duffield, John S. 1995. *World Power Forsaken: Political Culture, International Institutions, and Germany Security Policy after Unification*. Stanford, CA: Stanford University Press.

Duffield, John S. 2007. "What are International Institutions?" *International Studies Review* 9 (1): 1–22.

Durham, William H. 1991. *Coevolution: Genes, Culture, and Human Diversity*. Stanford, CA: Stanford University Press.

Earle, Timothy K. 1987. "Chiefdoms in Archaeological and Ethnohistorical Perspective." *Annual Review of Anthropology* 16: 279–308.

Eckstein, Arthur M. 2006. *Mediterranean Anarchy, Interstate War, and the Rise of Rome*. Berkeley, CA: University of California Press.

Eckstein, Arthur M. 2007. "Intra-Greek Balancing, the Mediterranean Crisis of c. 201–200 BCE, and the Rise of Rome." In *The Balance of Power in World History*, eds. Stuart J. Kaufman, Richard Little, and William C. Wohlforth. New York, NY: Palgrave Macmillan, 71–98.

Edelstein, David. 2004. "Occupation Hazards: Why Military Occupations Succeed or Fail?" *International Security* 29 (1): 49–91.

Eldredge, Niles, and Stephen Jay Gould. 1972. "Punctuated Equilibria: An Alternative to Phyletic Gradualism." In *Models in Paleobiology*, ed. Thomas J.M. Schopf. San Francisco, CA: Freeman Cooper, 82–115.

Elias, Norbert. [1939] 1991. *The Society of Individuals*. Oxford: Blackwell.

Elias, Norbert. [1939] 1994. *The Civilizing Process*. Rev. ed., Oxford: Blackwell.

Elias, Norbert. [1970] 1978. *What Is Sociology?* New York, NY: Columbia University Press.

Elman, Colin. 1996. "Horses for Courses: Why not neorealist theory of foreign policy?" *Security Studies* 6: 3–53.

Elman, Colin. 2004. "Extending Offensive Realism: The Louisiana Purchase and America's Rise to Regional Hegemony." *American Political Science Review* 98: 563–76.

Elman, Colin, and Miriam Fendius Elman. 1995. "Correspondence: History vs. Neorealism: A Second Look." *International Security* 20 (1): 182–93.

Ember, Carol. R. and Melvin Ember. 1992. "Resource Unpredictability, Mistrust, and War: A Cross-Cultural Study." *Journal of Conflict Resolution* 36 (2): 242–62.

Ember, Melvin, and Carol R. Ember. 1994. "Cross-Cultural Studies of War and Peace: Recent Achievements and Future Possibilities." In *Studying War: Anthropological Perspectives*, eds. Stephan P. Reyna and R. E. Downs, Langhorne, PA: Gordon and Breach, 185–208.

Ember, Carol. R. and Melvin Ember. 1994. "War, Socialization, and Interpersonal Violence: A Cross-Cultural Study." *Journal of Conflict Resolution* 38 (4): 620–46.

Ember, Carol. R. and Melvin Ember. 1998. "Violence in the Ethnographic Record: Results of Cross-Cultural Research on War and Aggression." In *Troubled Times: Violence and Warfare in the Past,* eds. Debra L. Martin and David W. Frayer. Langhorne, PA: Gordon and Breach, 1–20.

Epstein Charlotte. 2012. "Stop Telling Us How to Behave: Socialization or Infantilization?" *International Studies Perspectives* 13 (2): 135–45.

Epstude, Kai and Neal J. Roese. 2008. "The Functional Theory of Counterfactual Thinking." *Personality and Social Psychology Review* 12 (2): 168–92.

Erdal, O. D. 2012. "A Possible Massacre at Early Bronze Age Titriş Höyük Titris, Anatolia." *International Journal of Osteoarchaeology* 22 (1): 1–21.

Evans, Tony, and Peter Wilson, 1992. "Regime Theory and the English School of International Relations: A Comparison." *Millennium: Journal of International Studies* 21 (3): 329–51.

Fabbro, David. 1978. "Peaceful Societies: An Introduction," *Journal of Peace Research* 15 (1): 67–83.

Falger Vincent S. E. 2001. "Evolutionary World Politics Enriched: The Biological Foundations of International Relations." In *Evolutionary Interpretations of World Politics,* ed. William R. Thompson. New York, NY: Routledge, 30–51.

Farkas, Andrew. 1996. "Evolutionary Models in Foreign Policy Analysis." *International Studies Quarterly* 40 (3) 343–61.

Farris, W. Wayne. 1999. "Japan to 1300." In *War and society in the ancient and medieval worlds: Asia, the Mediterranean, Europe, and Mesoamerica,* eds. Kurt A. Raaflaub and Nathan Stewart Rosenstein. Cambridge, MA: Harvard University Press, 47–70.

Fazal, Tanisha M. 2004. "State Death in the International System." *International Organization* 58 (2): 311–44.

Fazal, Tanisha M. 2007. *State Death: The Politics and Geography of Conquest, Occupation, and Annexation.* Princeton, NJ: Princeton University Press.

Fearon, James D. 1995. "Rationalist Explanations for War." *International Organization* 49 (3): 379–414.

Feaver; Peter D. et al. (with Gunther Hellman; Randall L. Schweller; Jeffery W. Taliaferro; William C. Wohlforth; Jeffery W. Lergo; Andrew Moravcsik). 2000. "Brother, Can You Spare a Paradigm? (Or Was Anybody Ever a Realist?)" *International Security* 25 (1): 165–93.

Ferguson, Adam. [1765] 1995. *An Essay on the History of Civil Society,* ed. Fania Oz-Salberger. Cambridge: Cambridge University Press.

Ferguson, Brian R. 1989. "Game Wars? Ecology and Conflict in Amazonia." *Journal of Anthropological Research* 45 (2): 179–206.

Ferguson, Brian R. 1990. "Explaining War." In *The Anthropology of War,* ed. J. Haas. Cambridge: Cambridge University Press, 26–55.

Ferguson, Brian R. 1994. "The General Consequences of War: An Amazonian Perspective." In *Studying War: Anthropological Perspectives,* eds. Stephen P. Reyna and R. E. Downs. Amsterdam: Gordon and Breach, 85–111.

Ferguson, Brian R. 1995. *Yanomami Warfare: A Political History.* Santa Fe, N.M.: School of American Research.

Ferguson, Brian R. 1998. "Violence and War in Prehistory." In *Troubled Times: Violence and Warfare in the Past,* eds. Debra L. Martin and David W. Frayer. Langhorne, PA: Gordon and Breach, 321–55.

Ferguson, Brian R. 2000. "The Causes and Origins of 'Primitive Warfare': on Evolved Motivations for War." *Anthropological Quarterly* 73 (3): 159–64.

Ferguson, Brian R. 2006. "Archaeology, Cultural Anthropology, and the Origins and Intensifications of War." In *The Archaeology of Warfare: Prehistories of Raiding and Conquest,* eds. Elizabeth N. Arkush and Mark W. Allen. Gainesville, FL: University Press of Florida, 469–523.

Ferguson, Brian R. 2008. "Ten Points on War." *Social Analysis* 52 (2): 32–49.

Ferguson, Brian R. 2010. "Review of David Livingstone Smith's The Most Dangerous Animal: Human Nature and the Origins of War." *Peace & Change* 35 (1): 163–7.

Ferrill, Arther. 1985. *The Origins of War: From the Stone Age to Alexander the Great.* London: Thames and Hudson.

Fettweis, Christopher J. 2004. "Evaluating IR's Crystal Balls: How Predictions of the Future Have Withstood Fourteen Years of Unipolarity." *International Studies Review* 6 (1): 79–104.

Fiani, Ronaldo. n.d. "Was Hayek Really an Evolutionist?" <http://citeseerx.ist.psu.edu/viewdoc/summary?doi=10.1.1.9.5178> (accessed July 2012).

Flannery, Kent V. 1999. "Process and Agency in Early State Formation." *Cambridge Archaeological Journal* 9 (1): 3–21.

Flannery, Kent V., and Joyce Marcus. 2003. "The Origin of War: New 14C Dates from Ancient Mexico." *Proceedings of the National Academy of Sciences of U. S. A.* 100 (20): 11801–5.

Flenley, John R., and Paul Bahn. 2002. *The Enigmas of Easter Island: Island on Edge.* New York, NY: Oxford University Press.

Fiorini, Ann. 1996. "The Evolution of International Norms." *International Studies Quarterly* 40 (3): 363–89.

Fort, Bertrand, and Douglas Webber (eds.). 2006. *Regional Integration in East Asia and Europe: Convergence or Divergence*. London: Routledge.

Foucault, Michel. [1972]1977. "Intellectuals and Power." In *Language, Counter-memory, Practice: Selected Essays and Interviews*. Trans. and ed. Donald F. Bouchard and Sherry Simon. Ithaca, NY: Cornell University Press, 205–17.

Foucault, Michel. [1976] 1990. *An Introduction*. Vol. 1 of *The History of Sexuality*. Trans. Robert Hurley. New York, NY: Vintage.

Foucault, Michel. 1980. *Power/Knowledge: Selected Interviews and Other Writings, 1972–1977*, ed. Colin Gordon. New York, NY: Pantheon.

Foucault, Michel. [1984] 1997. "What is Enlightenment?" In *Ethics: Subjectivity and Truth*. Vol. 1 of *Essential Works of Michel Foucault*. New York, NY: The New Press, 303–21.

Foucault, Michel. 1988. *Politics, Philosophy, Culture: interviews and other writings 1977–1984*, ed. Lawrence D. Kirtzman. London: Routledge.

Foucault, Michel. 2000. *Power*. Vol. 3 of *Essential Works of Foucault (1954–1984)*, ed. James D. Faubion. New York, NY: The New Press.

Fracchia, Joseph, and Richard C. Lewontin. 1999. "Does Culture Evolve?" *History and Theory* 38 (4): 52–78.

Frank, Robert H. 1985. *Choosing the Right Pond: Human Behavior and the Quest for Status*. Oxford: Oxford University Press.

Frankel, Benjamin. 1996. "Restating the Realist Case: An Introduction." *Security Studies* 5 (3): ix–xx.

Frazier, Derrick, and Robert Stewart-Ingersoll. 2010. "Regional Powers and Security: A framework for Understanding Order within Regional Security Complexes." *European Journal of International Relations* 16 (4): 731–53.

Freud, Sigmund. 1961. *Civilization and Its Discontents*. Trans. James Strachecv. New York, NY: W. W. Norton and Co.

Fry, Douglas P. 2006. *Beyond War: The Human Potential for Peace: An Anthropological Challenge to Assumptions about War and Violence*. New York, NY: Oxford University Press.

Fulbrook, Mary, ed. 1997. *German History since 1800*. London: Arnold.

Futuyma, David J. 1998. *Evolutionary Biology*. 5th ed. Boston, MA: Sinauer Associates.

Gaertner, Samuel et al. 1993. "The Common Ingroup Identity Model: Recategorization and the Reduction of Intergroup Bias." *European Review of Social Psychology* 4 (1): 1–26.

Gaertner, Samuel et al. 2000. "The Common Ingroup Identity Model for Reducing Intergroup Bias: Progress and Challenges." In *Social Identity Processes: Trends in Theory and Research*, eds. Dora Capozza and Rupert Brown. Thousand Oaks, CA: Sage, 133–48.

Gat, Azar. 1999. "The Pattern of Fighting in Simple, Small-Scale, Prestate Societies." *Journal of Anthropological Research* 55 (4): 563–83.

Gat, Azar. 2000a. "The Human Motivational Complex: Evolutionary Theory and the Causes of Hunter-Gatherer Fighting. Part I. Primary Somatic and Reproductive Causes." *Anthropological Quarterly* 73 (1): 20–34.

Gat, Azar. 2000b. "The Human Motivational Complex: Evolutionary Theory and the Causes of Hunter-Gatherer Fighting, Part II. Proximate, Subordinate, and Derivative Causes." *Anthropological Quarterly* 73 (2): 74–88.

Gat, Azar. 2006. *War in Human Civilization*. Oxford: Oxford University Press.

Gat, Azar. 2009. "So Why do People Fight? Evolutionary Theory and the Causes of War." *European Journal of International Relations* 15 (4): 571–99.

Geddes, Barbara. 2003. *Paradigms and Sand Castles: Theory Building and Research Design in Comparative Politics*. Ann Arbor, MI: University of Michigan Press.

Geertz, Clifford. 1973. *The Interpretation of Cultures: Selected Essays*. New York, NY: Basic Books.

Gellner, Ernest. 1983. *Nations and Nationalism*. Ithaca, NY: Cornell University Press.

Giddens, Anthony. [1976] 1993. *New Rules of Sociological Method*. 2nd ed. London: Polity.

Giddens, Anthony. 1979. *Central Problems in Social Theory: Action, Structure and Contradiction in Social Analysis*. Berkeley. CA: University of California Press.

Giddens, Anthony. 1984. *The Constitution of Society: Outline of the Theory of Structuration*. London: Polity.

Giddens, Anthony. 2006. *Sociology*. 5th ed. London: Polity.

Gilpin, Robert. 1981. *War and Change in World Politics*. New York, NY: Cambridge University Press.

Glaser, Charles L. 1992. "Political Consequences of Military Strategy: Expanding and Refining the Spiral and Deterrence Models." *World Politics* 44 (4): 497–538.

Glaser, Charles L. 1994–95. "Realists as Optimists: Cooperation as Self-help." *International Security* 19 (3): 50–90.

Glaser, Charles L. 2010. *Rational Theory of International Politics: The Logic of Competition and Cooperation*. Princeton, NJ: Princeton University Press.

Gnirs, M, Andrea. 1999. "Ancient Egypt." In *War and society in the ancient and medieval worlds: Asia, the Mediterranean, Europe, and Mesoamerica*, eds. Kurt A. Raaflaub and Nathan Stewart Rosenstein. Cambridge, MA: Harvard University Press, 71–104.

Goddard, Stacie E., and Daniel H. Nexon. 2005. "Paradigm Lost? Reassessing *Theory of International Politics*." *European Journal of International Relations* 11 (1): 9–61.

Godfrey-Smith, Peter. 2000. "The Replicator in Retrospect." *Biology and Philosophy* 15 (3): 403–23.

Goldstein, Avery. 2001. "The Diplomatic Face of China's Grand Strategy: A Rising Power's Emerging Choice." *China Quarterly* 168: 835–64.

Goldstein, Joshua S. 1987. "The Emperor's New Genes: Sociobiology and War." *International Studies Quarterly* 31 (1): 33–43.

Gooch, Brison D. 1970. *Europe in the Nineteenth Century: A History*. London: Collier-Macmillan.

Gould, Harry D. 1998. "What Is at Stake in the Agent-Structure Debate?" In *International Relations in a Constructed World*, eds. Vendulka Kubálková, Nicholas Onuf, Paul Kowert. Armonk, NY: M. E. Sharpe, 79–98.

Gould, Stephen Jay. 1982. "Introduction." In *Genetics and the Origins of Species*, ed. Theodosius Dobzhansky. New York, NY: Columbia University Press.

Gowa, Joanne. 1986. "Anarchy, Egoism, and Third Images: The Evolution of Cooperation and International Relations." *International Organization* 40 (1): 167–86.

Gramsci, Antonio. [1926–1937] 1992–1996. *Prison Notebooks*. New York, NY: Columbia University Press.

Grieco, Joseph. 1990. *Cooperation among Nations: Europe, America, and Non-Tariff Barriers to Trade.* Ithaca, NY: Cornell University Press.

Gries, Peter H. 2005. "Social Psychology and the Identity-Conflict Debate: Is a 'China Threat' Inevitable?" *European Journal of International Relations* 11 (2): 235–65.

Gruber, Llyold. 2000. *Ruling the World: Power Politics and the Rise of Supranational Institutions.* Princeton, NJ: Princeton Univeristy Press.

Guilaine, Jean, and Jean Zammit. 2005. *The Origins of War: Violence in Prehistory.* Trans. Melanie Hersey. Malden, MA: Blackwell.

Guzman, Andrew T. 2002. "A Compliance-Based Theory of International Law." *California Law Review* 90 (6): 1823–87.

Guzman, Andrew T. 2008. *How International Law Works: A Rational Choice Theory.* Oxford: Oxford University Press.

Guzzini, Stefano. 1993. "Structural Power: The Limits of Neorealist Power Analysis." *International Organization* 47 (3): 443–78.

Guzzini, Stefano. 2000. "The Use and Misuse of Power Analysis in International Theory." In *Global Political Economy: Contemporary Theories,* ed. Ronen Palan. London: Routledge, 53–66.

Guzzini, Stefano. 2005. "The Concept of Power: A Constructivist Analysis." *Millennium: Journal of International Studies.* 33 (3): 495–521.

Haas, Jonathan, Shelia Pozorski, and Thomas Pozorski, eds. 1987. *The Origins and Development of the Andean State.* Cambridge: Cambridge University Press.

Hager, Robert P. Jr., and David A. Lake. 2000. "Balancing Empires: Competitive Decolonization in International Politics." *Security Studies* 9 (3): 108–48.

Hall, Rodney Bruce. 1999. *National Collective Identity: Social Constructs and International Systems.* New York, NY: Columbia University Press.

Hallpike, Christopher Robert. 1986. *The Principles of Social Evolution.* Oxford: Clarendon.

Hamblin, William J. 2006. *Warfare in the Ancient Near East to 1600 BC: Holy Warriors at the Dawn of History.* London: Routlege.

Han Fei Zi (韩非子). ~280–233BC. *Han Fei Zi* [韩非子] <http://www.guoxue.com/zibu/hanfeizi/hfzml.htm> (accessed July 2010).

Hanson, Donald W. 1984. "Thomas Hobbes's 'Highway to Peace'." *International Organization* 38 (2): 329–54.

Hanson, Victor Davis. 2009. *The Western Way of War: Infantry Battle in Classical Greece.* 2nd ed. Berkeley, CA: University of California Press.

Harris, William V. 1979. *War and Imperialism in Republican Rome, 327–70 B.C.* Oxford: Clarendon.

Hasenclever, Andreas, Peter Mayer and Volker Rittberger. 2000. "Integrating Theories of International Regimes." *Review of International Studies* 26 (1): 3–33.

Hasenclever, Andreas, and Brigitte Weiffen. 2006. "International Institutions Are the Key: A New Perspective on the Democratic Peace." *Review of International Studies* 32 (4): 563–85.

Hassig, Ross. 1992. *War and Society in Ancient Mesoamerica.* Berkeley, CA: University of California Press.

Hassig, Ross. 1999. "The Aztec World." In *War and society in the ancient and medieval worlds: Asia, the Mediterranean, Europe, and Mesoamerica* eds. Kurt A. Raaflaub and Nathan Stewart Rosenstein. Cambridge, MA: Harvard University Press, 361–87.

Haugaard, Mark. 1997. *The Constitution of power: a theoretical analysis of power, knowledge and structure.* Manchester, UK: Manchester University Press.

Hayek, Friedrich A. 1967. *Studies in Philosophy, Politics and Economics.* Chicago, IL: University of Chicago Press.

Hayek, Friedrich A. 1973, 1976, 1979 [1982]. *Law, Legislation, and Liberty.* 3 vols. London: Routledge.

Hayek, Friedrich A. 1978. *New Studies in Philosophy, Politics, Economics and the History of Ideas.* London: Routledge and Kegan Paul.

He, Kai, and Huiyun Feng. 2012. "'Why Is There No NATO in Asia?' Revisited: Prospect Theory, Balance of Threat and US Alliance Strategies." *European Journal of International Relations* 18 (2): 227–50.

He, Yinan. 2009. *The Search for Reconciliation: Sino-Japanese and German-Polish Relations after World War II.* Cambridge: Cambridge University Press.

Heather, Peter. 2006. *The Fall of the Roman Empire: A New History of Rome and the Barbarians.* Oxford: Oxford University Press.

Heller, Mark A. 1980. "The Use & Abuse of Hobbes: The State of Nature in International Relations." *Polity* 13 (1) 1: 21–32.

Hemmer, Christopher J., and Peter Katzenstein. 2002. "Why is There No NATO in Asia? Collective Identity, Regionalism, and the Origins of Multilateralism." *International Organization* 56 (3): 575–607.

Hershey, Amos S. 1911. "The History of International Relations during Antiquity and the Middle Ages." *American Journal of International Law* 5 (4): 901–33.

Hill, J. 1989. "Concepts as Units of Cultural Replication." *Journal of Social and Biological Structures* 12 (4): 343–55.

Hinsley, F. H. 1986, *Sovereignty.* 2nd ed. Cambridge: Cambridge University Press.

Hirsch, Fred. 1977. *Social Limits to Growth.* London: Routledge.

Hirschman, Albert O. 1970. "The Search for Paradigms as a Hindrance to Understanding." *World Politics* 22 (3): 329–43.

Hobbes, Thomas. [1651] 1985. *Leviathan,* ed. C. B. Macpherson. London: Penguin.

Hobsbawn, Eric J. 1990. *Nations and Nationalism since 1780.* Cambridge: Cambridge University Press.

Hodgson, Geoffrey M. 1993. *Economics and Evolution: Bringing Life Back into Economics.* London: Polity.

Hodgson, Geoffrey M. 2001. "Is Social Evolution Lamarckian or Darwinian?" In *Darwinism and Evolutionary Economics,* eds. John Laurent and John Nightingale. Cheltenham, UK: Edward Elgar, 87–118.

Hodgson, Geoffrey M. 2002. "Darwinism in Economics: From Analogy to Ontology." *Journal of Evolutionary Economics* 12 (3): 259–81.

Hodgson, Geoffrey M. 2005. "Generalizing Darwinism to Social Evolution: Some Early Attempts." *Journal of Economic Issues* 39 (4): 899–914.

Hodgson, Geoffrey M. 2006. "What Are Institutions?" *Journal of Economic Issues* 40 (1): 1–25.

Hodgson, Geoffrey M., and Thorbjørn Knudsen. 2010a. "Generative Replication and the Evolution of Complexity." *Journal of Economic Behavior and Organization* 75 (1): 12–24.

Hodgson, Geoffrey M., and Thorbjørn Knudsen. 2010b. *Darwin's Conjecture: The Search for General Principles of Social and Economic Evolution.* Chicago, IL: University of Chicago Press.

Hollis, Martin. 1988. *The Cunning of Reason.* New York, NY: Cambridge University Press.

Hollis, Martin, and Steve Smith. 1991. *Explaining and Understanding International Relations.* Oxford: Clarendon.

Holsti, Kal J. 1998. "The Study of International Politics during the Cold War." pp. 17–47 in *The Eighty Years' Crisis: International Relations 1919–1999,* eds. Tim Dunne, Michael Cox, and Ken Booth. Cambridge: Cambridge University Press.

Holsti, Kal J. 2002. "Interview." *Review of International Studies* 29: 619–33.

Holsti, Kal J. 2004. *Taming the Sovereigns: Institutional Change in International Politics.* Cambridge: Cambridge University Press.

Horowitz, Donald L. 1985. *Ethnic Groups in Conflict.* Berkeley, CA: University of California Press.

Houghton, David Patrick. 2009. "The Role of Self-Fulfilling and Self-Negating Prophecies in International Relations." *International Studies Review* 11 (3): 552–84.

Hui, Victoria Tin-bor. 2005. *War and State Formation in Ancient China and Early Modern Europe.* Cambridge: Cambridge University Press.

Hull, David L. 1980. "Individuality and Selection." *Annual Review of Ecology and Systematics* 11. 311–32.

Hull, David L. 1982. "The Naked Meme." In *Learning, Development and Culture: Essays in Evolutionary Epistemology,* ed. Henry C. Plotkin. New York, NY: Wiley, 273–327.

Hunt, Terry L. 2006. "Rethinking the Fall of Easter Island: New Evidence Points to an Alternative Explanation for a Civilization's Collapse." *American Scientist* 94 (5): 412–19.

Hunt, Terry L., and Carl R. Lipo. 2009. "Revisiting Rapa Nui (Easter Island) 'Ecocide'." *Pacific Science* 63 (4): 601–16.

Huntley, Wade L. 1996. "Kant's Third Image: Systemic Sources of the Liberal Peace." *International Studies Quarterly* 40 (1): 45–76.

Hurd, Ian. 1999. "Legitimacy and Authority in International Politics." *International Organization* 53 (2): 379–408.

Hurrell, Andrew. 1998. "An Emerging Security Community in South America?" In *Security Communities,* eds. Emanuel Adler and Michael Barnett. Cambridge: Cambridge University Press, 228–64.

Huxley, Julian. 1942. *Evolution: The Modern Synthesis.* 3rd ed. London: Allen and Unwin.

Huxley, Julian. 1956. "Evolution: Biological and Cultural." In *Current Anthropology: A Supplement to "Anthropology Today",* ed. William L. Thomas. Chicago, IL: University of Chicago Press, 3–25.

Ibn-Khaldun. [1377] 1967. *An Introduction to History* (abridged edition). Trans. Franz Rosenthal Ed. and Abr. N. J. Dawood. Princeton, NJ: Princeton University Press.

Ikenberry, G. John. 2000. *After Victory: Institutions, Strategic Restraint, and the Rebuilding of Order after Major Wars.* Princeton, NJ: Princeton University Press.

Ikenberry, G. John. 2008. "The Rise of China and the Future of the West: Can the Liberal System Survive?" *Foreign Affairs* 87 (1): 23–37.

Ikenberry, G. John., and Charles A. Kupchan. 1990. "Socialization and Hegemonic Power." *International Organization* 44 (3): 283–315.

Jablonka, Eva, and Marion J. Lamb. 2006. *Evolution in Four Dimensions: Genetic, Epigenetic, Behavioral, and Symbolic Variation in the History of Life.* Cambridge, MA: MIT Press.

Jackson, Patrick Thaddeus, and Daniel Nexon. 2004. "Constructivist Realism or Realist-Constructivism?" *International Studies Review* 6 (2): 337–41.

Jackson, Robert H. 1990. *Quasi-states: Sovereignty, International Relations and the Third World.* Cambridge: Cambridge University Press.

Jepperson, Ronald L., Alexander Wendt, and Peter Katzenstein. 1996. "Norms, Identity, and Culture in National Security." In *The Culture of National Security: Norms and Identity in World Politics,* ed. Peter J. Katzenstein. New York, NY: Columbia University Press, 33–75.

Jervis, Robert. 1970. *The Logic of Images in International Relations.* Princeton, NJ: Princeton University Press.

Jervis, Robert. 1976. *Perception and Misperception in International Politics.* Princeton, NJ: Princeton University Press.

Jervis, Robert. 1978. "Cooperation Under the Security Dilemma." *World Politics* 30(2): 167–214.

Jervis, Robert. 1982. "Security Regimes." *International Organization* 36 (2): 357–78.

Jervis, Robert. 1991–1992. "The Future of World Politics: Will It Resemble the Past?" *International Security* 16 (3): 39–73.

Jervis, Robert. 1997. *System Effects: Complexity in Political and Social Life.* Princeton, NJ: Princeton University Press.

Jervis, Robert. 1999. "Realism, Neoliberalism, and Cooperation: Understanding the Debate." *International Security* 24(1): 42–63.

Jervis, Robert. 2002. "Theories of War in an Era of Leading-Power Peace." *American Political Science Review* 96 (1): 1–14.

Jervis, Robert (with Thierry Balzacq). 2004. "The Logic of Mind: Interview with Robert Jervis," *Review of International Studies* 30 (2): 559–82.

Jiang, Xiaoyuan and Weixing Niu. 1999. "Establishing the Timing of King Wu's War against King Zhou with astronomy." *Zhong Guo Ke Xue* [中国科学 Science in China], 51: 20–8.

Johnson, Allen W., and Timothy Earle. 2000. *The Evolution of Human Societies: From Foraging Groups to Agrarian State.* 2nd ed. Stanford, CA: Stanford University Press.

Johnston, Alastair Iain. 1995. *Cultural Realism: Strategic Culture and Grand Strategy in Chinese History.* Princeton, NJ: Princeton University Press.

Johnston, Alastair Iain. 2001. "Treating International Institutions as Social Environment." *International Studies Quarterly* 45 (4): 487–515.

Johnston, Alastair Iain. 2008. *Social States: China in International Institutions, 1980–2000.* Princeton, NJ: Princeton University Press.

Jones, Charles, I. 2005. "Ideas and Growth." In *Handbook of Economic Growth.* Vol. 1b, eds. Phillippe Aghion and Steven N. Durlauf. North-Holland: Elsevier, 1064–111.

Joseph, Jonathan. 2010. "The Limits of Governmentality: Social Theory and the International." *European Journal of International Relations* 16 (2): 223–46.

Joyce, Arthur A. 2010. *Mixtecs, Zapotes, and Chatinos: Ancient Poeples of Southern Mexico.* Malden, MA: Wiley-Blackwell.

Kacowicz, Arie M. 1998. *Zones of Peace in the Third World: South America and West Africa in Comparative Perspective.* Albany, NY: SUNY Press.

Kahler, Miles. 1999. "Evolution, Choice, and International Change." In *Strategic Choices and International Relations,* eds. David A. Lake and Robert Powell. Princeton, NJ: Princeton University Press, 165–96.

Kang, David A. 2003. "Getting Asia Wrong: The Need for New Analytical Frameworks." *International Security* 27 (4): 57–85.

Kang, David A. 2005. "Hierarchy in Asian International Relations: 1300 1900." *Asian Security* 1 (1): 53–79.

Kant, Immanuel. [1784]1991. "Idea for a Universal History with a Cosmopolitan Purpose." In *Kant: Political Writings,* ed. Hans S. Reiss. Cambridge: Cambridge Univeristy Press, 41–54.

Kaplan, Morton A. 1957. *System and Process in International Politics.* New York, NY: Wiley.

Katzenstein, Peter J. (ed.) 1996. *The Culture of National Security.* New York, NY: Columbia University Press.

Katzenstein, Peter J. 1996. *Cultural Norms and National Security: Police and Military in Postwar Japan.* Ithaca, NY: Cornell University Press.

Katzenstein, Peter J. 2005. *A World of Regions: Asia and Europe in the American Imperium.* Ithaca, NY: Cornell University Press.

Kaufman, Stuart J., and William C. Wohlforth. 2007. "Balancing and Balcning Failure in Biblical Times: Assyria and the Ancient Middle Eastern System, 900–600 BEC." In *The Balance of Power in World History,* eds. Stuart J. Kaufman, Richard Little, and William C. Wohlforth. New York, NY: Palgrave Macmillan, 22–46.

Kautilya. [1915] 1967. *Arthasastra.* Trans. R. Shamasastry. Mysore, India, Mysore Printing and Publishing House. <http://en.wikisource.org/w/index.php?oldid= 607637> (Accessed August 2010).

Kaye, Howard L. 1986. *The Social Meaning of Modern Biology: From Social Darwinism to Sociobiology.* New Haven, CT: Yale University Press.

Keal, Paul. 2003. *European Conquest and the Rights of Indigenous Peoples: The Moral Backwardness of International Society.* Cambridge: Cambridge University Press.

Keegan, John. 1993. *A History of Warfare.* New York, NY: Vintage Books.

Keeley, James. 1990. "Toward a Foucauldian Analysis of International Regimes." *International Organization* 44 (1): 83–105.

Keeley, Lawrence H. 1988. "Hunter-gatherer Economic Complexity and 'Population Pressure': A Cross-Cultural Analysis." *Journal of Anthropological Archaeology* 7 (4): 373–411.

Keeley, Lawrence H. 1996. *War before Civilization: The Myth of the Peaceful Savage.* New York, NY: Oxford University Press.

Keeley, Lawrence H. 1998. "Frontier Warfare in the Early Neolithic." In *Troubled Times: Violence and Warfare in the Past,* eds. Debra L. Martin and David W. Frayer. Langhorne, PA: Gordon and Breach, 303–20.

Keeley, Lawrence H. 2004. "Warfare and Conquest." In *Ancient Europe 8000 B.C.— A.D. 1000: An Encyclopedia of the Barbarian World.* Vol. 1, eds. Peter Bogucki and Pam J. Crabtree. New York, NY: Thomson and Gale, 110–8.

Keeley, Lawrence H., and Daniel Cahen. 1989. "Early Neolithic Forts and Villages in NE Belgium: A Preliminary Report." *Journal of Field Archaeology* 16 (2): 157–76.

Kelly, Philip. 1997. *Checkerboards and Shatterbelts: The Geopolitics of South America.* Austin, TX: University of Texas Press.

Kelly, Raymond C. 2000. *Warless Societies and the Origin of War.* Ann Arbor, MI: University of Michigan Press.

Kelly, Raymond C. 2005. "The Evolution of Lethal Intergroup Violence." *Proceedings of the National Academy of Sciences of U.S.A.* 102 (43): 15294–8.

Kemp, Barry J. 1989. *Ancient Egypt: The Anatomy of a Civilization.* London: Routledge.

Kent, Susan. 1989. "And Justice for All: The Development of Political Centralization among Newly Sedentary Foragers." *American Anthropologist* 91 (3): 703–12.

Keohane, Robert O. 1984. *After Hegemony: Cooperation and Discord in the World Political Economy.* Princeton, NJ: Princeton University Press.

Keohane, Robert O., ed. 1986. *Neorealism and Its Critics.* New York, NY: Columbia University Press.

Keohane, Robert O. 1989. *International Institutions and State Power.* Boulder, CO: Westview.

Keohane, Robert O. 1993. "Institutional Theory and the Realist Challenge after the Cold War." In *Neorealism and Neoliberalism: The Contemporary Debate,* ed. David A. Baldwin. New York, NY: Columbia University Press, 269–300.

Keohane, Robert O., and Lisa L. Martin. 1995. "The Promise of Institutionalist Theory." *International Security* 20 (1): 39–51.

Keohane, Robert O., and Lisa L. Martin. 2003. "Institutional Theory as Research Program." In *Progress in International Relations Theory,* eds. Colin Elman and Miriam Fendius Elam. Cambridge, MA: MIT Press, 71–107.

Keohane, Robert O., and Joseph S. Nye. [1977]1989. *Power and Interdependence: World Politics in Transition.* 2nd ed. Boston, MA: Little and Brown.

Keohane, Robert O., and Joseph S. Nye. 1987. "Power and Interdependence Revisited." *International Organization* 41 (4): 725–53.

Kertzer, Joshua D., and Kathleen M. McGraw. 2012. "Folk Realism: Testing the Microfoundations of Realism in Ordinary Citizens." *International Studies Quarterly* 56 (2): 245–58.

Kingdon, John W. 1995. *Agendas, Alternatives, and Public Policies.* 2nd ed., New York, NY: Harper Collins.

Kitcher, Philip. 1982. *Abusing Science: The Case Against Creationism.* Cambridge, MA: MIT Press.

Kitcher, Philip. 1985. *Vaulting Ambition: Sociobiology and the Quest for Human Nature*. Cambridge, MA: MIT Press.

Kitcher, Philip. 2003. "Give Darwin his Due." Unpublished manuscript. Columbia University.

Kitcher, Philip. 2007. *Living with Darwin: Evolution, Design, and the Future of Faith*. Oxford: Oxford University Press.

Knauft, Bruce M. 1990a. "Melanesian Warfare: a Theoretical History." *Oceania* 60 (4): 250–311.

Knauft, Bruce M. 1990b. "Violence among Newly Sedentary Foragers." *American Anthropologist* 92 (4): 1013–15.

Knauft, Bruce M. 1991. "Violence and Sociality in Human Evolution." *Current Anthropology* 32 (4): 391–409.

Knight, Jack. 1992. *Institutions and Social Conflict*. Princeton, NJ: Princeton University Press.

Knudsen, Thorbjørn. 2001. "Nesting Lamarckism within Darwinian Explanations· Necessity in Economics and Possibility in Biology?" In *Darwinism and Evolutionary Economics*, eds. John Laurent and John Nightingale. Cheltenham, UK: Edward Elgar, 121–59.

Kontopoulos, Kyriakos M. 1993. *The Logics of Social Structure*. Cambridge: Cambridge Univeristy Press.

Korman, Sharon. 1996. *The Right of Conquest: The Acquisition of Territory by Force in International Law and Practice*. Oxford: Clarendon Press.

Koskenniemi, Martti. 2009. "Miserable Comforters: International Relations as New Natural Law." *European Journal of International Relations* 15(3): 395–422.

Kosse, Krisztina. 1990. "Group Size and Societal Complexity: Thresholds in the Long-term Memory." *Journal of Anthropological Archaeology* 9 (3): 275–303.

Krasner, Stephen D. 1982a. "Structural Causes and Regime Consequences: Regimes as Intervening Variables." *International Organization* 36 (2): 185–205.

Krasner, Stephen D. 1982b. "Regimes and the Limits of Realism: Regimes as Autonomous Variables." *International Organization* 36 (2): 497–510.

Krasner, Stephen D. 1984. "Approaches to the State: Alternative Conceptions and Historical Dynamics." *Comparative Politics* 16 (2): 223–46.

Krasner, Stephen D. 1988. "Sovereignty: An Institutional Perspective." *Comparative Political Studies* 21 (1): 66–94.

Krasner, Stephen D. 1999. *Sovereignty: Organized Hypocrisy*. Princeton, NJ: Princeton University Press.

Kratochwil, Friedrich V. 1989. *Rules, Norms, and Decisions: On the Conditions of Practical and Legal Reasoning in International Relations and Domestic Affairs*. Cambridge: Cambridge University Press.

Kremer, Michael. 1993. "Population Growth and Technological Change: One Million B.C. to 1990." *Quarterly Journal of Economics* 108 (3): 681–716.

Kroeber, A. L., and Talcott Parsons. 1958. "The Concepts of Culture and Social System." *American Sociological Review* 23 (5): 582–3.

Kuhrt, Amélie. 1995. *The Ancient Near East, c. 3000–300 BC*. 2 vols. London: Routledge.

Kulke, Hermann, and Dietmar Rothermund. 1998. *A History of India*. 3rd ed. London: Routledge.

Kupchan, Charles A. 1984. *The Vulnerability of Empire*. Ithaca, NY: Cornell University Press.

Kupchan, Charles A. 2010. *How Enemies Become Friends: The Sources of Stable Peace*. Princeton, NJ: Princeton University Press.

Kydd, Andrew. 1997. "Sheep in Sheep's Clothing: Why Security Seekers do not Fight Each Other." *Security Studies* 7 (1): 114–55.

Kydd, Andrew. 2005. *Trust and Mistrust in International Relations*. Princeton, NJ: Princeton University Press.

Labs, Eric J. 1997. "Beyond Victory: Offensive Realism and the Expansion of War Aims." *Security Studies* 6 (4): 1–49.

Lake, David A. 2001. "Beyond Anarchy: The Importance of Security Institutions." *International Security* 26 (1): 129–60.

Lake, David A. and Patrick M. Morgan (eds.) 1997. *Regional Orders: Building Security in a New World*. University Park, PA: Pennsylvania State University Press.

Lamberg-Karolvsky, C. C., and Jeremy A. Sabloff. 1995. *Ancient Civilizations: The Near East and Mesoamerica*. Long Grove, IL: Wave Press.

Lambert, Patricia M. 1998. "Patterns of Violence in Prehistoric Hunter-Gatherer Societies of Coastal Southern California." In *Troubled Times: Violence and Warfare in the Past*, eds. Debra L. Martin and David W. Frayer. Langhorne, PA: Gordon and Breach, 77–110.

LeBlanc, Steven, and Katherine Register. 2003. *Constant Battles: The Myth of the Peaceful, Nobel Savage*. New York, NY: St. Martin's Press.

Lebow, Richard Ned. 1994. "The Long Peace, the End of the Cold War, and the Failure of Realism." *International Organization* 48 (2): 249–77.

Lebow, Richard Ned. 2007. *Coercion, Cooperation, and Ethics in International Relations*. London: Routledge.

Lebow, Richard Ned. 2008. *A Cultural Theory of International Relations*. Cambridge: Cambridge University Press.

Lebow, Richard Ned. 2010. *Why Nations Fight*. Cambridge: Cambridge University Press.

Lebow, Richard Ned, and Thomas Risse-Kappen. 1995. "Introduction: International Relations Theory and the End of the Cold War." In *International Relations Theory and the End of the Cold War*, eds. Richard Ned Lebow and Thomas Risse-Kappen. New York, NY: Columbia University Press, 1–22.

Legro, Jeffrey W. 2005. *Rethinking the World: Great Power Strategies and International Order*. Ithaca, NY: Cornell University Press.

LeVine, Robert A., and Donald T. Campbell. 1972. *Ethnocentrism: Theories of Conflict, Ethnic Attitudes, and Group Behaviors*. New York, NY: John Wiley & Sons.

Legro, Jeffrey W., and Andrew Moravcsik. 1999. "Is Anybody Still a Realist?" *International Security* 24 (2): 5–55.

Levins, Richard, and Richard Lewontin. 1985. *The Dialectical Biologist*. Cambridge, MA: Harvard University Press.

Levy, Jack S. 1983. *War in the Modern Great Power System, 1495–1975*. Lexington, KY: The University Press of Kentucky.

Levy, Jack S. 1994. "Learning and Foreign Policy: Sweeping a Conceptual Minefield." *International Organization* 48 (2): 279–312.

Levy, Jack S. 1997. "Prospect Theory, Rational Choice, and International Relations." *International Studies Quarterly* 41 (1): 87–112.

Levy, Jack S. 1998. "The Causes of War and the Conditions of Peace." *Annual Review of Political Sciences* 1: 139–65.

Levy, Jack S., and William Thompson. 2010. *Causes of War*. Malden, MA: Blackwell.

Lewis, Mark Edward. 1990. *Sanctioned Violence in Early China*. Albany, NY: State University of New York Press.

Lewontin, Richard C. 1970. "The Units of Selection." *Annual Review of Ecology and Systematics* 1: 1–18.

Lin, Justin Yifu. 1989. "An Economic Theory of Institutional Change: Induced and Imposed Change." *Cato Journal* 9 (1): 1–35.

Lin, Justin Yifu, and Jeffrey B. Nugent. 1995. "Institutions and Economic Development." In *Handbook of Development Economics*. Vol. 3A, eds. J. Behrman and T. N. Srinivasan. Amerstand: Elsevier Science, 2301–70.

Lin, Yun [林沄]. 1990. "Shang Dai Bing Zhi Guan Kui [商代兵制管窥/A Preliminary Inquiry into the Shang Military System]." *Journal of Jilin University, Social Sciences Edition* 1: 11–17.

Linklater, Andrew, and Hidemi Suganami. 2006. *The English School of International Relations: A Contemporary Reassessment*. Cambridge: Cambridge University Press.

Little, Richard D. 2000. "The English School's Contribution to the Study of International Relations." *European Journal of International Relations*, 6 (3): 395–422.

Liu, Li. 1996. "Settlement Patterns, Chiefdom Variability, and the Development of Early States in North China." *Journal of anthropological archaeology* 15 (3): 237–88.

Liu, Li. 2004. *The Chinese Neolithic: Trajectories to Early States*. Cambridge: Cambridge University Press.

Liu, Qing Zhu [刘庆柱] (eds.) 2010. *Zhong Guo Kao Gu Fa Xiang yu Yang Jiu, 1949-2009* [中国考古发现与研究, 1949-2009/Archaeological Discoveries and Researches in China, 1949-2009]. Beijing: Peoples' Publishing House

Liverani, Mario. 2005. *Israel's History and the History of Israel*. Trans. Chiara Peri and Philip R. Davies. London: Equinox.

Lobell, Steven E., Norrin M. Ripsman, and Jeffrey W. Taliaferro, eds. 2009. *Neoclassical Realism, the State, and Foreign Policy*. Cambridge: Cambridge University Press.

López, Jośe, and John Scott. 2000. *Social Structure*. Buckingham: Open University Press.

Lorenz, Konrad. 1966 [2002]. *On Aggression*. London: Routledge.

Loyal, Steven, and Barry Barnes. 2001. "'Agency' as a Red Herring in Social Theory." *Philosophy of the Social Sciences* 31 (4): 507–24.

Luo, Guanzhong [罗贯中]. [c.1330-1400] 1999. *Sanguo Yangyi* [Romance of the Three Kingdoms], Moss Roberts, trans. Berkeley, CA: University of California Press.

Machiavelli, Nicoolo. [1532] 2005. *The Prince*. Trans. Peter Bondanella. Oxford: Oxford University Press.

MacIntyre, Alasdair. 1984. *After Virtue: A Study in Moral Theory*. 2nd ed. Notre Dame, IN: University of Notre Dame Press.

Macqueen, J. G. 1995. "The History of Anatolia and of the Hittite Empire: An Overview." In *Civilizations of the Ancient Near East*, vol. II, eds. Jack M. Sasson et al. New York, NY: Charles Scribner's Sons, 1085–105.

Maisels, Charles Keith. 1993. *The Near East: Archaeology in the Cradle of Civilization.* London: Routledge.

Malinowski, Bronislaw. 1941. "An Anthropological Analysis of War." *American Journal of Sociology* 46 (4): 521–50.

Malthus, Thomas R. [1798]1951. *An Essay on the Principle of Population.* London: Everyman.

Mann, Michael. 1986. *A History of power from the beginning to A. D. 1760.* Vol.1 of *The Sources of Social Power.* Cambridge: Cambridge University Press.

Mansfield, Edward D., and Helen V. Milner, eds. 1997. *The Political Economy of Regionalism.* New York, NY: Columbia University Press.

Mansfield, Edward D., and Helen V. Milner. 1999. "The New Wave of Regionalism." *International Organization* 53 (3): 589–627.

Marcus, Joyce and Kent V. Flannery. 1996. *The Zapotec Civilization: How Urban Society Evolved in the Mexico's Oaxaca Valley.* London: Thames and Hudson.

Martin, Debra L., and David W. Frayer. 1998. *Troubled Times: Violence and Warfare in the Past.* Langhorne, PA: Gordon and Breach.

Martin, Lisa L., and Beth A. Simmons. 1998. "Theories and Empirical Studies of International Institutions." *International Organization* 52 (4): 729–57.

Marx, Karl, and Friedrich Engels. 1846. *The German Ideology.* <http://www.marxist.org/> (accessed November 2007).

Maschner, Herbert D. G. 1998. "The Evolution of Northwest Coast Warfare." In *Troubled Times: Violence and Warfare in the Past,* eds. Debra L. Martin and David W. Frayer. Langhorne, PA: Gordon and Breach, 267–302.

Maschner, Herbert D. G., and Katherine L. Reedy-Maschner. 1998. "Raid, Retreat, Defend (Repeat): The Archaeology and Ethnohistory of Warfare on the North Pacific Rim." *Journal of Anthropological Archaeology* 17(1): 19–51.

Mattern, Janice Bially. 2004. "Power in Realist-Constructivist Research." *International Studies Review* 6 (2): 343–6.

Matthews, Roger. 2003. *The Archaeology of Mesopotamia: Theories and Approaches.* London: Routledge.

Mayr, Ernst. 1969. "Footnotes on the Philosophy of Biology." *Philosophy of Science* 36 (2): 197–202.

Mayr, Ernst. 1997. "The Objects of Selection." *Proceedings of the National Academy of Sciences of U.S.A.* 94 (6): 2091–4.

McIntosh, Jane R. 2005. *Ancient Mesopotamia: New Perspectives.* Santa Barbara, CA: ABC-CLIO.

McMahon, Augusta, Arkadiusz Sołtysiak and Jill Weber. 2008. "Late Chalcolithic Mass Graves at Tell Brak, Syria, and violent conflict during the Growth of Early City-states." *Journal of Field Archaeology* 36 (3): 201–20.

Mead, Margaret. [1940] 1964. "Warfare Is Only an Invention—Not a Biological Necessity." In *War: Studies from Psychology, Sociology, and Anthropology,* eds. Leon Bramson and George W. Goethals. New York, NY: Basic Books, 19–22.

Mearsheimer, John J. 1990. "Back to the Future: Instability in Europe after the Cold War." *International Security* 15 (1): 5–56.

Mearsheimer, John J. 1994–95. "The False Promise of International Institutions." *International Security* 19 (3): 5–49.

Mearsheimer, John J. 1995. "A Realist Reply." *International Security* 20 (1): 82–93.

Mearsheimer, John J. 2001. *The Tragedy of Great Power Politics.* New York, NY: Norton.

Mearsheimer, John J. 2006. "Interview." *International Affairs* 20: 105–23, 231–243.

Mellaart, James. 1967. *Catal Huyuk: A Neolithic Town in Anatolia.* New York, NY: McGraw Hill.

Mercer, Jonathan. 1995. "Anarchy and Identity." *International Organization* 49: 229–52.

Mercer, Jonathan. 1996. *Reputation in International Relations.* Ithaca, NY: Cornell University Press.

Merton, Robert K. 1968. *Social theory and Social structure.* New York, NY: Free Press.

Meyer, Jörg. 2008. "The Concealed Violence of Modern Peace(-Making)." *Millennium: Journal of International Studies* 36 (3): 555–74.

Meyers, Eric, ed. 1997. *The Oxford Encyclopedia of Archaeology in the Near East.* 5 vols. Oxford: Oxford Univeristy Press.

Miller, Gary, and Kathleen Cook. 1998. "Leveling and Leadership: Hierarchy and Social Order." In *Institutions and Social Order,* eds. Karol Soltan, Eric M. Uslaner and Virginia Haufler. Ann Arbor, MI: University of Michigan Press, 67–100.

Milner, Helen. 1991. "The Assumption of Anarchy in International Relations Theory: A Critique." *Review of International Studies* 17: 67–85.

Milner, Helen. 1992. "International Theories of Cooperation Among Nations: Strengths and Weaknesses." *World Politics* 44 (3): 466–96.

Modelski, George. 1978. "The Long Cycle of Global Politics and the Nation-State." *Comparative Studies in Society and History* 20 (02): 214–35.

Modelski, George. 1987. *Long Cycles in World Politics.* Seattle, WA: University of Washington Press.

Modelski, George. 1990. "Is World Politics Evolutionary Learning?" *International Organization* 44: 1–24.

Modelski, George. 2005. "Long-Term Trends in World Politics." *Journal of World-Systems Research* 11 (2): 195–206.

Monteiro, Nuno P., and Keven G. Ruby. 2009. "IR and the False Promise of Philosophical Foundations." *International Theory* 1(1): 15–48.

Montgomery, Evan Braden. 2006. "Breaking out of the Security Dilemma: Realism, Reassurance, and the Problem of Uncertainty." *International Security* 31(2):151–85.

Morgenthau, Hans J. 1948. *Politics among Nations.* New York, NY: Knopf.

Morgenthau, Hans J. 1970. *Truth and Power: Essays of a Decade, 1960–70.* London: Pall Mall.

Morgenthau, Hans J. 1978. *Politics among Nations.* 5th ed. New York, NY: Knopf.

Morrow, James D. 1994. *Game Theory for Political Scientists.* Princeton, NJ: Princeton University Press.

Moravcsik, Andrew. 1998. *The Choice of Europe: Social Purposes and State Power from Messina to Maastricht.* Ithaca, NY: Cornell University Press.

Mueller, John. 1989. *Retreat from Doomsday: The Obsolescence of Major War.* New York, NY: Basic Books.

Muller, Hermann J. 1959. "One Hundred Years without Darwinism Are Enough." *Social Science and Mathematics* 59 (4): 304–16.

Murphy, Alexander B. 1996. "The Sovereign State System as Political-Territorial Ideal: Historical and Contemporary Considerations." In *State Sovereignty as Social Construct*, eds. Thomas J. Biersteker and Cynthia Veber. Cambridge, Cambridge University Press, 81–120.

Nayak, Meghana V., and Christopher Malone. 2009. "American Orientalism and American Exceptionalism: A Critical Rethinking of US Hegemony." *International Studies Review* 11: 253–76.

Nelson, Richard R. 2007. "Universal Darwinism and Evolutionary Social Science." *Biology and Philosophy* 22 (1): 73–94.

Nelson, Richard R., and Sidney G. Winter. 1982. *An Evolutionary Theory of Economic Change*. Cambridge, MA: Harvard University Press.

Neumann, Iver B. 2004. "Beware of Organicism: the Narrative Self of the State." *Review of International Studies* 30 (2): 259–67.

Niebuhr, Reinhold. 1932 [1960]. *Moral Man and Immoral Society: A Study in Ethics and Politics*. New York, NY: Charles Scribner's Sons.

Nolan, Patrick, and Gerhard E. Lenski. 2004. *Human Societies: An Introduction to Macrosociology*. Boulder, CO: Paradigm Publishers.

North, Douglass C. 1981. *Structure and Change in Economic History*. New York, NY: Norton.

North, Douglass C. 1990. *Institutions, Institutional Change and Economic Performance*. Cambridge: Cambridge University Press.

Nugent, Neill. 2006. *The Government and Politics of the European Union*. New York, NY: Palgrave Macmillan.

Nye, Joseph S. Jr. 1988. "Neorealism and Neoliberalism." *World Politics* 40 (2): 235–51.

Nye, Joseph S. Jr. 2004. *Soft Power: The Means to Success in World Politics*. New York, NY: Public Affairs.

O'Connell, Robert L. 1989. *Of Arms and Man: A History of War, Weapons, and Aggression*. Oxford: Oxford University Press.

Oates, Joan, et al. 2007. "Early Mesopotamian Urbanism: a New View from the North." *Antiquity* 81 (313): 585–600.

Oelsner, Andrea. 2005. *International Relations in Latin America: Peace and Security in the Southern Cone*. London: Routledge.

Okasha, Samir. 2006. *Evolution and the Levels of Selection*. Oxford: Oxford University Press.

Onuf, Nicholas G. 1989. *World of Our Making: Rules and Rule in Social Theory and International Relations*. Columbia, SC: University of South Carolina Press.

Onuf, Nicholas G. 1998. "Constructivism: A User's Manual." In *International Relations in a Constructed World*, eds. V. Kubálková, Nicholas G. Onuf, and Paul Kowert. Armonk, NY: M. E. Sharpe, 58–78.

Osiander, Andreas. 2001. "Sovereignty, International Relations, and the Westphalia Myth." *International Organization* 55 (2): 251–87.

Otterbein, Keith F. 1989. *The Evolution of War: A Cross-Cultural Study*. 3rd ed. New Haven, CT: Human Relations Area Files Press.

Otterbein, Keith F. 2000. "Killing of Captured Enemies: A Cross-Cultural Study." *Current Anthropology* 41 (3): 439–43.

Otterbein, Keith F. 2004. *How War Began*. College Station, TX: Texas A & M University Press.

Palan, Ronen. 2000. "A World of Their Making: An Evaluation of the Constuctivist Critique in International Relations." *Review of International Studies* 26 (4): 575–98.

Papkin, David P. 2001. "Obstacles to an Evolutionary Global Politics Research Program." In *Evolutionary Interpretations of World Politics*, ed. William R. Thompson. New York and London: Routledge, 52–60.

Paras, Eric. 2006. *Foucault 2.0: Beyond Power and Knowledge*. New York, NY: Other Press.

Parish, Randall, and Mark Peceny. 2002. "Kantian Liberalism and the Collective Defense of Democracy in Latin America." *Journal of Peace Research* 39 (2): 229–50.

Parsons, Talcott. 1937. *The Structure of Social Action: A Study in Social Theory with Special Reference to a Group of Recent European Writers*. New York, NY: Free Press.

Parsons, Talcott. 1951. *The Social System*. New York, NY: Free Press.

Patrick, Stewart. 2001. "The Evolution of International Norms: Choice, Learning, Power, and Identity." In *Evolutionary Interpretations of World Politics*, ed. William R. Thompson. New York and London: Routledge, 133–74.

Peceny, Mark, Caroline C. Beer, and Shannon Shchez-Terry. 2002. "Dictatorial Peace?" *American Political Science Review* 96 (1): 15–26.

Pettitt, Paul, and Alistair Pike. 2007. "Dating European Palaeolithic Cave Art: Progress, Prospects, Problems." *Journal of Archaeological Method and Theory* 14 (1): 27–47.

Pevehouse, Jon C. 2005. *Democracy from Above: Regional Organizations and Democratization*. Cambridge: Cambridge University Press.

Pinker, Steven. 2002. *The Blank Slate: The Modern Denial of Human Nature*. New York, NY: Viking.

Polanyi, Karl. [1944] 2001. *The Great Transformation: The Political and Economic Origins of Our Time*. Boston, MA: Beacon.

Pollock, Susan. 1999. *Ancient Mesopotamia*. Cambridge: Cambridge University Press.

Popper, Karl. [1937] 1959. *The Logic of Scientific Discovery*. London: Routledge.

Popper, Karl. [1945] 1967. *The Open Society and its Enemies*. London: Routledge.

Popper, Karl. [1963] 1991. *Conjectures and Refutations: The Growth of Scientific Knowledge*. London: Routledge.

Popper, Karl. 1972. *Objective Knowledge: An Evolutionary Approach*. Oxford: Claredon Press.

Porpora, Douglas V. [1989] 1998. "Four Concepts of Social Structure." *Journal for the Theory of Social Behaviour* 19 (2): 195–211. Reprinted in *Critical Realism: Essential Readings*, eds. Margaret Archer et al. London: Routledge, 339–355.

Porpora, Douglas V. 1993. "Cultural Rules and Material Relations." *Sociological Theory* 11 (2): 212–29.

Powell, Robert. 1994. "Anarchy in International Relations Theory: The Neorealist-Neoliberal Debate." *International Organization* 48 (2): 313–44.

Pozorski, Shelia. 1987. "Theocracy vs. Militarism: The Significance of the Casma Valley in Understanding Early State Formation." In *The Origins and Development of the Andean State*, eds. Jonathan Haas, Shelia Pozorski, and Thomas Pozorski. Cambridge: Cambridge University Press, 15–30.

Pozorski, Shelia, and Thomas Pozorski. 2006. "Las Haldas: An Expanding Initial Period Polity of Coastal Peru." *Journal of Anthropological Research* 62 (1): 27–52.

Premack, David and Marc D. Hauser. 2004. "Why Animals Do Not Have Culture." In *Evolution and Culture*, eds. Stephen C. Levinson and Pierre Jaisson. Cambridge, MA: MIT Press, 133–52.

Pritchett, William Kendrick. 1971–1991. *The Greek State at War*. 5 vols. Berkeley, CA: University of California Press.

Raaflaub, Kurt A. 1999. "Archaic and Classical Greece." In *War and Society in the Ancient and Medieval Worlds: Asia, the Mediterranean, Europe, and Mesoamerica*, eds. Kurt A. Raaflaub and Nathan Stewart Rosenstein. Cambridge, MA: Harvard University Press, 129–62.

Raaflaub, Kurt A., eds. 2007. *War and Peace in the Ancient World*. Malden, MA: Blackwell.

Rathbun, Brian C. 2007. "Uncertain about Uncertainty: Understanding the Multiple Meanings of a Crucial Concept in International Relations Theory." *International Studies Quarterly* 51 (3): 533–57.

Redmond, Elsa M. and Charles S. Spencer. 2006. "From Raiding to Conquest: Warfare Strategies and Early State Development in Oaxaca, Mexico." In, *The Archaeology of Warfare: Prehistories of Raiding and Conquest*, eds. Elizabeth N. Arkush and Mark W. Allen. Gainesville, FL: University of Florida Press, 336–93.

Redmond, Elsa M., and Charles S. Spencer. 2012. "Chiefdoms at the Threshold: The Competitive Origins of The Primary State." *Journal of Anthropological Archaeology* 31 (1): 22–37.

Rescher, Nicholas. 1997. *Process Metaphysics: An Introduction to Process Philosophy*. Albany, NY: SUNY Press.

Resende-Santos, João. 2002. "The Origins of Security Cooperation in the Southern Cone." *Latin American Politics and Society* 44 (4): 89–126.

Reus-Smit, Christian. 1997. "The Constitutional Structure of International Society and the Nature of Fundamental Institutions." *International Organization* 51 (4): 555–89.

Reus-Smit, Christian. 1999. *The Moral Purpose of the State: Culture, Social Identity, and Institutional Rationality in International Relations*. Princeton, NJ: Princeton University Press.

Reus-Smit, Christian. 2002. "Imaging Society: Constructivism and the English School." *British Journal of Politics and International Relations* 4 (3): 487–509.

Reyna, Stephan P., and R. E. Downs. 1994. *Studying War: Anthropological Perspectives*. Langhorne, PA: Gordon and Breach.

Richards, Robert J. 1987. *Darwin and the Emergence of Evolutionary Theories of Mind and Behavior*. Chicago, IL: University of Chicago Press.

Richards, Robert J. 1992. "The Structure of Narrative Explanation in History and Biology." In *History and Evolution*, eds. Matthew H. Nitecki and Doris V. Nitecki. Albany, NY: State University of New York Press, 19–53.

Richardson, Robert C. 2007. *Evolutionary Psychology as Maladapted Psychology*. Cambridge, MA: MIT Press.

Richerson, Peter J., and Robert Boyd. 2005. *Not by Genes Alone: How Culture Transformed Human Evolution*. Chicago, IL: University of Chicago Press.

Ringmar, Erik. 1997. "Alexander Wendt: A Social Scientist Struggling with History." In *The Future of International Relations: Masters in the Making*, eds. Iver B. Neumann and Ole Wæver. London: Routledge, 269–89.

Ringmar, Erik. 2012. "Performing International Systems: Two East-Asian Alternatives to the Westphalian Order." *International Organizations* 66 (1): 1–25.

Ripsman Norrin M. 2005. "Two Stages of Transition From a Region of War to a Region of Peace: Realist Transition and Liberal Endurance." *International Studies Quarterly* 49 (4): 669–94.

Risse-Kappen, Thomas. 1996. "Collective Identity in a Democratic Community: The Case of NATO." In *The Culture of National Security: Norms and Identity in World Politics*, ed. Peter J. Katzenstein. New York, NY: Columbia University Press, 357–99.

Roberts, Christopher. n.d. "ASEAN Regional Identity Survey, unpublished data."

Robinson, Robert J., Keltner, D., Ward, A., and Lee Ross. 1995. "Actual versus Assumed Differences in Construal: 'Native Realism' in Intergroup Perception and Conflict." *Journal of Personality and Social Psychology* 68 (2): 404–17.

Rodseth, Lars. 1991. "Comments on Knauft." *Current Anthropology* 32 (4): 414–16.

Roese, Neal J. 1997. Counterfactual Thinking. *Psychological Bulletin* 121 (1): 133–48.

Roper, Marilyn K. 1975. "Evidence of Warfare in the Near East from 10,000–4,300 BC." In, *War: Its Causes and Correlates*, eds. M. A. Nettleship, D. Givens, and A. Nettelship. The Hague: Mouton Publishers, 299–344.

Rosenstein, Nathan. 1999. "Republican Rome." In *War and Society in the Ancient and Medieval Worlds: Asia, the Mediterranean, Europe, and Mesoamerica*, eds. Kurt A. Raaflaub and Nathan Stewart Rosenstein. Cambridge, MA: Harvard University Press, 163–216.

Ross, John. 1998. "Violence and Gender in Early Italy." In *Troubled Times: Violence and Warfare in the Past*, eds. Debra L. Martin and David W. Frayer. Langhorne, PA: Gordon and Breach, 111–44.

Ross, Lee, and Andrew Ward. 1995. "Psychological Barriers to Dispute Resolution." *Advances in Experimental Social Psychology* 27: 255–304.

Ross, Marc Howard. 1985. "Internal and External Conflict and Violence: Cross-Cultural Evidence and a New Analysis." *Journal of Conflict Resolution* 29 (4): 547–79.

Roth, Jonathan P. 2009. *Roman Warfare*. Cambridge: Cambridge University Press.

Rousseau, Jean-Jacques. [1762] 1993. *The Social Contract and Other Essays*. London: Everyman.

Ruggie, John G. 1983. "Continuity and Transformation in the World Polity: Toward a Neorealist Synthesis." *World Politics* 35 (2): 261–85.

Ruggie, John G. 1995. "The False Premise of Realism." *International Security* 20 (1): 62–70.

Russett, Bruce M., and John Oneal. 2001. *Triangulating Peace: Democracy, Interdependence, and International Organizations*. New York, NY: W. W. Norton.

Sabin, Philip, Hans van Wees, and Michael Whitby, eds. 2007. *The Cambridge History of Greek and Roman Warfare*. 2 vols. Cambridge: Cambridge University Press.

Sagan, Scott D. 1997. "Culture, Strategy, and Selection in International Security." Unpublished manuscript, Stanford University.

Sage, Michael M. 1996. *Warfare in Ancient Greece: A Sourcebook*. London: Routledge.

Sagona, Antonia, and Paul Zimansky. 2009. *Ancient Turkey*. London: Routledge.

Sahlins, Marshall. 1960. "Evolution: Specific and General." *In Evolution and Culture*, eds. M. D. Sahlins and E. R. Service. Ann Arbor, MI: University of Michigan Press.

Sahlins, Marshall D., and Elman R. Service. 1960. *Evolution and Culture*. Ann Arbor, MI: University of Michigan Press.

Said, Edward. 1978. *Orientalism*. New York, NY: Vintage Books.

Said, Edward. 1993. *Culture and Imperialism*. New York, NY: Knopf.

Saidemen, Stephen, and Williams Ayers. 2007a. "Pie Crust Promises and the Sources of Foreign Policy: The Limited Impact of Accession and the Priority of Domestic Constituencies." *Foreign Policy Analysis* 3 (3): 189–210.

Saidemen, Stephen, and Williams Ayers. 2007b. "Predicting a State's Foreign Policy: State Preferences between Domestic and International Constraints." *Foreign Policy Analysis* 3 (3): 211–32.

Salazar, Lucy C. 2004. "Machu Picchu: Mysterious Royal Estate in the Cloud Forest." In *Machu Picchu: Unveiling the Mystery of the Incas*, eds., Richard L. Burger and Lucy C. Salazar. New Haven, CT: Yale University Press, 21–47.

Sanderson, Stephen. 2001. *The Evolution of Sociality: A Darwinian Conflict Perspective*. Lanham, MD: Rowman and Littlefield.

Sárváry, Katalin. 2006. "No Place for Politics? Truth, Progress, and the Neglected Role of Diplomacy in Wendt's Theory of History." In *Constructivism and International Relations: Alexander Wendt and his critics*, eds. Stefano Guzzini and Anna Leander. London: Routledge, 160–80.

Sasson, Jack M., et al. eds. 1995. *Civilizations of the Ancient Near East*, vol. II. New York, NY: Charles Scribner's Sons.

Sawyer, Ralph D. 1993. *The Seven Military Classics of Ancient China*, with the collaboration of Mei-chun Sawyer, translation with a commentary. Boulder, CO: Westview Press.

Sawyer, Ralph D. 1998. *The Tao of Spycraft: Intelligence Theory and Practice in Traditional China*, with the bibliographic collaboration of Mei-chun Lee Sawyer. New York, NY: Basic Books.

Sawyer, Ralph D. 2011. *Ancient Chinese Warfare*, with the bibliographic collaboration of Mei-chun Lee Sawyer. New York, NY: Basic Books.

Schotter, Andrew. 1981. *The Economic Theory of Social Institutions*. Cambridge: Cambridge University Press.

Schroeder, Paul. 1994a. "Historical Reality vs. Neo-realist Theory." *International Stdudies* 19 (1): 108–48.

Schroeder, Paul. 1994b. *The Transformation of Europe Politics 1763–1848*. Clarendon: Oxford University Press.

Schroeder, Paul. 1995. "Reply: History vs. Neorealism: Another Look." *International Security* 20 (1): 193–5.

Schweller, Randall L. 1996. "Neorealism's Status-Quo Bias: What Security Dilemma?" *Security Studies* 5 (3): 122–66.

Schweller, Randall L. 2001. "The Problem of International Order Revisited: A Review Essay." *International Security* 26 (1): 161–86.

Schweller, Randall L. 2006. *Unanswered Threats: Political Constraints on the Balance of Power*. Princeton, NJ: Princeton University Press.

Schweller, Randall L., and David Priess. 1997. "A Tale of Two Realisms: Expanding the Institutions Debate." *Mershon International Studies Review* 41 (1): 1–32.

Schweller, Randall L. and William Wohlforth. 2000. "Power Test: Evaluating Realism in Response to the End of the Cold War." *Security Studies* 9 (3): 60–107.

Schweller, Randall L., and Xiaoyu Pu. 2011. "After Unipolarity: China's Visions of International Order in an Era of U.S. Decline." *International Security* 36 (1): 41–72.

Scott, James C. 1985. *Weapons of the Weak: Everyday Forms of Peasant Resistance*. New Haven, CT: Yale University Press.

Scott, James C. 1990. *Domination and the Art of Resistance: Hidden Transcripts*. New Haven, CT: Yale University Press.

Scriven, Michael. 1959. "Explanation and Prediction in Evolutionary Theory." *Science* 130 (3374): 477–82.

Searle, John. 1995. *The Construction of Social Reality*. New York, NY: Free Press.

Service, Elman R. [1962] 1971. *Primitive Social Organization: An Evolutionary Perspective*. 2nd ed. New York, NY: Random House.

Service, Elman R. 1968. "The Prime-Mover of Cultural Evolution." *Southwestern Journal of Anthropology* 24 (4): 396–409.

Service, Elman R. 1975. *Origins of the State and Civilization: The Process of Cultural Evolution*. New York, NY: W. W. Norton.

Shang, Yang (商鞅/Lord Shang). ~339 B.C. *Shang Jun Shu* [商君书/Books of Lord Shang]. <http://wenku.baidu.com/view/66fd0788680203d8ce2f241e.html> (accessed January 2007). For an earlier translation, see *The Book of Lord Shang: A Classic of the Chinese School of Law*, trans. Duyvendak, J. J. L. Chicago, IL: University of Chicago Press ([1928] 1963).

Shao, Wangping. 2005. "The Formation of Civilization: The Interaction Sphere of the Longshan Period." In *The Formation of Chinese Civilization: An Archeological Perspective*, eds. Kwang-chih Chang and Pingfang Xu. New Haven, CT: Yale University Press, 85–124.

Shaughnessy, Edward L. 1985–1987. "The 'Current' *Bamboo Annals* and the Date of the Zhou Conquest of Shang." *Early China* 11–12: 33–60.

Shaw, Ian, ed. 2000. *The Oxford History of Ancient Egypt*. Oxford: Oxford University Press.

Shaw, R. Paul, and Yuwa Wong. 1987. "Ethnic Mobilization and the Seeds of Warfare: An Evolutionary Perspective." *International Studies Quarterly* 31 (1): 5–31.

Shea, John J. 2001. "The Middle Paleolithic: Early Modern Humans and Neandertals in the Levant." *Near Eastern Archaeology* 64 (1/2): 38–64.

Shea, John J. 2003. "Neanderthals, Competition, and the Origin of Modern Human Behavior in the Levant." *Evolutionary Anthropology* 12 (4): 173–87.

Shi, Xiaoting, Weinan Tao [石晓霆、陶威娜]. 2003. "Xia Shan Shi Qi de Ge yu Ye Zhan Fang Shi Qian Shuo [Ge in the Xia-Shang Period and its Battlefield Deployment/夏商时期的戈与野战方式浅说]." *Zhong Yuan Wen Wu* [《中原文物》/Antiques of Central China] 5: 39–42.

Shinko, Rosemary E. 2008 "Agonistic Peace: A Postmodern Reading." *Millennium: Journal of International Studies* 36 (3): 473–91.

Si-Ma, Qian [司马迁]. 1997 [~87 B.C.]. *Shi-ji* [*Historical Record*]. 2 vols. Shanghai: Shanghai Guji Chubanshe.

Simmel, Georg. 1964. *Conflict and the Web of Social Affiliations.* Trans. Kurt H. Wolff and Reinhard Bendix. New York, NY: Free Press.

Simmons. Beth A. 2000. "International Law and State Behavior: Commitment and Compliance in International Monetary Affairs." *American Political Science Review* 94 (4): 819–35.

Smith, Anthony. 1986. *The Ethnic Origins of Nations.* Oxford: Basil Blackwell.

Smith, David Livingston. 2007. *The Most Dangerous Animal: Human Nature and the Origins of War.* New York, NY: St. Martin's Press.

Smith, Maria Ostendorf. 1998. "Osteological Indications of Warfare in the Archaic Period of the Western Tennessee Valley." In *Troubled Times: Violence and Warfare in the Past,* eds. Debra L. Martin and David W. Frayer. Langhorne, PA: Gordon and Breach, 241–66.

Smith, Maynard John, and Szathmary Eors. 1997. *The Major Transitions in Evolution.* Oxford: Oxford University Press.

Smith, Tony. 1979. "The Underdevelopment of Development Literature: The Case of Dependency Theory." *World Politics* 31 (2): 247–88.

Snyder, Glenn H. 2002. "Mearsheimer's World: Offensive Realism and the Struggle for Security: A Review Essay." *International Security* 27 (1): 149–73.

Snyder, Jack. 1991. *Myths of Empire: Domestic Politics and International Ambition.* Ithaca, NY: Cornell University Press.

Snyder, Jack. 2002. "Anarchy and Culture: Insights from the Anthropology of War." *International Organization* 56 (1): 7–45.

Sober, Elliott. 1984. *The Nature of Selection: Evolutionary Theory in Philosophical Focus.* Cambridge, MA: Bradford Books-MIT Press.

Solingen, Etel. 1998. *Regional Orders at Century's Dawn: Global and Domestic Influences on Grand Strategy.* Princeton, NJ: Princeton University Press.

Solingen, Etel, 2007. "Pax Asiatica versus Bella Levantina: The Foundations of War and Peace in East Asia and the Middle East." *American Political Science Review* 101 (4): 757–80.

Solingen, Etel. 2008. "The Genesis, Design and Effects of Regional Institutions: Lessons from East Asia and the Middle East." *International Studies Quarterly* 52 (2): 261–94.

Soltan, Karol. 1998. "Institutions as Products of Politics." In *Institutions and Social Order,* eds. Karol Soltan, Eric M. Uslaner, and Virginia Haufler. Ann Arbor, MI: University of Michigan Press, 45–64.

Soltis, Joseph, Robert Boyd, and Peter J. Richerson. 1995. "Can Group-Functional Behaviors Evolve by Cultural Group Selection?: An Empirical Test." *Current Anthropology* 36 (3): 473–94.

Song, Zhenhao. 1991. "An Estimation of the Populations in Xia and Shang [*Xia Shang Ren Kou Chu Tan*]" *Studies of History (Li Shi Yan Jiu)* 4 (1991): 20–34.

Sørensen, Georg. 2008. "The Case for Combining Material Forces and Ideas in the Study of IR." *European Journal of International Relations* 14(1): 5–52.

Spalinger, Anthony J. 2005. *War in Ancient Egypt.* Malden, MA: Blackwell.

Spencer, Charles S., 2003. "War and Early State Formation in Oaxaca, Mexico." *Proceedings of the National Academy of Sciences of the U.S.A.* 100 (20): 11185–7.

Spencer, Charles S., and Elsa M. Redmond. 2001. "Multilevel Selection and Political Evolution in the Valley of Oaxaca, 500–100 B.C." *Journal of Anthropological Archaeology* 20 (2): 195–229.

Spencer, Charles S., and Elsa M. Redmond. 2003. "Militarism, Resistance, and Early State Development in Oaxaca, Mexico." *Social Evolution and History* 2 (1): 25–70.

Spencer, Charles S., and Elsa M. Redmond. 2004. "Primary State Formation in Mesoamerica." *Annual Review of Anthropology* 33: 173–99.

Spencer, Herbert. 1857 [1891]. "Progress: Its Law and Cause." Pp. 8–62 in *Essays: Scientific, Political, and Speculative*, Vol. 1. London: William and Norgate. (Online at <http://oll.libertyfund.org>).

Spencer, Herbert. 1873. *The Study of Sociology*. London: Henry S. King & Co. (Online at <http://oll.libertyfund.org>).

Spencer, Herbert. [1898] 2003. *The Principles of Sociology*. 3 vols. New Brunswick, NJ: Transaction Publishers.

Spirtas, Michael, 1996. "A House Divided: Tragedy and Evil in Realist Theory." *Security Studies* 5 (3): 385–423.

Spruyt, Hendrik. 1994a. "Institutional Selection in International Relations: State Anarchy as Order." *International Organization* 48: 527–57.

Spruyt, Hendrik. 1994b. *The Sovereign State and Its Competitors: An Analysis of Systems Change*. Princeton, NJ: Princeton University Press.

Spruyt, Hendrik. 2000. "The End of Empire and the Extension of the Westphalian System: The Normative Basis of the Modern State Order." *International Studies Review* 2 (2): 65–92.

Spruyt, Hendrik. 2006. "Normative Transformations in International Relations and the Waning of Major War." In *The Waning of Major War: Theories and Debates*, ed. Raimo Vayrynen. London: Routledge, 185–205.

Stanish, Charles. 2001. "The Origin of State Societies in South America." *Annual Review of Anthropology* 30: 41–64.

Stein, Burton. 2010. *A History of India*. 2nd ed. Malden, MA: Blackwell.

Sterling-Folker, Jennifer. 2000. "Competing Paradigms or Birds of a Feather? Constructivism and Neoliberal Institutionalism Compared." *International Studies Quarterly* 44 (1): 97–119.

Sterling-Folker, Jennifer. 2001. "Evolutionary Tendencies in Realist and Liberal IR Theory." In *Evolutionary Interpretations of World Politics*, ed. William R. Thompson. London: Routledge, 62–109.

Sterling-Folker, Jennifer. 2002. "Realism and the Constructivist Challenge: Rejecting, Reconstructing, or Rereading." *International Studies Review* 4 (1): 73–97.

Sterling-Folker, Jennifer. 2004. "Realist-Constructivism and Morality." *International Studies Review* 6 (2): 341–3.

Strang, David. 1991. "Anomaly and Commonplace in European Political Expansion: Realist and Institutional Accounts." *International Organization* 45 (2): 143–62.

Struch, Naomi, and Shalom Schwartz. 1989. "Intergroup Aggression: Its predicators and Distinctness from In-Group Bias." *Journal of Personality and Social Psychology* 56 (3): 364–73.

Stuart-Fox, Martin. 1986. "The Unit of Replication in Socio-Cultural Evolution." *Journal of Social and Biological Structures* 9 (1): 67–89.

Stuart-Fox, Martin. 1999. "Evolutionary Theory of History." *History and Theory* 38(4): 33–51.

Suganami, Hidemi. 2003. "British Institutionalists, or the English School, 20 Years On." *International Relations* 17 (3): 253–71.

Sumner, William Graham. [1906] 1959. *Folkways: A Study of the Sociological Importance of Usages, Manners, Customs, Mores, and Morals.* New York, NY: Dover Publications.

Suzuki, Shogo. 2009. *Civilization and Empire: China and Japan's Encounter with European International Society.* London: Routledge.

Tajfel, Henri. 1982. "Social Psychology of Intergroup Relations." *Annual Review of Psychology* 33: 1–39.

Taliaferro, Jeffery W. 2001. "Realism, Power Shifts, and Major War." *Security Studies* 10 (4): 145–78.

Taliaferro, Jeffrey W. 2000–1. "Security Seeking under Anarchy: Defensive Realism Revisited." *International Security* 25(3): 128–61.

Taliaferro, Jeffery W. 2004. *Balancing Risks: Great Power Intervention in the Periphery.* Ithaca, NY: Cornell University Press.

Tan, Qi-xian et al. 1991. *Zhongguo Lishi Ditu Ji* [中国历史地图集/Concise Historical Atlas of China]. Zhongguo ditu chubanshe [Beijing: Sinomaps Press].

Tang, Ji-Geng. 2010. "Xia-Shang-Zhou Kao Gu [夏商周考古/Archaeology of Xia, Shan, Zhou]." In *Zhong Guo Kao Gu Fa Xiang yu Yang Jiu, 1949–2009* [中国考古发现与研究, 1949–2009/Archaeological Discoveries and Researches in China, 1949–2009]. Beijing: Peoples' Publishing House, 196–205.

Tang, Shiping. 2000. "Economic Integration in Central Asia: The Russian and Chinese Relationship." *Asian Survey* 40 (2): 360–76.

Tang, Shiping. 2004. "A Systemic Theory of the Security Environment." *Journal of Strategic Studies* 27 (1): 1–32.

Tang, Shiping. 2005. "Reputation, Cult of Reputation, and International Conflict." *Security Studies* 14: 34–62.

Tang, Shiping. 2006. "Leadership in Institution Building: the case of ASEAN + 3." In *Regional Integration in East Asia and Europe: Convergence or Divergence*, eds., Bertrand Fort and Douglas Webber. London: Routledge, 69–84.

Tang, Shiping. 2008a. "Fear in International Politics: Two Positions." *International Studies Review* 10 (3): 451–71.

Tang, Shiping. 2008b. "From Offensive to Defensive Realism: A Social Evolutionary Interpretation of China's Security Strategy." In *China's Ascent: Power, Security, and the Future of International Politics*, eds. Robert Ross and Zhu Feng. Ithaca, NY: Cornell University Press, 141–62.

Tang, Shiping. 2009a. "The Social Evolutionary Psychology of Fear (and Trust): or why is international cooperation difficult." Presented at the 26th ISA Annual Convention, San Francisco, March 26–31, 2009.

Tang, Shiping. 2009b. "The Security Dilemma: A Conceptual Analysis." *Security Studies* 18 (3): 587–623.

Tang, Shiping. 2009c. "Taking Stock of Neoclassical Realism." *International Studies Review* 11 (4): 799–803.

Tang, Shiping. 2010a. "Social Evolution of International Politics: From Mearsheimer to Jervis." *European Journal of International Relations* 16 (1): 31–55.

Tang, Shiping. 2010b. *A Theory of Security Strategy for Our Time: Defensive Realism.* New York, NY: Palgrave-Macmillan.

Tang, Shiping. 2010d. "Offense-Defense Theory: Toward a Definite Critique." *Chinese Journal of International Politics* 3 (2): 213–60.

Tang, Shiping. 2010e. "The Positional Market and Economic Growth." *Journal of Economic Issues* 44 (4): 915–42.

Tang, Shiping. 2011a. *A General Theory of Institutional Change.* London: Routledge.

Tang, Shiping. 2011b. "Foundational Paradigms of Social Sciences." *Philosophy of the Social Sciences* 41 (2): 211–49.

Tang, Shiping. 2011c. "Review Article: Reconciliation and the Remaking of Anarchy." *World Politics* 63 (4): 713–51.

Tang, Shiping. 2012. "Outline of a New Theory of Attribution in IR: Dimensions of Uncertainty and Their Cognitive Challenges," *Chinese Journal of International Politics* 5 (3): 299–338.

Tang, Shiping. 2013. "Priority versus Weight in Social Sciences: Ontological and Epistemological," unpublished manuscript, Fudan University.

Tang, Shiping. 2014–15. *On Social Evolution: Phenomenon and Paradigm.* Forthcoming.

Tang, Shiping. n.d.-a. "Power: Toward a Unifying Framework." Unpublished manuscript.

Tang, Shiping. n.d.-b. "(Political and Social) Order: Definition and Measurement." unpublished manuscript.

Tang, Shiping. n.d.-c. "Social Evolutionary Psychology: A Manifesto." Unpublished manuscript.

Tang, Shiping, and Peter Hay Gries. 2002. "China's Security Strategy: From Offensive to Defensive Realism and Beyond." *EAI Working Paper* No. 97. East Asian Institute, National University of Singapore.

Tang, Shiping, and Joey Shi-Ruey Long. 2012. "American Military Interventionism: A Social Evolutionary Interpretation." *European Journal of International Relations* 18 (3): 507–36.

Tang, Shiping, Zhan Hu, and Yun Li. n.d. "Institution, Knowledge, and Growth: Toward a Unifying Economics of Growth." Unpublished manuscript.

Thapar, Romila. 2003. *The Penguin History of Early India: From the Origins to AD 1300.* London: Penguin.

Thayer, Bradley A. 2004. *Darwin and International Relations: On the Evolutionary Origins of War and Ethnic Conflict.* Lexington, KY: University of Kentucky Press.

Thompson, William R. ed. 2001. *Evolutionary Interpretations of World Politics.* London: Routledge.

Thucydides. [c.431 BC] 1954. *The Peloponnesian War.* Trans. Rex Warner. London: Penguine Books.

Tilly, Charles. 1984. *Big Structures, Large Processes, Huge Comparisons*. Malden, MA: Blackwell.

Tilly, Charles. 1985. "War Making and State Making as Organized Crime." In *Bringing the State Back In*, eds. Peter B. Evans, Dietrich Rueschemeyer, and Theda Skocpol. Cambridge: Cambridge University Press, 167–89.

Tilly, Charles. 1990. *Coercion, Capital, and European States, AD 990–1992*. Malden, MA: Blackwell.

Tilly, Charles, and Willem P. Blockmans, eds. 1994. *Cities and the Rise of States in Europe, A.D. 1000 to 1800*. Boulder, CO: Westview Press.

Tooby, John, and Leda Cosmides. 1990. "The past explains the present: Emotional adaptations and the structure of ancestral environments." *Ethology and sociobiology* 11: 375–424.

Tooby, John, and Leda Cosmides. 1992. "The Psychological Foundation of Culture." In *The Adapted Mind: Evolutionary Psychology and the Generation of Culture*, eds. J. H. Barkow, J. Tooby, and L. Cosmides. New York, NY: Columbia University Press, 99–136.

Topic, John, and Theresa Topic. 1987. "The Archaeological Investigation of Andean Militarism: Some Cautionary Observations." In *The Origins and Development of the Andean State*, eds. Jonathan Haas, Shelia Pozorski, and Thomas Pozorski. Cambridge: Cambridge University Press, 47–55.

Trigger, Bruce G. 2003. *Understanding Early Civilizations: A Comparative Study*. Cambridge: Cambridge University Press.

Trivers, Robert. 1985. *Social Evolution*. Menlo Park, CA: Benjamin/Cummins.

Turney-High, Harry Holbert. 1949 [1971]. *Primitive War: Its Practices and Concepts*. Columbia, SC: University of South Carolina Press.

Tylor Edward Burnett. 1871. *Primitive Culture: Researches into the Development of Mythology, Philosophy, Religion, Art, and Custom*. 2 vols. London: J. Murray.

UNESCO. 1986. "The Seville Statement." <http://www.unesco.org/cpp/uk/declarations/seville.pdf> (Accessed September 2011).

Van de Mieroop, March. 2007. *A History of the Ancient Near East, ca. 3000–323BC*, 2nd ed., Malden, MA: Blackwell.

van den Berghe, Pierre L. 1974. "Bringing Beasts Back In: Toward a Biosocial Theory of Aggression." *American Sociological Review* 39 (6): 777–88.

van der Dennen, Johan Matheus Gerardus. 1995. *The Origin of War: The Evolution of a Male-Coalitional Reproductive Strategy*. 2 vols. Groningen, Netherlands: Origin Press. http://rint.rechten.rug.nl/rth/dennen/dennen.htm (Accessed March 2012).

van der Dennen, Johan Matheus Gerardus. 2007. "Three Works on War." *Politics and the Life Sciences* 26 (1): 71–92.

Van Evera, Stephen. 1984. "The Cult of the Offensive and the Origins of the First World War." *International Security* 9 (1): 58–107.

Van Evera, Stephen. 1990–1991. "Primed for Peace: Europe after the Cold War." *International Security* 15 (3): 7–57.

Van Evera, Stephen. 1994. "Hypotheses on Nationalism and War." *International Security* 18 (4): 5–39.

Van Evera, Stephen. 1998. "Offense, Defense, and the Causes of War." *International Security* 22 (4): 5–43.

Van Evera, Stephen. 1999. *Causes of War: Power and the Roots of Conflict*. Ithaca, NY: Cornell University Press.

Vayrynen, Raimo. 2003. "Regionalism: Old and New." *International Studies Review* 5 (1): 25–51.

Vayrynen, Ramio. 2006. *The Waning of Major War: Theories and Debates*. London: Routledge.

Veblen, Thorstein. 1898. "Why isn't Economics an Evolutionary Science?" *Quarterly Journal of Economics* 12: 373–97.

Velázquez, Arturo C. Sotomayor. 2004. "Civil-Military Affairs and Security Institutions in the Southern Cone: The Sources of Argentine-Brazilian Nuclear Cooperation." *Latin America Politics and Society* 46 (4): 29–60.

Vencl, S. I. 1984. "War and Warfare in Archaeology," *Journal of Anthropological Archaeology* 3 (1): 116–32.

Wallander, Celeste, Helga Haftendorn, and Robert O. Keohane. 1999. *Imperfect Unions: Security Institutions over Time and Space*. New York, NY: Oxford University Press.

Walt, Stephen M. 1987a. "Alliance Formation and the Balance of World Power." *International Security* 9 (4): 3–43.

Walt, Stephen M. 1987b. *The Origins of Alliances*. Ithaca, NY: Cornell University Press.

Waltz, Kenneth N. 1959. *Man, the State and War*. New York, NY: Columbia University Press.

Waltz, Kenneth N. 1979. *Theory of International Politics*. Reading, MA: Addison-Wesley.

Waltz, Kenneth A. 1986. "Reflections on Theory of International Politics: A Response to My Critics." In *Neorealism and its Critics,* ed. Robert O. Keohane. New York, NY: Columbia University Press, 322–45.

Waltz, Kenneth N. 1988. "The Origins of War in Neorealist Theory." *Journal of Interdisciplinary History* 18 (4): 615–28.

Waltz, Kenneth N. 1996. "International Politics Is not Foreign Policy." *Security Studies* 6 (1): 54–7.

Waltz, Kenneth N. 2000. "Structural Realism after the Cold War." *International Security* 25(1): 5–41.

Wang, Yuan-Kuang. 2011. *Harmony and War: Confucian Culture and Chinese Power Politics*. New York, NY: Columbia University Press.

Watkins, Trevor. 1989. "The Beginnings of Warfare." In *Warfare in the Ancient World*, ed. John W. Hackett. London: Sidgwick & Jackson.

Watson, Adam. 1987. "Hedley Bull, State Systems, and International Societies." *Review of International Studies* 13 (1): 147–53.

Wæver, Ole. 1995. "Securitization and Desecuritization." In *On Security*, ed. Ronnie D. Lipschutz. New York, NY: Columbia University Press, 46–86.

Wæver, Ole. 1998. "Insecurity, Security, and Asecurity in the West European Non-War Community." In *Security Communities*, eds. Emmanuel Adler and Michael Barnett. Cambridge: Cambridge University Press, 69–118.

Weber, Max. 1978. *Economy and Society*. 2 vols. Berkeley, CA: University of California Press.

Webster, David. 1999. "Ancient Maya Warfare." In *War and society in the ancient and medieval worlds: Asia, the Mediterranean, Europe, and Mesoamerica*, eds. Kurt A. Raaflaub and Nathan Stewart Rosenstein. Cambridge, MA: Harvard University Press, 333–60.

Weiffen, Brigitte, et al. 2011. "Democracy, Regional Security Institutions, and Rivalry Mitigation: Evidence from Europe, South America, and Asia." *Security Studies* 20 (3): 378–415.

Welch, David A. 2003. "Why International Relations Theorists Should Stop Reading Thucydides." *Review of International Studies* 29 (2): 301–19.

Welch, David A. 2005. *Painful Choices: A Theory of Foreign Policy Change*. Princeton, NJ: Princeton University Press.

Wendt, Alexander. 1987. "The Agent-Structure Problem in International Relations Theory." *International Organization* 41 (3): 335–70.

Wendt, Alexander. 1992. "Anarchy Is What States Make of It: The Social Construction of Power Politics." *International Organization* 46(2): 391–425.

Wendt, Alexander. 1994. "Collective Identity Formation and the International State." *American Political Science Review* 88 (2): 384–96.

Wendt, Alexander. 1995. "Constructing International Politics." *International Security* 20 (1): 71–81.

Wendt, Alexander. 1999. *Social Theory of International Politics*. Cambridge: Cambridge University Press.

Wendt, Alexander. 2003. "Why a World State is Inevitable?" *European Journal of International Relations* 9 (4): 491–542.

Wendt, Alexander. 2004. "The State as Person in International Theory." *Review of International Studies* 30: 289–316.

Wenke, Robert J. 2009. *The Ancient Egyptian State: The Origins of Egyptian Culture (c. 8000–2000 BC)*. Cambridge: Cambridge University Press.

White, Leslie A. 1949. *The Science of Culture: A Study of Man and Civilization*. New York, NY: Farrar and Straus.

Whiting, Robert M. 1995. "Amorite Tribes and Nations of Second-Millenium Western Asia." In *Civilizations of the Ancient Near East*, vol. II, eds. Jack M. Sasson et al. New York, NY: Charles Scribner's Sons, 1231–42.

Wight, Colin. 2006. *Agents, Structures, and International Relations: Politics as Ontology*. Cambridge: Cambridge University Press.

Wilkins, John S. 2001. "The Appearance of Lamarckism in the Evolution of Culture." In *Darwinism and Evolutionary Economics*, eds. John Laurent and John Nightingale. Cheltenham, UK: Edward Elgar, 160–83.

Wilkinson, Toby A. H. 1999. *Early Dynastic Egypt*. London: Routledge.

Williams, George C. [1966] 1996. *Adaptation and Natural Selection: A Critique of Some Current Evolutionary Thought*. Princeton, NJ: Princeton University Press.

Williams, Michael C. 1996. "Hobbes and International Relations: A Reconsideration." *International Organization* 50 (2): 213–36.

Williamson, Oliver E. 1975. *Markets and Hierarchies: Analysis and Antitrust Implications*. New York, NY: Free Press.

Williamson, Oliver E. 1985. *The Institutional Foundation of Capitalism*. New York, NY: Free Press.

Wilson, David J. 1987. "Reconstructing Patterns of Early Warfare in the Lower Santa Valley: New Data on the Role of Conflict in the Origins of Complex North Coast Society." In *The Origins and Development of the Andean State*, eds. Jonathan Haas, Shelia Pozorski, and Thomas Pozorski. Cambridge: Cambridge University Press, 56–69.

Wilson, David Sloan. 1975. "A Theory of Group Selection." *Proceedings of the National Academy of Sciences of U.S.A.* 72 (1): 143–6.

Wilson, Edward O. [1975] 2000. *Sociobiology: the New Synthesis*. Cambridge, MA: Belknap Press of Harvard University Press.

Wilson, Edward O. 1978. *On Human Nature*. Cambridge, MA: Belknap Press of Harvard University Press.

Wilson, Michael L. and Richard W. Wrangham. 2003. "Intergroup Relations in Chimpanzees." *Annual Review of Anthropology* 32: 363–92.

Wolfers, Arnold. 1952. "'National Security' as an Ambiguous Symbol." *Political Science Quarterly* 67(4): 481–502.

Wolfers, Arnold. 1962. *Discord and Collaboration: Essays on International Politics*. Baltimore, MD: Johns Hopkins University Press.

Woods, Ngaire (ed.). 2000. *The Political Economy of Globalization*. Basingstoke, UK: Macmillan.

Worth, Owen. 2011. "Recasting Gramsci in International Politics." *Review of International Studies* 37 (1): 373–92.

Wrangham, R. W. 1999. "Evolution of Coalitionary Killing." *Yearbook of Physical Anthropology* 42: 1–30.

Wrangham, Richard and Peterson, Dale. 1996. *Demonic Males: Apes and the Origins of Human Violence*. London: Bloomsbury.

Wright, Henry T. 1977. "Recent Research on the Origin of the State." *Annual Review of Anthropology* 6: 379–97.

Wright, Henry T. 1984. "Prestate Political Formations." In *On the Evolution of Complex Societies: Essays in Honor of Harry Hoijer*, ed. Timothy K. Earle. Malibu, CA: Undena Press, 41–77.

Wright, Quincy. [1942] 1983. *A Study of War*. 2nd ed. Chicago, IL: University of Chicago Press.

Wrong, Dennis H. 1961. "The Oversocialized Conception of Man in Modern Sociology." *American Sociological Review* 26: 183–93.

Yang, Kuan [杨宽]. 2003. *History of the Warring States* [Zhan Guo Shi]. Shanghai: Shanghai People's Publishing House.

Yang, Shen Nan [杨升南]. 1991. "Xia Dai Jun Shi Zhi Du Chu Tan [夏代军事制度初探/A Preliminary Inquiry into the Xia Military System]." *Journal of Zhengzhou University, Social Sciences Edition* 3: 40–46 (in Chinese).

Yates, D. S. Robin. 1999. "Early China." In *War and society in the ancient and medieval worlds: Asia, the Mediterranean, Europe, and Mesoamerica*, eds. Kurt A. Raaflaub and Nathau Rosenstein. Cambridge, MA: Harvard University Press, 7–45.

Zacher, Mark W. 2001. "The Territorial Integrity Norm: International Boundaries and the Use of Force." *International Organization* 55 (2): 215–50.

Zakaria, Fareed. 1992. "Realism and Domestic Politics." *International Security* 17 (1): 177–98.

Zakaria, Fareed. 1998. *From Wealth to Power: The Unusual Origins of America's World Role*. Princeton, NJ: Princeton University Press.

Zehfuss, Maja. 2001. "Constructivism and Identity: A Dangerous Liaison." *European Journal of International Relations* 7(3): 315–48.

Zhang, Guo Shuo [张国硕]. 2008. "Xia Guo Jia Jun Shi Fang Yu Ti Xi Yan Jiu [夏国家军事防御体系研究/A Study of the Military Defense System of the Xia State]." *Zhong Yuan Wen Wu* [《中原文物》/*Antiques of Central China*] 4: 40–9.

Zheng, Jie-xiang [郑杰祥]. 2005. *Xin Shi Qi Wen Hua yu Xia Dai Wen Ming* [新石器文化和夏代文明/*Neolithic Culture and the Xia Civilization*]. Zhejiang, China: Jiangsu Education Press.

Zimansky, Paul E. 1995. "The Kingdom of Urartu in Eastern Anatolia." In *Civilizations of the Ancient Near East*, vol. II, eds. Jack M. Sasson et al. New York, NY: Charles Scribner's Sons, 1135–46.

Zhou, Yin [周膺]and Jin Wu[吴晶]. 2004. *The First Evidence of the 5000-year Civilization of China: Liangzhu Culture and Early State of Liangzhu.* [中国5000年文明第一证：良诸文化与良诸古国] Zhejiang, China: Zhe Jiang University Press.

Zhu, Nai-Cheng. 2010. "Zhong Guo Xin Shi Qi Shi Dai Kao Gu Yan Jiu [中国新石器时代考古研究/ Neolithic Archaeological Research in China]." In *Zhong Guo Kao Gu Fa Xiang yu Yang Jiu, 1949–2009* [中国考古发现与研究, 1949–2009/Archaeological Discoveries and Researches in China, 1949–2009]. Beijing: Peoples' Publishing House, 94–195.

Subject Index

adaptation 15, 18–9, 21–2, 27–8, 31–2, 34, 169, 204, 245, 273, 275
adaptationism
in biology 18–9, 21–2
in social sciences as functionalism 34, 205
Africa 64–5, 188, 203, 221, 226, 256
agency (or action) 228, 231, 249, 260
agency-structure, *see* agent-structure
agent-structure 151–2, 155, 161, 165, 167, 177–8, 204, 228, 230–1, 243, 247, 251, 275
aggression 48–9, 55, 61, 88, 104, 197, 207, 211, 248, 260, 263, 271, 273
definition of 43–4
see also violence, definition of
Anatolia, ancient xi, 69–70, 80–1, 87, 194, 212–4, 248, 260, 262, 277
anti-socialization 26, 142, 162, 171–4, 176, 207, 231–3
definition of 167, 231
see also ideational resistance
archaeological anthropology 51–3, 208
archaeology vii, 46–7, 51–2, 190–1, 193, 244, 247–9, 256–8, 260–2, 265, 268, 270–1, 274

Bible, The 16, 86, 90, 198, 213, 240
biological determinism 205
biological/biotic evolution ix, 5, 9–27, 30, 32–5, 44, 50–1, 92, 94, 142, 203–5, 207, 242–3
biotic system 12–3, 19–20, 33

Canaan (Levant) 73, 80, 197, 213–4, 236
causes of war (vs. Origin of War) 38, 47–8, 207, 211, 240, 251, 260, 273–4
Chalcolithic (Age) 166, 195, 244, 161
China, ancient xi, 6, 68–70, 76, 82–3, 85, 88, 91, 100, 191, 193, 200, 215–6, 244, 247, 254, 267
collective/common identity 115, 118, 121, 133–4, 146, 154, 156–7, 229, 252–3, 266, 275
conflict of interest 122, 126, 129, 140, 143
constraining/enabling 167, 172, 232–3
constructivism
general 3, 6–7, 31, 35–7, 122, 125–7, 131–7, 139–40, 154, 157–9, 162–3, 165–6, 174,
176, 201, 205, 222, 226–8, 230–3, 237, 239, 255, 263, 265, 267, 270, 277
structural 162–3, 165–6, 231
creationism 16–8, 203, 243, 257
critical theory 6, 227, 231
cultural anthropology 51, 243, 249
cultural evolution (or sociocultural evolution) 9, 39, 203–4, 238, 240, 242, 268, 271
culture, definition of 8–9

Darwinian nested within Super-Lamarckian 27–8, 33
Darwinism v–vi, 15–8, 20, 26, 179, 202, 238, 253, 258, 262, 275
Darwinism, universal 263
defensive realism, definition of 97–8
defensive realism world (Jervis's world, Lockeian world, Lockeian anarchy) x, 5–6, 96–9, 106–9, 113–5, 118, 124, 133, 144, 146, 160, 179, 181–3, 185, 209, 212, 216, 218, 221, 223–5, 232
defensive realist state 6, 45–6, 97–8, 104–5, 160, 185, 217, 222, 232
devolution 29
direct inheritance 14–5, 202
see also Lamarckian and Super-Lamarckian
directionality 15, 19, 28–9, 204–5
DNA (deoxyribonucleic acid) 14–5, 18, 22, 202–3

Egypt, ancient 65, 69–70, 73–5, 82, 85, 191, 197, 214–5, 239, 251, 257, 268–9, 275
English School
pluralist 125, 131, 139–40, 146, 158, 201, 228
solidarist 125–6, 131, 139–41, 158–9, 201
ethnocentrism 48, 50, 55, 63, 84–5, 136, 138, 143, 146, 204, 237, 259
ethnographic (anthropology) ix, 50–2, 68, 187, 248
ethology 273
Europe, ancient 257
European project, the 117, 120–1, 225
evolution, essential conditions of 12–3
evolutionary psychology (as a field of psychology and as a doctrine) 34, 48, 92, 241–2, 245–6, 273

fear, spreading of 57, 211
fitness *see* adaptation
Foucauldian 6, 137–9, 170, 231, 256
functionalism 8, 31–6, 38, 112, 114, 126,
132, 134, 136, 139–41, 173–4, 178, 205,
227, 233
see also adaptationism in social sciences,
especially sociology and anthropology

gene, definition of 202n.7
general theory of institutional change 6, 37,
110–5, 118, 128, 272
genetic material in biological evolution 13–5,
22, 202
genotype 13, 15, 18, 26, 202
geopolitics 35, 91–2, 174, 203, 257
see also Social Darwinism
God
the Creator 16–19, 203
military or war 73, 75, 85–7, 90
Yahweh 86, 90
Greece, ancient 66, 70, 83, 89, 91, 188, 198–9,
214, 252, 265–6
group
identity 50, 55–6, 58, 66, 68, 87, 94, 144,
208–10, 250
selection 25, 204, 208, 246, 269, 276

Holy Roman Empire 6, 100–2, 219
Homo sapiens sapiens (the modern) 66–7, 213

ideational forces 20, 23–4, 36, 39, 54, 56, 60,
93–4, 109, 128–9, 165–6, 218
inclusive fitness 13, 24, 49–50, 94, 208
India, ancient 83, 89, 199, 240–1
institution, definition of 8
institutional change 6, 11, 21, 24, 36–7,
110–2, 114–5, 118, 120–1, 125–8, 135,
139–4, 157, 205, 228, 237, 254, 260,
263, 272
intelligent design 16–7, 19, 203

Jervis's world (see defensive realism world)
just/holy/sacred war 63, 84, 86–87, 191

Lamarckian 14, 27–8, 202, 204, 253
Lamarckism 202, 258, 275
learning
negative 97, 105, 168–70, 173, 222
positive 105–6, 168–9, 173, 222, 231

material forces 20, 23–4, 31, 36–7, 39, 54–6,
60, 93–4, 128, 166, 209, 218, 269

material progress 24, 29
Mesolithic/Epipaleolithic 58, 65–7, 189,
198, 204
Mesopotamia, ancient xi, 65–6, 69–73, 75,
80–7, 187, 189–91, 197, 200, 213–5, 238,
244, 261, 263–4
Middle East 124, 226, 229, 269
military god *see* god, military or war
modern synthesis, the (of biological
evolution) 12–4, 202, 254
moral progress 29
mutant 93, 203, 222
mutation
genetic 13–4
ideational 22, 24

nationalism/patriotism 6, 50, 53, 85, 97,
106–7, 143, 173, 221, 223, 238, 243,
251, 253, 273
see also ethnocentrism
Neanderthal (*Homo Neanderthal*, the
archaic) 67, 212–3, 268
Neo-Darwinism 13, 15–20, 26, 33, 202
Neo-Lamarckian (epigenetic) 14, 27
neoliberalism 3, 6, 35–7, 110–1, 114–5,
120–1, 125–7, 131–3, 135–7, 139–40,
157–8, 161–2, 180, 182–5, 201, 205,
226–8, 234, 239, 255, 257, 263, 270
see also institutionalism or
neo-institutionalism
Neolithic 58, 65–8, 80, 189, 192–3, 195,
198–9, 204, 240, 244, 257, 260,
262, 277

Oaxaca, Mexicao xi, 69–70, 78–9, 86, 193–4,
213, 236, 240, 261, 265, 270
offensive realism, definition of 97
offensive realism world (or Mearsheimer's
World, Hobbesian World, Hobbesian
anarchy) ix–x, 5–6, 43, 45–7, 53–7, 61,
64, 70, 80, 90, 92–9, 103–9, 127, 133, 146,
160, 170, 179, 181–5, 198, 211–2, 215–7,
221–2, 224, 226, 232, 234
offensive realist state 6, 36, 45, 54, 57, 90–1,
93, 97, 99, 104–7, 160, 181, 215, 217,
229, 232

Paleolithic 64–67, 190, 204, 213,
240, 268
Peru (Chavin and Moche) 69, 82, 193–4
phenotype 13–5, 18, 21–7, 29, 32–4, 111,
202, 204
political realism (in IR) 47

RNA (ribonucleic acid) 14
Rome (republic and imperial) 66, 69–70,
    82–3, 85, 87, 89, 116, 198–200, 247,
    252–3, 266

selection
  artificial 23–4, 146, 204
  natural 13, 19, 23–4, 27, 34, 58, 202–4, 208,
    222, 246, 275
Social Darwinism 34–5, 91–2, 174, 203, 256
  see also Social Spencerism
social evolution (as a phenomenon, also
  societal evolution) vi–vii, ix, xi, 5, 9–14,
  20–35, 205–8, 230, 272–3
social evolution paradigm (SEP or social
  evolutionary approach) vi, 5–11, 30–40,
  43, 51, 94–7, 110–4, 120, 133, 137, 139,
  141, 151, 177–9, 218, 233
social evolutionary psychology 271–2
Social Spencerism (see Social Darwinism)
social system paradigm (SSP) 30, 32,
  156, 177
socialization 7, 26, 40, 88, 93, 131, 136, 142–3,
  152, 167, 169, 171, 207, 215, 228–9, 231,
  244, 248, 255

sociobiology 34, 39, 48–51, 92, 207–8, 240,
  251, 256, 258, 273, 276
sovereignty 6, 38, 97, 106, 109, 113–4, 133,
  137, 141, 173, 206, 221, 223, 238–40, 244,
  253, 255, 258, 263
Spring and Autumn period (of ancient
  China) 70, 77, 83
structuralism 6, 135, 140, 151–2, 161–6,
  177–8, 230–1
structuration 151, 155, 167, 228, 251
structure, definition of 8
Super-Lamarckian 14, 27–8, 33, 202
survival of the fitter 18, 207
survival of the fittest (in Social Spencerism/
  Darwinism) 17–8, 34, 203

unfolding of design/destiny 19, 35

violence, definition of 43–4
  see also aggression, definition of

war, definition of 44
Warring State period, ancient China 83
Weisman Barrier, the 15, 26
Westphalia 103, 182, 223, 228, 263, 266, 270

DISCARDED
CONCORDIA UNIV. LIBRARY
CONCORDIA UNIVERSITY LIBRARIES
MONTREAL